GATE OF THE HEART

Bahá'í Studies Series

This series features the study of the Sacred Texts, theology, law, teachings, and principles of the Bahá'í Faith as well as the history of the Bahá'í religion and the development of the Bahá'í community. Bahá'í Studies also encompasses the application of Bahá'í teachings to the contemporary needs of humanity.

Gate of the Heart

Understanding the Writings of the Báb

Nader Saiedi

Wilfrid Laurier University Press

WLU

Wilfrid Laurier University Press acknowledges the financial support of the Government of Canada through the Canada Book Fund for our publishing activities.

Library and Archives Canada Cataloguing in Publication

Saiedi, Nader, 1955–
Gate of the heart : understanding the writings of the Báb / Nader Saiedi.

(Bahá'í studies series)

Includes bibliographical references and index.

ISBN 978-1-55458-056-9 (paper)

1. Bab, Ali Muhammad Shirazi, 1819–1850. 2. Bahai Faith. I. Title. II. Series.

BP361.2.S34 2008 297.9′2 C2008-900044-7

Paper edition 2010

Cover photograph of the House of the Báb in Shiraz courtesy of the Bahá'í World Centre. Cover and text design by P. J. Woodland.

CONTENTS

PREFACE

THIS BOOK IS AN INTRODUCTION to the vast ocean of the writings of the Báb, the young and charismatic Persian Prophet and Forerunner of the Bahá'í religion. I spent my undergraduate years in the Báb's birthplace, the city of Shiraz, where I studied at Pahlavi University. Memorable occasional visits to the House of the Báb (which was demolished in 1979 by the Iranian Revolutionary Guards) were the ultimate inspiration for my future work on the Báb's writings. During those years, one of my best friends was my fellow student, Bahrám Yaldá'í. Being of the same age, we took many of the same courses, and I always sat beside him. He was the most selfless, gentle, quiet, and peaceful person I have ever met. Years later I received the shocking news that Bahrám, together with his kind and brave mother, had been put to death by the Islamic regime simply because they refused to recant their faith as Bahá'ís and renounce their right to freedom of conscience, their right to be human. The same fanatical and intolerant culture that had executed the Báb in 1850 was continuing to kill the Báb's spiritual heirs, the Bahá'ís, at the end of the twentieth century.

My actual research on the writings of the Báb began a decade ago when a dear friend gave me a most precious gift. It was a copy of the Persian Bayán, the most important of the Báb's works. When I opened it, I recognized instantly the name of the book's previous owner, written in his own handwriting on the first page. It was my martyred friend, Bahrám. The one who gave me this gift was unaware that Bahrám and I had been friends in our undergraduate years in Iran.

It was in this mysterious context that I began to read again the Persian Bayán, while remembering my friendship with Bahrám in Shiraz. I became entranced by the Báb's creativity and could not stop studying the works that flowed from His prolific pen. Thus began a journey of exploration that has culminated in this book. Through it I hope to share some of the vibrant and creative experience that I have had in studying the works of the Báb. Even so, it is only a beginning and an invitation to further study and research.

Many people have contributed in various ways to the realization of this book, and although it is impossible to mention them all, I am grateful to every one. A number of scholars including Dr. Muhammad Afnan, Dr. Nosratollah Mohammadhosseini, and Dr. Iskander Ha'i made contributions that were essential. I am also grateful to the Research Department of the Bahá'í World Centre for assistance with the provisional translations that are included in this volume. My research has benefited from the supporting environment of the Department of Sociology and Anthropology at Carleton College. My thanks go to my editor and the Association for Bahá'í Studies for publishing this book as the first volume of the Bahá'í Studies Series published by Wilfrid Laurier University Press. I would like to thank my wife Bita, who always eagerly read various drafts of the manuscript, gave me insightful comments, and enthusiastically supported my work.

Furthermore, I would like to express my love and gratitude to my parents who taught me from an early age the love of reading. This work is an expression of their love and sacrifices throughout my life. Finally, I wish to thank Arden Lee for loving me like a son these last thirty years.

I dedicate this book to my beloved and noble friend from Shiraz, Bahrám Yaldá'í.

INTRODUCTION

In the middle of the nineteenth century, the world of Shí'ih Islam was in a state of fervent messianic expectation. Devout believers were awaiting the advent of the holy figure known as the Twelfth Imám, who had been in concealment for a thousand years. According to the prophecies recorded in the Traditions, when the Hidden Imám reappeared he would arise, as the *Qá'im*, to unleash jihad—holy war—on the forces of evil and unbelief, and would usher in the Day of Judgment and the Resurrection. When in 1844 a mild and refined twenty-five-year-old merchant from Shiraz, Persia, declared that He was that promised figure of Islamic prophecy, it sent a shock wave through Persian society.[1] His name was Siyyid 'Alí-Muḥammad Shírází, and He took the title of *Báb* (the Gate). Response to the Báb and His teachings ranged from ecstatic embrace by those who became His followers, to hostile and violent rejection by the government and clerical hierarchy. Determined to extirpate the newborn religion, the authorities launched a campaign of brutal persecution against the Bábís, culminating in the execution of the Báb Himself before a firing squad in the public square of Tabriz on July 9, 1850.[2]

In fact, the Báb had made a claim even more startling than that of being the Qá'im. He also claimed to be both a new Prophet and the herald of yet another messianic figure even greater than Himself, referred to as "He Whom God shall make manifest" (*Man Yuẓhiruhu'lláh*). The essence and purpose of the Báb's own mission (as the Báb would always stress) was to prepare the people for this second and greater Advent. In 1863 one of the Báb's followers, Mírzá Ḥusayn 'Alíy-i-Núrí, Bahá'u'lláh, would publicly claim to be that Promised One. In the century that followed, the religion Bahá'u'lláh founded—the Bahá'í Faith—would attract adherents far beyond Iran and the Middle East and would become a world religion with millions of followers across the globe.[3]

This book is an exploration of the creative and revolutionary ideas of the Báb through a study of some of His numerous writings. It should be regarded as a preliminary attempt to analyze and describe the overall vision and the substantive message contained in the Báb's texts. For a number of reasons, including their formidable difficulty and apparently hermetic nature, the Báb's writings have scarcely been studied by scholars. When they have been studied, those texts have often been approached in a literalistic framework and without sufficient attention to their symbolism, and thus they have frequently been misunderstood. This book offers a new approach to the writings of the Báb. Going beyond literalism, it attempts to understand the individual texts within the context of the totality of the Báb's works as well as His world view and His own explanations of His intentions, His rhetorical choices, and, above all, the language of symbolism and metaphor He employs throughout His works. As a tentative and preliminary exploration, this book is not intended to be a comprehensive or comparative study of the writings of the Báb. Each of the Báb's texts discussed here could, and no doubt will, become the subject of many volumes of analysis and commentary in the future. In addition to the many topics that are only briefly touched on in this book, much more could be said about all the multiple allusions and meanings contained in the Báb's writings, as well as the theological and philosophical ideas they contain. For brevity's sake, all these aspects must be omitted here and left to future scholarship.

In the second half of the nineteenth century, the story of the Báb and His followers, and their torture and martyrdom at the hands of the Persian state authorities and fanatical Muslim clergy, touched a receptive chord in some Western intellectuals who learned of it. Prominent among those intellectuals was the Cambridge orientalist, Edward Granville Browne. Despite the scorn of his colleagues, who derided him for spending his time on what they considered a minor and ephemeral phenomenon, Browne dedicated his career to recording and studying the Bábí movement. He was convinced he was witnessing "one of the most remarkable phenomena of the present century," and he believed the Báb's religion was "destined to leave a permanent mark in the world." The religion of the Báb, he observed, "whatever its actual destiny may be, is of that stuff whereof world-religions are made."[4]

Those first Europeans who became intrigued by the story of the Báb were influenced by various currents of romanticism and tended to concentrate on celebrating the natural, innocent, and courageous character of the Báb and His Revelation.[5] Although their accounts did help to gain wider recognition for the Báb and His movement outside the Middle East, they generally failed to go beyond traditional simplistic categories and did not even scratch the surface of the complexity and rich symbolism of the mystical and theological system contained in His works. A recent wave of scholarly research, however, has enkindled new excitement and curiosity about the Báb, and there is now a growing body of literature on His history and writings.[6] Some authors, however, have tended to dismiss the Báb's works as mere "archaeological" phenomena devoid of any real significance, let alone relevance beyond a limited historical context.[7] Within the literalist interpretive approach, several common features have contributed to producing such conclusions. These features include the tendency to treat the Báb's writings as completely separate from the writings of Bahá'u'lláh, lack of attention to the complexity and creativity of both the form and the content of the Báb's texts, and overlooking the subtleties of the Báb's language and logic of expression, especially the rhetorical and symbolic uses of language through which He transforms traditional concepts and at times completely reverses their meanings.

Are the writings of the Báb merely of "archaeological" interest, or do they have a value and importance that transcends the limits of their historical moment and speaks with relevance to the present? In a sense, this book is an attempt to answer that question, for it is only by coming to a better understanding of the Báb's works that we can correctly judge their significance, both in historical perspective and in terms of their contemporary relevance. In this chapter I will address the issue through a general introductory methodological examination of the historical background and writings of the Báb.

The Báb's Critique of Islamic Traditionalism

Before September 11, 2001, few could have imagined that one of the effects of modern Western technological advancement would be the dramatic and violent intrusion, upon the Western world, of the seemingly remote and arcane internal conflicts of Islam. The events of September 11 placed Islam at the centre of Western cultural and political discourse as the West struggles to make sense of what seems a bewildering, medieval mindset centring around holy war or jihad as a religious duty. A series of troubling but crucial questions have come to the fore: Is religion, particularly Islam, ultimately only conducive to conflict and hatred? Is the "clash of civilizations" inevitable? What went wrong in the Middle East's encounter with modernity? Why has nothing comparable to Christianity's Reformation occurred within Islam? Does any possibility exist for genuine reconciliation, mutual respect, and peace among the religions of the world? The writings of the Báb provide a challenging, novel perspective from which to examine such questions.

Between the traditionalist rejection of modernity (including its postmodern modifications) on the one hand, and the atheist rejection of religion on the other, there has existed a third position within Islam—a modernist, eclectic, though somewhat inconsistent and contradictory, interpretation of Islamic holy texts. This approach sought to safeguard the sacredness of tradition while imposing upon it a limited and superficial modern form.[8] But modernist Islam failed to question certain fundamental assumptions, and thus its ideology essentially consisted of superficial revisions and borrowings from the West imposed over the same traditionalistic bases without a thorough reexamination of their underlying cultural and religious concepts. Not surprisingly, the modernist approach has been relatively unpersuasive and ineffectual in the Muslim world.

Against a background of intellectual and political impasse within Islam, the historic significance and revolutionary import of the writings of both the Báb and Bahá'u'lláh stand out. For there was indeed a radical reform movement in Islam—so radical in its transformation of Islamic concepts and categories that ultimately it has ceased to be perceived as a part of Islam at all—in much the same way that Christianity, although appearing at first to be a reform movement within Judaism, came to be recognized as a separate and independent religion. But the movement initiated by the Báb was far more than an Islamic Reformation. The Báb engaged in a foundational reexamination of traditional conceptions of religion and religious identity, expounding a spiritual world view that was dynamic, historical, and oriented toward progress and communication.

At a time when the Middle East was ignoring the West, and Muslim religious leaders were insisting on adherence to the old traditions and rituals, avoiding communication and contact with non-Muslims, and rejecting any form of learning that came from the inferior "infidels," the Western world was rapidly improving its technological, economic, political, military, and cultural institutions and extending its influence throughout the world—including the Middle East. While the Islamic world was dominated by the culture of traditionalism, which defined the old ways as sacred, eternally valid, and unalterable—and hence obstructed change and progress—the West was experiencing the exact opposite trend: the rise of the culture of rationalization and rationalism called *modernity*.

Modernity, of course, does not necessarily mean a rejection of all tradition. Yet it does imply a rational and deliberate reexamination of tradition in terms of consistent and universal criteria, a process that can lead to the selective retention of those aspects of tradition that are conducive to progress and universal moral principles. Social and economic advancement depends on such an open and dynamic attitude toward truth and values, while blind traditionalism obstructs progress and creativity in any society.

But religious traditionalism in the Middle East was very different from traditionalism as it was defined by Max Weber.[9] For Weber, traditional authority was based more on the idea of habit than on the deliberate elevation of tradition to the realm of the sacred. The kind of traditionalism Weber was concerned with is much easier to overcome because practices based on mere force of habit and on taken-for-granted institutions can easily crumble when confronted by the advantages of a rational, deliberative, calculative, and purposive orientation. The traditionalism of the Middle East (like most religious traditionalism in general) was much more entrenched and resistant to change because the eternal validity of tradition was grounded in the eternal validity and truth of divine revelation itself. Islamic traditions and rituals, the realm of the religious laws or *s̲h̲arī'ah*, were defined as binding because they were the Word of God. And because it was assumed that the Word of God was not only eternally valid but unchanging, traditions were perceived to be absolute and unalterable because they represented the eternal, unalterable will of God.

In Islam, this traditionalism was based on belief in the finality of the Islamic Revelation: after the Prophet Muḥammad, there would be no further revelation and no change in the religious law. So strong was this traditionalism that it was even projected into the past: all the previous revealed Holy Scriptures, it was reasoned, must have advocated the same laws and rituals as those found in the Qur'án since divine truth is absolute and the divine will is eternal. The apparent inconsistency of the sacred texts and laws of Judaism and Christianity with the those of the Qur'án was explained by the doctrine of "corruption of the texts": the followers of the older religions were presumed to have altered their own holy books for the sole purpose of refuting Islam.

In Islam, the static thesis of finality, or the "end of history," has remained the underlying force of a traditionalism that categorically rejects all that is modern (and, for that reason, by definition heretical), has blocked socioeconomic vitality and creativity, and has exacerbated the social and economic problems of Muslim nations, but which also finds its own difficulties to be a further vindication of its hatred of the "infidels." Even modernist Islam, while more progressive than militant traditionalism, remains imprisoned within the same set of traditional assumptions about the finality of the Islamic Revelation and the eternal, unchanging nature of religious law. While modernist Islam is more flexible in adopting some superficial elements of modern culture, it has never questioned the fundamental premises of the traditionalistic model. The result, for the world of Islam, has been the cultural and spiritual deadlock described above; continuing social, political, and economic problems; and the pervasive negative perception and suspicion of the West and its institutions.

The writings of the Báb offered a novel solution to Islam's cultural and spiritual impasse. The Báb's dynamic approach to truth questioned all forms of traditionalism. His transformative interpretation of the finality doctrine overturned the very foundations of Muslim traditionalism by explaining divine revelation—past, present, and future—as a continuous process that was cyclical and progressive. What had been the basis of traditionalism became, in the Báb's writings, the foundation of a thorough critique of the traditionalist orientation itself.

The Báb's approach to the challenge of modernity was utterly different from that of Islamic traditionalists. Muslim traditionalists attributed the Middle East's backwardness, and its political and economic subjugation to Europe, to the Muslims' own failure to adhere to the traditional practices of early Islam. The solution they proposed was fundamentalism:

the wholesale rejection of modernity and a return to the practices, institutions, and laws of over a thousand years ago. The traditionalist explanation is of course too simplistic and does not confront the real questions. The Muslims' failure to observe Islamic practices of the past cannot explain the rise of the Western "infidels" to power and their cultural creativity, for Western peoples were even further than the Muslims in their deviation from Islamic practices. Still, this view was a major factor that contributed to legitimizing traditionalism, and it has remained a great obstacle to development and creativity in the Middle East.

According to the Báb, however, it is absolutely true that the solution to the problems of Islam lies in a return to the original creative spirit and source of the religion. But this return to the source, as it unfolds in the writings of the Báb, is the exact opposite of a return to the former Islamic rituals and practices. In the Báb's theology, the creative spirit of Islam is the same divine spirit that has been the source of all the religions and civilizations of the past. The creative nature of that spirit is defined by the progressive and historically specific character of divine revelation. Thus the creativity of the divine spirit involves not the conservation but the abrogation of previous social laws and practices, and their periodic renewal in new forms.[10] Return to the creative spirit of Islam is thus simultaneously a return to the creative spirit that animated Judaism and Christianity. Such a return to the spirit of Islam, therefore, far from demanding adherence to certain historically specific social laws and practices, requires no less than a thorough questioning of the traditionalist logic behind those practices, as well as a dynamic spiritual orientation and a cultural transformation based on the requirements of justice and progress in the contemporary world. In this systematic reexamination, the Báb advocates adopting useful elements of Western modernity—for example, He encourages trade relations with the West and urges learning from the sciences, arts, and industries of the Christians (that is, Europeans). But He rejects the particularistic, materialistic, and morally harmful aspects of modernity that obstruct the progress of human civilization.

Beyond Fundamentalism and Sociologism

Although the writings of the Báb, and in even more explicit ways those of Bahá'u'lláh, offer an elegant solution to the crisis of Islam in the contemporary world, the relevance of the Báb and His writings goes far beyond the question of Islam and modernity. One of those aspects with wider import is the Báb's approach to all religions, an approach that addresses the fundamental sources of conflict between religious communities and which has relevance not only for traditional religious discourse but for the sociology of religion.

In discourse about sources of religious conflict, the positions represented by religious fundamentalism and sociological reductionism (sociologism) are regarded as essentially extreme opposites. Although these two views are assumed to represent contradictory perspectives and dissimilar methodologies, the reality is much more complex. In fact, the viewpoints and methodologies of these groups have much in common, and they share an important premise that is directly related to the persistence of religious conflict in the world. Thus the need for a thorough reexamination of the current approach to religion is not confined to varieties of religious fundamentalism; it is crucial for academic sociologism as well.

Religion is a multi-dimensional phenomenon, possessing a metaphysical/spiritual and a social/empirical aspect. Religion advocates a metaphysical vision as the revelation of a transcendent Absolute Reality; at the same time religion is embodied in particular forms of human beliefs, behaviours, organizations, and institutions that are subject to sociological and historical dynamics. Any adequate approach to the study of religion must recognize these two dimensions. Traditionalist religious discourse and classical sociology of religion, however, both deny the multi-dimensional character of religion, and both insist on reducing religion to one of those two aspects. Religious fundamentalism defines religion solely in terms of the transcendental/metaphysical dimension and denies the relevance of the social/historical aspect. In this dogmatic perspective, religion is absolute and the divine Word is an expression of the eternal, unchangeable will of God. It is not surprising that, from this standpoint, conflict between religions is inevitable: the absolute character of religion means that only one's own religion is true and all other religions must be false.

The dominant perspective in sociology of religion, while taking a position opposite to fundamentalism, actually culminates in some of the same implications. This view usually defines religion in terms of its social/cultural dimension and denies the reality of any transcendental/

metaphysical aspect. Some of the greatest sociologists have even turned the sociology of religion itself into an argument for the non-existence of God and the soul. In their theories, religion is viewed as a social construction that can be adequately explained by the culture of a particular society, while the notion of divine revelation is defined as an error that can be disproved through scientific reasoning and evidence. Marx and most of the Marxists reduced religion to the material and economic aspects of society; denied the possibility of the existence of God, revelation, or the soul; and dismissed the idea of God as an illusion. Following Feuerbach, who reduced theological propositions to products of human beings' alienation from their own nature, Marx explained religion in terms of material alienation within the civil society.[11] Durkheim considered the ideas of both the soul and God to be illusions misrepresenting the real nature of religion, which was the collective consciousness/conscience of society, its common culture, projected (that is, alienated) onto a distorted conceptual realm.[12] Freud defined God as the psychological misrecognition of the unconscious perception of the father that is projected onto an imaginary realm.[13] And Auguste Comte conceived sociology itself, "the positive science," as the refutation of theological and metaphysical perspectives.[14]

But when closely examined, all these forms of analysis, despite their claims to rest on scientific—that is, objective—methods, are themselves methodologically unscientific. Sociology as an empirical science cannot, by its own definition, make judgments on the truth value of any metaphysical or theological propositions. Whether God exists is not a question that can be resolved by using the empirical tools of sociological research. Thus when Marx, Comte, Durkheim, or others use the authority of sociology as "science" to deny the validity of the metaphysical dimension of religion, they are no longer speaking as scientists and sociologists. They are, instead, making a rhetorical appeal to the authority of science in order to persuade readers to adopt what, in reality, are their own particular metaphysical assumptions. While they are of course convinced that these assumptions are brute "scientific" facts about reality, the premises offered as axiomatic are actually metaphysical assumptions. These assumptions have led to oversimplified and inaccurate representations of religion, and as a result science is portrayed as an enemy of religion.

Within the boundaries of empirical inquiry, sociologists can justifiably discuss the social and psychological conditions under which people are more or less likely to believe in certain forms of religious beliefs and practices. They can also legitimately establish empirical regularities concerning the relation of certain social conditions to certain forms of conceptualizing the sacred. Yet none of these endeavours is the same as proving or disproving metaphysical propositions about religious phenomena such as the existence of God, the soul, or revelation. It is possible to assume that a God exists as a metaphysical truth, and yet to state that the understanding of that truth, as well as the forms of its conceptualization, are dependent on the dynamics of cultural development and the specific conditions of human social existence. Human inadequacy to comprehend the Absolute, and the dependence of various forms of conceptualization on social factors, have nothing to do with the metaphysical question of the existence or non-existence of that Absolute. Thus sociologism's denial of the existence of the transcendental/metaphysical dimension of religion is an expression of its own tacit materialistic metaphysics that masks the axiomatic nature of that metaphysics—that is, conceals the fact that something is being accepted as an assumption without proof—by labelling its particular metaphysical propositions as scientific facts.

Not all sociologists of religion, of course, go as far as Marx and Durkheim in subordinating religion to the social realm. Yet even contemporary liberal and postmodern approaches to religion usually view religion as conditioned by the particular social culture in which it develops. The differences between religions are ascribed to the differences between cultures, and because each of those cultures represents a series of unique historical conditions, those cultures (and religions) are considered incommensurable. The existence of any common universal truth among all religions is explained in material terms—that is, as resulting from the similarities in the basic universal conditions of human life to which every culture must respond in its own way.

Thus people are considered to be imprisoned within different closed theological/cultural universes, and all religions are doomed to eternal separation from one another. It is easy to see how this particular perspective unwittingly undergirds the alienation of religions from one another. Religions become conceived of as closed cultural frameworks, a situation leading inevitably to mutual rejection and conflict. In other words, despite the good intentions of theorists, sociologistic methodology's reduction of religion to sociocultural phenomena provides a "scientific" basis for justifying the alienation of religions from each other and thus contributes to a situation in which religion is a force for hatred and communal strife. While for decades this approach to religion was the accepted norm in academic disciplines, emerging trends have put into question these premises as well as the various assumptions associated with the now increasingly discredited doctrine of cultural relativism.[15]

The perspective advocated by the Báb in the 1840s transcends the limitations of both religious fundamentalism and the sociological reductionism just described. The key to this perspective is the recognition of religion's multi-dimensional character. Each religion, with its particular practices and laws, is explained as the product of the interaction between the divine Will and a specific set of historical, social, and cultural conditions. The Will of God is not static but ever-creative, renewing the form in which It manifests Itself in accordance with humanity's stage of development; the various religions are all viewed as diverse, sequential expressions of the same divine truth. The writings of the Báb direct attention away from the token or secondary manifestations of religion—those laws and practices that are diverse—and they focus attention instead on the one common source of all those varying expressions: the divine Will. In other words, the Báb's writings combine historical consciousness with mystical consciousness, encompassing both dimensions of religion and emphasizing that the core reality of all the religions is one and the same.

The Crisis of Modernity

The significance of the writings of the Báb, as well as those of Bahá'u'lláh, is not limited to questions of religion and religious truth; Their writings are also directly relevant to the contemporary social and political crises of Western civilization. For if the Middle East has failed to adequately address the challenge of modernity because of its own imprisonment within a predominantly traditionalist outlook, the West has equally failed to deal with its own crisis of modernity because it has not applied the spirit of systematic search and deliberation to the realm of spiritual truth. The consequence of this failure is the persistence of a contradiction at the heart of Western modernity, the effects of which are increasingly evident in the breakdown of its moral premises and an inevitable slide into relativism with regard to truth and values.

The Western achievement of modernity was founded on the realization and institutionalization of certain fundamental moral principles including equality, freedom, and tolerance, based on a definition of human beings as endowed with inalienable human rights. Various legal and cultural institutions were created to institutionalize the egalitarian moral individualism of Enlightenment philosophy at the levels of the family, civil society, and politics, and to protect people's rights and freedom. Rejecting traditionalism, Western intellectual leaders accomplished this moral construct in the name of logic and reason. Since they themselves did not question the static premises of religious traditionalism, they tended to equate revelation with traditionalism, and thus founded "the republic of reason" on "the ruins of religion."

The philosophers of the Enlightenment believed that human reason and logic alone could arrive at truth and infer right values. However, reason alone, absent any human spiritual dimension, is unable to deduce universal moral values. In fact, the system of morality advocated by Enlightenment philosophy was caught in a fundamental contradiction between the ethics of consequences (utilitarianism) and the ethics of inalienable human rights.[16] Enlightenment philosophy not only failed to recognize the tension between these two moral theories, but it also failed to realize that its own assumptions about the possession of rights by individuals were based on taken-for-granted spiritual principles derived from the sources of its own cultural and philosophical heritage—the teachings of Judaism and Christianity. Enlightenment philosophers assumed that they were rejecting religion even while they were tacitly using religious premises as the precondition for the operations of their own reason.

However, in the course of the nineteenth and twentieth centuries, many of the remnants of those religious underpinnings were increasingly detected and rejected by various political philosophers. The result was the emergence of a moral crisis: concepts such as equality and inalienable human rights are founded on metaphysical beliefs that posit the sacred nature of humans as created in the image of God—and, as even some who do not accept those religious origins have argued, such rights can only be founded on that kind of religious belief.[17]

With the rejection of any metaphysical construct as an illusion, Nietzsche, in the nineteenth century, announced the death of all truth and values. Throughout the twentieth century, the crisis of modernity deepened, and with disillusion came skepticism that reason could indeed solve all human problems. The optimism that had greeted promises of "scientific" models of society turned into revulsion as those models yielded totalitarianism and world war. In the mid-twentieth century, modernity itself was pronounced dead and a "postmodern" age was proclaimed. According to postmodernist theorists, modernism had simply made the same metaphysical mistake: by elevating reason to the status of a transcendent source of universal truth, modernism had only replaced one metaphysical illusion with another.

The thorough rooting out of metaphysical assumptions has led to the prevalent view that there are and can be no "foundations" for anything, that all values are relative, and that there is no objective and rational criterion of moral judgment that can transcend the values and ideas of specific cultures and traditions. The disturbing and ominous message of some contemporary theorists is that human beings have no universal human identity independent from their local, cultural identity. The only apparent source of authority that many could see as a basis for moral principles, or even human identity, was, ironically—tradition.

Thus, in the West, no less than in the Islamic world, tradition once again has been elevated to the realm of the sacred. The celebration of tradition and the reduction of human identity to cultural categories has become the ultimate message of a discursive reason stripped of all vestiges of spiritual values. Now that reason has been abandoned as a transcendent Absolute, the challenge of postmodernity is to locate some ground for values and ethics in order to safeguard the positive aspects of modernity—its egalitarian and democratic principles—without returning to repressive religious traditionalism. The forces of globalization have only exacerbated this crisis and thrust upon the world the imperative of finding an ethical framework to regulate relations between actors—whether nations, peoples, cultures, or corporations—in an interdependent global society.

The twenty-first century finds itself trapped between awareness of the need for a universal ethic and a global moral framework, and pervasive suspicion of universalism and of foundations. We are thus left with a cult of tradition that eliminates the possibility of any universal criterion for judging among contending cultures and normative practices in the world. The spirit of this contradiction is nowhere more visible than in the heart of the very idea of postmodernism and cultural relativism itself. Advocates of these theories venerate diversity and equality, and yet they do so by denying the possibility of any objective, rational, and universal ground for morality and truth. Thus the acceptance of diversity, which is a reflection of the consciousness of the equal value of all human beings, has become turned into the worship of tradition. The dark side of cultural diversity, however, is that racism, patriarchal suppression of women, ritual mutilation, genocide, colonialism, and other practices that oppress one segment of society and maintain the dominance of another are also venerable cultural traditions.[18] And it has not escaped some repressive regimes that Western postmodernist theories of cultural relativism can be invoked to rebuff demands from the world community that those regimes conform to international standards of human rights, by claiming that their repressive traditions and practices cannot be judged by outsiders employing culturally alien notions such as universal human rights.

The positive egalitarian and democratic principles of Western modernity can be safeguarded with integrity only if the spiritual foundations of those principles are rediscovered—but not by a return to traditionalism. What is called for, instead, is a reexamination of Western instrumental rationality's approach to religion and spiritual principles, and the application of the spirit of systematic search for truth to the spiritual as well as the material dimensions of life. Reason need not be alienated from the spiritual dimension of human reality. A dynamic understanding of human civilization and culture can be harmonized with a dynamic approach to the mystical and spiritual dimension of reality. Such an approach to truth is the heart of the message of the Báb.

The writings of the Báb, and those of Bahá'u'lláh, unfold a vision that is simultaneously historical and mystical, in which phenomenal reality is linked to its transcendental ground, the principle of the unity of all beings. Human reason, assisted and inspired by a spiritual perspective, becomes empowered to discover the basis of universal moral truth which is eternal in its principle while relative in its historical expression and realization. Although elements of the outline of such a new moral order can be found in the writings of the Báb, it is in the writings of Bahá'u'lláh that this complex mystic-historical consciousness is systematically realized as the global consciousness of the oneness of humanity.

Shí'ih Millenarianism and the Renewal of Charismatic Authority

In A.H. 1260 (A.D. 1844), when the Báb made His proclamation, millenarian expectations in the Shí'ih world had reached an intense pitch as the time for the return of the Hidden Twelfth Imám approached. In Shí'ih Islam, authority was charismatic, and was vested in the Imáms, in contrast to Sunni Islam, where the Qur'án and the oral Traditions (*Ḥadíth*) formed the basis of a routinized and traditional type of authority. The Shí'ih Imáms, beginning with 'Alí ibn Abí-Ṭálib (Muḥammad's cousin and son-in-law), were regarded as the only legitimate leaders of the Muslim community and as the vicegerents or successors of the Prophet. Later Shí'ih theology also defined them as endowed with infallible authority inspired by divine knowledge. But in A.H. 260 (A.D. 874), when the Eleventh Imám died, the Twelfth Imám went into concealment or "occultation." For more than seven decades afterwards, mediators called *Báb*s (Gates) or *Ná'ib*s (Representatives) communicated between the Hidden Imám and the people. The fourth of those Gates, however, claimed that the Imám had gone into an indefinite "Grand Occultation," during which time he would cease to communicate with the people. According to the doctrine, the Twelfth Imám remained alive but, because of the threat from his enemies, in concealment from which he would only emerge shortly before the Day of Judgment. Then, as the Qá'im (He who will arise) or *Mahdí* (He who is rightly guided), with his sword he would unleash holy war against the forces of evil, would vanquish the unjust and the unbelievers, and would initiate a reign of justice in the world. He would be followed by the return of Christ, along with Imám Ḥusayn as well as the other Imáms and holy figures of Islam.

During the Twelfth Imám's occultation, the question of leadership within the Shí'ih community became particularly problematic. The Imám's absence left a gap which became filled by the traditional authority of the *'ulamá*, the scholars of religious law, who increasingly attempted to extend and consolidate their power and influence in society. To legitimize their authority, these clerics increasingly defined themselves as the general representatives of the Hidden Imám on earth. During the eighteenth and nineteenth centuries, the 'ulamá's power was greatly expanded by the triumph of the Uṣúlí school of Shí'ih Islam. Uṣúlí doctrine held that true knowledge (*'ilm*) belonged only to the Hidden Imám, but in his absence conjecture (*ẓann*) was a valid basis for legal inferences by expert jurist-scholars. These scholars were certified by their professional education and by the permission or licence conferred on them by senior legal scholars, which allowed them to make independent judgments. Each S̲h̲í'ih believer was expected to follow and obey a particular religious scholar on matters of law. This ideology also encouraged the creation of a corporate hierarchy among S̲h̲í'ih scholars, one which was increasingly centralized and, with its increasing tendency to have a universal centre of imitation, resembled the Christian papacy.[19]

For centuries, the Islamic clergy had defined and determined all aspects of individual and community life, including the minutest details of the individual's private concerns, as phenomena subject to the regulation of the *s̲h̲arí'ah*. Since a correct understanding of those laws required expert knowledge possessed only by the 'ulamá, the clerical elite's function and authority became further entrenched. With the victory of Uṣúlí doctrine and its corporate centralization, the 'ulamá's power expanded to an unprecedented extent.

This form of authority, by its very nature, was based on tradition and acted to conserve and guard the sacred ways of the past. It was in this situation, in the decades preceding the Báb's proclamation, that S̲h̲ay<u>k</u>h Aḥmad-i-Aḥsá'í (1743–1828), and later his successor Siyyid Káẓim-i-Ras̲h̲tí (1793–1843), revived interest in charismatic authority by focusing attention on the Imáms, particularly the Hidden Imám. Moreover, they attributed their own authority not only to their traditional and professional education, but to mystical knowledge received directly from the Hidden Imám. The community of S̲h̲ay<u>k</u>h Aḥmad's adherents was characterized by fervent millenarian expectations, complex mystical and esoteric knowledge, insistence on the absolute transcendence of the divine Essence (and hence a categorical rejection of the Sufi pantheistic doctrine of the unity of existence, or *vaḥdatu'l-vujúd*), a reinterpretation of the traditional doctrine of the Day of Resurrection as physical but not material, and ambiguous assertions concerning the necessity of the presence of a living Gate (a Báb) to the Hidden Imám for the guidance of the S̲h̲í'ih community.[20]

On the fifth of Jumádí'l-Avval, 1260 (the eve of May 23, 1844), the Báb met with Mullá Ḥusayn, a young S̲h̲ay<u>k</u>hí leader and scholar whose journey in search of the Promised One had led him to Shiraz. According to the account of that meeting as recorded in *The Dawn-Breakers,* Mullá Ḥusayn had privately decided upon two tests he would put to anyone claiming to be the promised Qá'im. The first test was to explain the "mysterious allusions" in a treatise Mullá Ḥusayn had written on the esoteric teachings of Shaykh Aḥmad and Siyyid Káẓim. Anyone who could unravel these mysteries would then be asked to reveal a commentary on the Qur'án's Súrih of Joseph, but "in a style and language entirely different from the prevailing standards of the time." Mullá Ḥusayn had once asked Siyyid Káẓim to reveal such a commentary but Siyyid Káẓim had declined, saying that such a task was beyond him. However, he told Mullá Ḥusayn, "He, that great One, who comes after me will, unasked, reveal it for you. That commentary will constitute one of the weightiest testimonies of His truth, and one of the clearest evidences of the loftiness of His position." Mullá Ḥusayn's account, according to the *Dawn-Breakers,* continues:

> "'I was revolving these things in my mind, when my distinguished Host again remarked: "Observe attentively. Might not the Person intended by Siyyid Káẓim be none other than I?" I thereupon felt impelled to present to Him a copy of the treatise which I had with me. "Will you," I asked Him, "read this book of mine and look at its pages with indulgent eyes? I pray you to overlook my weaknesses and failings." He graciously complied with my wish. He opened the book, glanced at certain passages, closed it, and began to address me. Within a few minutes He had, with characteristic vigour and charm, unravelled all its mysteries and resolved all its problems. Having to my entire satisfaction accomplished, within so short a time, the task I had expected Him to perform, He further expounded to me certain truths which could be found neither in the reported sayings of the Imáms of the Faith nor in the writings of Shaykh Aḥmad and Siyyid Káẓim. These truths, which I had never heard before, seemed to be endowed with refreshing vividness and power. "Had you not been My guest," He afterwards observed, "your position would indeed have been a grievous one. The all-encompassing grace of God has saved you. It is for God to test His servants, and not for His servants to judge Him in accordance with their deficient standards. Were I to fail to resolve your perplexities, could the Reality that shines within Me be regarded as powerless, or My knowledge be accused as faulty? Nay, by the righteousness of God! it behooves, in this day, the peoples and nations of both

> the East and the West to hasten to this threshold, and here seek to obtain the reviving grace of the Merciful. Whoso hesitates will indeed be in grievous loss. . . ." He then proceeded to say: "Now is the time to reveal the commentary on the Súrih of Joseph." He took up His pen and with incredible rapidity revealed the entire Súrih of Mulk, the first chapter of His commentary on the Súrih of Joseph. The overpowering effect of the manner in which He wrote was heightened by the gentle intonation of His voice which accompanied His writing. Not for one moment did He interrupt the flow of the verses which streamed from His pen. Not once did He pause till the Súrih of Mulk was finished. I sat enraptured by the magic of His voice and the sweeping force of His revelation. At last I reluctantly arose from my seat and begged leave to depart. He smilingly bade me be seated, and said: "If you leave in such a state, whoever sees you will assuredly say: 'This poor youth has lost his mind.'"[21]

On that night, which marked the first day of the Bábí era, and which would be observed afterwards as a holy day, Mullá Ḥusayn became the first to acknowledge his belief in the Báb. After him seventeen others recognized the Báb through their own independent search. Together these first eighteen disciples, seventeen men and one woman, were designated the "Letters of the Living."

In the very work that the Báb began to write that night in the presence of Mullá Ḥusayn, the Commentary on the Súrih of Joseph, or Qayyúmu'l-Asmá' (The Self-Subsisting Lord of All Names) as the Báb preferred to call it,[22] the Báb refuted the traditional authority of the Muslim religious jurists, including the Uṣúlí justification of rational conjecture. He claimed that the age of true knowledge had begun, and henceforth no religious leader of any faith was justified in pronouncing binding judgments:

> O concourse of divines! Fear God from this day onwards in the views ye advance, for He Who is Our Remembrance in your midst, and Who cometh from Us, is, in very truth, the Judge and Witness. Turn away from that which ye lay hold of and which the Book of God, the True One, hath not sanctioned, for on the Day of Resurrection ye shall, upon the Bridge, be, in very truth, held answerable for the position ye occupied.
>
> In all His Tablets, God hath verily ordained vain imaginings and conjecture (*ẓann*) to be a manifest sin.[23] . . . God verily hath made it

> unlawful for you to pronounce, in clear defiance of truth, any injunction or to exercise any legal judgment while bereft of the absolute knowledge of this Book.[24]

With what authority did the Báb make such audacious statements, overturning the entire basis of the Shí'ih clerical establishment? One of the most significant yet misunderstood aspects of the Báb's writings is this very question—what station and authority He claimed for Himself, and specifically, the apparent change in that claim over the course of His mission. In the early writings it appears that the Báb is identifying Himself as the Gate (Báb) to the Hidden Imám. Less than halfway through the six years of His ministry, He begins to explicitly proclaim His station to be that of the Hidden Imám, a new Prophet, and the Manifestation of the Primal Will of God. But does this apparent difference in His claims represent, as some have said, a change in His own consciousness and perception of His station, or, as others suggest, is it accountable to mere concealment or dissimulation (*taqíyyih*)?[25]

I will argue that the works of the Báb throughout the seven years of His Revelation express a message that, rather than being discontinuous or reflecting an evolving consciousness, is unitary and coherent from beginning to end. Despite the prodigious diversity of His texts and the range of topics and symbols in His writings, all these elements can be seen to unveil systematic aspects of a single underlying logic. The gradual disclosure of the Báb's actual station signified neither a change of consciousness nor mere dissimulation; moreover, the multiple stations He claimed were a coherent and integral part of His message and theology. As we shall see, that message and that theology is defined by the principle of the unity in diversity of all reality. The history of the gradual disclosure of the Báb's identity will be shown to express the very principle that is the heart of that identity. What at first appears to be concealment, once placed in its full context, becomes visible as the consummate disclosure. In the Báb's early writings, the exalted nature of the station He claimed is unmistakably evident, but for rhetorical reasons related to the reception of the people, His writings appear to convey the impression that He is only the Gate to the Hidden Imám. Yet even when the Báb describes His station ambiguously, from the very beginning it is evident that He is defining it in an unprecedented way.

The Brief Ministry of the Báb

Many of the details and specific dates of various events in the life of the Báb are subject to differing opinions among various authors. The short historical account presented here is intended only to provide the general background necessary for the discussion that follows and is tentative and preliminary. This study concerns the works of the Báb and not the history of His life. For more extensive and complete accounts of the history of the Báb, readers should consult some of the works specifically devoted to that subject.[26]

After the eighteen Letters of the Living accepted the Báb, the Báb dispatched them to different regions to proclaim His advent. As evidence of the Báb's claim, they carried copies of two of the major works He had revealed during the first days following His declaration in Shiraz: the Commentary on the Súrih of Joseph (the Qayyúmu'l-Asmá') and the Hidden Treasured Epistle (Ṣaḥífiy-i-Ma<u>kh</u>zúnih). Bearing these testimonies, Mullá Ḥusayn, the first Letter of the Living, travelled to various parts of Iran, while the second Letter, Mullá 'Alí Basṭámí, departed for Baghdad and the <u>Sh</u>í'ih holy city of Karbila, then in the Ottoman empire. The last of the Letters of the Living, Mullá Muḥammad 'Alí, surnamed Quddús, accompanied the Báb to Mecca and Medina.

The Báb's journey to Mecca and His declaration of His station to the Muslims present there before the Ka'bah, the traditional Sacred House of God, have a unique symbolic significance.[27] In both His early and later writings the Báb makes it clear that the House of God in Mecca is sacred only because the divine Word, as revealed in the Qur'án, attributed that House to God. The true repository of the Sacred, however, is the divine Word itself, which is identical with the Recipient of divine revelation. All the laws of the Qur'án, the Báb asserts, including the duty of pilgrimage, were ordained in order to prepare the people for His advent; the true focal point of pilgrimage and the embodiment of the Sacred House of God is the Báb Himself. Seventy thousand pilgrims were gathered there in Mecca by virtue of His previous command (when the same spirit spoke in the person of Muḥammad) in His former book (the Qur'án). But now He Himself was present in that very spot, and yet all were paying homage to a mere token of His command while disregarding His own presence and His authority. This event decisively marked the end of the age of the appearance of truth in symbolic form (the Sacred House made of clay) and the inception of the age of the revelation of the inner truth (the Báb).

In the Báb's early works, including the Commentary on the Súrih of Joseph, He had called on His followers to gather in Karbila. Given the set of expectations associated with the rising of the Qá'im, this summons would have been understood as signalling preparation for the beginning of the apocalyptic holy war foretold in the Islamic Traditions. Yet, in issuing this call, what the Báb was actually doing was something very different. The most important function of that call was to implicitly announce His identity as not merely the Gate to the Hidden Imám, but as the Qá'im Himself. This point was not missed by those enemies of the Báb who were familiar with the esoteric language of the Shaykhí school. The Shaykhí leader Ḥáj Karím Khán-i-Kirmání declared that the author of the Commentary on the Súrih of Joseph must be claiming to be the Qá'im since only the living Imám could authorize holy war.[28]

Karím Khán was correct that the Báb was implicitly claiming to be the Qá'im, but was the Báb actually authorizing holy war? This question—the Báb's position toward holy war—is an aspect of the Báb's writings and teachings that has been widely misunderstood and requires close examination. I will argue that although the Báb makes use of Shí'ih millenarian symbols, and nominally appears to accept the idea of holy war, in fact He completely undermines the concept by defining holy war in such a way as to make it contingent on the realization of impossible conditions—thus, in effect, nullifying it. This topic will be fully explored later in this book, but as an example, one of those conditions He set was that waging holy war must not result in any sort of grief or sadness for the people. Although the Bábís had gathered in Karbila for the expected jihad, the Báb unexpectedly cancelled that decree, and instead of going to Karbila, He returned to Iran. He explained that the reason He did so was the persecution of His followers by the Muslim clergy, who had imprisoned the Báb's messenger and rejected His message. As the Báb explains, it was His desire to see no harm or sadness befall anyone that led Him to alter His previous command to gather in Karbila for the inception of the expected holy war. Although victory was not in doubt, the persecution of His disciples meant that such a holy war would surely cause grief and loss of life.[29] The Báb's alteration of the divine command in this instance represents an important expression of His interpretive reversal of the concept of holy war. That reinterpretation would become much more explicit in the later period of His mission, in the form of the new laws that He decrees.

While in Bú<u>sh</u>ihr, the Báb received the news of the Muslim clerics' opposition to His writings. As He explains in one of His works, each act of denial by the people was like the blow of a sword cutting His heart in pieces—a spiritual martyrdom far more painful than any physical death.[30] In an action similar to His decision to cancel His journey to Karbila, the Báb announced that because the people had displayed opposition to the divine bounty conferred upon them through His revelation, they would henceforth be deprived of receiving the divine words from Him. On Jumádi'<u>th</u>-<u>Th</u>ání 15, 1261 (June 21, 1845), the Báb wrote a number of letters indicating that He would withdraw from direct contact with the people, would not respond to their questions, and would not send them new revelations, and that this withdrawal and withholding would last for five years, beginning that same day.[31]

It is crucial to understand the reasons for this pattern of withdrawal. The Báb was not personally seeking to proclaim His station; rather, as He explains, He did it as His duty to transmit to the people the revelation entrusted to Him. But when they reacted to His message with opposition, denial, and persecution, He was saddened and decided they were not yet worthy of receiving it. Thus He withdrew from contact with them and in that period sometimes even spoke as if He had no prophetic message for them at all.

One of the Báb's tablets announcing the beginning of this period of withdrawal is the Kitábu'l-Fihrist (Indexical Tablet). In it the Báb states that from "this day" God has forbidden giving His words to the people for the duration of five years.[32] In the same text, the Báb lists His own writings up to that point, including some earlier works written before His declaration. The significance of this tablet is not merely that it provides the Báb's own catalogue of His writings up to that time. As the listing was made on the occasion of a turning point in the history of His mission—His decision to withhold further revelation—the Kitábu'l-Fihrist not only reflects on the list of His writings but also on crucial events in the Báb's life and mission. In this work He identifies His first Letter of the Living, Mullá Ḥusayn, as His representative among the people—the Gate to the Gate (a title by which Mullá Ḥusayn was already known) and as the one to whom all questions concerning the writings of the Báb should be directed.[33]

There has been some confusion about the meaning of the Báb's five years of withdrawal from contact with the people. Denis MacEoin has read this statement as referring to the fact that for five years after the Báb's declaration He would conceal His true station as the Qá'im.[34] But this point is unrelated to the five years mentioned in the Kitábu'l-Fihrist and similar texts of that time. As we saw, this five-year period begins thirteen months after the Báb's declaration and does not concern the concealment of His station. Instead, it concerns His abstention from responding to questions and His withholding the revelation of new works either as the Gate to the Qá'im or as the Qá'im Himself.

But the passionate insistence of the Báb's followers, as well as the Báb's own character, led the Báb to alter His decree, and gradually He began to respond to questions. About six months after the beginning of His withdrawal, on Muḥarram 15, 1262 (January 13, 1846), He wrote the Khuṭbiy-i-Dhikríyyih (Sermon of Remembrance), which presents a new account of His works up to the writing of that text. Together with the Kitábu'l-Fihrist, the Khuṭbiy-i-Dhikríyyih is a crucial source for dating various early works of the Báb.[35] In it, the Báb lists the works He wrote during the years A.H. 1260–1262 as fourteen, comprising four major books (*kutub;* singular, *kitáb*) and ten shorter books, or epistles (*ṣaḥáif;* singular, *ṣaḥífih*). He now identifies these fourteen texts as written by the fourteen sacred figures of Shí'ih Islam (the Prophet Muḥammad, His daughter Fáṭimih, and the twelve Imáms). It is noteworthy that the Báb is now implicitly identifying Himself not just as a Gate to the Hidden Imám, but also as the Gate to the Prophet and all the other sacred figures.

After the Báb returned to Shiraz around July 1845, He was under virtual house arrest for more than a year. Apparently in late September of 1846 He left Shiraz for Isfahan, staying there about six months, after which He was banished to the remote prison fortress of Mákú in the mountains of Azerbaijan. The Báb's arrival at the prison of Mákú, around July 1847, marks the most important turning point in His mission.[36] During the previous three years (May 1844 to July 1847) the Báb had alluded to His true station in veiled, symbolic language, but from this point onward, and through the last three years of His life (July 1847 to July 9, 1850), His writings are characterized by open and unambiguous proclamation of His true station and mission. In these writings the Báb formally abrogates the Islamic Dispensation and initiates a new Dispensation with new laws.

The Báb remained confined in the prison of Mákú for about nine months. In His writings He identifies Mákú with Makkah (Mecca)—alluding to the identity of His Revelation with all the previous Revelations. During the Mákú period the Báb wrote some of His most important works, including the Persian Bayán and the Arabic Bayán. At the end of this period, in April 1848, the Báb was exiled to the prison fortress of Chihríq.[37] During His incarceration there, He wrote many new works, including the greater part of the Kitábu'l-Asmá' (Book of Divine Names) and Panj Sha'n (Five Modes of Revelation).

In June 1848, a few months after arriving at Chihríq, the Báb was taken to Tabriz to be interrogated by the leading Shí'ih clerics, led by conservative segments of the Shaykhí leadership, who had now joined the orthodox clergy in opposing the Báb.[38] When asked about His revolutionary claims, the Báb formally announced to them that He was the Qá'im. In support of His claim, He began to reveal divine verses. The clerics interrupted Him rudely and questioned His authority since He was disregarding the traditional rules of grammar. They demanded that the Báb answer irrelevant questions concerning superstitious medieval conceptions of knowledge which were then current among the Shí'ih clergy. But their questions clearly indicated that the traditionalist clerics were failing to face the Báb's claim; they were treating Him as if He were merely claiming to be an ordinary divine and hence they insisted on testing His conformity to the same ossified tradition that He was fundamentally invalidating. The scene presented an ironic contrast between the forceful authority of the young revolutionary prophet and the priestly traditionalism and obscurantism of the scholar-guardians of the old religious order. Faced with the clerics' repetition of their own doctrines, the Báb reaffirmed His authority on the grounds of His ability to reveal divine verses, and He refused to dignify their questions with any answer. After the interrogation, the Báb was taken back to Chihríq.

In June 1848, during the first months of the Báb's imprisonment in Chihríq, some eighty-four of His followers, including Quddús, Ṭáhirih, and Bahá'u'lláh, gathered in a historic conference at the hamlet of Badasht.[39] Shoghi Effendi states that "The primary purpose of that gathering was to implement the revelation of the Bayán by a sudden, a complete and dramatic break with the past—with its order, its ecclesiasticism, its traditions, and ceremonials. The subsidiary purpose of the conference was to consider the means of emancipating the Báb from His cruel confinement in C͟hihríq. The first was eminently successful; the second was destined from the outset to fail."[40] It was at Bada͟sht that Ṭáhirih, who, although a woman, was one of the Báb's most prominent disciples and a Letter of the Living—dramatically proclaimed the formal abrogation of the Islamic Dispensation through the gesture of appearing unveiled in the presence of the male Bábís. Symbolically representing the formal break between Islam and the new religion, she declared: "I am the Word which the Qá'im is to utter, the Word which shall put to flight the chiefs and nobles of the earth!"[41]

The last two years of the Báb's imprisonment in C͟hihríq marked the beginning of a new and heightened stage of persecution by both the state authorities and the S͟hí'ih religious establishment. It was during this time that the first massive confrontation took place between government troops and the persecuted Bábís, who were forced to take shelter in the shrine of S͟hayk͟h Ṭabarsí in Mázandarán. The state, unable to defeat them, promised amnesty if the Bábís left the shrine and surrendered their weapons. That promise, however, was a cruel ruse and the innocent Bábís were slaughtered. Throughout this entire episode, which lasted from September 1848 to May 1849, hundreds of the Báb's followers, including half of the Letters of the Living, were killed, among them the first and the last Letters of the Living—Mullá Ḥusayn and Quddús.

The Báb was once again taken from C͟hihríq to Tabriz. This time, by order of the Grand Vizier Amír Kabír and the signed decree of many Muslim clerics, He was condemned to death and was executed by firing squad on July 9, 1850. First a regiment of soldiers in three files was ordered to open fire upon Him in turn. But after the clouds of smoke had dissipated, the astounded crowd of onlookers discovered that the Báb had disappeared. The bullets had only severed the ropes binding Him, and He was eventually located in His prison cell finishing a conversation with His amanuensis. The regiment refused to fire at Him again, and another was called in to complete the execution. At the time of His martyrdom the Báb was just thirty-two years old.[42]

Reading the Writings of the Báb

Most of the works that have been written about the Báb deal with the history of His religion rather than His writings. Even those few works related to His writings are usually concerned either with the chronology of major works, the discussion of rituals, or the analysis of individual texts. One reason that the content of the Báb's writings has not yet been adequately studied is the problem of accessibility. The vast majority of the Báb's writings have not yet been translated or published.[43] Almost all His works were written during a period of seven years, but the quantity of writings He produced in that short period is overwhelming. The amazing rapidity of revelation, the pace at which the words passed through His pen and His lips, appears as a constant theme in His writings. In contrast, all the revelation of the Islamic Dispensation took place over twenty-three years and is contained in one book, the Qur'án. The Báb frequently comments that He is able to reveal divine verses equal in volume to those of the Qur'án in just a few days and nights. Observing the flow of revelation was a powerful force that attracted many people to become believers in the Báb.

Even for those who read the original languages, the Báb's writings present formidable challenges. The complexity and the esoteric character of those texts has understandably baffled readers and translators. Moreover, the language the Báb uses is unique to Him. The majority of His writings are in Arabic but a significant number are in Persian; both His Arabic and Persian, however, are linguistically innovative and non-standard, and deliberately so. This point has been lost on many readers, who have all too quickly and simplistically attributed deviation from convention to mere error. Yet, more important than the linguistic style, it is the complexity of the ideas, their philosophical and mystical depth, as well as the multi-faceted symbolic character and highly subtle rhetorical coding of the Báb's discourse that make these texts so difficult to understand, but that also account for their richness, beauty, and fascination.

One notable aspect of these texts' difficulty—an aspect which at first glance may seem arcane and esoteric—is their extensive use of the symbolism of letters and numbers. In Arabic, as in Hebrew and other ancient languages, each letter has a numerical value (the numbers were originally written as their letter equivalents, similar to roman numerals). The use of letter-number symbolism in mystical texts is often associated with the gematria of the Cabala, but it was also an important component of esoteric Islamic traditions and was widely practised in Shaykhí circles. Over the centuries, the fact that the súrihs of the Qur'án usually begin with a series of disconnected letters led many Muslims to believe that those mysterious letters stood for secret knowledge. One of the signs expected of the

Qá'im was that he would unravel the mystery concealed within those letters and would disclose the inner meanings of the Holy Text. Hence, in accordance with such millenarian expectations, as well as to convey multiple levels of meaning and allusion, the Báb often employs letter-number equivalence as one of the many symbolic modes of His discourse.

Another aspect contributing to the difficulty of reading the Báb's writings is that they are heavily intertextual: the Báb often employs quotations from and allusions to the Qur'án and Islamic Traditions, which are so interwoven into the fabric of His text as to make them indistinguishable from His own words. This stylistic feature in itself is highly meaningful and symbolic. Intimate knowledge of the Qur'án is required to identify those allusions and quotations, but knowledge of their traditional meanings is only the first step toward understanding their meaning within the Báb's texts. The presence of references to esoteric terms and concepts from Shaykhí discourse further adds to the challenge of understanding the Báb's works. Yet, the most important reason for the complexity and difficulty of His writings is the intense creativity and symbolic nature of the Báb's thought. The meaning of individual texts cannot be understood except within the context of the totality of the Báb's own writings; when one single text or passage is extracted from that totality and read out of context, it becomes vulnerable to serious misinterpretation and even reversal of meaning. For all these reasons, the writings of the Báb have presented a daunting challenge to readers.

The Báb's writings can be grouped into three broad stages, each characterized by a particular dominant thematic focus. The early writings, up to the beginning of 1262 (A.D. 1846), are primarily defined by the *interpretive* mode of revelation. While the interpretive mode continues throughout all three stages of His writings, a progressive shift of emphasis takes place, moving from interpretation to philosophical elucidation and culminating in legislative pronouncements. The second, *philosophical,* stage begins with the gradual end of the Báb's withdrawal from contact with the believers and His willingness to answer questions in the Persian language—an innovative departure, for in the tradition established by the Qur'án, Arabic was the language of revelation. During this period, although the interpretive mode continues, centre stage is now taken by an elaborate set of explanations of the metaphysics of being and creation. With the exile of the Báb to Mákú, a new, *legislative* form of revelation is initiated. During this third stage the mystical and historical principles become explicitly united in the Báb's writings. Millenarian attention is now intensely focused on the new Promised One, "He Whom God shall make manifest," Who, according to some writings of the Báb, would appear nine years after the inception of the Báb's Dispensation.

In the year 9, (A.H. 1269/A.D. 1852) Bahá'u'lláh's Revelation began, and in 1863 He made public His claim to be Him Whom God shall make manifest. Bahá'u'lláh's Revelation, as it unfolded in the years of His ministry, would turn the mystic-historical message of the Báb into a world religion centring on the principle of the oneness of humankind. Thus the wider importance of the Báb's writings lies in their inextricable relation to those of Bahá'u'lláh. The theological foundations of the Bahá'í teachings are first articulated in the writings of the Báb; thus those writings are indispensable to understanding the theology as well as the history of the Bahá'í Faith. If the Báb reinterpreted the Islamic concept of holy war in ways that effectively excluded violence, Bahá'u'lláh would formally and unequivocally abrogate it altogether, making the removal of the sword (with its implications of the larger principle of the equality and unity of all human beings) the cornerstone of the religion that would become known to the world as the Bahá'í Faith.[44] Yet it was the writings of the Báb that set the stage for the message of Bahá'u'lláh.

A SHORT CHRONOLOGICAL LIST OF THE BÁB'S WRITINGS

THIS SECTION PROVIDES a brief annotated listing of some of the major, or more frequently mentioned, works of the Báb in chronological order. In this study, three stages of the Báb's writings are distinguished. The first, interpretive, stage comprises works written up to the middle of the first month of A.H. 1262 (A.D. 1846). This stage corresponds to the period covered in the Báb's own listing of His main works in the Khuṭbiy-i-Dhikríyyih. In addition, within this first stage the Báb made yet another listing (the Kitábu'l-Fihrist) of His works written up to thirteen months after His declaration. A comparison of these two texts can identify the precise date of the revelation of texts within the first stage.

The second, philosophical, stage consists of works the Báb wrote during the remainder of His stay in Shiraz and His six months of residence in Isfahan (January 1846–April 1847). In addition to other evidence for dating the texts of this stage, we have a manuscript written by one of the greatest direct witnesses and scholars of the Bábí Dispensation, Siyyid Yaḥyá Dárábí, surnamed Vaḥíd, who transcribed some of the main works the Báb wrote in Isfahan.

The third, legislative, stage encompasses works written during the period from the Báb's departure from Isfahan for Mákú in April 1847 to His martyrdom in July 1850. The writings of the third stage are easily identifiable because in these writings the Báb discloses His station explicitly and uses new categories and concepts that were only implicit in the earlier stages. However, there are countless other clues for dating each of the Báb's works, the most important of which clues are His own references to dates within His texts. Yet for many other works, a precise dating awaits further research.

Some Works of the First Stage

(To January 1846)

1 **Fi's-Sulúk I** (On the Virtuous Journey I). This very early work was written before the declaration of the Báb and even before the death of Siyyid Káẓim. A short text, it was most likely written for Mullá Ḥasan and is mentioned in the Kitábu'l-Fihrist. In the text the Báb refers to a work by Siyyid Káẓim with a similar title.[1] Unlike Siyyid Káẓim's work, the Báb's focuses on the inner and mystical meanings of religious law, turning ritual action into a spiritual journey. The mediating category is love for the four layers of the divine covenant in the Islamic Dispensation.

2 **Fi's-Sulúk II** (On the Virtuous Journey II). This work was written after the Báb's declaration, for Abú Ṭálibi'l-Ḥusaynávi, and is also mentioned in the Kitábu'l-Fihrist. It unites the question of ethics and moral conduct with the idea of spiritual journey by emphasizing the philosophical purpose of any action, namely, seeking contentment with and acquiescence to the will of God. It discusses various types of contentment with regard to different aspects of life.

3 **Tafsír-i-Súriy-i-Baqarih I** (Commentary on the Súrih of the Cow I). This work, written within a year, was completed at the end of A.H. 1260 (A.D. 1844) and is an interpretation of a *juzv,* or one-thirtieth, of the Qur'án. It interprets various verses of the Súrih of the Cow in terms of the self-referential and ultimate truth of the Word of God, namely, the Primal Will of God and its covenantal manifestations.

4 **Tafsír-i-Súriy-i-Yúsif** (Commentary on the Súrih of Joseph), commonly referred to as the **Qayyúmu'l-Asmá'** (The Self-Subsisting Lord of All Names). This crucial text, written in honour of Mullá Ḥusayn, was begun on the night of the Báb's declaration in May 1844 and completed during the next forty days. Consisting of 111 chapters, it interprets various verses of the Qur'ánic Súrih of Joseph in terms of the principle of progressive revelation, disclosing both the station of the Báb and of Bahá'u'lláh.

5 **Ṣaḥífiy-i-Ma<u>kh</u>zúnih** (Hidden Treasured Epistle). This work was written shortly after the declaration of the Báb and consists of fourteen prayers and visitation tablets, one of which is related to the night of the Báb's declaration. Sometimes it is assumed that this work was written before that event, but in addition to its content, even the terminology used in the title of the text shows that it must have been written afterwards:

"God, glorified be He, hath verily sent forth this mighty and hidden Epistle unto one of His Testimonies, Muḥammad the Son of Ḥasan, peace be upon both of them. And it hath verily been revealed through the Remnant of God and the Lord of the Age, peace be upon Him, unto His Gate, the Remembrance, that God's testimony may be delivered through the agency of His Remembrance to all the peoples of the world."[2]

6 **Kitábu'r-Rúḥ** (Book of the Spirit). This text was written at sea during the Báb's return journey from Mecca and is mentioned in the Kitábu'l-Fihrist. A large work, consisting of approximately seven-hundred short súrihs, it is written in the language of Qur'ánic revelation. Referring to the Qur'ánic prophecy of the descent of the Spirit, the Báb identifies Himself with Jesus and the Holy Spirit. Given the work's context—the journey returning from Mecca and the realities of the sea voyage—the Báb frequently mentions the beauty of natural phenomena such as the wind, the waves, dawn, and sunshine, and interprets their true meaning as vehicles and symbols of the inner spiritual journey to the real House of God, which is the truth of the Báb Himself.[3]

7 **Tafsír-i-Bismilláh** (Commentary on *Bismilláh*). A commentary on the opening phrase of the Qur'án, "In the name of God," this text is mentioned in the Kitábu'l-Fihrist. In this work the Báb discusses the four stations of mystery (*sirr*) and analyzes each of the nineteen letters of the opening phrase of the Qur'án as references to the four levels of the divine covenant, while at times equating each of those letters with one of the sacred figures of the Islamic covenant.

8 **Ṣaḥífiy-i-A'mál-i-Sanih** (Epistle on the Devotional Deeds of the Year). This work is mentioned in the Kitábu'l-Fihrist. Written in Shiraz, it consists of fourteen chapters and provides various prayers and visitation tablets related to the twelve months of the Islamic calendar.

9 **Ṣaḥífiy-i-Bayna'l-Ḥaramayn** (Epistle Revealed between the Twin Shrines). This text was written between Mecca and Medina, on the first day of A.H. 1261, in response to questions posed by Mírzá Muḥíṭ-i-Kirmání and Siyyid 'Alíy-i-Kirmání. It is mentioned in the Kitábu'l-Fihrist. Consisting of an introduction and seven chapters, it affirms the station of the Báb, answers various questions regarding talismanic symbols, and offers prayers and visitation tablets for the rites associated with both the process of spiritual journey and pilgrimage to the shrine of Imám Ḥusayn.

10 **Kitábu'l-Fihrist** (Indexical Tablet). This work was written in Búshihr on Jumádi'th-Thání 15, 1261 (June 21, 1845), shortly after the Báb returned to Iran from Mecca. It recounts the story of His life, lists the works He has written up to that date, and informs the believers of His decision to withdraw from them for five years.

11 **Ṣaḥífiy-i-Raḍavíyyih** (Epistle of Riḍá').[4] This work consists of fourteen sermons (*khuṭáb;* singular, *khuṭbih*), written at different times, many of them during the journey to Mecca and Medina. The first chapter, entitled Khuṭbiy-i-Dhikríyyih (Sermon of Remembrance), was written at the end of the first stage of the Báb's writings and gives His works up to that date as four books and ten epistles, identifying the Ṣaḥífiy-i-Raḍavíyyih as the sixth epistle. Other chapters emphasize the absolute transcendence of God, the meaning of the martyrdom of Imám Ḥusayn, and the station of the Báb; and assign exalted spiritual meanings to the history of the Báb's life and various dates during His journey to Mecca and Medina. In the Khuṭbiy-i-Jiddah (Sermon of Jiddah), the Báb also lists the names of His works that were stolen during that journey.

12 **Sharḥ-i-Du'á'-i-Ghaybat** (Commentary on the Occultation Prayer), also called **Tafsír-i-Há'** (Interpretation of the Letter Há') and **Ṣaḥífiy-i-Ja'faríyyih** (Epistle of Ja'far). This work, consisting of fourteen chapters, was written in the early to middle part of the first month of A.H. 1262 and was one of the last works to be produced during the first stage. It is an interpretation of a prayer enjoined by Ja'far aṣ-Ṣádiq, the sixth Imám, to be read during the occultation of the Qá'im. The Báb identifies occultation with the existential station of forgetting the divine revelation within, which requires prayer in order to regain true self-consciousness. Various chapters deal with the preconditions of true prayer, and in the last three chapters the occultation prayer is interpreted. This work frequently turns to a discussion of the letter Há'. It is quoted by Bahá'u'lláh in the Kitáb-i-Íqán, and parts of it were translated and discussed by Nicolas in his introduction to his French translation of the Persian Bayán.[5]

Some Works of the Second Stage

(January 1846–April 1847)

1 **Ṣaḥífiy-i-'Adlíyyih** (Epistle of Justice: Root Principles). This work, sometimes also called **Ṣaḥífiy-i-Uṣúl-i-'Adlíyyih**, on the fundamental or root

principles of religion, is one of the texts that announce the inception of the second stage of the Báb's writings. It was written in the second half of the first month of 1262 (late January 1846) and is the first major work that the Báb wrote in Persian.

2 **Ṣaḥífiy-i-Furú'-i-'Adlíyyih** (Epistle of Justice: Branches). This work is a discussion of some of the branches and main laws of the Islamic religion (such as obligatory prayer, alms, and jihad). It is sometimes assumed that it was written before the Epistle of Justice: Root Principles, but it seems to have been written after that work. It is not listed in either the Kitábu'l-Fihrist or the Khuṭbiy-i-Dhikríyyih (which was written just days before the Epistle of Justice: Root Principles). And at the end of the Epistle of Justice: Root Principles, the Báb refers to the branches of religion as a topic which follows that of the present work.

3 **Tafsír-i-Súriy-i-Kawthar** (Commentary on the Súrih of Abundance). This long work interprets the Qur'ánic Súrih of Abundance through various levels of meaning. It was written during the final months of the Báb's stay in Shiraz. Various authors have noted that it was written while the Báb was in Shiraz after His return from Mecca. Yet we can identify its date more precisely. It was written in honour of Siyyid Yaḥyá Dárábí (Vaḥíd) when he met the Báb in Shiraz. Vaḥíd himself has specified the date when this occurred, in a letter in which he says that he attained the Báb's presence in the month of Jumádi'l-Avval 1262 (April 27–May 27, 1846).[6] Thus this commentary must have been written around May 1846, about four months before the Báb's departure for Isfahan.

4 **Tafsír-i-Há'** (Commentary on the Letter Há'). This text was written after the Commentary on the Súrih of Abundance but before the Báb's departure for Isfahan. In it, the Báb asks the addressee of the tablet to read the Commentary on the Súrih of Abundance. The Commentary on the Letter Há' is usually thought to have been written in honour of Siyyid Yaḥyá Dárábí. But this cannot be accurate, for in the above-mentioned letter Vaḥíd himself identifies the recipient of the tablet as Abu'l-Ḥasani'l-Ḥusayní, a prominent notable of Shiraz.[7] Internal evidence also makes it clear that this work cannot have been written for Vaḥíd. The entire tablet is devoted to disclosing the structure of spiritual reality through an interpretation of the letter Há'. The tablet affirms that the seven stages of divine creative Action are identical with the seven stages of the hierarchy of spiritual stations, as diverse reflections of the reality of the Báb.

5 **Tafsír-i-Sirr-i-Há'** (Commentary on the Mystery of Há'). This work was written shortly after the Commentary on the Letter Há' and as a completion of the latter. In discussing the mystery of Há', the Báb emphasizes the incontrovertible testimony of His own writings and identifies recognition of His true station with recognition of the divine revelation that is present within all beings, as the ultimate mystery and truth of all reality.

6 **Tafsír-i-Súriy-i-Va'l-'Aṣr** (Commentary on the Súrih of the Afternoon). This work was written in one night, in October or November 1846, during the Báb's stay in Isfahan, in honour of the *imám jum'ih* (the mullá who leads the Friday prayers) of that city. Interpreting various parts of the short Qur'ánic súrih, the Báb discusses many fundamental issues in religion including how to recognize spiritual truth, the nature of the human being, the meaning of faith, the nature of good deeds, and the preconditions of spiritual journey.

7 **Risáliy-i-Ithbát-i-Nubuvvat-i-Kháṣṣih** (Epistle on the Proofs of the Prophethood of Muḥammad). This work was written in Isfahan in honour of the governor of that city, Manúchihr Khán. The Báb argues that nothing is random with respect to the reality of the Manifestations of God, including the Prophet Muḥammad. Thus in addition to the Qur'án, which is the supreme and sufficient testimony of His truth, every aspect of the Prophet's life (including the names of His parents, the place and date of His birth, and so on) possesses spiritual meanings and offers distinct signs for the seeker of truth.

8 **Tablet to Mírzá Sa'íd.** Written in Isfahan, this work addresses three philosophical questions asked by Mírzá Sa'íd-i-Ardistání. One of the most explicit and complex philosophical writings of the Báb, the tablet discusses the enigmatic concept of the True Indivisible Being (*Basíṭu'l-Ḥaqíqah*), the question of the eternality or origination of the world, and the issue of the emanation of plurality out of the One. The key ideas in the text are the absolute transcendence of the divine Essence and the creative action of the Primal Will.

9 **Risálah Fi'l-Ghiná'** (Treatise on Singing). A discourse that takes its point of departure from the Islamic law regarding music, this text was written in honour of Sultánu'dh-Dhákirín. Instead of offering a traditional discussion of the Islamic law related to singing and music, however, the Báb defines the philosophical conditions of moral or immoral action by discussing the dual station of the human being as possessing both an aspect

of divine revelation (existence) and an aspect of specific determination (essence). Like every other human action, singing becomes moral or immoral depending on the intention of the actor and the function of the act.

Some Works of the Third Stage

(April 1847–July 1850)

1 **Bayán-i-Fársí** (Persian Bayán). This crucial text is the Mother Book of the Bábí Dispensation. Comprising nine *váḥids* (unities) of nineteen chapters or *bábs* (gates)[8]—with the exception of the last unity, which has only ten gates—the greater part of the work was written in the prison of Mákú, but, contrary to some prevalent assumptions, the last parts may have been written in Chihríq, after the Báb was interrogated by the clerics in Tabriz. The Persian Bayán abrogates Islamic laws and traditions and sets down new laws and teachings. However, the various laws are discussed as symbols referring to deep spiritual meanings and vehicles to prepare the people for the advent of Him Whom God shall make manifest. Both the form and content of the book affirm the underlying metaphysics of unity in which all things are manifestations of an inner reality which is the revelation of God within them.

2 **Bayánu'l-'Arabí** (Arabic Bayán). This work is sometimes assumed to have been written before the Persian Bayán for the simple reason that it seems as if the latter is an elaboration of the former. In reality, however, like the Persian Bayán, most of the Arabic Bayán was written in Mákú, although the last sections may have been written in Chihríq. The text is a condensed form of the Persian Bayán, written in the language of divine verses. While much shorter in length than the Persian Bayán, the Arabic Bayán contains eleven full unities, whereas the Persian Bayán ends with gate 10 of the ninth unity. The parts of the Arabic Bayán that are not matched by the Persian Bayán (from gate 11 of the ninth unity to the end of the eleventh unity) were written after the Persian Bayán was completed.

3 **Dalá'il-i-Sab'ih** (Seven Proofs). This work was written in Mákú, as attested within the text. It discusses seven arguments vindicating the claim that the revelation of divine verses is the sufficient proof of the truth of the Báb. The addressees of this work have been identified as Mullá Aḥmad-i-Kátib and Ḥujjat-i-Zanjání.[9]

4 **Tablet to Mullá Báqir.** This tablet discusses the majesty of the Promised One of the Bábí Dispensation—Him Whom God shall make manifest—and the appropriate method to employ in approaching His claim and Revelation. It was written in honour of Mullá Báqir and was also sent to Siyyid Yaḥyá Dárábí (Vaḥíd).

5 **Kitábu'l-Asmá'** (Book of Divine Names). This work, the complete text of which is more than three thousand pages, is the largest revealed book in sacred history. It consists of nineteen unities and 361 gates (chapters). Many parts of the text are yet to be located. Some of the chapters were written during the Báb's imprisonment in Mákú, and others while He was in Chihríq. The dates are indicated in the text itself. This book approaches various categories of human beings as reflections of divine names and attributes and discusses ways that all of reality can be spiritualized through the recognition of the supreme Source of divine revelation.

6 **Kitáb-i-Panj Sha'n** (Book of the Five Modes of Revelation). One of the last major works of the Báb, this book was written within the first days of the spring of 1850, the final year of the Báb's life, three or four months before His martyrdom. Panj Sha'n consists of nineteen chapters, each dealing with one of the names of God, corresponding to the first nineteen days of the year, that is, the days of the month of Bahá (Glory). These names also correspond to the nineteen figures of the Bábí Primal Unity. Panj Sha'n explains many fundamental spiritual concepts such as nearness to God, light, beauty, and unity. Each chapter was written in honour of one of the Bábís, and the chapters can all be considered as independent tablets as well. The Tablet of Ḥurúfát, or Tablet of Nineteen Temples, is one of these chapters.

I
The Interpretive Revelation

1

The Mode of Interpretation

IN MANY WAYS, the religion founded by the Báb was unprecedented in sacred history. One of its most unusual and distinctive features concerns the Scriptures that record the Báb's revelations. Historically, the primary form in which revelation was communicated was the spoken word. Subsequent generations of believers had to rely on the indirect record of that revelation, transmitted first through the oral tradition and only set down in writing many years later. But with the Báb, for the first time, revelation has been recorded in writing—either directly by the Báb Himself in His own hand (although He also chanted the words as He wrote them down) or by the amanuensis who wrote down the words as the Báb spoke them. Unlike past Dispensations, when the Prophet addressed groups of people verbally, virtually all of the Báb's revelation was communicated to His followers in written form, with manuscripts being copied and passed from hand to hand. And indeed, only the written works of the Báb are regarded as authoritative Sacred Text.

Thus in studying the Báb's writings, we are not dealing with the interpretive paraphrase of successive generations of believers, but with the corpus of His own written works. Ascertaining the authenticity of the Sacred Text is no longer an insolvable issue as it was in previous Dispensations, when it was not possible to know which parts of the Scripture accurately represented the Prophet's words and which were paraphrase, interpretation, or error due to the vagaries of the oral tradition. The most significant issue regarding the authenticity of the Báb's writings is the presence of some, occasionally significant, transcription errors in some transcribed and published copies of His works. In Persian and Arabic the presence or absence of a single dot distinguishes one word from another, and such transcription errors have sometimes led scholars to misread certain texts. For this study, whenever possible, different versions of particular manuscript texts have been consulted and compared.

The cultural milieu in which the Báb lived was a highly literate one, in which the epistolary genre was extensively developed. Many of the Báb's writings are thus in the form of letters, called "tablets," and frequently were answers to questions asked of Him, often concerning the meaning of passages in the Qur'án. Hence much of the Báb's writing, especially in the early stage, consists of explanations or commentaries, sometimes very extensive, on verses or súrihs of the Qur'án or the Traditions attributed to the Prophet Muḥammad or the Imáms.[1] Revelation, in other words, in the writings of the Báb, often takes the form of interpretation and commentary on previous revelation. The discourse of commentary on the Qur'án has a long tradition in Islamic scholarship. But although the Báb uses the traditional form of commentary, He does not merely offer His interpretations as another contribution to that Islamic discourse. He uses the genre against the grain of the established tradition; He interprets the text, in fact, to transform that tradition, reversing and redefining conventional meanings.

The interpretive writings of the Báb, particularly those that are extant, belong chiefly to the first three years of His ministry. Some of His most famous interpretive works, written before His imprisonment in Mákú, include the commentaries on the Súrihs of the Cow, Joseph, Abundance, and the Afternoon.[2] It is reported that while in Mákú, the Báb wrote nine commentaries on the entire Qur'án, although these commentaries are not extant;[3] unfortunately, many of His commentaries were stolen or lost.[4] Although the Báb did continue to write commentaries during the second and third stages of His writings (such as the Commentary on the Verse of Light II, which belongs to the third stage),[5] it is the earliest stage, up to the middle of Muḥarram 1262 (mid-January 1846), which emphasizes, and is best defined by, the interpretive form of writing.

A Typology of the Modes of Revelation

The Báb's interpretations are utterly unlike any normal interpretive or exegetical work. Not only does the form of the interpretive writing undergo a fundamental transformation, but so does the entire role and meaning of the interpretive act itself. Therefore, before examining some of the Báb's commentaries in more detail, it is necessary to identify His hermeneutical principles and His approach to interpretation.

The Báb's interpretation is *interpretive revelation.* In interpretive revelation, the relation of the interpreted text and the interpreting text is qualitatively different from the relation between those two texts in a scholarly interpretation. Understanding this fact is a key to comprehending some of the enigmatic aspects of the early writings of the Báb. Yet, even before discussing the hermeneutical principles operating in the Báb's interpretive works, we must locate interpretation, as a mode of writing, within the overall typology of the modes of revelation found in the Báb's writings and examine how these different modes are related to those of the Islamic Dispensation.

A significant portion of the writings of the Báb is devoted to discussion of the typology of the modes of revelation (*sh͟u'ún-i-áyát*) in which His works are written.[6] This emphasis on the modes themselves is not a mere exercise in classification; it plays an important role in the structure of meaning that defines the writings of the Báb. The Báb connects the typology itself to many other metaphysical and theological matters and derives far-reaching conclusions from His analysis. Aside from the fact that understanding the typology, as we shall see, reṣolves any doubt about the Báb's real claim and station as those are expressed in His earlier writings, it must be noted that, as the typology of the Logos—the creative divine Word through which all things are called into being—these various modes of revelation are the constitutive principles of reality. Thus the modes themselves are keys for understanding the metaphysics, theology, and indeed the entire world view of the Báb.

The Islamic Revelation, as the Báb explains, was characterized by four modes of revelation: divine verses (*áyát*), prayers and supplications (*munáját, ad'íyih*), commentaries and sermons (*tafásír, k͟huṭáb*), and rational, educational, and philosophical discourse (*sh͟u'ún-i-'ilmíyyih va hikamíyyih*), while the Báb's revelation consisted of five modes, four of which parallel the four Islamic modes.[7] In linguistic terms, the modes of revelation can be understood, in part, as different *registers,* as they are defined by the relationship, relative station, and attitude of the speaker with respect to the addressee.[8] The mode of divine verses is the direct revelation of God, uttered in the voice of God as the speaker addressing His creation (an affirmation of "I am God"). This mode employs the language of divinity, ascendancy, and lordship. In this mode God declares, for example: "Verily, I am God and there is none other God but Me, the Lord of all things. Verily, all else other than Me is My creation. Therefore, O My creation, adore Me alone!"[9] The word "Say!"—often encountered in the Qur'án—distinctively precedes the utterance of revelation in the mode of divine verses, as the voice of God tells the Prophet to speak, as in this example: "Say! The verses of God are like unto life-giving water sent down out of the heaven of His Primal Will upon the earth of your nearness to Him. . . ."[10]

The mode of prayers and supplications is the reverse of the mode of divine verses. Here the language of revelation is uttered in the voice of the Prophet, but now speaking in the station of the creation, addressing the Creator with an attitude of servitude and effacement (an affirmation of "Thou art God"). This mode emphasizes the poverty and powerlessness of the creatures before their Creator; for example: "I bear witness by Thee, O My God, even as Thou didst bear witness unto Thyself, before the creation of Thy Primal Will, that verily Thou art God, the Peerless, the Single, the Self-Subsisting, the Eternal, the Everlasting. Thou hast ever been independent of any description by anyone besides Thee, and Thou wilt remain forever without the praise of anyone other than Thyself."[11] The discourse of prayers is fundamentally an expression of servitude and love—the love of the created being for God, as exemplified in this passage:

> Glorified be Thou, O my God! How sweet, therefore, is Thy praise in my inner and outer being; and how abounding are Thy favours in my hidden and manifest states. Thou art He Who hath taught Me Thy Self through Thy Self, inspired me with Thy Remembrance through Thy Remembrance, and called me to Thyself through Thy Holy Countenance. Were it not for Thee, I would cease to exist; and were it not for Thy confirmations, I would not have attained any glory.[12]

The mode of commentaries and sermons primarily expresses affirmation of the words of God. Commentaries and sermons are uttered in the voice of the Revelator speaking to human beings about God and His words (an affirmation of "He is God"). The commentaries are interpretive works that aim to explain, in expository form, the true meanings of the divine verses, as in this example: "Know thou that verily every 'food' is a reminder of something delightful. But when it is joined with the true meaning of 'all,' it referreth to the reality which containeth and embraceth everything. That, however, can only be realized in the Point of the Primal Will, inasmuch as verily all the created manifestations are indeed hidden within It."[13]

The sermons praise and describe transcendental spiritual realities that are the cosmic manifestations of the Word. Often the Báb begins a work with a brief or lengthy sermon that endeavours to connect the reader's heart and consciousness to the divine verities. For example:

> Praised be God, Who hath caused, through the pattern of His Signs of Power, all that is vibrant to vibrate in the branches of the concourse of the Heaven of Divinity. And praise be to God, Who hath caused, through the evidences of His Will, the beingness of all beings to be revealed within the branches of the concourse of the Heaven of the Manifestations. And praise be to God, Who hath, through the revelation of the mysterious depths of His earthly and heavenly Signs, caused all that is radiant to radiate in the Stations of His Determination.[14]

The fourth mode of revelation—rational, educational, and philosophical discourse—is again spoken in the voice of the Revelator addressing human beings, but this time using rational arguments to demonstrate the truth of the Word of God and explain the message expressed in the prayers (an affirmation of "He is God Who is"). The fundamental function of this mode is to analyze the phenomenal world and to link it to the transcendental realm, as in this passage:

> Verily hath God created within thyself the similitude of all that He hath fashioned in creation, that thou mayest not be veiled from any effulgence. Verily God hath generated within thy being the entirety of His manifestations. He hath ordained that His home be the heart of His servant; by it the reality of existence shall be recognized, and the Fashioner of men be praised, and the bounty of existence pour forth through His ever-flowing Pen.[15]

The purpose of this mode is to show the signs of the unseen within the visible realm, and to prove the world of divinity and dominion through its manifestations in the earthly world, as in this example:

> For verily the soul, while bound by the ephemeral and transitory things of this world, is confined, in its understanding, to limited phenomena only. However, once the soul hath soared beyond the realm of nature and becometh submerged in the ocean of absolute unity, then can it acquire the capacity to discern the reality of all sciences and knowledge in their full plenitude. Thus 'Alí said: "O Lord! Submerge me in the reviving ocean of Thy unity and the fathomless depths of the sea of Thy oneness."[16]

This mode frequently employs logical argumentation and analysis:

> Verily, that which hath forced some philosophers to conceive of the presence of the eternal intelligible forms (*a'yání'th-thábitah*) in the Essence of God, and the doctrine of the True Indivisible Being, was their desire to validate the concept of the knowledge of God, magnified be His station! For they stated that knowledge must needs have an object of knowledge, and hence the affirmation of divine knowledge indicateth the existence of pluralities within the Essence of God.[17]

To these four modes of revelation, which were present in the Islamic Dispensation, the Báb adds a fifth, which He designates the "Persian mode." In the Islamic Dispensation the Arabic language was the sole language of revelation, but the Báb employs both Arabic and Persian as vehicles of revelation. The Báb distinguishes His Persian writings as a distinct mode of revelation although the content of these works may be any of the four modes: divine verses, prayers, commentaries/sermons, or rational discourse. The Persian mode of revelation thus represents the integrative form of the other four modes.

In His writings, the Báb often discusses the typology of the modes of revelation as a vehicle that in itself is richly symbolic. For example, in the Persian Bayán we read:

> Whatever is revealed by the Point hath been designated as the "Bayán." However, this name referreth in its primary reality to the divine verses, and in its secondary reality to prayers, third to commentaries, fourth to

> educational forms, and fifth to the Persian words. Yet, this exalted appellation, on the basis of its intrinsic worth, solely denoteth the divine verses to the exclusion of all others.[18]

> As such, the merging of the five rivers should not be permitted: thus, divine verses should remain within their own sublimity, prayers in their own loftiness, commentaries in their own seat of glory, words [of knowledge] in their own sacred horizon, and the Persian words in their own inaccessible and exalted heights.[19]

> [I]n this Dispensation, the writings of the Letters of the Living all proceed directly from the Sun of Truth Himself. Divine verses especially pertain to the Point of the Bayán, prayers pertain to the Messenger of God [Muḥammad], commentaries to the Imáms of guidance, and educational discourse (*ṣuvar-i-ʻilmíyyih*) to the Gates. However, all of these proceed from this Ocean so that all people can behold the exalted sublimity of these Writings of the Primal Truth.[20]

This classification of the divine writings into either four or five modes of revelation is the basis on which many of the later works of the Báb are organized. Two major examples of such works are the Kitábu'l-Asmá' (Book of Divine Names), and Panj Sha'n (Five Modes of Revelation). The Kitábu'l-Asmá' discusses the meanings and implications of various names of God. Generally each name is discussed in four different chapters, and each chapter is written in a different mode of revelation. The title of the other work, Panj Sha'n (Five Modes), indicates its organizational structure: it discusses nineteen names of God, each of which is explained through five modes of revelation.[21]

The Logic of the Typology

The categories represented by this typology of the modes of revelation can be seen as the logical expressions of the central theological principle informing the writings of the Báb: the concept of the Point, a term referring to the Primal Will of God. The Primal Will is manifested in the world by the Prophet or divine Messenger, Who is the nexus between the Divinity and the created world. "The Point" thus refers to the Báb Himself. The concept will be discussed extensively throughout this book but, briefly, the Primal Will is the Word of God, the Logos, through which the creation of all things takes place. The four modes of revelation are logical reflections of the structure of the Point or Primal Will: thus they are the four modes of the creative Word of God.

In order to understand this subtle concept, we need to look at the Báb's description of the ontological reality and structure of the Point. According to the Báb, the Point possesses two stations. The first is the station of the Point's divinity, the station of pure divine revelation, while the second is the station of the Point's servitude, the station of createdness and subservience to God. The Báb explains:

> Verily the Point possesseth two stations. One is the station that speaketh from God. The other is the station that speaketh from that which is other than God, a station whereby He expresseth His servitude for the former station. By virtue of the former, the latter worshippeth God in the daytime and in the night season, and glorifieth Him at morn and at eventide.
>
> The substance of this gate is that God hath fashioned two stations for the Sun of Truth. One is the station of His unknown and unknowable Essence, the Manifestation of His Divinity. Thus, all His revealed divine verses stream forth on behalf of God. . . . All else beyond this supreme Sign present within Him is His creation. . . .
>
> And within the inmost reality of all things there hath been, and will forever continue to be, a sign from God through which the unity of the Lord is celebrated. This sign, however, is a reflection of His Will present within it, through which naught is seen but God. However, within the Will, that supreme Sign is the Will Itself, the Supreme Mirror of God, which hath never referred, nor will it ever refer, to aught but God. . . . He is the possessor of two signs, that of God and that of creation, and through the latter he worshippeth God and boweth in adoration before Him. In like manner, all things adore their Beloved through the sign of Creation, though it hath never reached, nor will it ever reach, beyond its own sign from God, which is present within it and pointeth unto Him.[22]

According to the Báb, in the station of divine transcendence and pure unity, the Point speaks *from* God and on behalf of God, in the mode of divine verses. In the station of servitude, the Point speaks *to* God, in worship and adoration of Him, in the mode of prayers and supplications. These two fundamental modes of revelation—divine verses and prayers—

directly reflect the two stations of the Will as the reflection of divinity and the sign of servitude.

The other two modes of revelation are further reflections of this same structure. The commentaries and sermons represent the interpretation of divine verses (and divine attributes) for the creatures. Rational discourse, the Báb explains, is the elaboration of the mode of prayer. It is the exposition of the spiritual truth of reality in the language of reason. The most direct expression of the intimate relation between commentaries and divine verses, on the one hand, and rational discourse and prayers, on the other, can be found in the Persian Bayán. Here, the Báb refers to the mode of rational discourse as a specific kind of commentary or interpretation. While the commentaries are interpretations of divine verses, rational discourse is referred to as "the answers and interpretations that pertain to the prayers."[23]

In the Kitábu'l-Asmá', the Báb explains that the essence of religion itself is derived from the two stations of divinity and servitude, and that the manifestation of these two stations is fourfold, corresponding to the four modes of revelation.[24] The logical basis of the typology of the four modes of revelation becomes more evident when we note that, often in His writings, the Báb equates His four modes of revelation with the first four stages of the process of divine creative Action through which all created things come into being, an equivalence that we will see explained in detail in the Commentary on the Súrih of Abundance.

A point should be noted about the term *áyat* (singular, *áyih*), translated as "divine verses." The Arabic word *áyát* is a most complex term, the nuances of which cannot be captured by any single word in English. It means "verses," "signs," and "miracles." Indeed the Báb's frequent discussion of the inimitable and incontrovertible character of the Word of God contains all these meanings at the same time: the divine words are God's supreme miracle, which is the sign of His majesty and glory, revealed in the world in the form of the Word—that is, the divine verses.

Although *áyát* specifically refers to the mode of divine verses, it is also used in a broader, general sense encompassing all four modes of divine revelation. In other words, *áyát*, as the divine words, includes the modes of divine verses, prayers, commentaries, and rational discourse. The same feature is apparent in the statement in the Persian Bayán in which the Báb applies the word *Bayán* specifically to the mode of divine verses as well as generally to all His writings, saying that "whatever is revealed by the Point hath been designated as the Bayán. However, this name referreth in its primary reality to the divine verses. . . ."[25]

The distinguishing feature of all the divine words, of course, is that they convey the divine revelation. That revelation is primarily due to the unique station of the Point as the Manifestation of Divinity. The mode that pertains to the station of Divinity, that is, the mode of divine verses, is thus the primary mode of divine revelation and the source of all the other modes. This point is discussed in the Persian Bayán in various ways. In the following passage, the Báb states that for the Manifestation of God the most beloved mode of revelation is that of divine verses. This primacy is rooted in the intimate relation of the inmost reality of the Point to the language of the divine verses:

> These divine verses are the Word of the Will Himself, which is naught but the Word of God. For the Essence of Eternity hath always been, and will continue forever to be, beyond any change. But speaking the Word pertaineth to the station of divine creation and generation. Inasmuch as naught is seen in the Will but God, therefore this Word is attributed unto God, for none but God is capable of producing its like. Those who have been, or will ever be, in the presence of This Tree recognize that these words proceed from His pure primordial nature, and that speaking in such a mode is easier and closer to Him than speaking in the mode of prayers, sermons, rational arguments, or the Persian modes. For this is the language of His Inmost Reality which referreth unto naught but God alone. It is for that reason that the divine verses are called the Words (*áyát*) of God and praised as the divine Logos.[26]

The Báb's Hermeneutic Principles

The Báb's interpretive mode of writing is based upon a unique and transcendental logic of interpretation, or hermeneutics.[27] This section will discuss some of the main metaphysical principles of that interpretive system.

The Báb's writings represent a harmonious and unified corpus, but the immense magnitude of those writings, their diverse stages, and the vast richness and complexity of the topics they address, all can make it difficult to recognize the harmony and unity of those works. From the beginning, scholars of the Báb's writings have testified to their own difficulty, and sometimes total failure, to understand these texts. They have occasionally found them vague, obscure, unsystematic, or simply incomprehensible—and have frequently ascribed the difficulty to the author of the text rather than to themselves as readers. E. G. Browne, for example, described the Báb's writings as "set down, for the most part, not in the language of the people, but in Arabic treatises of interminable length, at once florid and incorrect in style, teeming with grammatical errors the most glaring, iterations the most wearisome, and words the rarest and most incomprehensible." He found the "great conceptions, noble ideals, subtle metaphysical conceptions, and splendid, though ill-defined, aspirations" which, he acknowledged, "do, indeed exist in the Beyán" to be "so lost in trackless mazes of rhapsody and mysticism, so weighed down by trivial injunctions and impracticable ordinances, that no casual reader, but only a student of considerable diligence and perseverance, can hope to find them." About the books of the Báb, Browne wrote: "They were, for the most part, voluminous, hard to comprehend, uncouth in style, unsystematic in arrangement, filled with iterations and solecisms, and not unfrequently quite incoherent and unintelligible to any ordinary reader."[28] Denis MacEoin, similarly, speaks of "the innumerable obscurities and vagueness of even the most reliable texts"[29] and characterizes the Báb's Commentary on the Súrih of Abundance as "for the most part, almost unreadable, consisting of highly abstract and insubstantial speculations on the verses, words, and even letters of the Súra on which it is supposed to be a 'commentary.'"[30]

The Báb, however, has frequently attested that His writings are neither inconsistent nor contradictory, and that statements which may appear to be contradictory assertions are actually diverse expressions of a single underlying principle that is expressed in a particular manner in accordance with the capacities of differing audiences.[31] A careful analysis of the Báb's writings discloses that throughout the three stages, all His writings are animated by a common fundamental principle which has multiple dimensions and forms. We may term this foremost hermeneutic concept the principle of *metaphysical unity*. Although the principle becomes increasingly explicit in the metaphysical and legislative stages of the Báb's writings, its presence in His interpretive works is unmistakable. Indeed, understanding the Báb's commentaries is dependent on comprehending this central idea. The concept of metaphysical unity also defines the purpose and goal of those interpretive works. One of the most explicit expositions of the end purpose of the interpretive act can be found in the Báb's Commentary on the Súrih of the Cow II:

> Elevate the alphabetical letters of that divine verse unto the sublime station of the manifestation of their heart. . . . Verily that ascent is the spirit of the Elixir of true knowledge, so that the servant may advance all that is motionless unto the lofty station of vibrant motion, and make manifest the Causes of his existence within the stage of the effect, and reveal the fruit of the Final Cause in the rank and station of the receptive phenomena. That is the true meaning of the words of Imám Riḍá', peace be upon Him, that verily those endued with understanding cannot know that which is there, except through that which is here.[32]

To interpret something is to uncover its true meaning. The text that is to be interpreted consists of signs, specifically words, appearing as combinations of the letters of the alphabet. The supreme task of interpretation, the Báb explains in this passage, is to elevate these alphabetical signs (which constitute the text) to the highest level of their own reality, the station at which they reveal their true essential nature, or "heart." The concept of "heart" (*fu'ád*) is one of the most important principles in the writings of the Báb. The station of the heart is the highest stage of a created being's existential reality. It is the reflection of divine revelation itself within the inmost reality of things. To interpret the words, therefore, is in essence to transform them into mirrors of divine reality. A true interpretive act finds in the words, alphabetical phenomena, and signs of the text nothing but the expression of divine attributes. In this sense the text—and all reality—becomes a testimony to the unity of God, a praise of the divine names, and an affirmation of the divine creative Action. Finding the "thing in itself" in the realm of the "appearances" (in Kantian terms), manifesting the infinite kingdom of the heart in the finite phenomenal realm of the world, and beholding the world as reflecting nothing but the proofs of the sovereignty of God, thus constitutes the ultimate hermeneutical principle of the Báb.[33] The Báb's interpretation of the Tradition of Imám Riḍá' in the above passage concisely describes the central role of symbolism in this interpretive process, for the spiritual world ("that which is there") can only be known metaphorically through the symbolism of the phenomenal world ("that which is here").

To engage in the act of interpreting the text at the level of the heart, in terms of its supreme Origin, seeing the reflection of the divine mirrored in every atom of creation, is to transform the phenomenal realm into its ultimate spiritual reality. The interpretation of a text is simultaneously an act of self-interpretation and self-transformation: through the act of interpretation, the reader spiritualizes the self as well as the world. This transformative act takes place through the symbol of the elixir. The term *elixir*, of course, alludes to the symbolism of alchemy, which, as Jung has argued, was not merely concerned with changing base metal into gold; more significantly, the physical process was a complex, arcane symbolic system representing stages of the mystical transformation of the self.[34]

After saying that the alphabetical letters must be elevated to the station of the revelation of their heart, the Báb describes the spirit of this true hermeneutics as the uplifting, by the "servant," of "all that is motionless unto the lofty station of vibrant motion," and making manifest "the Causes of his existence within the stage of the effect." The Báb likens this self-transformative interpretive consciousness to the "spirit of the Elixir of true knowledge," as the supreme agent that transforms potentialities into actualities, the catalyst for the beautification and elevation of being. The true Elixir, therefore, is a form of spiritual orientation in which the receptive becomes active and the motionless becomes vibrant. For the Báb these terms imply distinctive meanings. The Essence of God itself is sanctified above any description of motion or repose. Such notions, therefore, can pertain only to the creation. The Action of the divine Primal Will, which is the First Creation, is the vibrant and moving Final Cause of phenomenal reality, and it is the Primal Will that brings into existence the reality of all things. Although the world has the appearance of an independent material reality, in and of itself it is only a shadow and a motionless non-existence. The task of true hermeneutics is to cause a fundamental transformation in the phenomenal realm: to elevate the phenomena to the station of the heart is to uncover the signs of divine revelation that are enshrined within the reality of those phenomena, and to connect that which is motionless to its true inner reality of vibrant spiritual motion. This transformation is accomplished within the consciousness of the interpreter.

These same vibrant and moving realities are more explicitly described, in the same passage, as the Causes of the very existence of the human interpreter as well. The ultimate Cause of these Causes is the Primal Will, or the Point, sometimes referred to as the "Tree of Truth" or the "Sun of Truth." The Primal Will is also the essence of the Prophets or Manifestations of God. The Will becomes the Cause of reality through its manifestation in the process of divine creative Action, which consists of seven stages. These stages of creation, then, are the specific sequential Causes of reality, which set reality into the vibrant motion of life.

True hermeneutics—the act of interpretation—thus is not separable from either epistemology or the truth of being. The Báb's interpretive works, like His theological and legislative works, all intend to spiritualize reality in all its diverse aspects. By relating phenomena to their fundamental transcendental Causes, the interpreter unveils the mystery of the inner reality of all things. In His commentary on the Súrih of Abundance, the Báb states: "The greatest achievement of the servant is to elevate all objects to their supreme station of detachment and unity."[35] The Báb's hermeneutics, which relates the meaning of the words to the ultimate Origin and End of all being, is thus a method of disclosing the truth.[36]

An important consequence of this principle is the self-referential character of interpretive revelation. Since the ultimate meaning of the Word of God is the inner truth of the phenomena it refers to—which in turn is nothing but the creative Word of God itself—any divine revelation ultimately describes the very source of that revelation, namely, the Point or the Primal Will. Thus interpretive revelation is characterized by the unity of the interpreter (the Word or the Will of God), the interpreted (the Word of God), and the interpretation (the Word of God), transcending the limitations of time and uniting past, present, and future. When the Báb interprets a Qur'ánic verse, the real meaning of the interpreted text is not something external to that act of interpretation. Rather, the act of interpretation itself renews and recreates the meaning of the interpreted verse. The ultimate meaning of the divine words is therefore an eternally creative process of progressive revelation.

This interpretive principle is the key that unlocks the door to understanding the Báb's diverse and complex exegetical texts. Amid the diversity of His interpretive writings, one can see that the animating principle that runs through works like the Qayyúmu'l-Asmá' and the commentaries on the Súrih of Abundance, the Súrih of the Cow, and the Súrih of the Afternoon, as well as others, is one and the same—a mystical love which sees in everything the Countenance of the Divine Beloved.[37]

Universal Hermeneutics

Failing to recognize these metaphysical principles underlying the Báb's hermeneutics, and their symbolic expression within His writings, however, inevitably leads to superficial readings that seriously misconstrue and underestimate those texts. Such particularly has been the case with some attempts to understand the Báb's discussions of the letters of the alphabet. The assumption that those discussions are meant literally has resulted in the conclusion that the Báb is merely expressing a superstitious belief in the magical powers of letters. Based on this and other similar misconceptions, the writings of the Báb have sometimes been judged to be similar to, or merely imitating, the Ḥurúfíyyih and Nuqṭavíyyih schools of thought.[38] But although some elements found in those two schools are confirmed in the writings of the Báb, the elements He confirms have little to do with the issue of letters or their assumed literal divine character. Instead, the common points concern the mystic world view and the sacred character of human beings as the image of God, while the literal and exaggerated emphasis that the Ḥurúfíyyih and Nuqṭavíyyih schools place on letters and their sounds as direct elements of divine creation, as well as frequent reference made to the human head as the primary representation of those letters, are foreign to the Báb's teachings.

Undoubtedly, the Báb's writings are filled with interpretations of alphabetical letters, and He often discusses the numerical equivalents of various words. He also often employs a variety of sacred images and designs. But all these phenomena are rooted in a mystical view of reality that confers new meanings on all things. The meaning of the letter/number symbolism in the writings of the Báb must be sought in the context of His own hermeneutical, theological, and moral principles.

According to the Báb, not only the realm of language but all other aspects of phenomenal reality, including natural and cultural objects, are symbolic signs that point toward spiritual meanings. Everything is a divine text, and the entirety of being is a mirror of divine reality: whatever exists in the world is a sign, a verse, and a miracle that proclaims the unity and sovereignty of God. From this perspective, reality itself is a kind of language, consisting of words and letters that proclaim and celebrate the divine revelation enshrined within all things. Since all of creation is a symbol of God, the Báb's writings find in all phenomenal reality—including statements, words, letters, and numbers—references to celestial reality and transcendental meanings.

As we shall see throughout this study, the writings of the Báb often ascribe spiritual meanings to natural events. The sun, heaven, rain, trees, water, fire, air, and earth, for example, are all interpreted as symbols of profound spiritual truths. This symbolism is not due to any particular property of a limited set of phenomena. Rather, being, as such, and existence in general are pointers to the divine beauty and divine love. So, for the Báb, words and letters are not the only things endowed with spiritual reference: He extensively interprets all things in this symbolic logic, and His use of linguistic signs is just one example of this universal semiotics. Yet, given the prevalence, particularly among the Shaykhís, of the millenarian expectation that the Qá'im would unveil the inner meanings of the disconnected letters of the Qur'án, it was inevitable that the Báb would often use this particular symbolic medium, focusing on alphabetical letters, to convey His message.

The other dimension of the Báb's universalization of hermeneutics relates specifically to the realm of language. For the Báb, linguistic signs carry an inexhaustible richness of meaning. He extends this richness of meaning, this symbolic function, to all the different levels of language, including the level of letters. In this way, He confers fresh and creative meanings upon words in ways that defy the limitations of normal hermeneutics, imbuing signs with infinite—although not arbitrary—meaning. Language, in the writings of the Báb, thus becomes a fathomless ocean of representation of the Divine.

This last point is directly relevant to one of the most important aspects of the Báb's writings, that is, His transformative approach to language. The details of this transformative logic will be examined in part 3, when His specific laws and ordinances are discussed. But this transformative aspect also permeates His hermeneutics. One of the Báb's most important goals was to fundamentally change the linguistic signs and the communicative acts of humanity in such a way that the human tongue and pen become sacred instruments of divine revelation. The Báb sought to educate humanity so that human language would become the "throne of God"[39]—purifying all aspects of language from selfish and hedonistic orientations and reflecting the universal love of God such that every atom of existence would proclaim the glory of divinity.

Again, insufficient attention to these aspects has contributed to some problems in reading the Báb's works. Denis MacEoin, for example, persistently gives the impression that the writings of the Báb are obsessed with the magical character of letters, and he devotes extensive space to discussing the Báb's Tablet of Nineteen Temples (also called the Tablet of the Letters, Lawḥ-i-Ḥurúfát) as evidence for that claim. MacEoin sees in this tablet only charms and magic devices and consistently translates the term *haykal*, meaning "temple" or "body," as "talisman" and "talismanic device." Such methodology leads to a literalistic and simplistic reading of the text, closing off the possibility that there is any deeper symbolic content to be found. For example, MacEoin writes: "Another early work, the *Ṣaḥífa bayna'l-ḥaramayn*, contains a section dealing with talismans, with general instructions for their construction."[40] In a footnote he explains: "Two forms of talisman (*tilism; haykal*) are referred to: rectangular (*shikl al-tarbí'*) and triangular (*shikl al-tathlíth*). . . . This latter would seem from the description on p. 30 (which says it should not be regarded as resembling a Christian cross) to be identical to the pentagram talisman which the Bab later made the Babi *haykal* proper."[41] Elsewhere he says: "It is not entirely clear what relationship (if any) exists between the *haykal*s described in the *Panj sha'n* and those in the shape of a pentagram commonly found by that name and evidently identical with the 'triangular' talisman referred to in the *Ṣaḥífa bayna'l-ḥaramayn*."[42]

Although an extensive discussion of the problems in the above statements is not possible here, a fuller understanding of the issues involved should emerge by the end of this study.[43] Nevertheless, a brief reference to the spiritual meanings of these particular symbols may be helpful at this point. As we will see, contrary to MacEoin's statement, the triangular form has nothing to do with the pentagram temple, nor is it a rejection of the way the cross is shaped. Furthermore, what is discussed in the Ṣaḥífiy-i-Bayna'l-Ḥaramayn are the various levels of spiritual symbolic meaning of the two signs—the triangle and the square—in relation to different stages of the spiritual journey. The meaning of the triangle and the square in the Báb's text is quite complex. In the passage referred to, the Báb is answering a question regarding the triangle and square as two talismans. However, He turns the question of these forms into an analysis of deep spiritual meanings. He states that the forms of the triangle and the square represent the seven stages of divine creative Action. The triangle represents the first three stages and thus symbolizes Imám 'Alí, whose name consists of three Arabic letters. The square, representing the next four stages, refers to Muḥammad, whose name has four letters. The name of the Báb ('Alí-Muḥammad) is the unity of both forms, uniting the stations of 'Alí and Muḥammad. These are the stations of vicegerency and prophethood, and at the same time they represent the stations of divinity and prophethood because 'Alí is a name of God (the Most Exalted) as well as the name of the vicegerent of Muḥammad.

This particular text takes on yet another level of metaphysical allusion when we note that the Báb is writing it while travelling between the two sacred shrines, Mecca (the House of God) and Medina (the shrine of Muḥammad). The full title of the work is "The Epistle Revealed between the Twin Sacred Shrines." Thus the Báb is physically situated between the two places that symbolize, respectively, divinity and prophethood: He is in between the "triangle" of 'Alí (Mecca, the House of Divinity) and the "square" of servitude (Medina, the Shrine of the Prophet). This relation defines the station of the Báb as the *Báb*, or Gate. As He says, He is an *A* (Alif, a vertical line) which is located between the two *B*'s (two horizontal lines). He is the nexus that brings the two stations together, the Gate through which divinity and servitude are integrated. Thus the word *Báb* (as written in three distinct Persian letters) is both the secret of the trinity and the truth of the Christian sign of the cross.

At the very beginning of the text, the Báb proclaims: "Hearken unto the command of the Remnant of God, and, for the sake of the Truth, ask ye from the Remembrance of the name of your Lord, this Arabian Youth, that which ye desire regarding the truth of the twin Sacred Shrines, the Word of the twin supreme Clouds of Subtlety, and the Upright Line standing betwixt the twin Worlds."[44] Later, the Báb refers to Qur'ánic statements regarding the duty of the believer to enter the sacred gate (*báb*) in a posture of kneeling, and connects this reference to entering the gate of the Sacred House.[45] In other words, the Báb is the Gate through which the presence of God can be attained. He is the Gate that unites the twin Sacred Shrines, just as He was at that moment literally situated between Mecca and Medina. Thus the "triangle" and the "square" are now realized in His own being. More specifically, the station of the Báb is the unity of the primordial twin stations of the Point: divinity and servitude. The first three stages of creation represent the same spiritual truth that has been misconstrued by some Christians, in their phenomenology of worship, as a trinity that includes the realm of the divine

Essence, resulting in a reading of the shape of the cross in which the realm of divinity is reduced to the realm of contingency. Although these issues will become clearer later in this study, the point here is to demonstrate the vastly more productive reading that is possible when one does not assume that the Báb is only talking about magic charms.

As the Báb explains, these signs are intended to lead the consciousness of the wayfarer to discover the underlying unity of all reality. Pilgrimage is a pilgrimage toward God, a journey that aims at attaining the presence of God. This encounter can only take place in the various levels of paradise. Thus the Báb connects seven levels of paradise to seven modes of meeting God and pilgrimage. These levels correspond to the seven stages of divine creative Action. Thus, at the highest stage of mystic consciousness, corresponding to the station of Will (*Mashíyyat*), there can be no talismanic sign and all such signs must be discarded, for this is the realm of unity, where no differentiation exists between triangle and square. At this stage, only God is seen, without the presence of any phenomenal indicator of the unseen reality. It is only at the second stage of such consciousness, corresponding to the station of Determination (*Irádih*), that duality comes into play and the two signs become distinguished from each other. After this comes the third stage of divine creative Action, corresponding to the station of Destiny (*Qadar*). This stage is the beginning of the realm of plurality, and of the appearance of the triangle. Next is the fourth stage, Decree (*Qadá'*), the first of the last four stages of divine creative Action, which together are represented by the form of the square. The signs of the triangle and square, therefore, as symbols of the stages of creation, refer to the divine names that are manifest within the inner reality of all created beings. The believers/readers are asked to recognize this same unity within their own inner being even while worshipping God.[46]

As to the Tablet of Nineteen Temples, the reason that the Báb designs a system of nineteen temples is not a belief in the magical powers of letters. These temples are symbolic designs which express spiritual meanings. As we shall see in later chapters, the Báb creates these symbols to represent a metaphysical world view of unity—a consciousness of the universal solidarity of all beings, of the presence of the sign of God within all reality, and of the need to see in nature and in society nothing but the manifestations of the same divine creative Action. Thus, as the Báb explains, through these Nineteen Temples will become manifest the hidden truth of the Islamic Tradition according to which all the truth of the Qur'án is present in the "point." These temples have many more complex mystical meanings, which are explicitly discussed in the writings of the Báb.[47] Also, as we shall see, these temples are the same as the concept of the pentagram temple (five-pointed star) mentioned in the Persian Bayán.[48]

Organic Unity and Reciprocity of Signification

Unlike the ordinary and practical perspective which perceives the universe as a combination of distinct material objects, and unlike the mechanistic world view that sees the world as a realm of differentiation without transcendental reference, the world view reflected in the writings of the Báb portrays all of reality as a unity in diversity, as diverse reflections of the same truth, and as an interconnected, living and organic body. According to the Báb, not only do all beings testify to the unity of God, but it is by virtue of that very fact that they are all organic, interconnected parts of the reciprocal system of signification we have been discussing. This reciprocal feature means that each and every thing, to the degree of its capacity, carries within itself all other things. Every individual thing refers to all things, and any particular thing can potentially be deciphered through any other thing. Each atom of existence is endowed with oceans of perfections and attributes which are all reflections of the Divine Unity. Nothing exists independent from any other thing, and nothing can be adequately understood without reference to the totality of being.

Since everything is a mirror of all things, a true and holistic hermeneutics will be able to unveil infinite meanings and the mysteries of the universe through the understanding of any single atom of existence. Thus a drop of water, a ray of sunlight, or a glance of the eye can potentially unravel the mysteries of the cosmos and the secrets of all that has been and all that is to come. The Báb asserts:

> Every created entity in itself reflecteth the Greater World. . . . Verily God hath fashioned all things in the form of His Divine Unity in such wise that when a servant is purified from all protestation and doubt and instead reflecteth the splendours of the divine revelation unto him and

> through him, in utmost equity, he will be naught but the sign of the Divine Self, that "verily there is none other God but Him, the Beloved, the Compassionate."[49]

Likewise, He says that those endued with true understanding can even learn all celestial mysteries from the most humble and minute of creatures: "Know thou, verily, that God revealed the Qur'án even as He hath created all things. Therefore, in this day, should a tiny ant desire to unravel all its verses, and its abstruse meanings, and its stations, through the black of its own eye, it shall be capable of achieving that, inasmuch as the mystery of Lordship and the effulgence of the Eternal vibrate within the very atoms of all created things."[50] But it is the human reality that is particularly reflective of the entire universe, and it is the human heart that is singled out for a unique favour: "Verily hath God created within thyself all that He hath fashioned in creation in His likeness, that thou mayest not be veiled from any effulgence. Verily God hath generated within thy being the entirety of His manifestations. He hath ordained that His home be the heart of His servant. . . ."[51]

This universal organic unity and interconnectedness of all things, and its consequent universal mutuality of meaning, is applied by the Báb to all the various aspects of phenomenal reality including the symbolic realm of language. A single verse, a single word, or a single letter of the divine Word potentially discloses all spiritual mysteries. His own interpretive writings are partly a realization of this principle. It is in this context that He writes: "Verily, each letter of the Qur'án is invested with as many manifest meanings (*tafsír*) as the number of the atoms of all things that are embraced by the knowledge of God. And each one of these manifest meanings hath a hidden meaning (*ta'víl*), and each of these hidden meanings possesseth an inward meaning (*báṭin*), and each inward meaning containeth an inner inward meaning (*báṭin-i-báṭin*), and so on, as God willeth."[52]

Understanding these various meanings, however, is dependent on the level of spiritual understanding possessed by the individual reader. In the following passage, the different levels of meaning are represented as wellsprings corresponding to different individual stations. Each of the wellsprings alludes to one of the rivers of paradise mentioned in the Qur'án, which are composed of crystal water, milk, honey, and wine:

> Since God hath invested every letter with the ordinances pertaining to all things, it is My intention, at this juncture, to allude to some of the manifestations of the Fountain of Abundance (*Kawthar*), that those who abide under the shade of the Garden of Innermost Paradise (*al-Ifrídaws*) may drink their fill, while in this nether world, of the crystal spring of incorruptible water, and beyond them, those established upon the loftiest seats within the Paradise (*al-Firdaws*) of the wellspring of pure milk, and beyond them those who recline upon the snow-white couches 'neath the shade of the tree of being within the tabernacle of time (*zamán*) of the choicest wholesome honey, and beyond them, those who walk upon the earth, as permitted by God, clad in robes of grandeur and beauty and with the stature of sovereignty and glory, from the wellspring of pure wine "delicious to those who quaff it."[53]

In yet another statement, the Báb reaffirms that not only letters and numbers, but all creatures contain within themselves infinite, mutually referential meanings and that the purpose behind the organization of creation in this way is to attain the knowledge of God:

> . . . God hath created in the truth-sign of any thing that is called a thing, the signs of all beings, that it would not be difficult for anyone to recognize the manifestations of the tokens of His grace, and the effulgences of His modes of justice, so that all beings may witness the revelation of His sovereignty in the creation of all things, manifestly and truly, in such wise that none may see anything but that he would behold Him before seeing that object.[54]

Plenitude and Hierarchy of Meaning

The principles outlined so far make it clear that, for the Báb, all created things symbolically point to an infinite realm of spiritual meanings. It is important, however, to note that the fact that the text has infinite meanings does not imply, relativistically, that all meanings are equally true or that they are indistinguishable in their truth value. Although there is plenitude of meaning, there is also hierarchy.

The inexhaustible richness of meaning particularly applies to the words of God as revealed by His Manifestations. Although many Islamic

Traditions have said that the verses of God have multiple meanings, the Báb maintains that such a multiplicity understates the actual truth: "That which hath been reported previously concerning the existence of seventy or seven hundred inner meanings for the Qur'án, know verily that such a limitation is due only to the people's lack of ability to bear the truth. Indeed, the meanings of the Qur'ánic letters far exceed such numbers as to equal the number of all the atoms and determinations that are encompassed within the knowledge of God. . . ."[55]

The principle of the plenitude of meaning is modified by the equally crucial principle of the hierarchy of meanings, which we find emphasized in almost all the Báb's writings. The summit of this hierarchy is the Word uttered by the Manifestation of God. In the following statement, the Báb explains that the words that are uttered by the Manifestation are not the same words when uttered by anyone else, even if they appear to consist of exactly the same letters and signs. The words as spoken by the Manifestation inherently contain all the multitude of His intention, while those same words as spoken, and as understood, by a human being are representations limited to that individual speaker's level of understanding, which is determined by the person's spiritual station. That spiritual station is conditioned, in turn, by the individual's recognition of the station of the Manifestation as Speaker:

> O ye people of the Bayán! We verily have revealed unto you the knowledge of the exalted station of your being, which lieth in the words of your Lord, that ye may not, in truth, be veiled from Him Whom God shall assuredly make manifest in the Day of Resurrection. For verily that which ye utter is but a reflection of His revealed words that stems from you, whereas that which He decreeth is God's own testimony unto Himself: "Verily there is none other God but Him, the Omnipotent, the Self-Subsisting."[56]

Discussing the meaning of "food" in the Qur'ánic passage, "All food was lawful to the children of Israel," the Báb uses an analogy to demonstrate the hierarchy of spiritual levels and their corresponding "food":

> Thus the food that God hath made lawful unto the Will doth not befit the one who abideth in the station of Determination. For verily I have

> demonstrated this truth to thee through thine outward body, whereby that which is partaken by the ear cannot be enjoyed by the eye. Thus, it is incumbent upon thee to comprehend, in a similar way, such manifestations, that each station hath its own food. That which delighteth the eye is not the same thing that delighteth the ear, inasmuch as the ear beholdeth not and the eye heareth not.[57]

In the writings of the Báb, the question of meaning has two different dimensions. The *reflective* dimension pertains to the degree of clarity with which the different layers of reality are reflected in a symbol. While all created beings potentially reveal all reality, they reflect this reality in differential degrees of clarity corresponding to their own existential level. Those who occupy high spiritual stations are able to perceive meanings that others at lower spiritual stations are unable to discern. The second dimension is the *creative* dimension of meaning. Here the meaning of a word is equivalent to the existential effect of the speaker's uttering that word. The word spoken by the Manifestation of God is qualitatively different from the word of an ordinary human because it is the Creative Word: it is *creative* in that it has the power to produce change at all levels of reality and to bring into existence new states. Ordinary human meanings can also produce creative results, although to a strictly limited degree. The hierarchy of the meanings of symbols is thus a result of both the reflective and creative dimensions of those symbols.

In a work explaining the Tradition "He hath known God who hath known himself," the Báb begins His interpretation by setting out the hermeneutical principles, or rules of reading, that are necessary to understand the words of the Sacred Text. These rules are actually attitudes with which the reader should approach that Text. The first rule is to purify the heart in order to attain an understanding that is unbiased and undistorted by traditional received rules and methods: "I adjure thee," He writes, "before any other utterance, to pay heed unto my counsels, that thou mayest attain and be not of those whose affairs suffer, for verily there is no path to recognition save through recognition of these counsels. First, thou must, before all else, purify thy heart from any rule that thou hast acquired from thy divines and learned ones. . . ."

The next rule is to be conscious of the principle of the hierarchy of creative meanings—that is, to refrain from reducing the divinely inspired, revealed Word to mere human discourse, and to recognize that these words possess a vastly superior spiritual potency and meaning which is expressed in particular terms according to the recipient's level of understanding:

> Second, thou shouldst never compare the words of thy Imáms with the words of the people, for verily utterance is a manifestation of the reality of the one who uttereth, and a mirror that reflecteth that which is in his heart. Thus, just as their own being is a sure testimony for all the worlds and an indisputable sign from God, glorified be He, so are their words . . . which do not resemble the words of any other creatures. Their utterance, which is at once all-encompassing and all-perfect, is the proof of God unto the people. . . . All existence is the outcome of one letter of their utterance. . . . Thus the word of the Imám, peace be upon him, embraceth all things and streameth forth in all the worlds according to the conditions of their inhabitants.

The final rule is to consciously apply the second principle in regard to the sacred words, as a safeguard against misinterpretation: "Third, thou must refrain from interpreting, to the best of thine ability, the words of the Immaculate Souls, in regard to any imperfections, but, rather, [interpret them] through exaltation and honour."[58] Any perception of imperfection in such texts is an error on the part of the reader and a failure to grasp the meaning of the text.

The words of the Manifestation are unique in the sense that they are the creative Logos through which all things come into existence. Infinitely creative at all levels of reality, those words give rise to infinite meanings. These infinite meanings are the intended meanings of the Manifestation. What is meant, thus, by "words" is not just the visible alphabetical signs and audible sounds—those are mere shadows or symbols of the divine Word. When the Báb speaks of the infinite meanings of the letters of the Qur'án, or when He deduces all reality from the Point, He is not speaking of the empirical words and letters that are accessible to human beings, but rather of the divine Word, which is identical to the Will of God. When the Manifestation of God utters this Word, it becomes the set of meanings that are realized at the level of the Manifestation, but when a human being utters that same word, he is expressing only a shadow of the word that was spoken by the Point of Truth. In His commentary on the Letter Há', the Báb writes:

> For verily each name hath infinite degrees, and the meaning of each thing that is named pertaineth to its own degree. Behold the soul and the bodies of the Family of God, and then examine their words. For instance, the commonly used word "justice" (*'adl*): when uttered by God, glorified be His mention, this word becometh the source of justice as destined within the realm of the Will. Thus when a word issueth forth from the Concourse on High, it assumeth its ultimate and supreme Meaning (the Will). . . . Were all to gather together to produce even a semblance of that "Justice," they would assuredly fail to do so, except for the same literal letters that spell the word, 'Ayn, Dál, and Lám, which are at the level of their own existence, while the spirit (inner meaning) of that word is utterly non-existent in the face of the Justice God hath fashioned for His own Self. The same is true with regard to the word "Justice" as spoken by the Apostle of God, for verily its spirit is derived from His Spirit, while its literal pronunciation is associated with His body. . . .[59]

The hierarchy of true interpretation is at the same time the hierarchy of the plenitude of meaning. The existential level of the Point is absolute and all-embracing: it encompasses all the infinite meanings of the divine words and their individual letters, but access to all those meanings is barred to ordinary humans. There is an important exception, however: those authorized interpreters who have been specifically conferred the authority to interpret the Word and have been granted access to the meanings of the Manifestation. Their interpretations alone are therefore reliably true and binding. Although the meanings of the Word that are accessible to the human mind are multiple—indeed, infinite—even this infinity of meanings itself is but a drop in the fathomless ocean of meanings that is created and intended by the Manifestation.

The principle of the hierarchy of meaning implies that not only are there limitless true meanings but also that there is a continuum of quality, in which all meanings are relatively more true or less true in relation to each other. Hence, there are an infinite number of false and distorted meanings as well. Only the meanings intended by the Manifestation, and those of His authorized representatives, are purely true. All other limited perspectives, depending on their level, can lead to insights or distortion, true or false meanings. In the Persian Bayán, for example, the Báb asserts that the true meaning of His own words is only accessible to Him Whom God shall make manifest and His representatives:

> The substance of this gate is that none shall encompass that which God hath revealed in the Bayán except Him Whom God shall make manifest, or the One Who is taught such knowledge by Him [Whom God shall make manifest], as well as the Exalted Tree from which the Bayán hath emerged. For should all the oceans in the heavens and on the earth turn into ink, all the beings into pens, and all the souls into those who inscribe, they would be incapable of interpreting even a single letter of the Bayán, inasmuch as God hath destined for any letter thereof neither a beginning nor an end.[60]

According to the Báb, true understanding of the revealed Word, thus, is a matter of spiritual receptivity, attained by purifying the heart and turning to the Source of the Word, rather than by exerting the intellect alone or applying learning acquired from others. Such received traditional learning as is the focus of clerical education indeed constitutes the greatest obstacle to understanding the truth. As the Báb points out, the interpretations prevalent among the masses and scholars alike are usually mistaken. Discussing the meaning of the Day of Resurrection, the Báb states that "[w]hat is intended by the Day of Resurrection is the Day of the appearance of the Tree of divine Reality, but it is not seen that any one of the followers of Shí'ih Islám hath understood the meaning of the Day of Resurrection; rather have they fancifully imagined a thing which with God hath no reality."[61] As we shall see in subsequent chapters, it is "the gaze of the heart, and not that of intellect," which is the right method of approach to truth: "For intellect conceives not save limited things. Verily, bound by the realm of limitations, men are unable to gaze upon things simultaneously in their manifold aspects. Thus it is perplexing for them to comprehend that lofty station. No one can recognize the truth of the Middle Way between the two extreme poles except after attaining unto the gate of the heart and beholding the realities of the worlds, visible and unseen."[62]

2
The Divine Chemistry of Fire, Water, Air, and Earth

As we saw in the previous chapter, the fundamental purpose of the Báb's hermeneutics is to uncover the signs of that Divine Reality which is the supreme Origin, foundational Cause, and ultimate end and goal of phenomenal reality. Thus in His writings the Báb ceaselessly engages in both the interpretation and construction of various spiritual symbols. The heavily symbolic nature of His discourse is precisely because of the symbolic character of reality itself.

Symbols have two aspects: they represent both the otherness of the symbol in relation to its referent (that is, in the symbol the referent is being represented by something other than itself) as well as their unity (for the symbol does after all represent or stand for the referent). In this sense Coleridge's distinction between *arbitrary* sign and *symbolic* sign is instructive. According to Coleridge, the relation of an arbitrary sign to its meaning is completely random. An example of an arbitrary sign is an octagonal shape meaning "stop": any other shape could be used because there is no common meaningful feature that necessarily connects octagons and stopping. It is only convention that links them together. Symbolic signs, in contrast, are distinct from their meanings while at the same time they participate in some way in the truth of that meaning because they share some attribute or characteristic. A stylized image of the palm of a hand meaning "stop" as a sign partakes of the symbolic because it depicts the action of preventing motion.[1]

Using this definition of "symbol," we can see that for the Báb the entire phenomenal world is symbolic. Although the created realm and all the beings within it are categorically different from the transcendental realm, nevertheless they are the manifestations, the tokens, the reflections, and the revelations of that spiritual realm. In the language of the Báb, the world is the mirror of divine attributes. The phenomena of the world are thus symbols in the sense that they reflect the transcendental realm: they are the shadows, traces, images, and representations of the Divine. The image of the sun that is reflected in the mirror, of course, is not the same as the actual sun. It is always a representation, never an incarnation or a literal embodiment. Any assumption of the identity of the two is erroneous. Nevertheless, the sun that appears in the mirror is a true reflection of the sun.

This symbolic structure of phenomenal reality permeates the Báb's writings, which treat reality and natural phenomena as the reflection of the Countenance of the Divine Beloved. His writings themselves are designed in various symbolic forms to remind people of the essential truth of all things, namely their Supreme Origin and End. This symbolic character is also present, as we shall see, in the way the Báb designs His laws.

One expression of this symbolic orientation is the Báb's interpretation of the most visible components that constitute our ordinary experience of the material world—the four classical elements of fire, air, water, and earth. The Báb's writings affirm and reinterpret the reverence that was shown toward nature by the pre-Socratic Greek philosophers who conceptualized the Primal Matter, the source of all things, in terms of these elements.[2] In the Báb's extensive discussions of fire, water, air, and earth, these elements serve as symbols of numerous spiritual concepts which are central to the Báb's metaphysics. This chapter will outline a general sketch of these interpretations.

Water and the Kawthár Fountain

In the opening chapter of the Báb's first work, the Qayyúmu'l-Asmá', water and fire are used, often in mystical conjunction, as symbols of the highest levels of spiritual reality. In that work, as He is revealing Himself to Mullá Ḥusayn, the Báb announces that the Day of Resurrection has begun: "We verily have moved the mountains upon the earth, and the stars upon the Throne, by the power of the one true God, around the Fire which burneth in the centre of Water, as ordained by this Remembrance."[3] Often in this work the Báb speaks of Himself as the "Burning Bush" within the "Point of Snow," and reaffirms the Qur'ánic verse according to which the Throne of God is "upon the water."[4] In all these passages, emphasis is on the unity of fire and water as a mystical union of opposites.

The most detailed use of water symbolism can be found in the Báb's Commentary on the Súrih of Abundance. Written in Shiraz around May 1846, the commentary is an extensive interpretation of a short súrih of the Qur'án that reads in full: "We verily have conferred upon Thee the Kawthar fountain of abundance. Therefore pray unto Thy Lord, and sacrifice. Verily, it is Thine enemy who will be without posterity."[5] This súrih was revealed in response to the taunts of the enemies of Islam who had derided Muḥammad, saying He would be left without posterity or trace in the future because His sons had died in infancy. In the súrih, God addresses the Prophet, telling Him that God has bestowed upon Him the fountain of Kawthar, and that it is, instead, Muḥammad's enemies who will be without posterity.

The Báb's interpretation of this súrih is very complex. Here I will address briefly only His interpretation of the term "Kawthar fountain" as an instance of water symbolism. Kawthar is a fountain that flows in paradise. In the Báb's interpretation, most visibly it represents the creative force of the Prophet Muḥammad which would produce, through His daughter Fáṭimih, His true and lasting posterity—the line of the Imáms through whom the creative spirit of Islam would be manifested in the world in the centuries that followed. But in an important sense, the Báb is also interpreting the súrih as an affirmation of His own station: the supreme Manifestation of the divine fountain of Kawthar is the Báb Himself, Who is a descendant of the Imáms, and Who is none other than the Qá'im, for it is through Him that God's promise to Muḥammad is fully realized. (According to a Tradition, on the Day of Resurrection those who have truly believed in God will be given a drink from the Kawthar fountain and will never thirst again.)

Aside from the direct reference to the Báb, the Kawthar fountain, as a symbol, embraces within itself the entire mystery of reality and the end (goal) of creation. In order to understand this point we must pay attention to one of the most important and most often discussed interpretive novelties of the Báb. He relates the Kawthar fountain, and the divine water that bubbles up from it, to the four rivers or springs of paradise mentioned in the Qur'án. These four rivers are composed of "incorruptible, crystal water," milk "whose taste changeth not," "pure honey," and wine "delicious to those who quaff it."[6] According to the Báb, the source of these four rivers is the Kawthar fountain. It is the source of creativity and plenitude, the wellspring that produces life and gives birth to civilization. The "posterity" now being created out of the Kawthar fountain is thus the new spiritual civilization being initiated by the Báb through His Revelation. Together, the four rivers of paradise refer to the four levels of the divine creative Word in both the realm of cosmic creation (*takvín*) and the realm of revelation (*tadvín*). In the realm of creation, the four rivers are the source of all reality and stand for the first four of the seven stages of creation: Will, Determination, Destiny, and Decree.

The first and foremost of these rivers is the "incorruptible, crystal water." Out of this river flow the other three. The incorruptible, crystal water refers to the station of the Primal Will of God. This is the realm of the Logos, the Word of God, and it is the agency through which all reality comes into existence. Kawthar, the "fountain of abundance and plenitude," symbolizes that creative Word of God which is the source of life and existence for all beings. The symbolic role of water as the creative agent is visible in the realm of nature, where water is the primordial source of life. The Qur'án refers to this creative role in passages such as "We made all things living by virtue of water."[7] As the Primal Will, this water is the pure revelation of God shed upon all things by virtue of their coming into existence. All beings thus share a reflection, a trace, a shadow, of that crystal water within their inmost reality. That trace is the sign of the unity of all things which hints only at God. The Báb explains:

> The first river is the stream of crystal, snow-white, and incorruptible water, the inner essence of which is eternal (*azalí*) fire, and the manifest form of which is everlasting (*sarmadí*) water. It is a river that hath neither beginning, save itself, nor end, save its own essence. Verily, God hath made it to flow out by itself for itself, without any mention of anything besides itself. It is the river of transcendent unity, the water of supreme detachment, and the ocean of divine oneness, which streameth forth by the leave of God and as a testimony unto His revelation.
>
> Shouldst thou declare that the bed of this river is established of water, and the ark moving upon it is made out of water, and the mariner and those who enter the ark are fashioned out of its water, and the waves and all that lieth deep within are from the same substance of its water, thou verily wouldst have uttered the truth. For verily the inner essence of that

> crystal water referreth to naught but its outer manifestation; likewise, its outer manifestation revealeth naught but its inner essence. . . .
>
> Those who traverse the path of this river and quaff thereof behold in it naught but the pure and absolute revelation of the divine outpouring, which only referreth unto the Sovereign Source of Revelation Who hath shed upon them, and through them, the splendours of His Revelation. It is a river that by its very essence drowneth all the names and attributes.[8]

Although this crystal water itself is sanctified beyond all things, a reflection of it exists in every being.[9] Indeed, the seat of this revelation and effulgence is the human heart:

> Verily, allusions are the share of the people of veils. But he who fixeth his gaze upon the Lord of Names will behold, at all times and before all times, that invigorating water within the retreats of the branches of Divinity (*Láhút*), clearly visible in the manifestations of the inmost reality of his own soul. God, verily, will sustain him in all his acts and endeavours according to his station.
>
> Behold thou, with the glance of thy heart, the loftiest outpouring of divine creation within thine own soul: thou wouldst find naught but the crystal river of the incorruptible water of Kawthar at the sublime station of divinity. It remindeth thee to testify that "there is none other God but God" as thou dost bear witness at all times and under all conditions, without the slightest change in thine outward appearance or inner essence.[10]

Since the crystal water is the Primal Will out of which everything comes into existence, the other three rivers—those of fresh milk, pure honey, and red wine—represent various manifestations—that is, various levels of differentiation and determination—of the crystal water. The pure water itself is defined in terms of its absolute transparency. This first stage of creation, Will (*Mas͟híyyat*), represents the state of unity which is not yet mixed with any specification. Therefore, the water lacks any colour, or, rather, its colour is colourlessness. The second stage of the divine creative Word is Determination (*Irádih*). At this stage, the pure water enters into differentiation and is represented by the river of milk. The water now has a colour but that colour—white—is the closest to colourlessness. The Báb writes:

> For the spring of fresh milk "whose taste changeth not" floweth through the utterance of the determined essence which referreth to its snow-white colour. Verily, as it appeareth in the first stage the crystal incorruptible water is sanctified above any colour whatsoever, on account of the transparent intensity of its purity, the shining glory of its station, and the lofty proximity of its inner mystery to its Source of Revelation. That the appellation of snow-white colour is attributed to it is merely due to its station of limitation.[11]

The third stage of divine creative Action is symbolized by pure honey. It refers to the station of Destiny (*Qadar*). The fourth stage is Decree (*Qaḍá'*), symbolized by red wine. According to the Báb, each of these four rivers flows out of one of the four pillars of the Throne of God and each of the four stages of creative Action corresponds to one of the names of God, referring to the divine functions of the Creator, the Ever-Living, the Quickener, and the Slayer.[12]

While at the level of cosmic creation, the Kawthar fountain of abundance symbolizes the creative, generative revelation of God, it also has meaning at the level of discursive revelation. Here, the Kawthar fountain represents the Word of God which is revealed in four modes of revelation. The four rivers of paradise, thus, also correspond to the four modes of revelation. Paradise is ultimately the reflection of divine revelation in the world. Thus, literally the ink that flows from the pen of the Manifestation of God is the Kawthar fountain itself.

The crystal water is the revelation of divine verses: "[The mode of verses is] the crystal, incorruptible water, which belongeth solely to God, glorified be He. Inasmuch as it is sanctified above any combination with anything that pertaineth to the realm of plurality, it referreth and attesteth to naught save the Countenance of Effulgence shining within the Sovereign Source of Revelation."[13] In this passage we can see that the divine verses pertain to the state of unity, the undifferentiated Point, the unmitigated revelation of God. Connecting the Kawthar imagery to that of the Elixir, the Báb explains that few are pure enough in heart to recognize the truth of the Manifestation by the divine verses alone:

> The waters of that river flow forth from my tongue and pen with that which God willeth, imperishable and everlasting. This water is the well-spring of the Elixir, whose drinker was described by the Imám, peace be

> upon Him, as "Verily, a true believer is rarer than the philosopher's stone." And so it is in reality, for fewer than the number of the philosopher's stone have attained the full recognition of the Religion of God through no other path than that of the crystal water of this supreme River. Verily, these are the chosen ones who have attained unto the summit of detachment. . . .[14]

All others, according to their level of sincerity, purity, and receptivity, can drink only from the other three rivers/modes of revelation, which are diverse reflections of the divine verses:

> Those who have not quaffed of the crystal water of this river are incapable of recognizing its sublime station. Verily they all, each according to his nature and his object of love, drink from the other three rivers and yield praise unto God, their Lord. But the true believer would not drink of the three rivers before he imbibeth the crystal water of that lofty river. For, in truth, the triple rivers are but diverse names of that primal river; indeed, they are endued with life through the everlasting life of its invigorating water.[15]

The second river, that of fresh milk, symbolizes the mode of prayers:

> [T]he river of milk "whose taste changeth not" . . . floweth through the depths of prayers and supplications. It is the fresh milk and the manifest mystery, whose inner essence revealeth the crystal, incorruptible water, the outward form of which is pure milk. It is the water of the spirit of prayer, through which man reacheth the summit of sanctity and reposeth within the heaven of eternal reunion.[16]

Discussing the spirit of prayer and the exalted station of His prayers, the Báb states: "By thy life! Were the people to taste the delight of that milk, they would assuredly be willing to rend, with their own hands, their own bodies, that they might be permitted to recite a single prayer. For verily, within each prayer vibrateth the spirit of divine Sovereignty, radiateth the mystery of Eternity, and shineth forth the uttermost word of Servitude before the Divine Justice."[17]

The third river of paradise is the river of pure honey, representing the mode of sermons. The sweet nature of this river makes it easier for the people to appreciate it:

> [T]he pure Honey . . . floweth out, by the leave of God, in the mode of sermons. Verily the denizens of the realm of veils find it sweeter than all other signs, for it withstandeth veils, by the leave of God, more so than the first and the second rivers. Thus most of the enemies of God have confessed to the eloquence of My sermons, notwithstanding the remoteness of their station and the intensity of their denials.[18]

Finally the fourth river, that of red wine, corresponds to the mode of rational and educational discourse. This is the easiest and most accessible mode of revelation for the majority of people:

> Verily, amongst the rivers is the river of crimson-coloured wine. Whosoever drinketh even a single drop thereof will be rapturously drawn unto the station of holiness and nearness, without the slightest trace of inebriation, headache, faintness, or disagreeable after-effects. Nay, rather, it is exultation within exultation, from exultation to exultation.
>
> When imbibed, every drop of this river attesteth to the first river, the mode of verses; and to the second river, the mode of prayers; and to the third river, the mode of sermons; as well as its own mode, which affirmeth the allusions of the realm of Divinity, the signs of the world of Dominion, the stations of the world, and the evidences of the domain of the Kingdom. For the people, for the most part, quaff of this river because no one is able to deny the mode of Knowledge; indeed, the people are enchanted by the revelation of this mode, which gusheth out through the river of wine that perisheth not. It is the most delightful beverage and is the mode of the ascendancy of Words within the world of veils.[19]

The supreme Kawthar fountain of abundance, however, is the heart of the Báb Himself:

> By thy Life! Deep in My Heart, verily, existeth a transcendent Knowledge that is purer than the crystal, incorruptible water, more delicate than the fresh milk, sweeter than the pure honey, and tastier than the crimson-coloured wine. Should I find conduits or pure hearts like thee, I would assuredly manifest this knowledge by the leave of God, notwithstanding that My mode of Knowledge profiteth not the veiled people, nor others except the sincere amongst men of understanding.[20]

Another significant feature of the Kaw<u>th</u>ar fountain is the force with which these divine rivers surge and flow. The Báb frequently attests to the speed with which revelation flowed from His lips and pen, as evidence of the inimitable nature of that revelation. How much more powerful was the inner experience of being the vehicle of revelation:

> Verily, by virtue of the rapidity of the flow of the fresh milk of this river, a complete book of prayer streameth forth from My Pen within the course of six hours. Such rapidity is, verily, a most glorious sign within the realm of miracles. For verily the outward rapidity of flow is evidence of the inner surge. This surge is a daunting and highly perplexing matter, recognized by all as being impossible to attain by anyone save the One Whom God willeth. For the supreme honour is not in the mere composition of the outward appearance of the words, but in traversing the kingdom of Names and Attributes in less than the twinkling of an eye.[21]

But in addition to this invigorating pure water there is another kind of water: the burning salt water that symbolizes death, remoteness, and attachment to selfish desires. In His writings, the Báb often opposes "the fresh and thirst-quenching waters" (*má'u'l-furát*) to the "salt that burneth bitterly" (*milḥu'l-ujáj*). The one streams forth in paradise, while the other flows in the nethermost regions of hell.[22]

Fire and the Word

Although the Báb uses water to represent the Source of all life, when He uses the four elements as symbols of the four stages of spiritual reality, it is not water but fire that is the ultimate symbol of the Primal Will. For example, in discussing the symbolic significance of the nineteen months of the Bábí year, the Báb writes:

> The first three months are the fire of God, the next four months, the air of eternity, and the subsequent six months are the water of divine unity which streameth forth upon all souls, descending from the atmosphere of eternity, which in turn is derived from the fire of God. The last six months pertain to earthly existence, whereby all that hath appeared from these three elements may be established within the element of dust, through which the fruit will be harvested.[23]

Fire symbolism thus has a prominent role throughout the Báb's writings. His first work after the declaration of His mission, the Qayyúmu'l-Asmá,' is filled with fire imagery. To understand some of these references, it is helpful to note the relation the Báb draws between fire and the water of Kaw<u>th</u>ar. In His commentary on the Súrih of Abundance, the Báb says that the "inner essence" of the "crystal, snow-white, and incorruptible water" "is the eternal (*azalí*) fire," although its outward, "manifest form . . . is everlasting (*sarmadí*) water."[24]

The paradoxical relation involved in the unity of fire and water is the key to understanding the complex meanings associated with this symbol in the writings of the Báb. In the Qayyúmu'l-Asmá', we encounter the fire-and-water symbolism in passages such as these:

> We have verily sent Thee in the midst of Fire. For, verily, God hath revealed unto Thee this Furqán amidst Water and Thou art verily inscribed by the Twin Names in the Mother Book.[25]

> Verily, God hath granted thee permission to kneel in adoration and approach that Fire. This Fire, which, for the one True God, burneth at the very heart of the Water, prostrateth itself before the Truth.[26]

> O peoples of the earth! Cleave ye tenaciously to the Cord of the All-Highest God, which is but this Arabian Youth, Our Remembrance—He Who standeth concealed at the point of ice amidst the ocean of fire.[27]

Fire refers to the Creative Word of God, the inmost reality of the Primal Will. This fire, that is at the same time water, represents the union of opposites, the synthesis of all oppositions, and the universal totality. The Primal Will is "All Things" (*Kullu-<u>Sh</u>ay'*) in the highest sense of the term, as "the reality that containeth and embraceth everything."[28] Most directly, however, the fire symbol is a reference to divine revelation and the Logos, as expressed in the call of God that emanates from the Burning Bush. The Burning Bush unites in a mystical symbol the three motifs of fire, the tree, and the voice of God.

The Burning Bush, of course, belongs to the story of Moses, and it is one of the most significant features of the Báb's self-definition in all His writings. In the Qayyúmu'l-Asmá' the voice of God that spoke to Moses through the Burning Bush is in fact the Báb: "O People of effacement!" the Báb writes, "Hearken ye unto My Call, appearing out of the Point of

Confirmation, from this Arabian Youth Who hath addressed, by the leave of God, Moses upon Mount Sinai. Verily God revealed, by the leave of God, the Pentateuch unto Moses, for mighty is the Cause of God as ordained in the Mother Book."[29]

This fire also symbolizes the ultimate paradise, the state of utmost joy, and the supreme end of human existence, as it denotes the state of attaining the presence of God and beholding the Countenance of the Divine Beloved. Consequently the fire is directly related to the Day of God, the day when the presence of God is attained. It is in this context that the Báb emphasizes the uniqueness of His station as compared to that of Moses.[30] While according to the appearance of the Scriptures, Moses' encounter with the Burning Bush was limited to a few occasions, for the Báb it is a ceaseless and eternal experience.[31]

Parallel to the distinction between the two types of water—the life-giving pure water and the burning salt water—there are also two types of fire. The fire of paradise, the fire of Divine Unity, is the fire of love, which represents nearness to and union with the Beloved. The other fire is the fire of hell; it is the fire of hatred, selfishness, and envy, and represents separation, remoteness, and deprivation of faith. The fire of unity burns away the veils and makes it possible to gaze upon the Countenance of God. The fire of remoteness is itself the very veil that obscures the eye of the heart.

A major difference between the two types of fire is already visible in the unique feature of the divine fire. As the symbol of the Primal Will, this fire is the unity of opposites: it is both burning fire and cool water. Consequently the reflection of this fire in the hearts of the faithful creates not only love and yearning, but also peace and tranquility. The fire of hate, on the other hand, is incapable of offering peace and life. It brings only distress and agitation, negation, and death. The Báb discusses the difference between these two types of fire in reference to the story of the fire with which the idol worshippers sought to burn Abraham. According to the Qur'án, God made that fire cool and safe.[32] The Báb describes this fire as the fire that burns away all the veils and manifests the Beloved within one's own being.[33] The divine fire is pure light, whereas the hellish fire is pure darkness. In the story of Moses and the Burning Bush, the fire is the light through which the vision of God becomes possible. It is for these reasons that the Manifestation as the Point of Fire is also the Sun of Truth: the Sun is the Point of Fire itself.

Turning away from the Manifestation of God, Who is the Source of light, vision, and guidance, deprives oneself of light and constitutes the fire of hell. One of the most significant symbolic expressions of the distinction between hellish fire and heavenly light is found in the very title of the Báb. The numerical value of the word "light" (*núr*) is 256. The word for "fire" is *nár*, which is equal to 251. The difference between light and fire, thus, is 5—which is exactly the value of the word *Báb*. The Báb thus is the touchstone determining whether one's lot is to be the fire or the light—perdition or paradise.[34]

Just as the incorruptible and crystal water is characterized by pure transparency, the celestial light is also defined in terms of its utter purity and clarity. But the light is not merely visible itself; through its sacrifice of itself it makes all other things visible. According to the Báb, light is also a reference to the idea of martyrdom, and thus both concepts (light and martyrdom) allude to the station of Imám Ḥusayn. The Báb expounds this point in relation to the S͟hí'ih Dawn Prayer, in which various names of God are celebrated. The first name mentioned is *Bahá* (Glory), while the fifth is *Núr* (Light):

> Consider the Dawn Prayer revealed by Imám Báqir. It beginneth with this: "O thou God! I beseech Thee by the most glorious of Thy Glory (*Bahá*), for all Thy Glory is glorious. O Thou God! I beseech Thee by all Thy Glory." The allusion to *Bahá* in this part referreth unto the Apostle of God, the blessings of God rest upon Him. Witness the second part of the prayer as a reference to the station of the Commander of the Faithful, till thou reachest the fifth part thereof, where it mentioneth the Light (*Núr*), which pointeth to the Prince of Martyrs. The station of light resembleth that of the lamp, which consumeth its own self in order to illumine others, for there remaineth no trace of identity in the light. Thus shouldst thou be alive, thou wouldst witness the lights of this Revelation who will relinquish, by their own will, their own being in order to render victorious the unity of God, and His ordinances and prohibitions.[35]

Air and the Word

After fire, the symbol of exalted spiritual mysteries is air. Like fire and water, air also ultimately symbolizes different stations of the divine creative Action and Logos. One of the most important expressions of the organic connection between air and the Word is the mystic concept of the "Breath of the All-Merciful" (*Nafas-i-Raḥmán*), which occurs in various mystic and spiritual traditions. The word is the motion of air and the breath that proceeds from the lips of the speaker. In the story of creation, God creates Adam by breathing spirit into his body. The breath of God is the source of life and reality, the spirit of the Word of God that calls all beings into existence.

In the Qayyúmu'l-Asmá', the Báb identifies the Breath of the All-Merciful as the Source of the divine Wind (the divine verses), which sows the seeds of godly attributes in the holy city of the heart: "Curse ye not the 'Winds,'" He writes, "for they verily have proceeded, in truth, from the 'Breath of the All-Merciful' by the Command of God. And We send them not except to the sacred city, by the leave of God, that the divine attributes may be manifested therefrom at the behest of the Most Exalted God. For He is God, Who is in truth the All-Praised."[36]

Discussing the four stages of the concept of "mystery," the Báb identifies the second station (the second stage of creation, or Determination) as the station of the "Breath of the All-Merciful."[37] At the same time, one of the literal meanings of air is the sweet fragrance which is so frequently praised by the Báb. Discussing the true "food" of different parts of the body, symbolizing the first four stages of divine creative Action, He writes:

> Next is the station of Destiny (*Qadar*), represented in thy body by the nose. It behooveth the faithful to inhale the fragrance of sweet savours, for, verily, that is the food ordained by God for it. Thus it hath been the tradition of the Prophets and the Messengers, from the day of Adam till this Day, to make use of the best pure perfumes. . . . That is for him who hath the means to obtain it; as for him who cannot, God hath made water a sweet fragrance for the faithful. . . .
>
> For, verily, perfume is created out of the Sea of Destiny. Whosoever is adorned with the virtues of God, glorified and exalted be He, must make use of perfumes, and inhale sweet-smelling substances such as clove or other creations of God, the Exalted, the Mighty. Verily God shall sustain such a soul in the station of truth through His name, the Ever-Living.[38]

Like fire, air is defined in terms of its subtlety and lightness and is a symbol of ascent to the Divine Beloved. In this context air and the wind become inseparable from heaven and flight. A related symbol thus is the divine bird, which plays a central role in the Báb's cosmic drama. The relation of the bird to the air is twofold: not only does the divine bird soar in the air of eternity, it also sings, through the vibrations of the transcendental air, the song of the celestial Word. The Báb Himself is often referred to as a celestial Bird. In His commentary on the Súrih of Abundance, He writes: "O thou who hast fixed thy gaze upon these sparkling and vibrant leaves of the Tree of the Supreme Cloud of Subtlety! Follow thou the buzzing melodies of the Bees of Sovereign Divinity (*Láhút*) in the inmost realities of these manifestations, and the songs of the Dove of Dominion (*Jabarút*) in the quintessences of these evidences, and the subtle plaintive cries of the Birds of the Kingdom of This World (*Mulk*) within the identities of these allusions. . . ."[39] In another statement, He relates the proclamation of the divine Word by the celestial Bird to the sufferings of the Prophet at the hands of the heedless people:

> Verily, that which We sprinkled upon thee out of the ocean of Names and Attributes is due to the sweet melodies of This Bird, Who hath first soared in the air of the Supreme Cloud of Subtlety and then warbled in the inner depths of these allusions; thereby it shone forth and was manifest, circled around and revolved, rose up and stood upright, . . . sighed and bemoaned, cried and wept, then fell with anguish upon the earth, trembling like unto a fish out of water, proclaiming the words of His Lord, as permitted by God: O My God! I plead My grief solely unto Thee. Ennoble My Cause, and fulfill that which Thou hast promised Me. . . .[40]

The Earth of Magnification

The last of the four elements is earth. Like the previous three elements, it is part of an interrelated spiritual symbolism. Earth, or dust, represents the fourth stage of creation, Decree (*Qaḍá'*).[41] The most frequent use of the symbol of "earth" in the writings of the Báb concerns the relation of earth to heaven. In an extensive chapter of the Kitábu'l-Asmá', the Báb characterizes God and His Prophets, particularly the Promised One of the Bayán, as a divine farmer who tills the soil of the hearts:

> Say! God verily cultivateth on earth as He pleaseth, at His bidding. Will ye not behold? Think ye that ye are the sowers? Say! Glorified be God! We

> are, verily, the Cultivators. Say! Gaze ye then upon all even as ye behold the most exalted of the renowned amongst you. Verily, that which is shared by both the rulers and those who farm the lands is one thing: they all abide by the bidding of God.
>
> Say! We verily sow through Our verses in the soil of your hearts, spirits, souls, and bodies. . . .
>
> Thus God instructeth you how to sow for your ultimate end and final abode, that haply in the Day of Resurrection, when He Whom God shall make manifest revealeth His verses unto your hearts, ye may, with utter love, become impregnated and show forth the noble fruits of what ye carry at the bidding of God as swiftly as ye can. . . .
>
> Say! The verses of God are like unto a living, invigorating water, which is sent down out of the heaven of the Primal Will upon the earth of your nearness to God. Turn ye, then, instantly to God, your Lord. Purify ye, then, your soil through that which He sendeth down out of the heaven of divinity, and yield ye, without delay, His fruits.[42]

At the human level, the reflection of the element of earth (dust) is the human body. Although it is but dust, the human body is also the temple of spiritual attributes and thus it is to be honoured and sanctified. According to the Báb, even the body is a symbol of the divine Word. In the passage, cited earlier, in which the Báb uses parts of the body (ear, eye, nose, and mouth) as symbols of the four stages of divine creative Action, He says:

> Then is the food of thine eyes, which is the gazing upon that which remindeth thee of God. . . . This is the station of Determination (*Irádih*) in thy body. Thus, make thou the food of the Will thy remembrance of "God," and the food of Determination His remembrance, once thou hast uttered the word of negation, "but Him." Next is the station of Destiny (*Qadar*). It is represented in thy body by the nose. It behooveth the faithful to inhale the fragrance of sweet savours, for verily that is the food ordained by God for it. . . . Then is the representative of the station of Decree (*Qaḍá'*), which is naught but the mouth. Upon its throne abideth the king of knowledge, which is the tongue.[43]

Finally, the complex symbolism of earth or dust in the writings of the Báb occurs in His discussion of those particular Houses, made of earth and clay, that become sacred temples, the Point of Adoration (*Qiblih*) for prayer, and places of pilgrimage. In the Persian Bayán, the Báb explains the reason that exalted temples should be constructed in the birthplace of the Promised One of the Bayán:

> [T]he first land wherein the very body of Him Whom God shall make manifest appeareth [His birthplace], hath always been, and will ever be, the Sacred Temple. . . . The purpose of this ordinance is this, that when a piece of earth is enobled by virtue of its association with His body, it attaineth such an exalted station that it becometh the place of pilgrimage through the act of circumambulation around His House; then how much more exalted would be the soil of the essential bodies that point unto His magnificence, and the soil of the souls that refer unto His unity, and the soil of the spirits that hint at His praise, and the soil of the hearts that mirror His glorification. For in the foremost station of the heart, the fire of love shineth forth; and in the second, the air of guardianship ascendeth; and in the third, the water of unity surgeth; and in the fourth, the dust of existence is elevated.[44]

In the writings of the Báb, symbols such as these comprise a mystical lexicon that conveys complex and often ineffable metaphysical concepts. Understanding this mystical lexicon, and how the Báb employs it to express, in condensed form, ideas that would need voluminous explication, is the key to deciphering what otherwise may seem bewildering and arcane references in His writings.

3
The Remembrance, the Gate, and the Dust

No discussion of the early writings of the Báb can fail to address the question of the nature of the claim to spiritual authority that He makes in those works. In those texts, written during the first three years of His ministry (May 1844–May 1847), the Báb claims to be the Gate to the hidden Twelfth Imám. He also frequently refers to Himself as the "Remembrance of God" (*Dhikru'lláh*). However, in His later writings, those set down during the last three years of His life (May 1847–July 1850), the Báb declares His real station to be not only that of the Twelfth Imám—the very Qá'im Himself—but also a new Prophet, a new Manifestation of God, with the authority to promulgate a new Holy Book with new laws.

Reconciling the apparent differences in the claims made by the Báb has been a matter of puzzlement to some scholars. Although some have found continuity in the Báb's claims,[1] others have assumed that the different stations the Báb attributed to Himself at various times reflect an alteration or evolution of consciousness on His part—indicating, in effect, that over time the Báb changed His mind about what station He actually held. But even those who espouse the theory that the Báb's claims changed substantively have had to account for the fact that His earliest claims to gatehood are accompanied by unmistakable indications of a status and authority far more exalted than anything that would normally apply to a Gate. MacEoin, for example, maintains that "for several years he regarded himself and was regarded by his followers as the *báb*, or representative on earth of the hidden Twelfth Imám. . . . Exactly how his claims developed after that is not entirely clear."[2] Yet MacEoin also notes what he calls a "tension" in the Qayyúmu'l-Asmá' between "the Báb's claims to be merely the gate of the Hidden Imám, the Remembrance of God (*dhikr Allah*), and Seal of the Gates (*khatim al-abwáb*) on the one hand and more dramatic proclamations of quasi-prophethood or even divinity on the other."[3] And MacEoin acknowledges that "Even at the earliest period, there is evidence that the Báb claimed for himself and his writings a level of inspirational authority well above that normally associated with the role of *bábu'l-imám*." But MacEoin explains away this crucial fact as the Báb's own personal and more expansive intepretation of His role as the Gate: "This is not to suggest that he entertained notions of a more exalted status for himself at this point, merely that the function of *bábiyya* (or *niyába*) as he understood and expressed it involved the ability to reveal inspired verses and to possess innate knowledge."[4]

Lawson correctly points out that the early claims of the Báb concealed an inward claim to prophetic consciousness.[5] Amanat, while arguing for the gradual development and evolving definition of the Báb's self-conception, suggests that the Báb's early references to gatehood are in fact concealed expressions of an inwardly self-conscious prophetic station.[6] MacEoin, however, although recognizing that the early claim of the Báb went far beyond the traditional conception of gatehood, seems to argue for a qualitative break in the Báb's own concept of the nature of His claim, with prophetic consciousness emerging only in the last two to three years of His life.[7]

Another possible theory is that the apparently different claims signify that the Báb was merely engaging in the traditional Shí'ih practice of dissimulation (*taqíyyih*), and was modifying His statements in a particular way at times because He did not want to be seen as making an exalted claim.[8] While it is undeniable that the Báb employed judicious concealment of the full truth (as He Himself has said), I suggest that the reality is far more complex, subtle, and meaningful than the explanation of mere dissimulation allows. To understand the nature of the Báb's claims as they unfold in His writings during the different stages of His ministry, we must examine in some detail several different, interrelated, crucial elements. These factors include the revolutionary nature of the Báb's assertions, set against the background context of the prevailing beliefs of Shí'ih Islam; the rhetorical considerations that the Báb Himself has cited as His reasons for couching His discourse in the terms He uses in particular texts; and the nature, meaning, and complex implications of the Báb's claims considered together and situated within the context of His metaphysics and theology.

The Revolutionary Nature of the Báb's Claims

Whether friend or foe, none of those who have come into contact with the teachings of the Báb has denied their revolutionary character. That His writings and claims were so radically challenging as to threaten S͟hí'ih traditionalism literally at its very roots becomes eminently clear when the Báb's claims are considered in light of traditional S͟hí'ih doctrine and eschatological expectations. The S͟hí'ih held a firm belief in the finality of the prophethood of Muḥammad, although it should be noted that a Tradition does assert that the Qá'im "will come with a new Cause—just as Muḥammad, at the beginning of Islam, summoned the people to a new Cause—and with a new book and a new religious law (s͟har'), which will be a severe test for the Arabs."[9] The Qá'im was expected to appear at the end of time, accompanied by specific signs, manifesting overt temporal sovereignty, and initiating a reign of justice that would precede the end of history and the Day of Judgment.[10]

The entrenched expectations about the Qá'im, based on various Traditions, were overwhelmingly in terms of violent imagery: war, blood, and conquest of the enemies of Islam and the unbelievers. Traditions said of the Qá'im that "his task is naught but the use of the sword, and he shall not accept repentance from any one." Unlike Imám 'Alí, who tolerated the presence of unbelievers in Iraq, the Qá'im was expected to act on the basis of the "red book" and would "reign by shedding blood and slaying the enemies of God"; he would "fight with the people and enslave them."[11] According to other Traditions, the Qá'im would offer Islam to the Jews, Christians, Sabeans (Ṣabi'ín), atheists, heretics, and infidels throughout the East and the West and "whoever refuses to accept Islam will have his throat slit by him so that there will be left not even a single disbeliever on earth, either in the East or the West."[12] The Imám Báqir is reported to have said that "the Qá'im will fill the earth with justice even as it was filled before him with oppression. God will conquer the East and the West for him, and he will kill so many of the people that none but the religion of Muḥammad will remain on earth."[13] In a Tradition attributed to Muḥammad, the Prophet foretold that two signs would herald the advent of the Qá'im. One was a banner which would unfurl itself at the time of his appearance and call out to the Qá'im, bidding him to "rise up and kill the enemies of God." The other was his sword, which would be unsheathed at the moment of his appearance and would address the Qá'im, saying, "Rise up, do not let the enemies of God get away," whereupon he would unveil himself and "slay all the enemies of God."[14] In another Tradition, Imám Ṣádiq is believed to have said, "In the reign of the Qá'im the Shí'ih will be the leaders and rulers of earth. Each one of them will possess the force of forty men . . . each one of them will be braver than a lion and swifter than an arrow, so that they will crush our enemies under their feet and kill them with their bare hands."[15]

Of course, the image of the Day of Judgment as a bloody Apocalypse and of the return of the promised prophetic figure wielding a sword and waging war, conquering and slaying the unbelievers, is not unique to Islam. Significant parallels can be found in Jewish and Christian Scriptures and history. At the time of Jesus, the Jews expected the awaited Messiah to demonstrate sovereignty—interpreted literally as military might and political dominion. Of course Jesus did not conform to those expectations and was accordingly dismissed by the Pharisees as an imposter yet was judged so threatening to the authority of the leadership that He was condemned to death.

Christian expectations of the Second Coming of Christ, as described in the Book of Revelation, predict the unleashing of the horsemen of the Apocalypse, who would wield "a great sword,"[16] and lead an army of "two hundred thousand thousand" to "slay the third part of men."[17] The vision of the "end time" recorded in the Book of Revelation is similar to the Shí'ih expectations of the Qá'im in terms of its imagery of the sword, war, blood, judgment, and the initiation of a reign of justice:

> And I saw heaven opened, and behold a white horse; and he that sat upon him *was* called Faithful and True, and in righteousness he doth judge and make war. His eyes *were* as a flame of fire, and on his head *were* many crowns; and he had a name written, that no man knew, but he himself. And he *was* clothed with a vesture dipped in blood: and his name is called The Word of God. And the armies *which were* in heaven followed him upon white horses, clothed in fine linen, white and clean. And out of his mouth goeth a sharp sword, that with it he should smite

> the nations; and he shall rule them with a rod of iron: and he treadeth the winepress of the fierceness and wrath of Almighty God. And he hath on *his* vesture and on his thigh a name written, KING OF KINGS, AND LORD OF LORDS.[18]

In the context of Shí'ih beliefs, to make any claim of prophethood was nothing less than heresy punishable by death. And when judged literally against some of the descriptions recorded in the Traditions, the Báb's claim to be the Twelfth Imám and the Qá'im could not but be regarded as false and blasphemous. After all, the Báb was a mild, refined young merchant from Shiraz, with well-known parents and life history: how could He possibly be the Imám who had been living in occultation for a thousand years? Moreover, the Báb showed no signs of demonstrating any sort of worldly sovereignty of the type promised in the Traditions, as they were literally understood.

Although the Báb certainly had ample reason to assume that if He openly claimed the station of the Qá'im—let alone the station of prophethood—He would be quickly put to death, mere dissimulation does not satisfactorily explain why He phrased His claims as He did in His early texts. For the exalted, extremely challenging, and even provocative, claims that the Báb made in those works were perfectly clear to some readers, including some of His most hostile opponents. Inflamed by what they saw in the Báb's Qayyúmu'l-Asmá', the Shí'ih and Sunní 'ulamá issued a joint decree condemning the book as a heretical claim to a new revelation.[19] And the first polemical work against the Báb, written by the prominent Shaykhí, Karím Khán-i-Kirmání, made several powerful arguments using statements in the Qayyúmu'l-Asmá' to support his charge that the Báb was patently claiming to be the Qá'im and the recipient of a new revelation equal to that of Muḥammad.[20]

To understand the meaning of the Báb's claims, we must understand the subtle connotations of the word *báb* as used in His texts. In His early writings, *báb* was apparently used to mean the Gate to the Hidden Imám. If we read this term in the sense it would have had in the Shí'ih context of the time, the obvious interpretation of such a claim to gatehood would be that it asserted attainment to a particular level of religious scholarship within the community of religious scholars and clerics. The traditional Shí'ih world view conceived of five root principles or pillars of the Faith: the unity of God, prophethood, the Day of Resurrection, divine justice, and the successorship of the Imáms. Shaykh Aḥmad-i-Aḥsá'í, in his writings, appeared to alter this rendering, however, and seemed to imply that there was, instead, a hierarchy of four principles: the unity of God, prophethood, the successorship of the Imáms, and the "Shí'ih."[21] The last element, which he seems intentionally to have left vague, referred to the leader or leaders of the community in the absence of the Imám. The early writings of the Báb appear to identify the Báb's station as this fourth category.

However, in traditional Twelver Shí'ih Islam, the term *báb* referred to the four representatives of the hidden Twelfth Imám during the decades following the Imám's Lesser Occultation. Shortly before the death of the fourth Gate, the Hidden Imám sent a final message instructing the Gate not to appoint a successor because "the second occultation has come and there will not now be a manifestation except by the permission of God and that after a long time has passed, and hearts have hardened and the earth become filled with tyranny. . . ."[22] The Báb, in His early writings, identified Shaykh Aḥmad and Siyyid Káẓim as two of the Gates of the Imám, while He identified Himself as the Supreme Gate, and His first believer, Mullá Ḥusayn, as the Gate of the Gate (*Bábu'l-Báb*).[23]

Although the Báb's early writings seem to indicate that He is claiming to be a mere representative of the Imám, a Gate among other Gates, a closer reading of His works reveals a very different picture. It becomes evident that the Báb was not using the familiar Shí'ih terms in their received meanings but in a new and different way, infusing fresh significance into those symbols in order to claim from the very beginning to be the Qá'im, a new Prophet, and the manifestation of the Primal Will. To perceive the continuity of the central elements of the Báb's writings, His self-conception, and His message, it is necessary to have an intimate understanding of the totality of His early and later works. Although a full discussion of the complexity of the Báb's early claims is only possible after we have considered the entire course of His writings, a general examination of the issue is necessary at this stage.

Dissimulation, Rhetoric, and Wisdom

Obviously the Báb was keenly aware of the rhetorical and psychological considerations inherent in attempting to communicate to an audience a message that not only contradicted their expectations and their most cherished beliefs, but which also profoundly threatened the very foundations of their religion and their entire world view. Ideas at the periphery of a belief system are usually more open to question and may even be subject to revision without causing alarm, although, in the realm of religion, so strong is the force of traditional conservatism that even the smallest details may be insisted upon as firmly as if they were core beliefs. The boundaries of normal discourse are determined by the point at which differing interpretations threaten the core of the belief system.[24] And the closer to the core the beliefs in question are located, the more resistance is encountered. To challenge core beliefs is to challenge the entire belief system itself. When faced by such a radical and alarming message, the normal initial reaction is some degree of shock and rejection. At that point, however, an individual faced by dissonance between the new claim and one's existing beliefs must decide whether to reexamine those beliefs in light of the challenging new idea, or whether to cling to the existing beliefs and to reject the new claim by defining it as erroneous because it does not conform to the standard of those beliefs.

In the case of the Báb's claims, there was another crucial aspect: His message not only challenged the foundations of traditional Shí'ih Islam as a set of beliefs, but more specifically it directly threatened the basis of the Muslim clergy's power and authority. His claims thus not only had spiritual implications but revolutionary social implications as well, implications that were deeply alarming to the powerful clerical establishment.

To be willing to subject to reexamination one's most deeply cherished beliefs—beliefs that constitute the foundation of one's personal identity—and accept the possibility that those beliefs may be mistaken requires an extremely high degree of psychological and spiritual maturity. It requires an absolute dedication to searching out the truth above all, no matter where that search leads, and a willingness to recognize the truth once one encounters it, no matter what the consequences. Few people possess such a level of absolute justice and love of truth that surpasses all other allegiances and inclinations. Thus the majority of the audience to whom the Báb would offer His message could be expected to respond to it initially with shock, denial, and rejection.

To cushion the shock for His audience, the Báb expresses His challenging message through His writings in such a way that the message will be less likely to evoke an automatic response of fear, defensiveness, and hostility. An important distinction must be made between the motivation for the Báb's concealment of the full and complete truth in this context, and the motivation generally associated with dissimulation. Traditionally, dissimulation was employed by the Shí'ih in times of persecution and danger; thus the main motivation was to avoid harm to oneself. But here, in contrast, the primary motivation concerns the audience's reception. In other words, the Báb is applying principles of wisdom in rhetoric in order to communicate His message effectively to His audience. Therefore, given His audience's state of receptivity, He initially couches His claims in terms that can be identified with beliefs located closer to the periphery of the Shí'ih belief system. To claim to be a Gate to the Qá'im, while surprising, was not seriously threatening to the core of the belief system. Once that station was accepted, the next level of the belief system could be approached—the fact that the Báb was not merely a Gate but the very Qá'im Himself. Having reached that level of reorganization of their internal belief structure, the Báb's followers would be better prepared to receive the most challenging fact about His station: that the Báb was claiming to be a Prophet and the recipient of a new revelation.

The Báb's rhetorical method is distinguished from mere dissimulation in another, profoundly significant respect: none of the apparently differing claims He advanced was untrue: each of the titles He ascribed to Himself in the successive stages of His writings was an integral facet of the complex reality of His own station. He revealed those aspects consecutively, like layers gradually unfolding to finally disclose the heart and the whole.

By the Báb's own account, it was the spiritual condition and level of receptivity of the people around Him that necessitated the gradual divulgence of His message. Accordingly, He explains, at the beginning of His mission He did not disclose His true station to the generality of the people because He knew that His claim to prophethood was far beyond the ability of the people to bear. In one of His later writings, the Seven Proofs, He explains:

> Consider the manifold favours vouchsafed by the Promised One, and the effusions of His bounty which have pervaded the concourse of the followers of Islám to enable them to attain unto salvation. Indeed observe how He Who representeth the origin of creation, He Who is the Exponent of the verse, "I, in very truth, am God," identified Himself as the Gate [Báb] for the advent of the promised Qá'im, a descendant of Muḥammad, and in His first Book enjoined the observance of the laws of the Qur'án,

so that the people might not be seized with perturbation by reason of a new Book and a new Revelation and might regard His Faith as similar to their own, perchance they would not turn away from the Truth and ignore the thing for which they had been called into being.[25]

In the Qayyúmu'l-Asmá', He writes that the reaction of the people to the full truth would be shock:

O Qurratu'l-'Ayn![26] Stretch not Thy hands wide open in the Cause, inasmuch as the people would find themselves in a state of stupor by reason of the Mystery, and I swear by the true, Almighty God that there is yet for Thee another turn after this Dispensation.

And when the appointed hour hath struck, do Thou, by the leave of God, the All-Wise, reveal from the heights of the Most Lofty and Mystic Mount a faint, an infinitesimal glimmer of Thy impenetrable Mystery, that they who have recognized the radiance of the Sinaic Splendour may faint away and die as they catch a lightning glimpse of the fierce and crimson Light that envelops Thy Revelation.[27]

In the Epistle on the Proofs of the Prophethood of Muḥammad, the Báb notes that if He disclosed the full truth of His station, the people would react with denial and rejection:

Verily, but for the recognition that the knowledge of that exalted station involveth endless conditions which none except God can reckon, and since not all that a servant knoweth can be disclosed, and had it not been for the duty of concealment and the dread, as alluded to by 'Alí, the Son of Ḥusayn, glorified be His mention: "How many are the essences of knowledge which, should I reveal them, I would be told that I am amongst the worshippers of idols," I would have divulged the true secret of that glorious station.[28]

In the Commentary on the Súrih of Abundance, writing to someone whom He judged to be receptive, and thus to whom He could impart more of the truth, the Báb explains:

For, verily, the people comprehend not that which I behold within these remarks, witness not that which I perceive within the words, and discern not the Repositories of the signs. Had I been questioned by anyone

> but thee, I would not have divulged these remarks, inasmuch as they are far more precious in Mine estimation than the crimson Elixir. This notwithstanding, I have refrained in some places, on account of the gaze of the foes, from explicit affirmation of the ocean of utmost tranquility, and enshrouded My words in the dark depths of the air, for those who fail to witness the Countenance of the Attributes within a darkness that is hard, thick, blind, intense, dusty, and gloomy, so that no wicked-doer may discover the true secrets of the Family of God, the blessings of God rest upon them, and thus spread disorder on the earth without the leave of the righteous.[29]

And yet, even though the Báb used the language of wisdom, His earlier writings did convey unmistakably the full magnitude of the station and spiritual authority He was in fact claiming. This disclosure is most evident in the modes of revelation the Báb employs in His writings and what can be inferred from His use of those modes, given the way He Himself defined them.

The Modes of Revelation and the Station of the Báb

Although in His early writings the Báb only claims to be the representative of the Hidden Imám, other levels of implied meaning are clearly present, and they are crucial to understanding the actual claim that the Báb is making in those texts. His first book, like many of His other works, is expressed as a direct revelation of God in the language of divine verses, similar to the verses of the Qur'án. However, if the Báb were only a human representative of the Imám, it would have been inconceivable to reveal divine verses like those of the Qur'án. No Imám (much less any of the Gates) had ever produced a single divine verse, for the revelation of divine verses was categorically confined to the station of the Primal Will. In Islam, even the words of the Prophet Muḥammad are not all considered to be divine verses. Muḥammad was able to reveal divine verses only when He was the vehicle of the Point of the Qur'án, receiving revelation from God imparted to Him through the angel Gabriel. His other words, although considered holy, were not believed to be the Word of God. But no Imám, and certainly no Gate, could ever be the Point of the Qur'án or the vehicle of the revelation of divine verses.

From the very beginning, however, even when the Báb was claiming to be the representative of one of the Imáms, the very statements in which He affirmed His own servitude and gatehood were expressed *in the form of divine verses*. This fact in itself implicitly testified to a far more exalted claim on the part of the author of those words. In effect, to speak or write in the mode of divine verses was a speech act that inherently claimed the station of a Prophet of God.

To read the Báb's claim as ascribing to Himself a station equivalent to that of the four Gates of the Hidden Imám, therefore, would be to misunderstand every aspect of the Báb's writings. The four Gates had been messengers who transmitted questions, money, and the like, to the Imám and brought back his instructions or tablets. But they themselves were never able to be the direct vehicles of the words of the Imám, let alone the words of the Prophet or the words of God.

Similarly, to take the Báb's claim as equating His station with that of the Imáms falls far short of the mark. All the early writings of the Báb claimed that the heart of the Báb was the vehicle of the revelation of the direct Word of God, that whoever rejected the Báb had rejected God, and whoever accepted Him had entered paradise. Again, no Imám had ever adduced the ability to reveal the verses of the Qur'án as evidence of his truth. From the beginning, thus, through the very form and manner of His writings, the Báb was making a claim to prophethood—to be the bearer of another revelation.

The Báb Himself says as much in many of His writings, in which He explains the true intention of His early statements. In a prayer written in Chihríq, in answer to twenty-four questions posed to Him by Mullá Aḥmad, the Báb writes:

> Should a man be endued with knowledge, and behold Thy [God's] divine verses revealed during earlier times, he would assuredly recognize that this was naught but Thy divine revelation sent down upon the Point of the Furqán but appearing in the name of Thy Testimony [Qá'im] and Thy Guardian [Imám]. For all the divine names belong to Thee, from the First to the Last, the Manifest to the Hidden. Had this been a Cause that could possibly be manifested by the Imáms of the Faith or the Gates of guidance, then divine revelation would never have ceased after Muḥammad, Thy Friend. Nay, rather, this revelation is that which Thou

hast singled out for The Manifestation of Thine Own Self. Had such a revelation been possible from anyone else besides Thee, then at least one soul would have brought forth a single verse during the long interval from the ascension of Muḥammad till the year 1260.[30]

In the Persian Bayán the Báb explains that the realm that pertains to the Primal Will (referred to here as the first *dharr*), has become manifested in the name of the realm of the Gates (the fourth *dharr*):

> In like manner, gaze upon the revelation of the Point of the Bayán. . . . For at that time, He revealed Himself by that title, and described Himself as the appearance of one of the Gates. It is for that reason that the first *dharr* was manifest in the fourth *dharr*, inasmuch as in that very fourth *dharr* He revealed the supreme words, "Verily I, Myself, am God; none other God is there but Me." Should there be a man of discernment in the world, he would be able to tread the path and attain certitude that the Last is the same as the First, and the Manifest but the Hidden. . . .[31]

In addition to the revelation of divine verses, the totality of the Báb's modes of revelation also testifies to the true nature of His earlier claim. The Báb's four modes of revelation symbolize the four levels of the divine covenant: the mode of divine verses belongs to God, revealed through the Primal Will, or the Point. The mode of prayers pertains to the station of the Prophet as a servant of God. The mode of sermons and interpretations refers to the station of the Imáms, and the mode of rational and educational discourse corresponds to the station of the Gates. In the "Commentary on the Verse of Light II," the Báb explains:

> Although that which is created is fashioned by the words, "There is none other God but God," and that which is provided for is provided for by the statement, "Muḥammad is the Apostle of God," and that which is slain dieth by the words, "Verily 'Alí and the Twelve Sacred Lights are the Testimonies of God," and that which quickeneth doeth so by the four Pillars . . . , He Who is manifest in those Mirrors is one and the same, and that is none other than Me. Should one, on this day, desire to behold all the nineteen, the supports of Divine Unity, prophethood, guardianship, and the Shí'ih, he must behold Me, for verily they all proceeded from Me and return unto Me.[32]

Thus from the first year of His mission, the Báb defined His station as the manifestation of all the four modes of revelation, encompassing the entire range of divine revelation as sent down in all the previous Dispensations. Even when referring to Himself as a Gate in the early writings, He was simultaneously speaking in all the other stations of divine manifestation as well—as the Point of the Qur'án, the Apostle of God, and all the Imáms. All the modes of spiritual truth, in other words, are manifested by His pen and by His being.

The Word of God and the Divine Remembrance

In addition to the form of His writing and the modes of His revelation, the titles that the Báb assumed in His early writings also disclose the true nature of His claim. One of the most important of these appellations is the "Remembrance (*Dhikr*) of God."[33] *Dhikr* or "Remembrance" is the most frequently encountered title of the Báb in the Qayyúmu'l-Asmá', in which He is called the Most Great or the Most Mighty Remembrance of God.

A careful study of the earlier writings of the Báb shows that the word *dhikr* is ultimately a reference to the Logos, the Word of God, the Primal Will, and the essence of all the Prophets of God. *Dhikr* simultaneously means "utterance," "making mention of," and "remembrance." But the Most Great *Dhikr* of God is the Greatest Word of God, the Greatest Remembrance of God. This is nothing less than the Word and the Will through which God calls reality into being. In all the stages of the Báb's writings, earlier and later alike, He frequently and systematically stresses that the term "Remembrance" refers to the station of the Primal Will.

In His early writings the Báb identifies *dhikr* with the creative Word of God, and in a tablet to Mírzá Sa'íd He explains that the Primal *Dhikr* is the Primal Will:

> Concerning thy question about the meaning of the philosopher's saying, "From the One proceedeth only One": The statement is incorrect when the Cause is meant to be the Absolute Essence.... However, when the intention behind the statement is to refer to the Primal Utterance, which is created by God by Itself, for Itself, then verily it is the truth.... As the Imám said, glorified be his mention: "O thou Yúnus! Knowest

> thou what the Primal Will is?" He replied, "Nay." Then the Imám stated: "It is the Primal Utterance (D̲h̲ikr)."[34]

In another early text, interpreting the Islamic Tradition, "He hath known God who hath known himself," the Báb states:

> He [God] hath not begotten anything; rather He hath created all beings by His Will, and created the Will by Itself. Verily that Will is the First Point mentioned at the level of the contingent world. And the Will is the First Utterance (D̲h̲ikr) confirmed by God Himself as His own praise: "Verily, I am God; there is none other God but Me. I was a Hidden Treasure. I wished to be made known, and thus I called creation into being in order that I might be made known."[35]

This reading of *d̲h̲ikr* is not an arbitrary one; as the Báb states above, even the Islamic Traditions have identified *d̲h̲ikr* as the creative Word of God. Therefore, the self-definition of the Báb as the Most Great Remembrance of God in His early writings must be taken as a subtle but unmistakable allusion to His true claim, and the references to Himself as "the Remembrance" in the early writings unequivocally demonstrate the continuity of the Báb's self-conception throughout His ministry.

A related allusion in the Báb's earlier works can be seen in His frequent reference to Himself as the "Word," or the "Word of God." In the Qur'án, as in the Gospel of John, Jesus is identified as the "Word of God."[36] Various Holy Scriptures characterize divine revelation as the revelation of the Word, the Logos—the utterance of God which calls creation into being. The Remembrance and the Word are one and the same, and each discloses the meaning of the other. The Qayyúmu'l-Asmá' repeatedly refers to the Báb, and His book, as the Word of God. The text states: "This is indeed the eternal Truth which God, the Ancient of Days, hath revealed unto His omnipotent Word—He Who hath been raised up from the midst of the Burning Bush."[37]

Identifying the Remembrance with the Word, the Báb writes elsewhere in that work, "We, of a truth, choose the Messengers through the potency of Our Word, and We exalt Their offspring, some over others, through the Great Remembrance of God as decreed in the Book and concealed therein. . . ."[38] And in yet another passage, He says: "O People of Persia! Are ye not satisfied with this glorious honour which the supreme

Remembrance of God hath conferred upon you? Verily ye have been especially favoured by God through this mighty Word."[39]

The Gate and the Burning Bush

The word *báb* (gate) is a general term that refers to the concepts of mediation, manifestation, reference, and symbolism. Although the four Gates to the Hidden Imám were called by that title, the Islamic usage of the term *báb* is not restricted to their level of mediation. In fact, the most famous Shí'ih usage of the word occurs in the Tradition attributed to the Prophet Muḥammad, Who said, "I am the City of knowledge, and 'Alí is the Gate (*Báb*) thereof." Here we can see that "Gate" (*Báb*) describes the Imám.

In other words, the term *báb* in itself does not signify any particular level of mediation or manifestation, but rather the function and role of mediation. In this sense, all the levels of the divine covenant represent some aspect of gatehood, as they all mediate between the divine realm and that of creation. The early writings of the Báb define the gatehood of the Gates, including the Báb Himself, in multiple levels. He is not only the Gate to the Hidden Imám, but also, as He writes in the Qayyúmu'l-Asmá', "the Sublime Gate of God."[40] In another passage in that book He declares: "Say: Verily I am the 'Gate of God' and I give you to drink, by the leave of God, the sovereign Truth, of the crystal-pure waters of His Revelation which are gushing out from the incorruptible Fountain situate upon the Holy Mount."[41] Later writings of the Báb make it clear that as well as the Gate to divine knowledge for His Dispensation, He was the Gate to the next Manifestation of God.

But the real meaning of this sense of gatehood is already apparent in the manifold, complex self-descriptions of the Báb found in His earlier writings. Prominent among these terms is the Burning Bush. In the Qayyúmu'l-Asmá' the Báb writes, "O People of effacement! Hearken unto My Voice arising out of the Point of Confirmation, from this Arabian Youth Who speaketh forth amidst Mount Sinai, by the leave of God, unto Moses. Verily God hath revealed unto Moses the Pentateuch, for mighty is the Cause of God in the judgment of the Mother Book."[42] The Voice of God that spoke to Moses of course came out of the midst of a burning bush.[43] Here the Báb is saying that He is the intermediary or

Gate through which God spoke to Moses, that Moses in fact attained the presence of God *through the mediation of the Báb*. Although Moses was believed to have spoken with God on only a few occasions, the Báb claims to live ceaselessly in that sublime station of intimate converse with the Divine. In fact, the Báb declares that for, the first time, the realm of divinity has become inseparable from the realm of servitude, in the form of a human temple, namely the Báb Himself:

> The words of God shine forth from naught but their own source. This element is the very Tree Which hath spoken in the Dispensation of Moses, the Son of 'Imrán.... Verily that Primal Reality rose above the limitations of words and beyond the confines of comparison, until It was united with the human station, whereupon the realms of the invisible shone forth above the horizon of the visible.... [V]erily the archetypal realm of *dharr* is now speaking forth in this human station. Many a time, so often that none except God can know, it is crying out ceaselessly and without interruption: "Verily I truly am God, the Almighty, the All-Wise," as God had spoken unto Moses through the Tree.[44]

The same distinction is made in the early writings of the Báb with regard to Muḥammad. In His commentary on the Súrih of Abundance, the Báb claims that the direct divine revelation imparted to Him (the revelation of divine verses) is continuous and ceaseless, unlike the assumed discontinuous way the Qur'án was revealed to Muḥammad. The reason, it should be noted, is the differing receptivity of the audience: "Verily, during the stage of the Prophet Muḥammad, the true flow of this river did not take place," the Báb explains, "inasmuch as God did not grant such leave unto His Apostle, for the lack of capacity of the people of that age. Today, the waters of the crystal river stream forth ceaselessly from My Tongue and Pen, by the will of God, and neither decline nor abate."[45]

Various of the Báb's writings, both earlier and later, indicate that in the language of the new Revelation the word *báb* implies meanings that are unprecedented in Islamic tradition. More will be said about these new meanings later, but a brief listing of some of them will provide a glimpse of their variety and symbolic depth, and therefore of the allusive fecundity of the word in the Báb's discourse. First, the equivalence of *báb* with the letter Há' (both equal to 5) signifies that the Báb is the manifestation of God, with Há' standing for *Huva* (He). Second, the term alludes to the concept of light since the word *báb* equals the difference between fire and light. Third, the word consists of an upright vertical line (Alif or *A*) which unites two horizontal lines (two *B*'s), symbolizing that the Báb is the unity of the first and second stages of creation through their linkage by the third stage. Thus He is the unity of Will and Determination, or the divinity and the servitude of the Point. Fourth, the Báb represents the Middle Path, the unity of the two extremes of freedom and determinism, which is the reality of justice. Fifth, He represents the truth of the trinity, the real meaning of the shape of the cross—as a vertical line between two horizontal lines. Sixth, the term *báb* represents the ultimate purpose of life, the realization of divine revelation within one's being. Seventh, it refers to the unity of trinity and quaternity, or the names *'Alí* and *Muḥammad*. The numerical value of both names of the Báb (202) is equal to that of the word *Rabb* or "Lord." Eighth, given the equivalence of the *haykal* or "temple" (consisting of five lines) with the word *báb*, the term refers to the reality of the Temple, as the Perfect Human Being, or the Manifestation of God. Finally, the term represents the unity of various other sacred binary structures in the reality of the Báb. Thus it can be see that the word *báb* acquires complex meanings which are irreducible to the conventional meaning of the term in Islamic discourse.

The Unity in Diversity of the Four Layers of the Covenant

The most important key to understanding the meaning of the Báb's self-definition in His early writings can be found in the explicit and systematic explanations of this very issue that He provides in His later writings. Those retrospective explanations of the Báb's intentions help us to put into context many other aspects of the early works. One example of such an explanation occurs at the beginning of the Persian Bayán. The Báb is speaking of the return of the Point of the Furqán (the Qur'án), Muḥammad, and the Qá'im as three different symbolic figures (who are represented by Himself and two of His Letters of Living), even if He alone also represents all of those symbolic figures. He says:

> Though the Point of the Bayán was mentioned in the first gate, the Point of the Furqán [Muḥammad] in the second, and the revelation of

> the Qá'im in the fifteenth gate, the secret lieth in that the Point, while occupying the station of pure transcendence, which is naught but the pure revelation of God Himself manifested by the name "Divinity," was indeed mentioned in the first gate, while in Its station of Determination, which is the rank of the Primal Will, It is mentioned in the second gate. Finally, the manifestation of the Point in Its station of standing supreme over (*qá'imíyyat*) all souls, which is a glory restricted to the revelation of the fourteenth Sacred Soul, was mentioned in the fifteenth gate. . . .
>
> Thus, when the name "Divinity" is present, the name "Lordship," as well as all other names, are also present therein. . . . For He is the First while also being the Last, the Hidden and the Manifest, and the One Who is praised by all names while glorified above the praise of any name. There is none other God but Him, the Upright (*Qá'im*), the Self-Subsisting (*Qayyúm*).[46]

In this passage, we can discern one of the most important principles of the Báb's theology. According to the Qur'án's description of God, "He is the First and the Last, the Seen and the Hidden."[47] For the Báb this statement primarily describes the station of the Point in its aspect of pure unity. In this sense, all things are mirrors of the Point of Truth, and nothing is seen in those mirrors except the Point. This is true as well for the divine manifestations in the form of the four layers of the divine covenant between God and human beings. These four levels of the covenant are the Point, the Apostle, the Imáms, and the Gates. In one respect—as the conduits through which God's will is made known to humans—they are all one and the same, while in another respect—as specific individuals—they are diverse and distinct. The Point is the First and the Last, the Manifest and the Hidden; the Báb as the Point of the Bayán is the Sun whose image and radiance are reflected in the mirrors below Him. Thus He is also the Apostle and the Imám, as well as the Gate to the Imám. And even when He says, "I am the Gate to the Imám," He is at the same time the Imám, the Prophet, and the Point. This theological principle, however, is not only central to the message of the Persian Bayán, but it is present throughout the writings of the Báb in all the stages of His Revelation.

Thus, as in the Báb's hermeneutical principle of metaphysical unity, all the manifestations of divine revelation are elevated to the level of their supreme Origin and End, which is the divinity of the Primal Will. For this reason, the Báb attributes all four layers of the divine covenant to Himself as the Point of Truth. In all His early writings, He is emphasizing the ultimate unity of all the divine manifestations. No perceptive reader of the Qayyúmu'l-Asmá' can fail to note the central role of this perspective of unity in the Báb's interpretation of the story of Joseph. As we shall see shortly, the story of Joseph is actually a story of the stage of *Aḥadíyyat*, or Absolute Unity. The self-definition of the Báb in the Qayyúmu'l-Asmá' should also be understood in light of this interpretive principle.[48]

A parallel point is expressed in the discussion of the Báb's own name, 'Alí, in His early writings. This discussion furnishes a subtle but unmistakable allusion to the Báb's true self-conception at that stage. He plays upon the name *'Alí* and alludes to the unity of its diverse manifestations. The Qayyúmu'l-Asmá' frequently refers to the Báb as *'Alí* and *Ḥakím*. These two terms allude to Qur'ánic verses in which God is described as *'Alí* (the Exalted) and *Ḥakím* (the Wise). The particular verses in the Qur'án where these terms occur are tremendously significant in explaining the allusion.

In the Qur'án, *'Alí* (the Exalted), and *Ḥakím* (the Wise) are attributes of both God and the Qur'án. The first verse speaks of God and His revelation: "And it was not vouchsafed to any mortal that God should speak to him unless by revelation or from behind a veil, or that He sendeth a messenger to reveal what He willeth by His leave. Verily He is the Exalted (*'Alí*), the Wise (*Ḥakím*)."[49] The second verse refers to the Qur'án itself: "And verily, it [the Qur'án] is in the Mother Book, before Us, the Exalted (*'Alí*), the Wise (*Ḥakím*)."[50] At the beginning of the Qayyúmu'l-Asmá, the Báb identifies Himself directly with the Qur'ánic *'Alí* and *Ḥakím*, saying: "Verily, this is the straight Path ascribed to 'Alí before Thy Lord, as laid out in the Mother Book. And He is that *'Alí* (Exalted One), Who is praised before Us as the Wise (*Ḥakím*) in the Mother Book. Verily, He is the Truth from God, registered in the Mother Book as endued with the uncorrupted Religion in the midst of Sinai."[51] In another passage the Báb describes Himself as "the Arabian Youth, Who is called in the Mother Book *'Alí* and *Ḥakím*."[52] Elsewhere He links the "Remembrance" to these titles: "This Remembrance is indeed the Most Mighty Remembrance . . . and He is the *'Alí* described before God as *Ḥakím* in the Mother Book."[53]

In His early writings the Báb often points out that *'Alí* (the Exalted) was the first name that God ascribed to Himself.[54] It was also the name of the first Imám. Reference to Imám 'Alí and his exalted station is present throughout the Báb's writings.[55] Finally, *'Alí* was of course the Báb's own given name. His constant allusive emphasis on this name signifies that the hierarchy of all the stations implied by the term is present within His own being: He is the Gate to the Imám, the Imám 'Alí, and the Point, the Supreme Representative of God. All these allusions are present in the Báb's own name.

The Heart, Spirit, Soul, and Body of the Báb

With an understanding of the unity of the four layers of the covenant in mind, we can now begin to see in a new way the enigma of the Báb's apparently diverse claims in His writings. As we will explore later in more detail, the Báb employs a symbolic schema to represent human reality in terms of four levels: *heart, spirit, soul,* and *body*. These levels of reality represent a hierarchy of spiritual stations, and each of these levels of reality corresponds to a layer of the covenant.

The highest of these levels is the heart. "Heart" here should not be interpreted in the Western sense in which the heart is associated with emotion or sentiment. It is, rather, the supreme seat of spiritual truth, the abode of divine revelation. After the heart are the three lower stages of spirit, soul, and body. In terms of the layers of the covenant, the level of the heart corresponds to the station of the Point, while the level of the body corresponds to the station of the Gate. These four stages also correspond to the first four stages of divine creative Action.

It is now possible to see with clarity the full meaning of the early claims of the Báb. All His stations—the Gate to the Hidden Imám, the Imám himself, the Prophet and Apostle of God, the Point of the Qur'án, and the Point of the Bayán—are simultaneously true. They all refer to different aspects of His being, and each of these aspects corresponds to one of the levels or layers of reality: His body represents the station of the Gate to the Imám, His soul represents the station of the Imám, His spirit reflects the station of the Prophet (servitude), and His heart represents the station of the unity (divinity) of the Prophet, that is, the station of the Point. All the levels of spiritual reality are thus united in the being of the Báb. This is exactly what the Báb has said in Commentary on the Verse of Light II:

> Naught is seen in Me in in the station of My heart save God alone, which is the manifestation of Lordship from God, My Lord and My Fashioner. Naught is witnessed in the station of My spirit, the indivisible substantive Intellect . . . , but Muḥammad, the Apostle of God. . . . That which thou observeth in the station of My soul is naught but all the thirteen Sacred Manifestations . . . , nor canst thou perceive in the station of My body aught but the station of the dust for the realization of the three stations of fire, air, and water. . . .
>
> Should I proclaim, "I am the First Who is manifest in the first support," I would indeed have stated the truth . . . , and were I to say, "I verily am the bearer of the second support," I verily would have spoken the truth. . . . And I am, verily, the One Who is resplendent in all the Sacred Souls of the third support, as well as in the fourth support. . . .[56]

Literally speaking, the body of the Prophet is the gate to His soul. Human beings can have no direct contact with the soul of the Prophet except through its appearance in a physical body. However, the soul and the spirit of the Prophet are also successive gates to His heart. The heart of the Prophet is the Primal Will, the Source of divine revelation, or, as we saw earlier, the fountain of Kaw<u>th</u>ar. Given this symbolic structure, we can understand how the Báb can claim to be the Gate to the Imám, and at the same time the Voice in Sinai that spoke to Moses, the Word of God, and the Remembrance of God. This mystical schema also explains why the Báb appears with all the proofs that previously vindicated the truth of the Point, the Apostle, the Imám, and the Gate. Using the symbolism of the four rivers as standing for the four stations, the Báb writes in the Commentary on the Súrih of Abundance: "After thou hast partaken of a drop of this water, thou must know of a certainty that no man can ever attain perfection in his existence unless he hath achieved the power to cause all the four rivers to stream forth within the realm of true exposition (*bayán*). Thus God hath conferred upon Me, as an incontrovertible Testimony, the revelation of all the four rivers."[57]

In that same early text, and in a most explicit and detailed form, the Báb explains the true nature of His claim. He emphasizes the unity of all the stations in His own being, and explains that since we are now in the arc of ascent, or return to God, all the four layers of the divine covenant, which were manifested from the day of Adam to the present, are now manifest at one and the same time in the being of the Báb. Both the lowest and the highest levels of the divine covenant—the Point and the Gate, the heart and the dust—are now united in him:

> Shouldst thou behold the arc of descent (*maqám-i-nuzúl*), thou wouldst perceive the advance of the river of crystal, incorruptible water pass the other three rivers, as observed in the world thus. Verily, from the day of Adam, the first wondrous creation of the Primal Will, there streamed forth the crystal, incorruptible water, that Divine Unity might be praised: "There is none other God but Him." Then, on the day of the revelation of Muḥammad, the Apostle of God, the blessings of God rest upon Him, God made the wellspring of milk "whose taste changeth not" to flow, that it might be witnessed that "verily, Muḥammad is the Messenger of God." Subsequently, in the Day of the Brook (*Ghadír*), God caused the wellspring of purest honey to gush forth, that the souls might testify unto the vicegerency of the Family of God, the Imáms of the Faith. . . .
>
> Finally, from the day of the revelation of this wondrous and unique new Cause, God, glorified and exalted be He, hath caused the river of wine, "delicious to those who quaff it," to surge, that the hearts might acknowledge what God hath destined for it, in the form of a human Countenance and the transcendent Temple of 'Alí (*Ṣúrati'l-Anza'íyyah*), from the eternal Revelation and everlasting Concealment. Therein lieth the order of the stations of descent.
>
> Shouldst thou desire to discern the principle of ascent, thou shouldst recognize that the first step is the wellspring of wine, followed by honey, then milk, and finally water. Thus, at the Hour of the coming together of the two worlds of descent and ascent, there streameth forth the wellspring of the Twin Wines, manifesting both Vicegerency and Prophethood within the one and the same Soul.
>
> This, in truth, is a sublime guide to the mystery of the Transcendent and Exalted World of This 'Alí (*'Álami'l-'Alaví*). Thus, thou shouldst recognize the glorious station of this Wine, Who is at once the inner mystery of the Heart in [the stages of] descent, and the first Dust, the station of the body, in [the stages of] ascent.[58]

The Báb as the Elixir

The concept of the elixir was mentioned earlier in connection with the spiritual process of transformative interpretation which turns the phenomenal world into a reflection of its divine Origin. In the symbolism of alchemy, in texts that became known to the West during the medieval period through Arabic translations, the mysterious agent of transformation, the elixir (from Arabic, *al-iksír*), was also referred to as the "philosopher's stone" and, interestingly, was associated with the symbol of the "point" as the "starting point of creation."[59] Medieval Christian alchemists associated the elixir with Christ.

The elixir frequently appears in the Báb's writings as a mystical symbol representing absolute actualization: the stage of the realization of truth, which is the realization of the Supreme Origin and End at the level of phenomenal being. When, for example, the "dust" becomes a complete manifestation of "fire," making visible the essential unity of reality, the divine sign enshrined within the phenomenal world is disclosed. More specifically, the elixir represents the union of opposites, the unity of the First and the Last, or the clear manifestation of the truth of the First within the Last. It is by virtue of this perfect self-realization that the elixir can attain ascendancy over other things and is the catalyst which enables them to realize their latent qualities. Since the sign of God is present within all beings, a trace of the elixir exists within all things.

The early writings of the Báb refer to His station as the station of the "true Elixir." Although the station of the Gate represents the fourth layer of the covenant, this Gate integrates within itself the reality of all the other three stations. In other words, in the station of gatehood, the four causes are united together in the Final Cause, and in this way "fire" is made visible at the level of "dust."[60]

The writings of the Báb discuss this station as the realization of the Most Great Name of God. The Báb often refers to an Islamic Tradition which states that the Most Great Name consists of four names. Three of these have been revealed but the fourth has been kept hidden. The Tradition identifies the first name as "God" (*Alláh*), the second as "the Blessed" (*Tabáraka*), and the third as "the Exalted" (*Ta'álá*, from the same root as *'Alí*). The fourth is the hidden name of God, through which the complete form of the Most Great Name is disclosed. The Báb interprets this Tradition as a reference to the four levels of the divine covenant, the totality of which is a manifestation of the Most Great Name. That name is made visible in the unity of the stations of divinity, prophethood, the vicegerency of the Imáms, and the gatehood of the Báb. In this way, the Báb represents the hidden name of God.

But those same writings affirm that all the perfections of the first three stations are revealed in the fourth station, that of dust: its inner reality is none other than the fire of divinity. That is why the Báb equates the Most Great Name with the fourth station, the station of the Báb. It is for the same reason that the Báb is endowed with the four modes of revelation which represent all four layers of the covenant.[61] He is a Gate Who contains within Himself all the stations of divine revelation.

In His commentary on the Súrih of Unity (*Tawḥíd*), the Báb interprets the name of God, He (*Huva*, equal to 11). He says that *Huva* is the Most Great Name of God, and that it is equal to the name "the All-Sufficing" (*Káfí*). *Káfí* is numerically equal to 111, which is a further reflection of 11. The name of the Báb (and of Bahá'u'lláh), 'Alí, is equal to 110 and 111 (the letters together equal 110, but the Báb takes the word as equalling 111 as well, calculating not only the sum of the letters but also the form of their unity as 1). Then He writes that *Huva* is the Most Great Name of God, provided that one observes the hidden divine name within the third of the four names that constitute the Most Great Name of God.[62] As the third name is "the Exalted" (*Ta'álá*), the hidden divine name present within it is obviously *'Alí*.[63]

Although the writings of the Báb identify Him as the realization of the Most Great Name of God, they also indicate that the ultimate realization of the Most Great Name is actually *Bahá*. We already have seen how the Báb identifies the Most Great Name with *'Alí*, the name shared by the Báb and Bahá'u'lláh. Yet it is *Huva* (He) that represents the Most Great Name of God. To express this, the Báb consistently fashions symbolic divine "Temples" consisting of eleven lines of text, which He frequently equates with the word *Huva*. These eleven lines of text consist, first, of letters of the alphabet; second, of points; and then, of the numbers 1 through 9.[64] *Huva*, or 11, always is the equivalent of 9, or *Bahá*. In this passage the Báb identifies the hidden reality of the Most Great Name with *Bahá* and 9, which becomes manifest in the world as 19:

> For verily God hath created, in the furthermost oceans of plurality, beyond the Alif (1), countless numerical letters according to His will. Verily these stations are nine in the unseen realm and nineteen in the manifest world. For this reason, the Mystery of the Point appeared in nineteen letters at the beginning of the Book of God (the Qur'án and the Bayán) without a single letter being added thereto or subtracted therefrom. . . . The

manifest name is *Váḥid* (Unity), and the Hidden Name is *Bahá* since it is equal to 9, while the former equalleth 19. The first is the Most Great Name in the hidden station, hence the revelation in all the exalted prayers: "O thou God! I beseech Thee by the most glorious of Thy Glory (*Bahá*), for all Thy Glory is glorious."[65]

Bahá'u'lláh's concealed revelation in the Síyáh Chál dungeon occurred in the year 9, and His public declaration in the year 19 (after the inception of the Báb's revelation). It is noteworthy that in the above passage the Báb confirms what was implied by earlier some Islamic authors, that the Most Great Name of God is the first divine name mentioned in the Dawn Prayer, which the Báb quotes in this statement.[66] Furthermore, we often see the Báb identify the Most Great Name with *Ḥusayn*, which was also the name of Bahá'u'lláh.[67]

The Name 'Alí-Muḥammad

Another subtle indication of the Báb's true station that can be found in His early writings is His analysis of His own name, 'Alí-Muḥammad. According to the Báb nothing about a Prophet is accidental: all aspects of His being and His life refer to His spiritual truth.[68] The same principle applies to the Báb; His very name is a sign that points to His inner truth. Even through the coded language in which the Báb talks about His true station in the early years, His many discussions of the significance of His name leave little room for doubt about His self-conception during that period.

The Báb defines His station as uniting the functions of prophethood and vicegerency. His name, 'Alí-Muḥammad, symbolizes that unity, with "Muḥammad" representing prophethood and "'Alí" vicegerency. Referring to His own name, the Báb writes in the Qayyúmu'l-Asmá': "We have verily sent Thee in the midst of Fire. For, verily, God hath revealed unto Thee this Furqán amidst Water and Thou art verily inscribed by the Twin Names in the Mother Book."[69] And in His Commentary on the Súrih of Abundance, He states that "God hath refused to manifest this sublime Station from amongst the succession of men save in the Twin Names."[70]

Not only does the Báb reveal the modes of revelation that were previously revealed by Muḥammad and 'Alí, but He also declares that the realization of both their stations is found in His own being: "Thus," He writes,"at the Hour of the coming together of the two worlds of descent and ascent, there streameth forth the wellspring of the Twin Wines, manifesting both vicegerency and prophethood within the one and the same Soul."[71] A further expression of this point can be found in the Báb's many references to the sun and the moon in relation to His own station. In passages such as the following, He interprets the sun as referring to the prophethood of Muḥammad, and the moon as the vicegerency of 'Alí:

> Know thou of a certainty that the existence of sunrise is only realized through the existence of the sun, which in turn is naught but the garment of prophethood appearing in the Countenance of Muḥammad, the blessings of God rest upon Him. It is when the sun goeth down that sunset is realized, when the most darksome night approacheth, and the moon, the sign of vicegerency, shineth forth with the most radiant light.[72]

The Báb's name, then, brings together the true "sun" and the true "moon." This coming together of the sun and the moon is also one of the chief signs of the Day of Resurrection mentioned in the Qur'án: "and the sun and the moon shall be together."[73] In other words, His name also signifies the commencement of the Day of Resurrection.

A related group of symbols in the early writings of the Báb refers to Him as the representative of the triangle and the square, or the trinity and the quaternity. The triangle or trinity refers to a sequence of three stages of creation, while the square or quaternity refers to four stages of creation.[74] The triangle is also a symbol for 'Alí because in Arabic *'Alí* consists of three letters, while the square or quaternity refers to the name *Muḥammad*, which has four letters. Together they constitute seven letters. Alluding to the unity of these two names, the later writings of the Báb, including the Persian Bayán, refer to the Báb as the "Lord of the Seven Letters." In the Qayyúmu'l-Asmá', the Báb describes His own station in these coded terms:

> O Qurratu'l-'Ayn! Soon the people of the Supreme Cloud of Subtlety shall utter: "Thou assuredly art the Joseph of Divine Unity. Say! Yea, by My Lord! I, in the shape of a square, am the Joseph of the Supreme Origin, and here is My Brother in the shape of a triangle, the form of the Seal. Verily, God hath favoured Me with the Twin Mysteries within the Twin Sinais, and the Twin Names in the Twin Luminaries.[75]

And, in His later work, the Kitábu'l-Asmá', the Báb writes of Himself: "Verily the Essence of the letters of the triangle preceding the square is the Manifestation of His Self in the kingdoms of heaven and earth, and whatever lieth between them."[76]

The Manifestation of the Qá'im in the Year 1260

Another significant indication of the Báb's self-conception in His early writings is found in His interpretation of the Tradition of Abú Lubayd-i-Makhzúmí concerning the date of the Qá'im's manifestation. This Tradition states that the disconnected letters in the Qur'án disclose the date when the Qá'im would appear. Discussing the sequence of those mysterious letters, which begin with "A-L-M," the Tradition states: "Our Qá'im riseth up after the end of A-L-M-R." The Báb explains that previous interpretations of this Tradition have missed the point. Then He writes:

> Verily, the appearance of the day of Muḥammad, the Apostle of God, the blessings of God rest upon Him and His kin, was associated with the revelation of "A-L-M. This is a Book that is beyond a shadow of doubt a guidance unto the virtuous," as it is explicitly stated in the tradition of Abí Ja'far, peace be upon him, addressing Abí Lubayd-i-Makhzúmí. Verily, the Days of God have been decreed for the proponents of truth and error [that they may last] until the time of the end of days, as promised by the Imám, peace be upon him, in his verdict. Those days do not come to an end except by the word "A-L-M-R." When the days come to pass at the conclusion of these letters, then may God remove the difficulties of all His servants by His grace. Thus God hath later revealed those seven disconnected words—He hath sent them down in this form: A-L-M, A-L-M, A-L-M-S, A-L-R, A-L-R, A-L-R, A-L-M-R—and the verse: "The Cause of God is come. Refrain ye from calling for its hastening."[77]

This early work was written in response to the questions of Siyyid Yaḥyá Dárábí, surnamed Vaḥíd. Although the tablet is written in veiled language, and apparently denies any station for the Báb except servitude to God, it also makes it clear that the Báb considers His time to be the time of the Revelation of the Qá'im and the termination of the Islamic Dispensation. He fixes the beginning of that Dispensation at the inception of the revelation of the Qur'án, and says that the manifestation of the Qá'im will be according to the number of the seven disconnected words of the Qur'án (in the passage quoted above). However, the numerical value of those numbers is 1267. Since the Islamic calendar begins with the hegira—the migration of the Prophet to Medina—which occurred about a decade after the beginning of the revelation of the Qur'án, we can see that the Báb is actually speaking of the year A.H. 1260 (A.D. 1844) as the year the Qá'im would appear. It is unmistakably clear that even in this early period of concealed revelation, the Báb perceived the year of His declaration to be the year of the rise of the Qá'im.

Finally, the very fact that the early writings of the Báb exhibit a form of dissimulation is itself a testimony to His true station. One of the famous Traditions concerning the signs that would mark the appearance of the Qá'im is: "In our Qá'im there shall be four signs from four Prophets, Moses, Jesus, Joseph, and Muḥammad. The sign from Moses is fear and expectation; from Jesus, that which was spoken of Him; from Joseph, imprisonment and dissimulation; from Muḥammad, the revelation of a Book similar to the Qur'án."[78] In the Qayyúmu'l-Asmá', as we will see in more detail in the next chapter, the Báb interprets Joseph as an expression of the unity of Muḥammad, Ḥusayn, and Himself. But one of the most distinctive features of Joseph was his practice of dissimulation, as he veiled his true station even from his brothers. Therefore, the Báb's concealment of His true station in fact fulfills one of the signs of the advent of the Qá'im.

4
The Structure of the Qayyúmu'l-Asmá'

In this and the next chapter we will explore in more detail one of the Báb's major interpretive works, the Commentary on the Súrih of Joseph, or Qayyúmu'l-Asmá'. We begin by comparing this text to three other interpretive works by the Báb.

In addition to several smaller works, four of the major existing books of the Báb are commentaries on súrihs of the Qur'án—the Súrihs of the Cow, Joseph, Abundance, and the Afternoon. The first of these commentaries was written between January 1844 and January 1845. The second was written during forty days, beginning on the night of the Báb's declaration (May 23, 1844). The third was written in one night sometime around May 1846, during the final months of His stay in Shiraz. The fourth was also produced in just one night during October or November of 1846 while the Báb was in Isfahan.

Plenitude of Meaning in the Commentaries

Structurally, the first two commentaries can be clearly differentiated from the last two. The Commentary on the Súrih of the Cow and the Commentary on the Súrih of Joseph are extended glosses on the verses of those súrihs: each verse of the súrih is quoted, followed by explanations and interpretations. This particular structure may have been chosen because the súrihs are long, and the interpretation of just the verse units alone constitutes a lengthy book.

The other two texts are organized differently. The Commentary on the Súrih of Abundance and the Commentary on the Súrih of the Afternoon interpret not only the verse units of these súrihs, but also the phrases and letters, as well as the text as a whole. Unlike the first two súrihs mentioned, the Súrihs of Abundance and the Afternoon are very short, each consisting of just two or three lines. Nevertheless, the Báb's commentary on the Súrih of Abundance is almost as long as the two commentaries that interpret much longer texts. The shortness of the súrih makes it possible to interpret the text in great depth, exploring many different dimensions of interpretation. In other words, the first two commentaries are more *extensive*, while the last two are more *intensive*. Because of this fact, the last two commentaries manifest even more explicitly the Báb's hermeneutical principle of the plenitude and infinity of the meanings contained within the divine words. The very structure of these intensive interpretive works can be seen as a symbolic representation of the Báb's view of the Word and of reality as both one and many. For the Báb, each súrih of the Qur'án, and indeed each unit of the divine Word, can be interpreted in several different dimensions.

The process of interpretation has several different aspects or levels: in addition to the *author*, there is the *text*, a *reader*, a *referential object*, and a *modality* of the interpretive act. The Báb addresses each of these aspects. The textual level concerns the differentiation and organizational level of the text. The reader's level refers to the hierarchy of readers' stations, determined by their degree of understanding. The level of the referential object points to the different connotations and levels of application of signs in various realms of being. Finally, the level of the modality of the interpretive act involves the depth of interpretation and analysis, defined by the various layers of manifest and hidden meanings. These dimensions are sometimes parallel to each other and sometimes constitute a permutation of the possibilities of meaning. The result is that even a single letter of the divine Word can yield hundreds or thousands of meanings.[1]

The Textual Level

The first aspect is the level of organization and differentiation of the text. A súrih, a chapter of the divine words, is perceived by the Báb as reflecting the Point and its various levels of abstraction or differentiation. Since the Point is the supreme Source of all beings, the structure of an intensive interpretation mirrors all of reality. At the first and highest level of abstraction, the entire súrih is considered as an undifferentiated point: here only totality and unity are seen. The type of interpretation that focuses on this level of the text is the most sublime form of interpretation, corresponding to an all-encompassing, transcendent epistemological perspective, or the perspective of unity. From this standpoint, all the parts, all the verses, all the sentences, phrases, words, and letters are seen as one and the same. This level of interpretation transcends the limitations of words and is attained in the station of knowledge and understanding called the *perspective* (or *sanctuary*) *of the heart* or the *sanctuary of unity*.

Many of the Báb's writings speak of this station or perspective of the heart, which indeed constitutes the cornerstone of His entire approach to reality. Thus in the Commentary on the Súrih of Abundance, He writes:

> Shouldst thou abide in the land of divinity, and recite that blessed súrih whilst in the Ocean of Absolute Unity, beyond the Sea of Dominion, thou wouldst know of a certainty that, verily, all the letters of this súrih are but one single letter. All variations in the words and meanings therein revert to a single point. That point is, verily, the station of the heart and the sanctuary of unity. God hath created its elements out of the one crystal water of Kawthar. They are all fire, all air, all water, all dust, and all are the vessel of majestic identity, the everlasting bestowal, and the effulgent Kawthar.[2]

At the lowest level of abstraction—the level of extreme differentiation and specificity—are the individual letters, the basic units comprising the words of the súrih. Here the interpretive focus is on the specific symbolic meanings of each letter. Accordingly, the intensive commentaries of the Báb usually contain a letter-by-letter interpretation of the súrih. As we have seen before, the Báb emphasizes that a reflection of the beauty of God is present in all reality, and the letters are just one instance of this universal principle. In the Commentary on the Súrih of Abundance He writes:

> Shouldst thou abide beneath the shadow of the Primal Will, within the station of Determination, upon the land of Dominion, and recite this holy súrih, thou wouldst comprehend the meaning of the letters of the first word of the súrih: the letter Alif referreth to the fire of divine creation; the letter Nún intendeth the air of divine generation; the manifest letter of Alif, the water of divine fashioning; while the invisible letter, the

Hidden Pillar, constituted for the manifestation of the other three pillars, hinteth at the element of dust. . . .

Shouldst thou descend from the stations of divine Action, and occupy the summit of the Throne, and desire to scrutinize each single word, thou wouldst acknowledge that the letter Alif in the first word of the súrih referreth first to the favours (*álá'*) of thy Lord, then the favours of thy Lord within the immensity of the Supreme Cloud of Subtlety (*'Amá'*), then the favours of thy Lord upon the Throne of radiant Praise, and then the favours of thy Lord in the Heaven of Decree, and then the favours of thy Lord upon the Throne of Bahá. Then the letter Nún referreth to the radiant light (*núr*) of thy Lord. . . .[3]

Between the two extremes of abstraction or undifferentiated unity, and differentiation or utmost diversity, are many levels of structure and meaning in the text, including the verses, sentences, phrases, and words. The Báb explains the overall unity of the Súrih of Abundance by relating all its different phrases and sentences together as expressions of the general meaning of the súrih, in terms of the two modalities of *outward* and *inward* meaning, where the outward meaning pertains to historical reality, and the inward to metaphysical reality:

Know thou that, verily, this blessed súrih is endowed outwardly with universal meanings. Amongst them is what thou knowest, that the Kawthar fount referreth to the ordinance of the vicegerency [of 'Alí] conferred upon Muḥammad the Apostle of God, the blessings of God rest upon Him, when He addressed Him, saying that God hath verily "conferred upon Thee [Muḥammad]" the vicegerency of 'Alí, peace be upon him. The exalted verse of God, "Therefore pray unto Thy Lord," referreth to the vicegerency of Ḥasan, peace be upon him, while His magnified word, "sacrifice" pointeth to the martyrdom of Ḥusayn, peace be upon him. Finally, His glorified words, "Verily, it is Thine enemies who are bereft of posterity," allude to the fate of the wicked and the nethermost levels of the chiefs of the inhabitants of the fire. . . .

Consider thou, in its inward meaning, the One Who conferreth the bestowal to be the Will Itself, while the One who is being addressed as "Thou" is the essence of Determination, and the Kawthar fount the essence of Destiny. What came after these words referreth to the other stations of divine Action.[4]

Individual words can also be units of analysis. In addition to commenting on other levels of interpretation, the Báb interprets all the words of the Súrih of the Afternoon one by one. The entire súrih reads as follows: "By the afternoon! Verily, man is in grievous loss, save those who have attained faith, and do righteous deeds, and enjoin the truth, and enjoin patience."[5] In the process of elucidating the words of the text including "by," "afternoon," "man," "grievous loss," "faith," "righteous deeds," "truth," and "patience," the Báb touches on many fundamental issues of religion including the nature of the human being, the meaning of faith and its opposite (that is, "grievous loss"), the nature of good deeds, and the true function of patience in attaining the ultimate Truth.[6]

The Báb explains the phrase "By the afternoon" (*Va'l-'aṣr*) by analyzing the meaning of the letter Váv (here meaning "By") as well as "afternoon" (*'aṣr*) and their mutual connection. Váv is the second letter of the name of God, *Huva* (He), consisting of the letters Há' and Váv. Váv (6) is the immediate (succeeding) manifestation of Há' (5), and they appear successively in the name that refers to the unseen Essence of God. In this way Váv is a reflection of "He." However, "He" itself, which is equal to 11, is manifested in the name of God, *'Alí* (the Most Exalted), because *'Alí* is equal to 110, which is a reflection of 11, and thus of "He." "Afternoon," according to the Báb, refers to the station of Imám 'Alí because the station of the Prophet Muḥammad is that of the sun at its zenith, and the immediate manifestation or successor of the noon is the afternoon; moreover, it was 'Alí who led the afternoon prayer on behalf of the Prophet.[7]

The Reader's Level

The second aspect of the interpretive act refers to the level of the reader. One of the interpretive styles most often employed by the Báb is to present various meanings of the same sign according to the station of the reader. Each reader belongs to a distinct level or perspective, which depends on the individual's existential spiritual station and corresponds to certain possible forms of understanding. In His hermeneutics, the Báb often distinguishes these levels of comprehension in terms of the seven stages of divine Action and their corresponding realms of existence. For example, those who live in the realm of the Will, which is the highest station as it is nearest to God, possess a greater, more ample perspective than those who abide in the (lower) realm of Determination, and so on.

One of the most frequently found typologies of these levels classifies readers according to their place in the hierarchy of metaphysical realms on a continuum of nearness to or remoteness from the Divine—described (in descending order) as the realms of *Láhút* (Divinity), *Jabarút* (the Celestial Dominion), *Malakút* (the Heavenly Kingdom), and *Mulk* (the Earthly Kingdom). However, the number of stages, as well as their designations and order, are flexible and they vary in the Báb's writings. In the Commentary on the Súrih of the Afternoon, for example, interpreting the letter Rá' (the last letter of *'aṣr*, or "afternoon") as a reference to *raḥmah* (grace), the Báb gives different meanings for "grace" as the concept applies at each of the levels of creation, from high to low:

> Then there is the sixth letter of the súrih, Rá', which referreth first to that universal Grace by which God created the Primal Will, prior to all things, by the Will's own causation, whereby He ordained It to be the Cause of all essences. [The letter Rá' also pointeth unto] the Grace of oneness by which God fashioned the souls of all who are embraced by His knowledge in the Book. Next, it hinteth at the universal Grace which descendeth unto the station of Destiny, that surging and bountiful sea within which all the creatures are distinguished. . . . Finally, it indicateth the Mercy that hath encompassed all things . . . the all-embracing Grace which encompasseth the believer, the unbeliever, and all beings.[8]

The Referential Level

The third aspect of the interpretive process concerns the objective reference of the signs. Since the divine words are considered to be creative as well as descriptive, each word has specific applications and manifestations at all levels of objective reality. Each divine utterance is understood as penetrating all grades of existence, giving rise to various meanings at each level. An example of reference to the grades of existence is the eight stages in the longitudinal chain of being. These stages correspond to the eight levels of paradise, beginning with the level of Absolute Unity, and continuing with the seven stages of divine creative

Action. The stages of being also correspond to the hierarchy of spiritual stations (after Absolute Unity, seven stages beginning with Bayán or True Exposition) as well as the hierarchy of beings (the realms of eternal paradise, prophets, humans, angels, jinn, animals, plants, and minerals). Thus words like "faithful" or "grace" in the passage quoted above have distinct meanings at different levels of objective reality. Although all beings are embodiments of divine grace, all participate in faith in their Creator, and all sing His praise, the words "faith" and "praise" mean very different things at the level of the Prophet and at the level of ordinary humans, and so on.[9]

The Modality Level

Finally, the modality of interpretation provides yet another source of diversification of meaning within the interpretive act. Each sign can be interpreted in its outward and manifest, or inward and hidden, aspect. These dimensions, in turn, can be further divided into a range of other levels such as the "hidden of the hidden" and the "manifest of the manifest." The continuum of levels extends from the most subtle, mystical, divine, essential, abstract, and immaterial, to the tangible, concrete, earthly, material, and historical levels of reality.

In the following passage, the Báb refers to some of these dimensions of interpretation that manifest aspects of the plenitude of meaning:

> Know thou that each letter thereof [the Morning Prayer of Imám 'Alí] pertaineth to seven stations that were enjoined by the Imám to Jábir in reference to true recognition. Every one of these stations referreth to the four worlds that are at times referred to as Divinity (*Láhút*), which is the realm of the heart and the first dharr; Dominion (*Jabarút*), which is the realm of the intellect and the second dharr; and the Contingent Kingdom (*Mulk*), which is the realm of the soul as well as the third witnessing spot and the declarative word of Divine Unity; and finally the Kingdom (*Malakút*), which is the station of testimony as well as the fourth witnessing spot and the word of magnification. Each one of these realms applieth to all the eight rings of the chain of being, as realized by the people of truth.[10]

History and Text in Two Commentaries

The existing commentary on the Súrih of the Cow consists of two parts. The first part is an interpretation of the first *juzv* (one-thirtieth) of the Qur'án (which includes the first 141 verses of the Súrih of the Cow), while the existing copy of the second part interprets only a few verses of the second *juzv* and remains incomplete. I will refer to the latter work as Commentary on the Súrih of the Cow II. Both parts are written in the mode of educational/rational discourse. Yet the Báb has mentioned that during His journey to Mecca and Medina He also revealed in the language of divine verses a complete interpretation of the second part of the Súrih of the Cow. Some authors refer to this work as the Commentary on the Súrih of the Cow II. Unfortunately this text was stolen on that same journey to Mecca. It seems that the Báb began to reveal the (later stolen) text, which was in the mode of divine verses, before completing the existing first part, which is in the educational/rational mode.

Opinions differ on when the existing first part was written, and various dates for the completion of the text have been proposed, including the beginning of the year A.H. 1259, the beginning of 1261, and the beginning of 1260.[11] The Báb Himself specifies within the text that He began to write it on the night of Siyyid Káẓim's passing, which occurred at the end of 1259 (corresponding to December 31, 1843). Thus the Báb began to write this work five months before His declaration. He also tells us that the work was completed at the end of 1260. This chronology is confirmed by the fact that within the final parts of the text the Báb refers to His meeting with Mírzá Muḥíṭ-i-Kirmání while He was in Mecca.[12]

In both the Commentary on the Súrih of the Cow and the Commentary on the Súrih of Joseph, which deal with long Qur'ánic chapters, the basic unit of analysis is the verse. Nevertheless, the structures of the two commentaries are different. The Commentary on the Súrih of the Cow is a continuous text without division into chapters, while the Commentary on the Súrih of Joseph is divided into 111 chapters or súrihs corresponding to the verses in the Qur'ánic súrih. The main difference between the two works, however, lies in their substantive interpretive framework, which involves the relation of the text to history. The Súrih of the Cow (the second and longest chapter of the Qur'án) addresses many subjects including the progression of prophets and cultures in time: it relates the story of creation, Adam and Eve, their fall, their children, Noah,

Abraham, the children of Israel, Moses, Jesus, and Muḥammad, as well as the story of various communities and their relationship to God's covenant and justice. The Báb's commentary on this súrih, however, interprets all the verses of the Qur'ánic text as referring to the stations of 'Alí, Muḥammad, Ḥusayn, and other sacred figures of the Islamic covenant. 'Alí and Ḥusayn are often presented as the ultimate intended meanings of all the verses of the súrih including those verses that deal with various historical figures, such as Adam, Israel, and Moses, as well as those that describe various laws and ordinances, and even those verses that refer to objects such as stone, rivers, and bread. The Súrih of Joseph, in contrast, relates the story of the life of one person, Joseph. But the Báb's commentary interprets Joseph's life as symbolizing major turning points in sacred history and Joseph himself as a progression of historical figures: in addition to representing himself, Joseph also symbolizes Imám Ḥusayn, the Báb, and the Promised One of the Bábí Dispensation.

The Súrih of the Cow begins with the three disconnected letters Alif, Lám, Mím (*A, L, M*). Interpreting those letters, the Báb writes:

> For the people of truth, this verse representeth the recognition of God, glorified be He, for they recognize all the Qur'ánic letters as one letter, and all their meanings as a single meaning, regardless of the difference in letters and the diversity of meanings. . . . For verily they behold naught but God. . . .
>
> The letter Alif referreth to Muḥammad, the blessings of God rest upon Him, for He representeth the Guardianship of God (*A*lláh); the letter Lám referreth to 'A*l*í, peace be upon Him, while the letter Mím standeth for Fáṭ*im*ih, the blessings of God rest upon Her. Verily, God hath created Lám and Mím by His bidding, so that when joined together they signify the word Be (*Kun*), whereby the heavens and earth were raised up by His Command.[13]

In the first part of this passage, the disconnected letters of the Qur'án are understood as references to the sanctuary of the heart and the undifferentiated unity of the Word or Logos, where the diversity of súrihs, verses, phrases, and words all merges into the unity of those letters. Then at the level of divine Action and differentiation of those letters, the letter *A* is interpreted as *A*lláh and His representative Muḥammad, which becomes the cause of the letters *L* and *M*—standing for 'A*l*í and Fáṭ*im*ih.

These two letters together, the Báb says, constitute the creative Word "Be," which calls all reality into being. The numerical value of *L* and *M* together equals the value of the letters comprising the word "Be" (*K* and *N*, or *kun*), or seventy. Out of the union of 'Alí and Fáṭimih, the Imáms were created. In terms of the stages of creation alluded to here, *A* corresponds to the Primal Will in its pure unity and transcendence, while *L* and *M* represent Will and Determination, whose union makes possible the third stage of creation, Destiny. Out of this union all reality comes into existence.

In interpreting the verse, "O Adam! Dwell thou and thy wife in heaven, and partake ye plentifully therefrom wheresoever ye desire; but unto this tree draw not nigh, lest ye become of the transgressors,"[14] the Báb says:

> The Primal Adam is the Will, Who is the Primal Utterance (*D̲h̲ikr*), manifested in the primal realm of contingency. His consort is Determination, which is the resolution regarding the Primal Utterance, and heaven is the heaven of Oneness and not that of Absolute Unity (*Aḥadíyyát*). This is so inasmuch as therein no mention can there be of proximity to the tree, whether in the realm of probability or in reality. For it is the eternal heaven; whoever is admitted therein doth not leave, and he who is kept out shall never enter. . . .
>
> The heaven of the Primal Adam is the Sea of Absolute Unity. After he [Adam] became intimate with his wife, who is naught but the station of the definition of Adam, their Lord made them to dwell in the heaven of unity, and commanded them to approach Him through the ways of divine unity and the manners of celestial qualities, and the awareness of that which they desire, endlessly and infinitely. He then covenanted with them not to approach the tree, which is the sign of Absolute Unity. For, verily, whoever gazeth upon it with the eye of contingency shall never recognize it and would thus punish himself, whilst he who gazeth upon it with the eye of the tree itself will truly recognize the tree because then the one who hath recognized it and the object of his recognition become one (Absolute Unity). This tree is the tree of Muḥammad, wherein the sign of Absolute Unity is manifest, and it is the furthermost direction of the Will. But the Primal Adam and His wife approached it through their knowledge, but not action, and thus they became transgressors. . . . And the first child born in the realm of contingency after their transgression is the Sea of Destiny, which remaineth beyond the comprehension of anyone save God.[15]

In this passage, the process of creation—that is, the descent of the Primal Will through the seven stages of creation—is designated symbolically as the transgression of Adam and Eve, representing the first and second stages of divine creative Action, respectively.

Regarding the Qur'ánic verse, "O Children of Israel! Remember My favour wherewith I showed favour upon you; and be true to your covenant with Me, I will be true to My covenant with you,"[16] the Báb states:

> Israel is in truth 'Alí, peace be upon him, and those who were addressed by him are his progeny, who are the eleven Imáms, peace be upon them. God thus hath commanded them to reveal their guardianship within themselves, inasmuch as God hath verily shed the splendours of His revelation upon them and through them. "Be true to your covenant with Me": this covenant is the epitome of servitude on their part, that "I will be true to My covenant with you"; thus it bestoweth the lordship of God on them and through them.[17]

Explaining the verse, "And remember when We rescued you from the people of Pharaoh. . . . They slew your male children . . . ,"[18] the Báb says:

> This verse is addressed to Fáṭimih, her husband, and her father, the blessings of God rest upon them, and Pharaoh, the father of all evils . . . and the object of this, Yazíd, the curse of God be upon him.[19] The reference to slaying pertaineth to the progeny of the Apostle, and their Prince, Ḥusayn. . . . By God! Through his martyrdom the signs of glorification and the tokens of praise were slain, causing all who dwell in the worlds of creation and generation to weep and lament for the intensity of his affliction.[20]

Interpreting the verse, "And when Moses asked drink for His people, We said, 'Strike the rock with thy rod'; and from it there gushed twelve fountains . . . ,"[21] the Báb states: "The striker is Muḥammad, the blessings of God rest upon Him and His kin; the rod is 'Alí, peace be upon him; the rock is Fáṭimih, the blessings of God rest upon her; and the fountains, the twelve Imáms, peace be upon them. For 'Alí, peace be upon him, occupieth two stations: one is the station of guardianship amongst them, while in the station of the rod he remaineth separate from them."[22] Finally, the Báb interprets the verse, "Thus We have made you a middle people . . . ,"[23] as follows: "Verily, God hath ordained that, within the stages of divine Action, the middle people indicate the six stages of Determination, Destiny, Decree, Permission, Term, and Book. These are the Causes of creation and are the Witnesses unto the people of the Supreme Cloud of Subtlety."[24]

The interpretive structure of the Commentary on the Súrih of Joseph reverses this pattern. Where the Commentary on the Súrih of the Cow took historical events as symbolizing spiritual figures, the Commentary on the Súrih of Joseph sees the account of one spiritual figure as symbolizing the progression of historical events. The two commentaries, taken together, thus express two different sides of the same truth. This essential mutual interdependence of the commentaries has largely been neglected, however, and, instead, qualitative breaks between the two texts have been emphasized.[25] But in fact the unity of apparently opposite interpretive logics which we see in these commentaries is the hallmark of the Báb's theology: the two seemingly opposite types of relation between phenomenal history and the Sacred Word are expressions of the principle of progressive revelation.

In the Commentary on the Súrih of the Cow, we see the unity of all the Manifestations of God. Here, all the Prophets are one with Muḥammad, and all refer to the inner station of 'Alí and Ḥusayn. In this commentary, it is the creative Word of God, the Logos, and the creative divine Action that are the innermost truth of all the Prophets, of all beings, and of all the divine verses. In other words, while the Qur'ánic súrih describes various events and cultures in history, the Báb's commentary consistently explains the meaningful, teleological, and purposive character of history. History in all its manifestations is the expression of an ultimate spiritual reality, namely, the divine Action or the Primal Will, where origin and end are one and the same. Conversely, the Commentary on the Súrih of Joseph shows the progressive march of history as interrelated stages of the realization of the same spiritual meaning and purpose.

As we have seen before, this unity of the two approaches is the essence of the supreme interpretive principle of all the works of the Báb: to disclose, through the interpretive act, the supreme Origin, Cause, and End of all things within the phenomenal realm so that all things are seen as the mirror of their underlying reality and truth—the revelation of God enshrined within them. For the Báb, the truth of all phenomena is that essential unity, or the reflection of the Countenance of the Beloved, within the heart of all things. As the Word of God, in the Holy Scripture, treats phenomenal reality in terms of its hidden truth, everything then points to the Will, Muḥammad, and the other manifestations of the Logos.

But if the Commentary on the Súrih of the Cow emphasizes the oneness of all religions, all Prophets, all divine Revelations, and all beings, the Commentary on the Súrih of Joseph emphasizes the other side of this truth. The spiritual truth that is the inner reality of Joseph is manifested within the phenomenal realm in a progressive and historically specific form. The aspect of unity is inseparable from the aspect of historicity and progress. Together they constitute the principle of progressive revelation, the bedrock of the Báb's metaphysics.

Dating the Qayyúmu'l-Asmá'

Before discussing the structural features of the Commentary on the Súrih of Joseph, the Qayyúmu'l-Asmá', two points need to be clarified. First, the writings of the central figures of the Bahá'í Faith usually identify this work as the Báb's "First Book." However, in *Sources for Early Bábí Doctrine and History,* Denis MacEoin faults 'Abdu'l-Bahá for "mistakenly" referring to the Qayyúmu'l-Asmá' as the "first book" of the Báb, as if this reference were evidence that 'Abdu'l-Bahá was unaware that the Báb had written other works previously, including the Commentary on the Súrih of the Cow.[26] However, MacEoin himself says that such references "must be taken as meaning the first work composed subsequent to the inception of [the Báb's] prophetic career," although he is unwilling to ascribe this understanding to 'Abdu'l-Bahá.[27]

It is obvious, however, that 'Abdu'l-Bahá is referring to the fact that, within the ministry of the Báb—that is, within the category of books written by the Báb as the founder of a new religion—the Qayyúmu'l-Asmá' was the Báb's first work. In fact 'Abdu'l-Bahá is following exactly the Báb's own usage. In the Epistle of Justice: Root Principles (Ṣaḥífiy-i-'Adlíyyih), the Báb designates Mullá Ḥusayn as the first learned one of the "First Book" (the Qayyúmu'l-Asmá').[28] And in the Seven Proofs the Báb speaks of enjoining the laws of the Qur'án "in His first Book," again referring to the Qayyúmu'l-Asmá'.[29]

The second point relates to the date when the Qayyúmu'l-Asmá' was written. MacEoin has argued that this work was composed over a long period stretching from the night of the Báb's declaration in Shiraz to the time when the Báb was in Mecca and Medina. He bases this inference on textual evidence within the Qayyúmu'l-Asmá' including "two references to 'this month of Ramadán,'" which he assumes to be "most probably Ramadán 1260/August–September 1844." He also cites various references to Mecca, the Sacred House of God (the Ka'bah), such as "his call 'from this protected land, the station of Abraham,'" which he takes as "apparently Mecca," and the Báb's statement, "'when I went to the Ka'ba (*al-bayt*), I found the house raised up on square supports before the Báb; and, when I sought to perform the circumambulation around the Ka'ba, I found that the duty imposed in truth in the Mother of the Book was seven times,'" which he interprets as referring to "what seems to have been yet another experience in Mecca." MacEoin adds that "these references, all of which occur in the later sections of the book, strongly suggest that it was completed during the Báb's pilgrimage to Mecca."[30]

Although a categorical conclusion would require further research, there are reasons to doubt the accuracy of this argument. The Báb Himself says that the text was written within forty days. In a letter written in Bú<u>sh</u>ihr (or possibly Muscat), on the return journey from Mecca, the Báb says: "This lowly One hath completed the Commentary on the Súrih of Joseph in forty days, during which I wrote parts thereof each day."[31] MacEoin as well as Lawson have argued that this "forty days" cannot mean forty successive days, but must indicate forty days scattered over many months. But there are problems with that interpretation. In none of His works does the Báb speak in this way. Furthermore, the full context of the statement does not fit that reading.

The Báb is discussing the miraculous speed of His writing as a proof that His revelation is inimitable. As evidence, He refers to the writing of the Commentary on the Súrih of Joseph in forty days, and of a previous Epistle (most likely the Hidden Treasured Epistle) in one night. In that context, forty days cannot mean many months. The Báb frequently compares the speed of His revelation to that of the revelation of the Qur'án. The latter was revealed over twenty-three years while the Báb reveals the equivalent amount in just a few days. But obviously, with respect to the Qur'án, "twenty-three years" does not mean 8,395 consecutive days of revelation. If "forty days" means almost a year, then the comparison with the Qur'án in terms of the speed of revelation is meaningless.

In fact, other textual evidence within the same letter further confirms that the Commentary on the Súrih of Joseph may have been written in forty consecutive days. In the letter, the Báb writes: "Now it is ten months that the Commentary on the Súrih of Joseph hath been circulating amongst the people . . . yet no one hath even completed an accurate transcription thereof." He adds that those parts that have been sent from Shiraz are filled with mistakes. But how could anyone *complete* an accurate copy in the last ten months if the commentary itself had not already been finished at least ten months before that date? And if the commentary had just been completed *after* the trip to Mecca, how could the Báb expect there to be a complete copy many months *before* He had finished writing the text?

The fact that the Báb revealed the commentary in forty days itself is quite meaningful. As we will see shortly, the Qayyúmu'l-Asmá' is structured around forty units (each chapter consisting of forty verses) because this number symbolizes "before Me" (*lí*, equal to 40). As to the textual evidence within the Qayyúmu'l-Asmá mentioned by MacEoin, the Báb's references to the month of Ramaḍán or the House of God in Mecca seem, rather, to be signifying deeper symbolic spiritual meanings: the Qayyúmu'l-Asmá' interprets all the Qur'ánic terms as references to their inner truth, which is the reality of the Báb Himself. The month of Ramaḍán and the House of God are no exceptions to this rule.

MacEoin, however, reads the Báb's references to the month of Ramaḍán literally, taking them as evidence that those parts of the text were written in Ramaḍán of 1260, four months after the declaration of the Báb. But this cannot be the case. One of these references is in the Súrih of the Book (*Kitáb*), which is Súrih 41 of the text:

> O Concourse of Light! Hearken unto My Call in this Sacred Month: this verily is "the month of Ramaḍán, in which the Qur'án was revealed."[32] I verily am God, none other God is there but Me.
>
> God hath verily sent down unto Me, on this Night of Power (*Laylatu'l-Qadr*), His Revelation. . . .
>
> Say, verily, I am the Sacred House, and My True Month, according to the Book of God, is 'Á<u>sh</u>úrá, the tenth of Muḥarram, the Sacred Month.

> Whoso glorifieth the Month of God and His Book, which is revealed in very truth to proclaim My truth and the Mighty Truth, and reciteth during that month a single letter thereof, shall assuredly receive the blessings of the All-Merciful, His angels, and those endued with knowledge amongst His servants.[33]

When we examine this statement, it becomes clear that the Báb is identifying Himself and His Revelation symbolically as both the month of Ramaḍán and the tenth of Muḥarram, rather than literally recording the date of writing. Since the Qayyúmu'l-Asmá' is the hidden truth of the Qur'án, like the Qur'án it is (symbolically) being revealed in the month of Ramaḍán, on the Night of Power. And since the Báb is the reality of Ḥusayn, each day of the revelation of the text is also the tenth of Muḥarram—the day of the martyrdom of Ḥusayn. In other words, all the days of all the revelations of the Báb are, metaphorically, the Night of Power, the twenty-third of Ramaḍán, and the tenth of Muḥarram. It is significant that Islamic Traditions frequently mention that the Qá'im's call from heaven would be heard on the Night of Power in the month of Ramaḍán and that he would announce that he would arise on the tenth of Muḥarram.[34] In other works, the Báb uses the Night of Power to refer to His own reality. The word for "power," *qadr*, is numerically equal to 304. Since zero can be ignored in the calculation, according to the Báb the number is actually $3 + 4 = 7$, which stands for the Báb's name, 'Alí-Muḥammad (also $3 + 4 = 7$).[35] Some Traditions have interpreted the Qur'ánic verse referring to the revelation of the Qur'án on the Night of Power as signifying the revelation of the Qá'im.[36]

Further evidence that the Báb's references are metaphorical and symbolic is afforded by the description, in the same chapter of the Qayyúmu'l-Asmá', of the Báb as being present on Mount Sinai. This, once again, obviously cannot be meant literally. But there is yet another reason why we can be sure that this chapter could not have been written after the Báb's departure from Shiraz. We know that shortly after His declaration, the Báb sent one of the Letters of the Living, Mullá 'Alí Basṭámí, to Iraq to proclaim the new Cause to the major learned figures of that area. Basṭámí carried with him a copy of the Qayyúmu'l-Asmá' as evidence of the truth of the Báb's claim. Basṭámí was imprisoned, and a joint council of Shí'ih and Sunní clergy tried Him and condemned the author of the Qayyúmu'l-Asmá'. In their decree they quote from various parts of the text to support their indictment. This important document proves that it is most likely that Basṭámí's copy contained at least half of the book because the clerics' decree includes quotations from chapters 62 and 65.[37] Basṭámí had left Shiraz about two months after the Báb's declaration. Since the Súrih of the Book is the forty-first chapter of the text, it must have been written before Basṭámí's departure, in which case the mention of the month of Ramaḍán cannot be a literal reference to the date of writing.[38]

The Báb's references to Mecca and the House of God must also be taken as metaphorical. We can see that every one of them is an interpretation of Qur'ánic verses, and they all describe the reality of the Báb. From the very beginning, the Báb refers to Himself as the "Sacred House"—for His reality is the true place of pilgrimage. In the Súrih of the Book, quoted earlier, the Báb says, "Say! I verily am the Sacred House, and My True Month, according to the Book of God, is 'Á<u>sh</u>úrá, the tenth of Muḥarram." This passage was written long before the Báb's journey to Mecca.

In His early writings the Báb identifies the four levels of the divine covenant with the four true Points of Adoration to which one turns in prayer (the *Qiblih*, which is the Sacred House). The heart's Point of Adoration is God; the intellect's is the Prophet Muḥammad; the soul's is the Imám; and the body's is the station of the Báb, Who is the Sacred House of God.[39] Since He is the Sacred House, the entire text is being revealed "in the Sacred House," and the term "Protected Land" (*Baladu'l-Amín*) becomes the designation for Shiraz, where the Báb then resided. Furthermore, the "Twin Sacred Shrines" (which normally refer to Mecca and Medina) now refer to the places of the Báb's birth and declaration in Shiraz.[40] The identification of the Báb as the House of God is explicitly affirmed in the earlier parts of the Qayyúmu'l-Asmá' itself, passages that we know were revealed in Shiraz. For example, in the Súrih of He (*Huva*), chapter 45, we read: "Praise be to God, Who hath revealed this Book, in truth, unto His Servant, and ordained the angels of the heavens and earth to be Its bearers, that they may circle round this Báb. For verily We have appointed the Sacred House, in truth, to be in His heart."[41]

The same symbolic equivalence occurs in the statement quoted by MacEoin. MacEoin's translation is: "'when I went to the Ka'ba (*al-bayt*), I found the house raised up on square supports before the Báb; and, when I sought to perform the circumambulation around the Ka'ba, I found that the duty imposed in truth in the Mother of the Book was seven times." The Báb's original text, however, is more nuanced. It does not say "when I went to the House of God"; rather, it says, "when I sought (*aradtu*) the House of God."[42] Such a "visit" to the Ka'bah may in fact have been a metaphorical and spiritual "journey." The point of the Báb's statement is to disclose the hidden meaning of the pilgrimage laws in the Qur'án. The Báb is saying that they all refer to the being of the Báb. Thus the House of God is based on "four supports"—the four levels of the covenant, which are united in the fourth support (the Báb); and the duty of circumambulating is seven times, as a reference to the name of the Báb.

However, the exact date of the revelation of the Qayyúmu'l-Asmá' cannot be ascertained with certainty and needs more research. A complicating aspect is that toward the end of the book (chapter 92) the Báb speaks of five people from the holy land who have just been accepted as those who have preceded in faith, including the "youth from Qazvín," and mentions the Báb's dispute with "the remote soul" within the twin sacred shrines. If we assume that these references are to Letters of the Living coming to Shiraz to find the Báb, then we can say that the text was revealed in approximately forty consecutive days—approximately, because within forty days of the Báb's declaration no one had accepted Him other than Mullá Ḥusayn.

The Structure of the Commentary on the Súrih of Joseph

The Báb's decision to use His interpretation of the Súrih of Joseph as a vehicle to declare His mission is not accidental. The first message conveyed by the very form of the commentary concerns the Báb's true station. To understand this fact, we must note that in the writings of the Báb, one specific Qur'ánic verse holds particular significance. This verse, which is repeated twice in the Qur'án, says, "God, there is none other God but Him, the Ever-Living (*Ḥayy*), the Self-Subsisting (*Qayyúm*)."[43] According to the Báb, this verse is realized in His own Revelation, which manifests the names of God "the Ever-Living" and "the Self-Subsisting." In the Báb's later works, He Himself represents the name "the Self-Subsisting," while His first eighteen believers symbolize the name "the Ever-Living." *Qayyúm* (Self-Subsisting) implies not only that which exists in itself, but also that which is the source of the existence of everything else: all other things depend on it. The Manifestation of God, as the Point of the Will, is the *Qayyúm*, whereas all things are created by it and depend upon it for their existence.

The first eighteen believers in the Báb are the representatives of the name "the Ever-Living" (*Ḥayy*); their lives are dependent on the *Qayyúm*, the Self-Subsisting. Numerically *Qayyúm* is equivalent to the word "Joseph," both being 156. "Joseph," therefore, stands for the divine name *Qayyúm* (which also, as the Báb says, refers to *Qá'im*), and thus Joseph becomes the vehicle for the proclamation of the new Revelation. In other words, the Báb is the *Qayyúm* and, ultimately, the true Joseph.

The Báb makes these connections explicitly in a letter addressed to His uncle Mírzá Siyyid Muḥammad, which explains His station as the realization of the "Mystery" of Muḥammad:

> Inasmuch as every morning I saw thee reciting these words, "I believe in the Mystery of the Family of Muḥammad," I now intend to lift the veil, that thy deed may mirror thy words. . . . The inception of the year 1260 [1844] was the beginning of the revelation of "Mystery." Hence it was revealed: "There is no power nor strength except in God, the Exalted (*'Alí*), the Mighty (*'Aẓím*)." For after the period of negation, the cycle of affirmation is completed by the year 1260, which is the beginning of the Mystery of Muḥammad and His Family, the blessings of God and all His glory rest upon them. Inasmuch as the revelation of this Mystery is the revelation of God Himself—that is, a revelation in the station of divine Lordship rather than mere prophethood or guardianship—He revealed Himself through the proclamation: "Verily, I Myself am God; there is none other God but Me."
>
> At the time of this Revelation, the first to recognize Him was Muḥammad, the blessings of God rest upon Him—as it is explicitly mentioned in the Tradition—then the Commander of the Faithful, peace be upon him, and then the Imáms, peace be upon them. This is the mystery of the Qur'ánic verse, "When Joseph addressed His Father, saying, 'O My Father! I saw eleven stars, and the sun and the moon; I saw them bowing down before Me.'"[44]

That statement provides us with the crucial terms to understand the complex layers of symbolism in the Commentary on the Súrih of Joseph.

The reference to the concept of "Mystery" is perhaps the most significant key unlocking the entire text. Although it will be discussed in more detail later, the passage just quoted needs some initial clarification.

Let us examine the following part first: "The inception of the year 1260 [1844] was the beginning of the revelation of 'Mystery.' Hence it was revealed: 'There is no power nor strength except in God, the Exalted (*'Alí*), the Mighty (*'Aẓím*).' For after the period of negation, the cycle of affirmation is completed by the year 1260, which is the beginning of the Mystery of Muḥammad and His Family. . . ." Here the Báb connects the date of the inception of His Revelation, the year A.H. 1260 (A.D. 1844), to a famous Islamic Tradition frequently mentioned in His own writings. The Tradition consists of a negation ("There is no power nor strength") and a letter of affirmation, "except," which is followed by the affirmation ("in God, the Exalted [*'Alí*], the Mighty [*'Aẓím*]"). The Báb is saying that the entire cycle of Islam is the affirmation subsequent to the negation. The completion of the affirmation becomes the beginning point of the appearance of the Mystery of the Islamic Revelation. It symbolizes the inception of the age of the disclosure of hidden meanings and the inner truth of Islam.

The numerical value of the words of affirmation, "in God, the Exalted, the Mighty" (*Billáhi'l-'Alíyyi'l-'Aẓím*), is 1260 (68 + 141 + 1051). Note that here God is referred to by the name *'Alí* (the Exalted). As we will see, the identity of the name of God with the name of the Báb plays a significant role in the Commentary on the Súrih of Joseph. In addition, in His writings the Báb often refers to Himself as the "Great" or "Mighty" (*'Aẓím*), while referring to the Promised One (Bahá'u'lláh) as the "Most Great" or "Most Mighty" (*A'ẓam*).

In the last part of the statement, the Báb makes it clear that "Joseph" is equal to the divine name *Qayyúm*, which is the truth and inner reality of the Qá'im. Thus the Báb interprets the súrih of His own name as the means of declaring Himself to the world. And indeed, "Qayyúmu'l-Asmá'" was the Báb's favourite name for the commentary. This title can be translated as "The Self-Subsisting Lord of All Names," implying that all names, including the names of God, subsist by virtue of the name *Qayyúm*.

But the most visible clue to the secret of the Qayyúmu'l-Asmá' is found in the Báb's reference to the sun, the moon, and the eleven stars bowing down or prostrating themselves before Joseph. Here, the Báb links the Qayyúmu'l-Asmá' to the secrets revealed in His later works. The statement in fact provides one of the most interesting examples of the continuity of the Báb's early and later writings.

The organizational structure of the Qayyúmu'l-Asmá' itself refers to the spiritual meanings that are unveiled in the text. In the tablet quoted above, the Báb explains: "And He prefaced each súrih with two of the verses of the Qur'án, that it should indicate that He is the Point of the Furqán in the letter Bá' of the opening phrase of the Qur'án (*Bismilláh*), upon Whom, according to the Tradition, all depend for their existence. And He ordained each súrih to consist of forty verses that it might point to the number of the words 'before Me' (*lí*, equal to 40) in the verse 'bowing down before Me.'" The number of verses in each chapter is therefore a testimony to the station of the Báb as the *Qayyúm*, the One before whom Muḥammad, 'Alí, and the Imáms bow down. However, in the Khuṭbiy-i-Dhikríyyih, the Báb describes the number of verses in the Qayyúmu'l-Asmá' slightly differently. Calling the Qayyúmu'l-Asmá' "the Book of Ḥusayn" (Kitábu'l-Ḥusayníyyah), He explains that it is "an interpretation of the Súrih of Joseph, peace be upon Him. The entire book consisteth of 111 perspicuous súrihs, each containing forty-two verses."[45]

The number 42 is equal to the word *balí* (read as *balá*) or "yea," referring to the affirmative response uttered by the faithful to the primordial covenantal call of God, "Am I not your Lord?" However, both numbers of verses, forty and forty-two, are literally correct. In fact the identity of the two is the key to understanding the statement of the Báb. As the Báb mentioned, each súrih consists of forty verses preceded by two Qur'ánic verses: the opening phrase of the Qur'án ("In the name of God, the Most Gracious, the Most Merciful"), followed by the specific Qur'ánic verse that is interpreted in that particular chapter. Forty verses then follow in the interpretive body of the chapter. As we saw, the Báb identifies the two opening verses with the Letter Bá', the first letter of the opening phrase of the Qur'án, which is considered to contain all spiritual mysteries, and which is the Point of the Qur'án. The forty-two verses of each súrih equal *balí* (yea), and of these, the first two represent Bá', and the next forty represent *lí*. The difference between the words *balí* (which is written *blí*) and *lí* is the letter Bá'. Thus the Báb is saying that each súrih of His text expresses the fact that the Báb Himself is the Point of the Qur'án, hidden within the first two Qur'ánic verses. This *B*, representing the Báb, precedes the concept of *lí* (before Me, for Me). The word *lí* itself refers to the absolute sovereignty of the Point. Thus the station of the Point, the hidden truth of the Qur'án, has now become manifest in the sovereignty of the Báb. It is this unity that represents the fulfillment of the divine covenant.

Both the Qur'ánic Súrih of Joseph and the Qayyúmu'l-Asmá' consist of 111 súrihs. But there is a minor organizational point here that has gone unnoticed. Various writers have assumed that each súrih of the Báb's text is an interpretation of one of the verses of the Súrih of Joseph. Since the latter has 111 verses, the commentary contains 111 súrihs. However, the first súrih of the Qayyúmu'l-Asmá' is an introductory chapter which does not interpret any of the verses of the Súrih of Joseph. The interpretation of the Súrih of Joseph begins with the second chapter of the Qayyúmu'l-Asmá'. Yet the number of súrihs in the Qayyúmu'l-Asmá' is 111. This puzzle is easily solved when we note that súrih 81 of the Qayyúmu'l-Asmá' actually interprets two consecutive verses, 80 and 81, of the Súrih of Joseph.

The number of chapters in the Qayyúmu'l-Asmá' also conveys an important symbolic meaning. For the Báb, both 110 and 111 (110 + 1 as the integrative form of all the letters) are the numerical value of His own name, 'Alí—a point He makes clear in another early work, the Commentary on *Bismilláh*. In this text, which is a detailed interpretation of the opening phrase of the Qur'án, the Báb writes: "Verily the number of the name of 'Alí, peace be upon Him, is 111."[46] Then the Báb explains that the name *'Alí* consists of three repetitions of the number 1. The unity of these three 1's refers to the unity of God, Muḥammad, and 'Alí in the person of the Báb, whose name is 'Alí. The Súrih of Joseph, then, consists of 111 verses because the hidden meaning of "Joseph" is "'Alí"—the Báb.

The Unity of Divine Verses and Interpretation

Like its structure, the form in which the Qayyúmu'l-Asmá' was revealed also communicates much about its message and the station of its author. A perceptive reader will immediately notice a fundamental paradox in the Qayyúmu'l-Asmá', a paradox which is at the same time the most visible clue to the content of this complex work. Although the text is a commentary—an interpretive work—it is written in the mode of divine verses. As we have seen, the mode of divine verses is the language of revelation associated with the Primal Will and the Point of the Qur'án. The mode of commentary, which explains the meaning of the divine verses, is primarily the language of the Imáms, who were the interpreters of the Holy Word.[47] These two modes of revelation thus normally pertain to two different sacred stations. In the Islamic Dispensation, only God revealed divine verses, and only the Prophet Muḥammad, in His role as the Point of the Furqán, was the recipient of such revelation. The Imáms were subordinate in station to the Apostle of God, and their interpretations were never, and could never be, considered to be divine verses.

This relationship is completely transformed by the Qayyúmu'l-Asmá'. Here we have a work which is ostensibly an interpretation of a súrih of the Qur'án, and yet which is itself written in the mode of divine verses. It is simultaneously divine verses and interpretation of divine verses. The Báb penned many other interpretive works that were not in the mode of divine verses: the existing commentaries on the Súrihs of Abundance, the Afternoon, and the Cow are written in other modes. However, none of those works was the manifesto of the new Revelation. The significance of the Qayyúmu'l-Asmá' as the Báb's declarative testimony of His mission is thus mirrored in the form in which it was revealed.

The immediate meaning implicitly communicated by this unique form is that its author, the Báb, is both the Qá'im (the Twelfth Imám) and the Point of the Qur'án (a new Manifestation of God). Simultaneously, the fundamental hidden message of the text is the identity of these two stations in the reality of the Báb. The Qayyúmu'l-Asmá' announces the advent of the "Great Announcement" foretold in the Qur'án, the inception of a new prophetic cycle, the commencement of the age of the disclosure of hidden meanings and inner secrets. The Imám is now the vehicle of the Point of the Will, speaking through the Báb by means of the direct revelation of divine verses. The Báb Himself is the identity of different grades of spiritual reality, the manifestation of divine attributes, and therefore He is the First and the Last, the Manifest and the Hidden.

The formal paradox of the Qayyúmu'l-Asmá' explains the ambiguity of the use of the first person plural ("We"), as found throughout the text. Although the first person plural, as the voice of the Point of the Will, is the vehicle of the direct revelation of divine verses, here it actually refers most of the time to the reality of the Imám, who is now the Point of the Will, and thus the Speaker of the verses of God. This paradox is also echoed in many substantive features of the text. Next, we will examine four types of textual paradoxes, those of mystery, fire, colour, and glorification. These paradoxes are the most often repeated themes in the Qayyúmu'l-Asmá', and as we will see, they are also crucial keys for unlocking the enigmas of this work.

Four Levels of Mystery

The concept of "Mystery" is perhaps the most frequent topic encountered in the entire Commentary on the Súrih of Joseph. Hardly any of the 111 súrihs of the text is without explicit references to it. The Báb uses the various expressions and types of mystery to allude to the reality of His own station and the secret of the text itself. For example:

> Seek ye eagerly God's Most Mighty Reward, through the Báb, for the Báb of Truth, the Exalted Mystery of God, this 'Alí, Who is evident in the Mother Book. . . . O people of Glory! Hearken ye unto the call of God, raised within the Inscribed Mystery, out of these Crimson Leaves, that hath descended from the Throne upon this Snow-White Leaf, to bow down upon the Yellow Dust.[48]

> O people of the Supreme Cloud of Subtlety! Hearken unto My call from this Radiant Moon, Whose Countenance shall never eclipse the Face of this Youth of the East and the West, the One ye find mentioned in all the Holy Scriptures as the Mystery that is hidden upon the Written Line. . . . He verily is the Truth in the accent of Muḥammad, and He is the Mystery Who shineth forth out of the body of 'Alí, the hidden Dove-like Light within the heart of Fáṭimih. . . . This is verily the Mystery of Mysteries, Who hath been inscribed in the vicinity of the Water. . . .[49]

Of course, references to "Mystery" are not limited to the Qayyúmu'l-Asmá'. In the Báb's commentary on the Tradition of Truth, for example, we find: "Such a station cannot be described by any allusion, notwithstanding that its absolute nearness is remote, and its absolute remoteness is near. The veils are powerless to conceal it. He is Supreme over all things, Hidden by the Mystery, and Veiled by the Hidden Mystery, that cannot be unraveled except through Mystery."[50]

These passages give a sampling of the many references to the Báb as the "Mystery," the "Mystery of Mysteries," the "Hidden Mystery," and the "Mystery veiled by Mystery." The ultimate meaning of these references is already evident in the Báb's own explanation of the "Mystery of the Family of Muḥammad" as explained in the letter to His uncle, Mírzá Siyyid Muḥammad. In that tablet, the Báb refers to "the inception of the year 1260" as "the beginning of the Mystery of Muḥammad and His Family," and states that "the revelation of this Mystery is the revelation of God Himself—that is, a revelation in the station of divine Lordship rather than mere prophethood or guardianship. . . ."[51] This passage not only shows that the references in the Qayyúmu'l-Asmá' to "Mystery" indicate that the Báb is the inner truth of Islam and the Qur'án, but they also demonstrate that the concept of Mystery refers solely to the station of the Primal Will, the Point of the Qur'án. As the revelation of Mystery is the revelation of God, it is primarily expressed in the mode of divine verses. It is interesting that the Arabic word for mystery (*sirr*) is numerically equivalent to 260—which itself points directly to the year in which the Báb's Revelation began.

Yet this Mystery has multiple layers: the Qayyúmu'l-Asmá' often speaks of the Báb as the manifestation of Mystery at various levels, including the "Hidden Mystery." The interplay between various levels of Mystery alludes to the realization of all the layers of the divine covenant in the reality of the Báb. He is the Mystery revealed in the form of the Hidden Mystery: in other words, He is the Point of the Will that speaks as the Imám, the Qá'im. The most detailed explanation of the meaning of "Mystery" can be found in the Báb's commentary on *Bismilláh*, where He writes of four levels or stations of Mystery:

> Verily God, glorified be He, hath ordained for His revelation unto His creation, through His creation, four stations, which are referred to symbolically within the writings of the Family of God, peace be upon Them, as Mysteries. These stations are Mystery (*Sirr*), the Mystery of Mystery (*Sirru's-sirr*), the Hidden Mystery (*Sirru'l-mustasirr*), and the Mystery veiled by Mystery (*Sirru'l-muqanna'-i-bi's-sirr*). Likewise, they allude to the First Station as the Point, which is the Pivot of the Book of God in both Creation and Revelation.[52]

The Báb explains that the Point is "the Blessed Tree," "the Fire in the Blessed Tree," "the Snow White Pearl," "The Primary Utterance," "the

Glory (*Jalál*)," "the Eternal Sun," and "the Truth of Muḥammad"—all metaphors and designations indicating that this is the station of the Primal Will.[53] He goes on to explain:

> The second station is that of the Mystery of Mystery. On our part, we have referred to it as the Tree that burgeoneth forth from Mount Sinai, bringing forth oil, colour, and food. We have also called it the gold-coloured Pearl, the creative station of Determination—which is naught but the determination of that which hath been willed—the eradication of vain imaginings and upholding of the Supreme Object of knowledge, the Breath of the All-Merciful, the Command of God, and the absolute, complete, exalted, and lofty guardianship of 'Alí.[54]

The third station, the Hidden Mystery, is "the station of Imám Ḥasan, Who is represented by Us as the Pure Tree, the Green Pearl, the Sea of Destiny, the Most Exalted Mystery, and the Sublime Secret. . . ."[55] Finally, the Báb explains the fourth station: "The Mystery veiled by Mystery is the Temple of Absolute Unity. . . . Former Traditions referred to this station as the Holy Tree, the Crimson Reed, the Fixed Decree, the Morn of Eternity, the All-Embracing Mercy, and the Rank of Ḥusayn. He, peace be upon Him, abideth in the Station of manifested Unity after the concealment of the Trinity."[56] In this passage, the Báb is equating the four stations of Mystery with the first four stages of divine creative Action, as well as the station of the Point and the three stations of the first alphabetical letter, Alif. The four stations of Mystery also refer to the stations of Muḥammad, 'Alí, Ḥasan, and Ḥusayn, as well as the four levels of the covenant. The entire text of the Qayyúmu'l-Asmá' defines the station of the Báb as the manifestation of Mystery, or the Primal Will, in the name of other levels of Mystery, including the stations of the Imám and the Gate.

The Fire amidst the Snow

Another figurative pattern frequently emphasized in the Qayyúmu'l-Asmá' is the unity of the elements of fire, air, water, and earth or dust. The Báb is variously referred to as the "Burning Bush," the "Voice of the Burning Bush," the "The Fire within the Point of Ice," the "Celestial Heaven around the Fire," and the "Sacred Earth of Revelation." The four elements symbolize, in metaphorical language, the four layers of the divine covenant, representing stations that originate from the Primal Will and which end in the Gate. When the Báb indicates, as He does frequently in the Qayyúmu'l-Asmá', that all these elements are united in His own being, He is alluding to many spiritual secrets, including the true nature of His mission. In addition, the description of the Báb as the "Fire amidst the Snow" also alludes to His station as the Primal Will, in which the opposites are united. The Báb, thus, is the Point that is the Source and the Beginning of all creation and all revelation.

Colour symbolism plays a central role in the writings of the Báb, and a significant symbolic reference often encountered in the Qayyúmu'l-Asmá' is to the colour of the leaves, branches, roots, and soil of the Burning Bush, as in the following passages:

> O people of the Throne! Incline your ears unto My voice, calling unto you from this Yellow Leaf, burgeoning from the Green Branch that hath risen from out of the Snow-White Tree, and brought forth, by the leave of God, within the depths of the Seventh Sea, around the Point of Fire, that: Verily, I am God, there is none other God but Me.[57]

> O people of the Supreme Cloud of Subtlety! Listen unto My call from this Crimson Leaf, burgeoning from the Branches of this Green Tree, resting upon the Yellow Tree that hath risen from out of the Snow-White Root in this Soil of holiness: This is the Arabian Youth, Who is, in truth, evident amongst you.[58]

Here the Báb is identified with the various colours of the leaf, the branch, or the tree. These colours express symbolically the synthesis, in the Báb, of the four levels of the covenant. This point becomes clear when we note the symbolic meaning of colours in both the early and later writings of the Báb: in terms of the stages of divine creative Action, white is the colour of the Primal Will; yellow indicates Determination, green represents Destiny, and crimson corresponds to Decree.[59] This colour symbolism enables us to understand why the Báb is simultaneously the Snow-White Tree, the Yellow Leaf, and the Green Branch, as well as the Crimson Leaf of that Tree.

A further significant expression of the unity of diverse spiritual stations in the Báb is found in the Qayyúmu'l-Asmá's reference to the four stations of divine praise. We will return to examine this topic in more detail later; but briefly, the station of glorification (*tasbíḥ*) refers to the station of the Primal Will, whereas the celebration of God's praise (*taḥmíd*) corresponds to the station of Muḥammad as the Apostle of God. The exaltation of Divine Unity (*Tawḥíd* and *Tahlíl*), alludes to the station of the Imáms, while the station of magnification (*takbír*) points to the rank of the Gate. With this key we can approach the following passage and can perceive something of the complexity and levels of meaning that are contained in it:

> [I]n this mighty Paradise naught have I ever witnessed save that which proclaimeth the Remembrance of God by extolling the virtues of this Arabian Youth. . . . Magnify ye, then, His station, for behold, He is poised in the midmost heart of the All-Highest Paradise as the embodiment of the [glorification] (*tasbíḥ*) of God in the Tabernacle wherein [exaltation of His unity] (*tahlíl*) is intoned.
>
> At one time I hear His Voice as He acclaimeth Him Who is the Ever-Living, the Ancient of Days, and at another time as He speaketh of the mystery of His most august Name. And when He intoneth the anthems of the [magnification] (*takbír*) of God all Paradise waileth in its longing to gaze on His Beauty, and when He chanteth words of . . . glorification of God all Paradise becomes motionless like unto ice locked in the heart of a frost-bound mountain.[60]

Recurring expressions in the Qayyúmu'l-Asmá' speak of the appearance of "glorification"—indicating the Primal Will—at other stages of divine praise, including that of "magnification"—the rank of the Gates. Through such expressions, the Báb is divulging, in symbolic language, that He is the Primal Will Who has appeared in the name of gatehood, as well as a Prophet Who is manifested as the Imám.

5
The Qayyúmu'l-Asmá' as Interpretation

In this chapter we will focus on the substantive message of the Qayyúmu'l-Asmá', the Báb's commentary on the Súrih of Joseph, as the unveiling of the hidden mysteries of that Qur'ánic súrih. Identifying the message of the Báb's commentary, however, has proved an elusive goal for some readers, who have been baffled by the way it defies expectations that it should conform to the standard features characterizing the genre of commentary in Islamic discourse.

Existing discussions of the Qayyúmu'l-Asmá' are frequently a testimony to the failure of readers to understand it. The often-quoted statement of Browne is a good example: "A commentary in the strict sense of the word it is not, but rather a mystical and often unintelligible rhapsody."[1] As we have seen, it certainly is apt to term this work mystical, and perhaps even a rhapsody, but once we decode its symbolic lexicon, the references and allusions that at first may have been baffling or "unintelligible" become clear.

The Word and the Remembrance

One of the distinctive messages of the Qayyúmu'l-Asmá' is the unity of Author and Text. The identification of the Báb with the Qayyúmu'l-Asmá' so pervades the book—many chapters begin with that very message—that it would be impossible to touch on all the references to it. In a sense, the Qayyúmu'l-Asmá' represents a theological synthesis of the apparently differing definitions of the Word of God—the Logos—that occur in the Gospel and in the Qur'án.

The Gospel defines the reality of Jesus as "the Word." But the Qur'án reserves that status for the Qur'án itself—*Qur'án* means "recitation," "reading," and "the Word." Muḥammad as the Apostle of God received the divine Word through the angel Gabriel, but according to the typical interpretations held by Muslims, Muḥammad Himself was not considered to be the Word of God. Thus, for Muslims, the ultimate repository of sacred reality is the Qur'án and not the Prophet. However, the Qur'án does confirm that Jesus was the Word and the Spirit of God.[2] Thus within the Qur'án itself there is already a hint at their unity.

But it is the Qayyúmu'l-Asmá' that most directly indicates that the Word of God signifies both the scriptural revelation and the heart of the Prophet: the inner reality of the Báb is the Word, and the truth of the inscribed, revealed Word of God is the same as the existential, living Word of God. The Báb terms the scriptural Word the "Silent Book," while characterizing the Manifestation of God, the Prophet, as the "Speaking Book." The Speaking Book is authoritatively prior to the Silent Book: the Silent Book owes its binding character to the fact that it is uttered by the Speaking Book, and the utterances of the Speaking Book supersede all that has been previously recorded in the Silent Book. This key fact becomes an integral and central part of the historical consciousness that permeates all the Báb's theological writings.

In the Qayyúmu'l-Asmá', both the text and the Báb are frequently called the *Dhikr* (Remembrance, Utterance), as well as the *Kalimah* (the Word). The Qayyúmu'l-Asmá' is also frequently called the "Qur'án" or the "Inner Qur'án." The Báb is variously referred to as the Word of God speaking through the Burning Bush to Moses, as the reality of Jesus, and as God's testimony to humankind. For example, at the beginning of the Súrih of the Friend (*Khalíl*) the Báb speaks of the dialectic of *Dhikr* as the Text, the Báb, and the Word: "Praise be to God, Who hath revealed this Utterance (*Dhikr*), in truth, unto the Remembrance (*Dhikr*), that the people may be mentioned in the Mother Book by virtue of the Most Great Remembrance (*Dhikr*)."[3] The following statements from the Qayyúmu'l-Asmá' represent just a few instances of the same principle: "This is the Utterance (*Dhikr*) of the Power of God, that appeareth through the Most Great Word (*Kalimah*), this Youth, Whom the faithful call in truth by the name 'Alí. . . . We have verily revealed this Book unto the Most Great Word and ordained Him, in truth, to be the Midmost

Point in the realm of justice";[4] "This book is the Remembrance of God that, in truth, is revealed unto the Most Great Word for the entire world."[5]

This principle of the identification of Author and Text explains why the verses of the Qayyúmu'l-Asmá' alternate between using *Dhikr* to refer to the Báb and to refer to the Qayyúmu'l-Asmá'. In a similar way, throughout the text the Qayyúmu'l-Asmá' is called "the Path of God," and the Báb is referred to as the "Exalted Path of God, this 'Alí." The Báb is also often identified as the "upright Alif"—the letter *A*, a vertical line which is unwavering and straight, and thus the symbol of the true Path of God, the supreme Standard of truth, the straight line of justice and moderation. The close interplay between the Qá'im, the essence of justice, and the divine Path is a frequent feature of all the writings of the Báb, particularly the Commentary on the Súrih of Joseph.

The First Chapter of the Qayyúmu'l-Asmá'

Before discussing the details of the Báb's interpretation of the Súrih of Joseph, it is useful to examine some aspects of the opening chapter of this work. Given the structure of the book, the first chapter is a general commentary on the entire Súrih of Joseph. The title of this chapter is "Mulk" (Sovereignty). The first three chapters that follow it contain statements to the rulers, the divines, and the entirety of the faithful; the Báb addresses them in a sequence of descending authority, beginning with those whose authority encompasses all the people. As we shall see later, this is also the sequence in which the Báb called upon the leaders of the people to propagate His mission: first the rulers, then the divines. The reason for this order was that the concept of "rendering the Cause of God victorious"—a prominent principle in the Qur'án—is dependent on the acceptance of the Faith by the kings and leaders of the nations. The individual's role in that duty was to follow the initiatives made by the kings and the rulers in helping the new Cause.

In the title and content of the chapter, we can already get a glimpse of the interpretive style that characterizes the Qayyúmu'l-Asmá'. The chapter affirms the dominion of God and the sovereignty of the Báb, and the fact that the legitimacy of temporal authority is derived from the Báb's absolute dominion and kingship:

> O concourse of kings and of the sons of kings! Lay aside, one and all, your dominion which belongeth unto God. . . .
>
> O King of Islam! Aid thou, with the truth, after having aided the Book, Him Who is Our Most Great Remembrance, for God hath, in very truth, destined for thee, and for such as circle round thee, on the Day of Judgement, a responsible position in His Path. . . . God, verily, hath prescribed to thee to submit unto Him Who is His Remembrance, and unto His Cause, and to subdue, with the truth and by His leave, the countries, for in this world thou hast been mercifully invested with sovereignty, and wilt, in the next, dwell, nigh unto the Seat of Holiness, with the inmates of the Paradise of His good-pleasure. . . .[6]

The concept of sovereignty and the announcement of the Báb's sovereignty are directly related to the Qur'ánic súrih being interpreted in this text. The Súrih of Joseph is in fact the account of how divine sovereignty became realized in the life of Joseph, who was invested with authority and dominion after enduring much suffering. The title and the message of the introductory chapter of the Qayyúmu'l-Asmá' allude to verse 101 of the súrih, which reads: "O My Lord! Thou hast invested me with sovereignty (*mulk*), and hast taught me to expound the signs. Thou art the Creator of the heavens and of the earth. My Guardian art Thou in this world and the world to come. Cause Thou me to die a Muslim [submissive to God], and join me with the just." The beginning of the Qayyúmu'l-Asmá' thus captures the essence of the story of Joseph by announcing the sovereignty of the Báb. One can already perceive that Joseph symbolizes the Báb Himself.

The Qur'ánic verse just quoted, which is the last verse in the portion of the súrih that recounts the story of Joseph, expresses Joseph's prayer to die a Muslim. The introductory chapter of the Qayyúmu'l-Asmá', however, announces a startlingly new definition of Islam: "Verily, the essence of religion is none other than submission unto This Remembrance. Thus whoso seeketh Islam (submission to God), let him submit unto this Remembrance. For God will inscribe his name in the Book of the Righteous as a true Muslim, and he will be praised as one who is faithful. Whoso rejecteth this true Islam, God shall not accept, on the Day of Resurrection, any of his deeds."[7] Here, in this very first chapter, which declares the mission of the Báb, we have a direct assertion of the Báb' spiritual sovereignty: belief in and submission to Him is the new standard and criterion of faith, and the acceptance of righteous deeds is dependent on His recognition. Now we can more clearly see why this chapter is titled "Sovereignty."[8]

A related fundamental feature of the Qayyúmu'l-Asmá', which is expressed in its introductory chapter and confirmed throughout the text, is the association of the Báb with *'Alí* and *Ḥakím*, as previously mentioned. In the opening paragraph we read: "Verily, this is the straight Path ascribed to 'Alí before Thy Lord, as laid out in the Mother Book. And He is that *'Alí* (Exalted One), Who is praised before Us as the Wise (*Ḥakím*) in the Mother Book. Verily, He is the Truth from God, registered in the Mother Book as endued with the uncorrupted Religion in the midst of Sinai."[9] As we saw before, this passage alludes to passages in the Qur'án in which God and the Qur'án are described as "the Exalted (*Alí*), the Wise (*Ḥakím*)," and the Báb fulfills both Qur'ánic meanings of these terms.[10]

But the reference to *'Alí*, the Exalted, who is *Ḥakím*, the Wise, also implies subtle meanings that are directly related to the Qur'ánic Súrih of Joseph. According to that súrih, God conferred sovereignty upon Joseph because of Joseph's wisdom and his interpretive ability; he attained that authority because he could interpret dreams, stories, and signs in general. The Báb not only engages in an interpretation of the supreme Sign, which is the Word of God, but He also is the *Ḥakím*, the Wise, and thus the sovereign. In verse 23 of the Súrih of Joseph, it is written: "And when he had reached his age of strength, We bestowed on him judgment (*ḥukm*) and knowledge; for thus We recompense the well-doers." The word *ḥukm* means both wisdom (or judgment) and authority. Hence we can see that Joseph was endowed with the knowledge of interpretation as well as *ḥukm*, or wisdom and dominion: in short, he was invested with authority because of his wisdom. The Báb is invested with supreme authority by God, and He is called by God the exalted *Alí* who is *Ḥakím*, the Wise.

Although the Qayyúmu'l-Asmá' defines the Báb as the ultimate truth of Joseph, here again the station of Joseph is defined as a shadow of the Báb. If Joseph was granted wisdom in his age of maturity, the Báb, according to the Qayyúmu'l-Asmá' attained it in childhood:

> O Spirit of God! Call to mind My bounty to Thee, when I conversed with Thee in the centre of holiness, and assisted Thee through the Holy Spirit, that Thou mayest address the people, with the new wondrous

> tongue of God, with that which God hath wondrously ordained concerning the mystery of the heart. Verily God hath taught Thee the Book and the Wisdom (*Ḥikmah*) in Thy childhood, and shown favour unto the people of the earth by virtue of thy Most Great Name.[11]

Finally, the term most often encountered in the first chapter, and which plays an important role throughout the text, is *Dhikr*, the Remembrance of God. We have discussed the meaning and significance of this term as a title of the Báb. However, it should be noted that the frequent identification of the Báb in the Qayyúmu'l-Asmá' as the *Dhikr* (the Remembrance, the Utterance) is directly related to the Qur'ánic Súrih of Joseph. Toward the end of the súrih, after the account of Joseph's life, we read that the Súrih of Joseph and the Qur'án are in fact a *Dhikr* for the people of the world: "This is one of the secret histories which We reveal unto Thee. . . . Thou shalt not ask of them any recompense for this. It is simply a Remembrance (*Dhikr*) for all humankind." Clearly, in the Súrih of Joseph, *Dhikr* is the Word of God, the Qur'ánic súrih itself. The Báb's interpretation of that súrih identifies the Báb as that very Word of God which is being interpreted. In the Commentary on the Súrih of Joseph, the interpreter, the object of interpretation, and the interpretation are all one and the same.

The Interpretation of the Story of Joseph

Although the Qayyúmu'l-Asmá' is an interpretation of the Qur'ánic story of Joseph, this interpretation is so subtle that it has been frequently missed by various commentators on the text, who have sometimes concluded that Qayyúmu'l-Asmá' does not interpret the Súrih of Joseph or its story in any methodical way at all.[12] But when the Báb's text is read in light of the specific principles of interpretation, symbolism, and context that we have been identifying, it becomes possible to see the coherence and systematicity of the text: the Qayyúmu'l-Asmá' does indeed interpret the story of Joseph in a systematic manner, and the essence of this interpretation affirms the station and mission of the Báb as well as that of Bahá'u'lláh.

It is important, at this point, to recall the ultimate hermeneutical principle of the Báb's writings. The supreme interpretive act manifests the sanctuary of the heart, the moment of divine revelation, the sublime Origin and the ultimate End of all beings—within the object of interpretation.

Hence, for the Báb the Súrih of Joseph must also be referring, in its ultimate truth, to the station of the Primal Will, to the Manifestation of God, to divine revelation in human history, to the Promised One of all ages, to the Báb Himself, as well as to Bahá'u'lláh. In other words, it is precisely the substantive interpretation of the story of Joseph that makes the Qayyúmu'l-Asmá' an announcement of the station and mission of the Báb. In that interpretation, the figure of Joseph is a shadow of Ḥusayn, the Báb, and Bahá'u'lláh. And indeed it is stated at the beginning of an early chapter (titled the "Súrih of Joseph"), which speaks of the "beauty" of Joseph: "Inasmuch as We found him (Joseph) to be One of Our sincerely devoted Shí'ih, He was adorned by God, even as Our Beauty, with a radiant shadow; for God hath never intended aught but Us when referring to the word 'beautiful' in the inner heart of the Book."[13] In other words, any "beauty" that is mentioned in the Qur'án refers to the revealer of the Qayyúmu'l-Asmá' (the Point of the Will), and thus Joseph partakes of that eternal beauty. The story of Joseph, therefore, is about both Joseph and the Countenance of the Divine Beloved that is reflected in his heart. But this Countenance is most radiantly visible, at its zenith of revelation, in the figure of the Báb and His Promised One, Bahá'u'lláh.

No attempt to generalize about the Báb's commentary on the Súrih of Joseph can be truly adequate because of the complexity, subtlety, and nuances that characterize the interpretation the Báb gives each of the súrih's 111 verses. In fact, a discussion of the interpretation of each verse would require at least a full chapter on its own. But in addition to the various levels of interpretation that unfold in each chapter, we can discern in the Qayyúmu'l-Asmá' the presence of an overall interpretation of the story of Joseph as a whole. The Báb has said that He is interpreting the súrih of His own name, and that both the name of Joseph and the number of the verses of that súrih (111) refer to His own being. At the same time, the earlier parts of the Qayyúmu'l-Asmá' identify Joseph as Imám Ḥusayn while Joseph's eleven brothers stand for the other Imáms. Yet we soon discover that the text introduces Joseph as the Báb Himself, and later passages frequently interpret Joseph's brothers as the ones who were the first to recognize the Báb. It becomes clear that the Qayyúmu'l-Asmá' is presenting the story of Joseph as the dynamics of sacred history, culminating in the Revelation of the Báb. And at another, higher level of interpretation, the same story also refers to the return of the Báb in the next Revelation as Bahá'u'lláh. Shoghi Effendi has thus described the purpose of the Qayyúmu'l-Asmá' as "to forecast what the true Joseph (Bahá'u'lláh) would, in a succeeding Dispensation, endure at the hands of one who was at once His arch-enemy and blood brother."[14]

The account of Joseph given in the Qur'án is ostensibly a straightforward narrative of Joseph's life. Yet in the Báb's interpretation that story becomes a complex, symbolic, mystical code in which the meanings of the concrete details of the narrative are read at a higher level of abstraction. These are indeed "symbolic," not "arbitrary," signs: the link between the sign and its referent is made from the lower to the higher level through the particular motif, feature, or attribute that is singled out as meaningful. In His interpretations, the Báb abstracts a particular feature, which relates to the metaphysical nature of the object or event, and this feature is the relevant one that defines the essence of the symbol. For example, the dark well refers to the abyss of undifferentiated unity; silver coins stand for worldly passions; a caravan signifies spiritual search. To interpret things at a high level of abstraction is in fact to see those things in terms of their ultimate metaphysical reality.

Joseph's Dream and the Well of Absolute Unity

Examining the story of Joseph as narrated in the Qur'án, we can distinguish three stages in Joseph's life history. Each of these stages becomes the occasion for new interpretive turns in the Qayyúmu'l-Asmá'. The first stage comprises Joseph's childhood, ending in his being abandoned in a dark well by his brothers. The second stage includes the discovery of Joseph by a caravan journeying to Egypt and Joseph's adolescent life in the Egyptian family that adopts him as their son, and it ends in intrigues against him by various women. The third stage includes the story of Joseph's imprisonment, sovereignty, and reunion with his beloved father. Let us examine each of these stages briefly.

Regarding the first stage—Joseph's childhood and the conspiracy of his brothers, who cast him into the well—the Báb offers a radically inward interpretation, in which Joseph stands for the Imám Ḥusayn, while the brothers represent the eleven other Imáms. This interpretation is particularly challenging and, on the face of it, counterintuitive, because in the story of Joseph, his brothers commit a most evil act, and yet the Báb identifies them with the Imáms, who are sinless. Although the interpretive logic may seem puzzling, once its mystical premises are grasped it becomes understandable as both consistent and systematic.

From beginning to end, the story of Joseph is the story of a dream and its fulfillment. The story begins with Joseph telling his father of his dream, and the final resolution of the story is the interpretation and realization of that dream. The Qur'án describes Joseph's dream thus: "When Joseph said to His Father, 'O My Father! I saw eleven stars, and the sun and the moon; I saw them bowing down before Me.'" Interpreting this verse in the fifth chapter of the Qayyúmu'l-Asmá', the Báb writes:

> Verily, the Most Gracious God hath unmistakably intended [by reference to Joseph], naught but Ḥusayn, the Self of the Apostle, the Fruit of the Chaste One [Fáṭimih], and the Son of 'Alí, begotten of Abí Ṭálib. God hath verily shown Ḥusayn within the Sanctuary of His Heart (*Mas͟h'arihi'l-Fu'ád*), and above the Throne, that the Sun, the Moon, and the Stars have manifestly knelt before Him in adoration of the One True God. Hence when Ḥusayn addressed His Father, saying, "I saw eleven Stars, and the Sun and the Moon; I saw them in very truth bowing down for the Eternal God, by virtue of the embracing truth of My Cause." . . .
>
> Verily the stars of the Throne in the Book of God have bowed down in very truth for the martyrdom of Ḥusayn, and they were indeed, according to the Mother Book, eleven in number. It is God Who hath infused the very essences of all things, willingly or otherwise, with the absolute truth of His Unity through the Rays of His Light. He is the One Who, in very truth, hath created the letters as a sign of Himself. It is He Who hath ordained the Letters of His Transcendent Essence (*Huvíyyat*) which refer to His Absolute Unity (*Aḥadíyyat*), to be eleven in number. He is the One Who hath ordained the Imáms to constitute His Word of Unity, and to manifest them in writing. And it is He Who hath commanded the mystical kneeling down of the sun, the moon, and the stars in the Mother Book, as decreed in this Book. . . .
>
> God hath verily intended by the sun, Fáṭimih; by the moon, Muḥammad; and by the stars, the true Imáms. They are the ones who, by the leave of God, weep ceaselessly for Joseph, whether kneeling or standing. Verily all men, even as a dark cloud, lament with tears for that which befell Ḥusayn, bowing down in utter humility.[15]

This dream is particularly significant because it is the frame for the story of Joseph in the Qur'án—it begins the story, which recounts the process of that dream's realization, and the story concludes with Joseph's words to his father, after all have bowed down before his throne in Egypt: "O my father! This is the meaning of my dream of old. My Lord hath now made it true. . . ." In the Báb's interpretation, the dream takes place in the archetypal realm of the divine covenant and creation. The realization of the dream in the realm of phenomena is the historical revelation of the invisible and eternal divine truth. The throne in the dream is the Throne of God, and the "bowing down" occurs in the everlasting divine Kingdom that transcends time and space.

The Báb describes Joseph's dream as a dream vision in which God has shown Joseph's true station in the realm of Absolute Unity. This Joseph is, according to the Báb, none other than Imám Ḥusayn. Dreaming now becomes "witnessing." The Báb's subtle interpretive play here is not to be missed. He uses the similarity of the Arabic terms *ru'yá* (dream) and *shahádah* (witnessing/martyrdom) to connect Joseph's dream to witnessing and to the martyrdom of Ḥusayn. The word for "dream" in Arabic also has the connotation of vision or witnessing, just as "martyrdom" also means witnessing or beholding. Thus Joseph's dream is actually Ḥusayn's dream in which Ḥusayn, through his martyrdom, is testifying to the unity of God. But this is a vision shown to Ḥusayn by God, and it is because God is disclosing Ḥusayn's reality and the reality of all beings to him, that Ḥusayn can bear witness to the unity of God. In this sense the Witness and that which is Witnessed, the Beholder and the Beloved that is gazed upon, become one and the same thing. This complex interplay between dream vision and witnessing/martyrdom is explained by the Báb in the same chapter:

> Praise be to God, Who hath interpreted the truth of Ḥusayn's vision in a clear manner upon the land of the Heart in full truth. God verily hath ordained that Ḥusayn's testimony of martyrdom, bearing witness unto the Unity of God, by virtue of His very soul, is utterly pleasing and acceptable to God. For God hath manifestly shown Ḥusayn his own soul, through God's Testimony of Unity.[16]

Here, dreaming and witnessing become a declaration of the Logos and an affirmation of the declarative testimony of the unity of God. The dream takes place in the celestial witnessing spot—the sanctuary of the heart. The Imáms who bow down before, and witness, the majesty of

Ḥusayn are the letters of this Word of witnessing. The Báb explains that the eleven other Imáms refer to the word "He" (*Huva*, equal to 11), and that the twelve Imáms together refer to the twelve letters of the declarative testimony of the unity of God: "There is none other God but God" (*Lá iláha illa'lláh*, which in Arabic has twelve letters).

The Imáms bear witness by bowing down before God, but at a higher level their obeisance is also a reflection of the witnessing, or self-description, of God. Ḥusayn's station pertains to the realm of Absolute Unity, where nothing exists except God. In that celestial state, Ḥusayn's witnessing is the same as God's self-witnessing. In the realm below that of Absolute Unity—the realm of divine oneness—this transcendental witnessing becomes differentiated in the form of the Imáms and their witnessing.

The martyrdom of Ḥusayn symbolizes his unique station as the "light"—that is, true annihilation in God and submersion in the Sea of Absolute Unity. But within the Dispensation of the Báb, the truth of Ḥusayn is manifested through the Báb. As we have seen before, in His letter to His uncle Mírzá Siyyid Muḥammad, the Báb interpreted the ultimate meaning of the obeisance of the moon, the sun, and the eleven stars before Joseph as recognition of the Báb by Muḥammad and the Imáms.[17]

Other subsequent chapters of the Qayyúmu'l-Asmá' deal with the intrigue of Joseph's brothers against him, ending in their abandoning him at the bottom of the dark well. The Báb consistently interprets these events in creative, transformative ways. The well stands for the well of Absolute Unity. It is deep and dark, a place where all differentiations and distinctions are obliterated—the unfathomable realm of utter effacement and nothingness. The Imáms left Ḥusayn in the transcendental depths of the well of Absolute Unity while they themselves returned to the realm of divine Oneness, the realm of the Names and Attributes, where differentiation and creation begins. Interpreting the brothers' words to their father, Jacob—that they left Joseph with their possessions and a wolf devoured him—the Báb writes:

> God hath verily informed the believers of the truth regarding the brothers of Joseph upon their return from the realm of Oneness (*Váḥidíyyat*), on account of that which, in truth, they had committed with regard to Joseph. Verily, God is the knower of all things. Upon Their return, they said, "O Our Father! We went off racing upon the land of *'Amá'* (the Supreme Cloud of Subtlety), and We left Joseph with the

> priceless gift of Absolute Unity (*Aḥadíyyat*), from Our Lord, besides Whom there is none other God. Thus he was devoured in what had been alluded to as the Sea of the Beginning, by those who fix their gaze upon the names of God. For this reason they were described in the Mother Book as wolves.[18]

The "wolves" thus stand for the people of the time who understood the truth of Ḥusayn in limited terms, within the realm of differentiation and distinction, which was tantamount to denying him.

Interpreting other similar verses of the story, the Báb explains that it was because the Imáms decided not to divulge the Mystery of Ḥusayn to the people that they left him in the hidden state of the well, waiting to be discovered by future generations. The unveiling of the Mystery of Ḥusayn to the people would take place through the Revelation of the Báb. Therefore, the story of Joseph in Egypt symbolizes the story of the life and Revelation of the Báb, and the next stages of the story refer to the stages of divine revelation through the author of the Qayyúmu'l-Asmá' Himself. The Báb is the Ḥusayn who is appearing now with a new intensity of revelation that was not possible at the time of the Imáms. The Day of God, the Day of the Revelation of the Speaker to Moses is now at hand: the Báb is the Mystery of God unveiled.

A crucial point which relates the transition from Ḥusayn to the Báb is discussed in the Súrih of the Throne. The Báb writes:

> Thus it was when the brothers of Joseph joined him in their journey to the land of Absolute Unity. . . . these Letters of Absolute Unity concealed the Letter Há' within the dark well of the Mystery of the heart, amidst the fire. And We verily revealed unto Joseph that which warneth them of their doings. Erelong God shall manifest this Letter to them within the abode of Mystery as it circleth around the Báb.[19]

Here the eleven brothers stand for the numerical value of the letters of the word *Huva* (He), concealing the Letter Há' in the land of Absolute Unity. The Báb often emphasizes that the letter Há' represents both Imám Ḥusayn and the Báb. Há', or 5, refers to Ḥusayn because he was the fifth sacred figure (after Muḥammad, 'Alí, Fáṭimih, and Ḥasan); Há' also numerically stands for the title of the Báb. This passage clearly explains that the appearance of Ḥusayn (Joseph) as the concealed Letter Há' would take place in the form of the Revelation of the Báb.

The Family of Joseph and the Maid of Heaven

In the story of Joseph, a turning point occurs when a caravan stops at the well and the drawer of water, letting his bucket down the well, discovers Joseph. Joseph is concealed, brought to Egypt, and sold to the family of an official, who adopt him as their own son. The official's wife falls in love with Joseph but, failing to win his affection, she intrigues against him. Later the other wives of the city, who had reproached her, cut their own fingers after seeing Joseph's beauty. Joseph is then sent to prison. The Qayyúmu'l-Asmá' transforms this turning point into the story of the childhood and the mystic experience of the Báb, Who is to reveal the hidden mystery of Ḥusayn.

The chapters of the Qayyúmu'l-Asmá' that interpret the verses related to this part of the story emphasize three main elements: the caravan and the journey to Egypt; the story of Joseph's (or Ḥusayn's) new family; and the story of the female figures in the life of Joseph. Let us examine each of these elements briefly.

The lowering of the bucket into the well is interpreted by the Báb as the gaze of love. The drawer of water beheld the Báb, Who was in the Sea of Absolute Unity, with the eye of the heart and announced the glad tidings of His appearance. But the other travellers failed to see Him because they did not share that elevated perspective; thus they "sold" the Báb for the paltry price of evil passions and worldly desires.[20] The Egyptian official looked upon Him with the eye of the heart and "purchased" Him: he entered the Sea of Absolute Unity by setting aside all but God.[21]

The caravan is also discussed in connection with the brothers' journey to Egypt. The Báb identifies the caravan as the caravan of love, which has embarked upon a spiritual journey. Egypt stands for the land of the heart, where Joseph is waiting to be found. The caravan passes through many cities and villages before reaching its destination. The Báb interprets the reference, in verse 82 of the Qur'ánic súrih, to the "city" as alluding to Himself as the destiny of that spiritual journey.[22] Recognition of Him is the ultimate end and goal of the mystic journey. Likewise, in the Súrih of Remembrance (*Dhikr*), discussing Joseph's call to his brothers when they were returning to their homeland, the Báb announces: "Verily God hath ordained Me to be the most excellent Abode for the travellers and the most excellent Seat for those who attain."[23] In the Súrih of Lawful (*Ḥill*), He writes: "O ye the faithful! Wherefore keep ye afar, in your journeys, from the Abodes of God, this Báb, your true Habitation?"[24] In the Súrih of Those Who Have Preceded in Faith (*Sábiqín*) the Báb interprets the verse, "And We placed between them and the cities which We have blessed, manifest cities, and We ordained your journey therein,"[25] as a reference to the mediation of the Letters of the Living (the manifest cities) between the Báb (the Blessed City) and the people.[26] The spiritual voyage goes through the Letters of the Living to the Báb Himself.

The second theme concerns Joseph's new family in Egypt. The Báb interprets this family as the one into which He Himself was born. Thus, a number of chapters of the Qayyúmu'l-Asmá' at this stage of the story concern the Báb's own family. The most detailed of such discussions is the Súrih of Kinship (*Qarábah*). Here the Báb implies that the sign of His true station can be found in the names of His parents such that His identity as the Prophet and the Imám is symbolically disclosed in this outward form. He also states that His grandfather is Ibráhím (Abraham), implying thereby that the Báb is also Joseph. Thus both Joseph and Ḥusayn as well as 'Alí and Muḥammad can be seen in His being:

> Verily I have hailed this Remembrance by My Twin Names ['Alí-Muḥammad], which are the names of My Twin Friends amongst My servants. Verily I have called, upon the Throne, His grandfather Ibráhím, and His father the name of the twin first Friends [Muḥammad-Riḍá'], and His mother the pure Fáṭimih, that they who are endued with an understanding heart may bear witness, as soon as His Message is proclaimed, to that Mystery of splendours that proceedeth from the All-Glorious, the Ever-Forgiving.[27]

In the same chapter the Báb addresses His male and female kinsmen, His mother and His wife, and remembers His son Aḥmad, who died in infancy:

> O ye kinsmen of the Most Great Remembrance! This Tree of Holiness, dyed crimson with the oil of servitude, hath verily sprung forth out of your own soil in the midst of the Burning Bush. . . .
>
> O Qurratu'l-'Ayn! Deliver the summons of the most exalted Word unto the handmaids among Thy kindred. . . .
>
> O Thou Mother of the Remembrance! May the peace and salutation of God rest upon thee. Indeed thou hast endured patiently in Him Who

is the sublime Self of God. Recognize then the station of thy Son Who is none other than the mighty Word of God. . . .

O thou who art loved by the Supreme Beloved of My Lover! Thou art unique amongst women. . . . Verily thy son Aḥmad is, in very truth, with the exalted Fáṭimih, nurtured by knowledge in the heaven of holiness.[28]

Finally, the Qur'ánic story, in the section of the súrih concerning Joseph's family in Egypt, deals with female figures in relation to Joseph. The women appear to be embodiments of deceit and corruption, as well as worldly desires and deception. The wife of the Egyptian official tries to seduce Joseph, but when she fails, she accuses him of approaching her. The women of the city were talking behind her back and ridiculing her. She invites them to her home and shows them Joseph, whereupon they all fall in love with him. But they all become part of the intrigue against Joseph, who is sent to prison.

The interpretation offered by the Qayyúmu'l-Asmá' concerning the female figures is most complex. In contrast to the apparent message of the story of Joseph, where the female figures represent negative qualities, the Báb interprets the female figures as representing the supreme spiritual reality, the Primal Will. The female character stands for a Maid of Heaven (*Ḥúrí*) who proclaims the Word of God to all humanity. It is noteworthy that the Báb identifies this figure as "begotten by the Spirit of Bahá." This Maid of Heaven descends from her celestial chamber to the world, but in a concealed manner. The Báb states that at this stage the faithful are unable to understand or to bear His truth. Thus she appears among them arrayed in what He terms a "coarse" attire.

O Qurratu'l-'Ayn! Let the Maid of Heaven, the inmate of the Exalted Paradise, drape Herself in a coarse vesture and put on a veil of the most beautiful silk. Then let Her step out of Her mansion, appearing by Herself, upon the earth, in the beauty of the black-eyed damsel. Let Her listen to the sweet praise out of Thy holy breaths upon the Seat of the Throne and in the celestial spheres, that haply those intoxicated and bewildered amongst the dwellers on earth may be awakened by Thy Cause, to an extent less than a single hair from the back of Her head, as ordained by God. God verily knoweth all things. . . .

"O People of the earth! By the righteousness of the One true God, I am the Maid of Heaven begotten by the Spirit of Bahá, abiding within the Mansion hewn out of a mass of ruby, tender and vibrant; and in this mighty Paradise naught have I ever witnessed save that which proclaimeth the Remembrance of God by extolling the virtues of this Arabian Youth. Verily there is none other God but your Lord, the All-Merciful. Magnify ye, then, His station, for behold, He is poised in the midmost heart of the All-Highest Paradise as the embodiment of the [glorification] (*tasbíḥ*) of God in the Tabernacle wherein [exaltation of His unity] (*tahlíl*) is intoned. . . ."

O Qurratu'l-'Ayn! Permit Her to divest Herself of Her coarse robe, put on the garment She donneth in Her reserved Chamber. For verily the dwellers of heaven have wailed out of their yearning for Her hair, arrayed (*malfúf*) beneath Her veil. God is verily merciful unto His believing servants.

Return, O Thou Immortal Maid of Heaven, unto the holy Sanctuary within Thy Mansion. Thou wouldst receive Thy reward solely from Me, written down, verily, by Mine own hand in this Book through a single letter of My Command that hath been inscribed around the Fire.[29]

The Báb's identification of the female figure as the Primal Will, the Logos, and the Remembrance of God represents a reversal of the traditional patriarchal representation of the female in many previous religions.[30] But the female figure here is not only a symbol of the Primal Will; she also stands for Determination, the second stage of divine creative Action, which represents differentiation, duality, and the station of oneness below the station of Absolute Unity. In this sense, the female figure is mentioned in a "negative" way, relatively speaking, as the realm of creation and differentiation, which is ontologically a step below the level of Absolute Unity. In the same chapter of the Qayyúmu'l-Asmá', the Báb interprets the Qur'ánic verse, "When he saw that His garment was torn from behind, he said, verily this is one of your womanish tricks, for surely your cunning is serious,"[31] in terms of the story of Adam and Eve, with Eve as the symbol of duality and the perspective of differentiation (that is, representing the existence of another human besides the primal Adam). In other words, the "cunning of women" stands for the allusions of the people who are veiled (from the truth) in the perspective from which they behold the Countenance of the Beloved. The point is that to behold anything other than God is to fail to grasp the truth of Divine Unity: "Verily those who find themselves, within the Book of God, in the sanctuary of the twin limits, are indeed identified by the angels as 'women.'[32] And We acquaint them, in truth, with that which the Most Compassionate God hath attested in His mighty truth: verily this is one of your feminine ploys, for surely your cunning is momentous in all the Tablets."[33]

Just as the female figure stood for both the Primal Will and Determination, the Egyptian's wife has two different levels of significance; she stands for a person of veils who is confined to the realm of allusions, and she also represents the sacred and brave sister of Ḥusayn who gave the weapons of holy war (knives) to Ḥusayn's devoted followers (represented by the women of the city) so that they could fight in the path of God and be martyred like Ḥusayn for his love, cutting themselves in their divine ecstasy.[34]

Prison and Sovereignty

The last part of the story of Joseph deals with his adult life: first in prison, interpreting dreams, and then in Egypt, where he ultimately attains sovereignty. Joseph's brothers, with the exception of the youngest, come to Egypt to buy corn. But Joseph asks for his younger brother, Benjamin, to be brought to him. Promising their father to protect Benjamin, the brothers bring the young brother to Egypt. But Joseph hides his cup in Benjamin's saddlebag, accuses him of theft, and arrests him. The brothers return to their father and inform him of events. The father does not believe them and sends them back to find both Joseph and Benjamin. When they return to Joseph they offer a little money in exchange for Benjamin. Joseph now reveals his secret and sends for his parents, and all come to Egypt and bow down before Joseph's throne. He declares to his father that this is the fulfillment of his childhood dream.

The Báb interprets this part of the story as symbolizing present and future events of His own Revelation: all these verses are portrayed in terms of the dynamics of the concealed revelation of the Báb, the Báb's own dreams, His recognition by the Letters of the Living, the gatehood of His first believer, the journey of the Letters of the Living to find Him, and their eternal return to the city of the heart. Finally, the story becomes the account of the future exaltation and sovereignty of the Cause of God. The question of Joseph's authority becomes the fulfillment of divine holy war, the conquest of hearts, and the establishment of divine sovereignty on earth. Thus the Báb's own celestial dream and the Sea of Absolute Unity are now realized in the form of a spiritualized world.

This part of the story is parallel to the previous one. In that part, the Báb emerged from the dark well of Absolute Unity. He was Joseph and Ḥusayn returning to manifest the divine mystery in His new appearance. In the last part of the story, Joseph's brothers, here interpreted as the Imáms, return in a new form as the Báb's first believers, the *Sábiqún* or *Sábiqín* (those who have preceded in faith), or the Letters of the Living. The journey of Joseph's brothers to Egypt and their final settling there is the completion of what would later be called by the Báb the "Primal Unity" of the Bábí Dispensation. In this sense, the Qayyúmu'l-Asmá' represents the entire future metaphysics of the Báb.

In discussing the dreams of Joseph's two fellow-prisoners as well as the dream of the king of Egypt, the Báb interprets them in terms of the contrast between those who would recognize Him and those who would deny Him. The prisoners' dreams relate to the letters of affirmation and the letters of negation. In the king's dream, the king sees seven green ears and seven withered ones, which Joseph interprets as seven years of prosperous harvest and seven years of hardship. The Báb, Who interprets the king's dream through His own "most beautiful dream," now interprets Joseph's interpretation: the seven green ears are the seven letters of His own name and the seven years of His mission. The seven withered ears represent the seven gates of hell—the first opponents who would deny the Báb. The Báb writes: "O people of the earth! God shall cause you to journey through seven green ears by virtue of this Most Great Word, that ye may find refuge in the one True God, and learn the path of the Remembrance."[35]

Joseph's brothers who came to Egypt for corn saw Joseph but failed to recognize him until he later made himself known to them. Throughout this last part of the story, the brothers represent the *Sábiqún* (the Letters of the Living), the Concourse of Light, the people of truth, and the faithful. They come from the holy land of Karbila in search of the Promised One, and they meet the Báb but are unaware that He is the object of their search. For example, in the Súrih of Hearts (*Af'idah*), the Báb writes: "O concourse of Light! Verily, God hath ordained you to be the brothers of Joseph. Ye attain His presence, and yet ye shall never recognize Him except when He maketh Himself known to you. It is when ye recognize a glimpse of His Cause, that ye, in truth, shall be mentioned around the Throne."[36] In the Súrih of Grace (*Raḥmah*), interpreting Joseph's command to place money, without the brothers' knowledge, in their saddlebags so that they might return with Benjamin to Egypt, the Báb writes: "We verily say, by the leave of God, unto the angels: 'Place the sign of the Remembrance in the sacks of the souls of those who have preceded in faith, that they may recognize it when they proceed to the city of Absolute Unity, and that they may return to God through this Most Mighty Path.'"[37]

The Letters of the Living can recognize the Báb by beholding the sign of the Báb within their hearts in the city of Absolute Unity. In other words, beholding the divine revelation within their own hearts, they can recognize the Báb through His verses. The Qayyúmu'l-Asmá', therefore, is itself the first "sack of corn" that was taken by the brothers to their home. Again, the text which is interpreting becomes identical with that which is being interpreted.

In the Súrih of the Pen (*Qalam*), explaining Joseph's order to put his drinking cup in his brother's saddlebag, the Báb writes: "We verily have commanded angels, by the leave of the Exalted God, to place the drinking cup of the Remembrance in the saddlebag of the faithful. . . . O Crier! Call out with verses unto the travellers that, verily, ye are the thieves, for ye have hidden the drinking-cup of the Remembrance within the uttermost sanctuary of your being."[38] From this "cup" gushes out the invigorating water of life to the Letters of the Living. The love of the Báb is hidden within the sanctuary of their hearts, the pure divine revelation shed upon their being. Here the Báb is in fact defining the Letters of the Living in subtle ways as the return of the sacred figures of Islam, an identification that will be made explicitly in His later writings.

Similarly, the later chapters of the Qayyúmu'l-Asmá' often speak of those who have "preceded in faith." Mullá Ḥusayn, the first believer, is particularly addressed as "the Beloved Siyyid, the exalted Ḥusayn," and is designated the *báb*, or gate, to the Báb.[39] In the Súrih of Glorious (*Mujallal*), the Báb speaks of His first followers who have come to Shiraz from Karbila, and affirms their faith in the new Cause.[40] It is important to recognize that this chapter is the interpretation of the verse in the Súrih of Joseph in which Joseph discloses his true identity to his brothers and tells them that today God has forgiven them. The affirmation of the faith of the Letters of the Living is the fulfillment of this verse. The Báb writes: "God verily hath forgiven those who, prior to this Dispensation, left the

Sacred Land (Karbila) to find the Most Great Remembrance. For they have followed Thee at the time of Thy oneness, when no one was aware of Thy Most Great Cause."[41] In the Súrih of Those Who Have Preceeded in Faith (*Sábiqín*), the Báb addresses His first believers, calling Mullá Ḥusayn the gate to the Báb and one of the *Sábiqín*, and calling the Letters of the Living the "manifest cities" between the people and the "Blessed City," the Báb.[42]

The final chapters of the Qayyúmu'l-Asmá' are particularly revealing of the Báb's true station. The Báb defines His own station in complex and sublime symbols corresponding to the unveiling of Joseph's true identity. The Qayyúmu'l-Asmá' is filled with pronouncements like this:

> O people of the Supreme Cloud of Subtlety! Hearken unto My call from this Radiant Moon, Whose Countenance shall never eclipse the Face of this Youth of the East and the West, the One ye find mentioned in all the Holy Scriptures as the Mystery that is hidden upon the Written Line. . . . O people of the earth! Verily the Point hath reached Its Abode. . . . God verily hath enjoined upon you, through this Book, to write with the most exquisite writing, in golden ink. . . . O Qurratu'l-'Ayn! Say! When I sought the Sacred House, I found that the Ka'bah is erected upon four pillars of support standing before the Báb; and when I desired to circumambulate the House, I found that the Mother Book hath enjoined seven repetitions; and when I wished to make mention of God upon earth, I found the Fane (*Mash'ar*) and Mount 'Arafát existing around the Báb. . . .
>
> Verily this is the Light of the Fire on Sinai, He Who revealeth the names of God through the hosts of manifestation. . . . He verily is the Truth in the accent of Muḥammad, and He is the Mystery Who shineth forth out of the body of 'Alí, the hidden Dove-like Light within the heart of Fáṭimih. . . . This is verily the Mystery of Mysteries, Who hath been inscribed in the vicinity of the Water. . . . Verily this is the inscribed Mystery that hath been hidden in the heart of the Prophet. Verily this is the Unseen Secret, hidden in the heart of the shining Arabian Guardian ('Alí), which hath been written around the Fire. . . . Thou art, in truth, in the realm of holiness, the pillar of glorification, and art, in very truth, and with utter majesty, the essence of magnification.[43]

It is important to note a particular aspect of the Báb's commentary on the Súrih of Joseph as a unique interpretive work. A normal exegetical work deals with the material of the past—an archaic text, a historical narrative, a set of events that have already taken place—and interprets them in that context. This is not the case here. In the Qayyúmu'l-Asmá', the meaning that is assigned to the story of Joseph is prophetic: the inner truth of Joseph and his brothers is the inner truth of the Báb and His Letters of the Living. Yet, when the Báb was beginning to write the Qayyúmu'l-Asmá', those Letters of the Living were yet to recognize Him. This recognition would take place precisely through their encounter with the text of the Qayyúmu'l-Asmá'. In other words, the Qayyúmu'l-Asmá' is actually creating the very (future) reality that it is interpreting.

The story of Joseph was the story of a dream and its subsequent fulfillment. Yet here the dynamic of dream and reality is the dynamic of true reality and its shadow representation in the world. Thus it is the dream that represents the supreme reality—the realm of divine creative Action—while the historical realization of the dream in the world is a mere phenomenal reflection of that eternal truth.

No analysis of the Qayyúmu'l-Asmá' can be adequate if it fails to appreciate that this text is not only an interpretation of the Súrih of Joseph, but also a commentary on the entire Qur'án itself. The various chapters of the Qayyúmu'l-Asmá' are filled with interpretations of various súrihs, and the entire text of the Qayyúmu'l-Asmá' is written like the Qur'án, with frequent usage of Qur'ánic concepts interpreted in new ways. From the signs of the Day of Resurrection, to the stories of Khiḍr and Moses, the people of the cave, Dhu'l-Qarnayn (Alexander the Great), Adam and Eve, Pharaoh and Moses, Noah, Abraham, and Jesus—all are interpreted in the Qayyúmu'l-Asmá'. Analysis of these aspects of the text, however, would be a book in itself. Suffice it to say that the Báb consistently interprets them all as a reference to His own Revelation. In this sense, the Qayyúmu'l-Asmá' represents itself as the Hidden Secret of the Qur'án, while that secret is none other than the Mystery of God—the Báb Himself.

The Qayyúmu'l-Asmá' represents the station of unity, the realization of the perspective of the heart: the interpretation (the Qayyúmu'l-Asmá') is seen to be the same as the interpreter (the Báb), and it is identical with the Qur'án and the súrih that is the object of its interpretation. The story which it interprets is the story of the Báb, the very Qayyúmu'l-Asmá' itself. Past, present, and future are intertwined and merged in its transcendental perspective of unity.

II

The Metaphysics of the Primal Will and Divine Action

6

The Sanctuary of the Heart and the Path to Truth

WE HAVE SEEN that the Báb interprets all the phenomena that are mentioned in the Holy Scriptures ultimately as references to their supreme Beginning and End, seeing in all things only the signs and traces of the divine Effulgence that permeates and constitutes all creation. The mode of interpretation was based on the perspective of unity that is attained in the sanctuary of the heart. In this chapter we address the methodology and the epistemology that the Báb prescribes as most conducive to the discovery of spiritual truth. In the following chapters we will examine His conception of being, with particular emphasis on the analytics of the Point and the arc of descent.

Discussions of the question of truth and the conditions that govern the process of spiritual search are found throughout the writings of the Báb, but several of His works directly address in detail the subject of truth and methodology. Of these texts we will focus on two: an early work, the Commentary on the Tradition of Truth, and a later one, His analysis of the name of God, the Most Near, which is found in the book Panj Sha'n.

Truth and the Declarative Testimony

The Persian Bayán defines the fundamental principle of faith as the declarative testimony of Divine Unity, which affirms that "there is none other God but God." The entirety of the Báb's religion can be derived from that statement. As He says:

> In chapter 1 of the number of all things, that which is enjoined by God, glorified and exalted be He, is the recognition of these words: "There is none other God but God, the Absolute and Utter Truth." For the whole of the Bayán returneth unto these words, and the gathering of the next creation shall proceed thereof. But the recognition of these words dependeth upon the recognition of the Point of the Bayán, Whom God hath ordained to be the Lord of the Seven Letters.[1]

The declaration of Divine Unity consists of two parts: a statement of negation and a statement of affirmation. First all but God are negated, and then the sovereignty of God is affirmed. This dialectic of negation and affirmation is central to the Báb's discourse on truth. Its structure corresponds to the Báb's conception of the sanctuary of the heart, within which the vision of truth is possible. In this state, only when all but God are cast away can the revelation of the Countenance of the Beloved be witnessed in the heart. Phenomenal things are then discerned to be the manifestations of their supreme Origin and End: nothing is seen in anything but the signs and traces of divine revelation.

One of the most important aspects of the Báb's epistemology is the concept of *servitude:* it runs through the Báb's self-conception, His mode of revelation, His ethics, and His approach to the mystic journey as the necessary precondition for attaining truth. To know truth, one must attain the station of servitude, which means to travel the path of humility, self-effacement, and negation of all but God. As long as the obscuring layers of selfish desires, arrogance, and reliance on anything but God still exist, one cannot become worthy of beholding the Divine Beauty. When the station of servitude is realized, then the divine light will shine upon the pure mirror of the heart. In this way servitude becomes, paradoxically, the substance of divinity. That fact is the reason the Báb often refers to the statement of Imám Ṣádiq that "servitude is a substance the essence of which is divinity."

One of the Báb's works on this topic is an interpretation of the Tradition of Truth (or the Tradition of Kumayl), which reports a conversation between Imám 'Alí and one of his disciples, Kumayl. One day 'Alí permitted Kumayl to ride with him on his camel. Kumayl asked: "O my Lord! What is the truth?" At first 'Alí refused to answer his question, replying: "What hast thou to do with truth?" Then Kumayl said, "Am I not trustworthy of Thy mysteries?" to which 'Alí replied, "But that which is sprinkled upon thee is but that which overfloweth from Me." Kumayl pleaded humbly, "Would a Bountiful One like Thee disappoint the hope of a lowly beseecher?" 'Alí responded to Kumayl's question with five successive statements about truth. Since Kumayl did not understand the full import of the answers, he replied after each answer, "Please confer upon me further explanation." After the fifth statement, 'Alí concluded his response, indicating that the dawn had broken, the truth had appeared, and no further question was relevant.[2]

The five sequential statements of 'Alí concerning truth are as follows:

> "Pierce the veils of glory with no allusion."
> "Efface the vain imaginings and confirm the Supreme Object of knowledge."
> "Rend asunder the veil for the ascendancy of the Mystery."
> "Be thou attracted, by the rapture of Absolute Unity (*Aḥadíyyat*), unto the Divine attribute of Oneness."
> "Behold, a light hath shone forth out of the Morn of eternity, and lo! Its waves have penetrated the inmost reality of all [Temples of Unity]."

In His commentary, the Báb interprets these statements, as well as Kumayl's conversation with Imám 'Alí, in terms of the dialectic of negation and affirmation, which is the logic of servitude and the path to knowledge. The Báb explains:

> [T]hou must know that Kumayl's response reflecteth his condition; for he was not attired with the vesture of utter servitude, otherwise he would not have questioned the truth. . . . For the truth of his being (*ḥaqíqatah*) is a sprinkling out of His Glory that overflowed, for how can a ray compete with the Countenance (*Qamṣ*) of the Sun? That is impossible, for no being surpasseth its Origin (*Mabda'*). . . . Then 'Alí said unto him, "What hast thou to do with truth?" indicating that thou art in the station of duality, which is utter blasphemy . . . for He, the Truth, is closer to thee than thy life-vein; thus, "What hast thou to do with truth?"
>
> When Kumayl hearkened to the call of Truth and recognized his blasphemy, he was reduced to insignificance before his Fashioner, dispelled the thick darkness of his self, and pleaded, "Am I not trustworthy of Thy mysteries?" This time 'Alí said yea, on account of His loving-kindness to him, that the fire of his love would not be extinguished. He sprinkled upon him out of that which overflowed from Him. . . .

> After Kumayl understood the issue of his remoteness, he raised himself up to occupy the station of servitude. With utter humility before his Lord, he said, "Would a Bountiful One like Thee disappoint the hope of a lowly beseecher?" This time he intended to tear away the veils to become worthy of reflecting the lights of the Beauty of His truth, which are naught but His effulgence upon him and through him. . . .[3]

In this passage, which is filled with complex allusions, the Báb explains that Kumayl's very question and his mode of questioning were based upon the wrong assumptions, wrong categories, and wrong method. Kumayl could not recognize the truth because he was in the station of duality—the spiritual level that perceives differentiation and plurality rather than oneness and unity. He had to pass beyond this realm of duality to raise himself up to the station of servitude, where he could behold the truth. But in this passage, the Báb speaks of the perspective of unity in two apparently opposing ways. First, He states that 'Alí is the essence of that truth which Kumayl seeks. But He also says:

> Behold with the eye of thy heart, for, verily, the truth of thy being is the Divinity of thy Lord, revealed unto thee and through thee. Thou art He Himself, and He is thou thyself, except that indeed thou art that thou art, and He is that He is. . . .
>
> Verily, God, magnified be He, ceaselessly sheddeth His effulgence, gazeth upon thee through thee, and embraceth thee through thee. This station is thine uttermost paradise and ultimate Goal. For verily the inmates of the everlasting paradise make mention of naught but the Most Great Remembrance of God and His Most Mighty, Most Wondrous Name.[4]

Here the Báb indicates that the truth Kumayl seeks is nothing less than his own true being. The station of duality has obscured Kumayl's vision and prevented him from realizing that the truth is present within him, at the core of his being, and it is only his alienation from his own being that bars him from attaining the truth. In the above passage as well as in other parts of the work, the Báb says that the essential truth of anyone (or, indeed, of any created thing) is the station of divine revelation enshrined within, and through, that being, in one's heart. This divine effulgence shed upon each creature is the divine self-description for that being. It is important to note that although the Bab appears to be talking about the Imám 'Alí in the Tradition, He really is talking about God as well as Himself— *'Alí* being a name of God and as well as of the Báb. Thus it is not 'Alí as the Imám, but the Source of revelation which the Imám is receiving that is the "truth of 'Alí" being discussed.

The Báb finds Kumayl's inability to recognize the truth to be rooted in the paradoxical fact that Kumayl could neither perceive the truth—'Alí—that was manifest before him, nor could he behold the truth that was so near to him—the reality of his own being. Although to the eye of duality this phenomenon may seem a contradiction, it is precisely the unity of both aspects that the Báb emphasizes: the truth is 'Alí, while the truth that is Kumayl's own being is a reflection of the revelation of 'Alí upon Kumayl's heart. To recognize this truth, Kumayl must humble himself, purify his heart, behold his own inner being, and discover the revelation of the Countenance of the Beloved—the face of 'Alí—within his own reality.

This mystical unity is further emphasized at the end of the passage, where "the uttermost paradise" is described as the realization of the truth of one's own reality, through the all-encompassing gaze of the eye of the heart within the sanctuary of unity. Significantly, the Báb also terms this same paradise "the Most Great Remembrance of God," which, of course, is the Báb Himself. In other words, the Báb is none other than 'Alí, and the truth of each soul is a reflection of the Báb's revelation upon the heart of that person: "He made him to know his own self, through His statement, 'But that which is sprinkled upon thee is but that which overfloweth from Me'; thus the truth of thy being, O Kumayl, is a mere sprinkling from the station of the Prophets, which in turn is that which overfloweth from Me."[5]

As the Báb interprets the conversation between 'Alí and Kumayl in terms of the logic of servitude, He also explains 'Alí's five statements on truth as diverse expressions of the dialectic of negation and affirmation. The first statement is discussed in more detail. The Imám commands Kumayl, who now has become worthy of witnessing the truth, to "pierce the veils of glory with no allusion." According to the Báb, this statement asks for the veils to be torn away as the precondition for the divine glory to shine forth. To "pierce the veils" means to transcend the realm of plurality, the realm of allusion to this or that, to self and other: "Thus 'Alí replied, 'Pierce the veils of glory with no allusion.' He meant: O thou Kumayl! Rend all veils asunder, for they are the creation of God. Be established within the ocean of the Glory, their Creator, and forsake them all without alluding to either Me or thyself. . . ."[6]

As the Báb explains, the other four statements convey the same truth in different ways. In the second statement, "Efface the vain imaginings, and confirm the Supreme Object of knowledge," the vain imaginings are the "veils" to be negated, and the Supreme Object of knowledge to be affirmed is the "Glory." The Báb defines the "truth" in the first four statements as "Glory," the "Supreme Object of knowledge," "Mystery," and "Absolute Unity." As for the fifth statement, the Báb explains that the truth is "light," which ultimately derives from the Sun of Eternity, the Prophet Muḥammad. The Báb also interprets the fifth statement in terms of the stages of divine creative Action. In other words, the essential truth of human beings is a reflection of the divine creative Action and its stages. In this way, the interpretation of the Tradition of Truth expresses the same interpretive principle which was operative in the Qayyúmu'l-Asmá' and the Báb's other interpretive works. As He explains:

> When Kumayl pleaded, "Please confer upon me further explanation," 'Alí responded, "Behold, a light hath shone forth out of the Morn of eternity, and lo! Its waves have penetrated the inmost reality of all [Temples of Unity]." His goal, peace be upon Him, was to instruct Kumayl in the diverse stations of Divine Action (*Fi'l*) and its effects: meaning, "O thou Kumayl! The 'Morn of Eternity' is 'Alí; the 'Sun of Eternity' is Muḥammad; 'Out of' is Ḥasan and Ḥusayn; 'Hath shone forth' are the Imáms; 'light' is Faṭimih; 'Temples of Unity' are the prophets and the chosen ones; and 'Its waves' are thy station, O Kumayl, and the station of all Shí'ih beyond thyself.[7]

The five statements of truth are followed by a final comment by 'Alí which refers to the concrete realization of truth in his own being and in the heart of Kumayl. 'Alí says, "Extinguish the lamp; for verily the morn hath now broken." The Báb then explains: "He meant that 'O Kumayl! Extinguish the lamp by whose aid thou walkest in the darkness of the intellect, soul, and spirit, that haply the heart, which is the morn, may shine forth within thee.' He thus alluded to the true meaning of truth in this context, that 'O Kumayl! Extinguish the lamp, for I am the Morn.'"[8] The "lamp" refers to those modes and methods of search that are imprisoned within the lower levels of limitation and plurality and which must be discarded just as lamps are extinguished when the sun rises. As an epistemic perspective, the "lamp" is what the Báb refers to (sometimes in varying terminology) as the sanctuaries of intellect, soul, and body, while the "morning" is the sanctuary of the heart. But this also means, the Báb asserts, that 'Alí himself is that morn of truth, and that Kumayl must realize the truth which is manifest before his very eyes.

The Tradition of Truth and the Chronology of Revelation

The Báb interprets the Tradition of Truth at multiple levels. Even as He had explained the five statements of Imám 'Alí as they applied at the individual level, signifying the stages in the soul's journey to the sanctuary of the heart in order to attain truth, so He also interprets those five statements as they apply at the collective level, referring to the chronology of His own Revelation, which saw the gradual disclosure of His truth to the people through a sequence of stages. The Báb indicates that His entire mission itself is the realization of the Tradition of Kumayl. The first five statements on truth symbolize the first five years, when His truth was divulged gradually. The last of these statements, on the dawning of the light, signifies the stage in which the truth of the Báb's station, and the true meaning of the word *Báb,* became manifest. In the Seven Proofs, He explains:

> Examine the exalted answers offered twice previously, that thou mayest attain certitude that the manifestation of the Awaited Promised One is the very manifestation of the responsible Truth that thou hast observed in the tradition of Kumayl: Behold in the first year, "Pierce the veils of glory with no allusion"; in the second year, "Efface the vain imaginings and confirm the Supreme Object of knowledge"; in the third year, "Rend asunder the veil for the ascendancy of the Mystery"; in the fourth, "Be thou attracted, by the rapture of Absolute Unity, unto the Divine attribute of Oneness"; and in the fifth, "Behold, a light hath shone forth out of the Morn of eternity, and lo! Its waves have penetrated the inmost reality of all [Temples of Unity]." Thou assuredly wilt see the light that shineth forth out of the Morn of Eternity, as long as thou flee not and fear not.[9]

Given the significance of this chronology, it is necessary to determine precisely which years are being referred to. In the Báb's later writings such as Panj Sha'n, He says that during the first four years of His ministry He appeared among the people as the Báb and they assumed Him to be the Gate to the Hidden Imám. Then in the year 5, the true meaning of the title of the Báb became manifest publicly so that the people would realize that He was the supreme divine Light, and the difference between light and fire. At this time, His station as both the Qá'im and a new Manifestation of God would be apparent.[10] In that same discussion, the Báb notes that the date when He is writing this marks the passing of two complete years after the termination of those first four years. In other words, it was the end of the year 6, and the beginning of the year 7.[11] We know precisely what that date was, as the Báb mentions it in that same text: Jumádí'l-Avval 5, 1266 (March 19, 1850), which was also the anniversary of His declaration, as well as the eve of the first day of spring, and thus the eve of the first day of the Bábí year.

The first year of the Báb's Dispensation began, not at the start of the Muslim year 1260, but on the day of His declaration, Jumádí'l-Avval 5, 1260 (May 23, 1844). Thus the ministry of the Báb comprises seven years: the first four years correspond to the number of the Gates and the first four statements on truth in the Tradition of Truth. The fifth year is the year of the letter Há', the fifth statement in the Tradition, and the revelation of the true meaning of the title *Báb*. The sixth year is the year of the letter Váv. Thus in the years 5 and 6, the letters Há' and Váv are combined, forming the word *Huva* (He). In other words, after the first four years of preparation, the truth of the Báb, as the manifestation of divine revelation (the manifestation of "He") appears in the two next years. Shortly after the end of the sixth year, the ministry of the Báb comes to an end. The Báb calls the seventh year the year of *Abad* (Eternity), the year of His martyrdom, which occurred on July 9, 1850. Thus the beginning of the year 5 was April 9, 1848. It was also in July 1848 that the Báb was examined by the clerics in Tabriz and publicly proclaimed to them His station as the promised Qá'im.

The Tradition of Truth designated the fifth stage of truth as the stage of light and the morn of eternity. In the Qur'án, light is associated with God, as in this passage: "God is the light of the heavens and the earth."[12] Although in the Báb's writings the terms "Light," "Morn of Eternity," and "Sun of Truth" all primarily refer to the Báb, the first reflection of this

Light is the Báb's first believer, Mullá Ḥusayn.[13] In addition, the fifth stage, the year of Light, was the stage of the heroic sacrifice and martyrdom of Mullá Ḥusayn and many of the Báb's other disciples during the Ṭabarsí upheaval. For the Báb, such martyrdom is the concrete realization and testimony of annihilation in God, the attainment of consummate servitude, and ascent to the sanctuary of the heart. Just like the martyrdom of Imám Ḥusayn, the martyrdom of Mullá Ḥusayn and other believers announced the vision of truth, a testimony which was acceptable to God. The Báb says:

> Consider the Dawn Prayer revealed by Imám Báqir. It beginneth with this: "O thou God! I beseech Thee by the most glorious of Thy Glory (*Bahá*), for all Thy Glory is glorious. O Thou God! I beseech Thee by all Thy Glory (*Bahá*)." The allusion to Bahá in this part referreth unto the Apostle of God, the blessings of God rest upon Him. Witness the second part of the prayer as a reference to the station of the Commander of the Faithful, till thou reachest the fifth part thereof, where it mentioneth the Light (*Núr*), which pointeth to the Prince of Martyrs. The station of light resembleth that of the lamp, which consumeth its own self in order to illumine others, for there remaineth no trace of identity in the light. Thus shouldst thou be alive, thou wouldst witness the lights of this Revelation who will relinquish, by their own will, their own being in order to render victorious the unity of God, and His ordinances and prohibitions.[14]

In this statement from the Seven Proofs, written in the Prison of Mákú, the Báb is clearly speaking of the year 5 as a year which is yet to come. He also refers to the realization of the light in that year, through the self-sacrifice of the believers, as an event in the future. The martyrdom of Mullá Ḥusayn, and a number of other Bábís, took place at the end of the year 5, on February 2, 1849.

In a short letter written during His imprisonment in Chihríq, the Báb states that His Cause is the very Truth that was asked of by Kumayl. Then the Báb explains that the first five years of His ministry correspond to the five statements on truth in the Tradition. After mentioning the fifth, referring to the shining of the light out of the morn of eternity, the Báb adds that "verily, at this time, the Sun of Truth hath reached the Point of midday zenith."[15] The year 5, then, denotes the breaking of the dawn, and the year 6 is the time of the Sun's rise to its zenith. The year 7 is the year of the setting of the Sun of Truth.

Another important document which further confirms the accuracy of this chronology is found in the Kitábu'l-Asmá', in a passage in which the Báb recounts where He has been on that particular night in each of the years of His ministry. There are indications in that work that it was written around the night of the anniversary of the martyrdom of Imám Ḥusayn, that is, Muḥarram 10, 1266 (November 26, 1849). The Báb states that, in the first year, on this night He was mentioning his Lord before Muḥammad, while no one was with Him except "the Last Name" (Quddús). This is most likely a reference to the time when the Báb was in Medina, where the shrine of Muḥammad is located, accompanied only by Quddús, the last Letter of the Living (around Muḥarram 10, 1261/January 19, 1845). Then the Báb says that in the second year, on this night, He was in His own home, while only "the Most Exalted Name" (*A'lá*) was with Him. This must be a reference to His house arrest in Shiraz. "The Most Exalted Name" probably refers to His uncle Siyyid 'Alí. The date would have been around Muḥarram 10, 1262 (January 8, 1846). In the third year, He continues, He was alone in the city of Isfahan. This is a reference to His early solitary stay in the house of the governor of that city (around Muḥarram 10, 1263/December 29, 1846). Next the Báb states that in the fourth year He was in the Prison of Mákú, where only two people were permitted by the guards to attain His presence. This would have been about Muḥarram 10, 1264 (December 18, 1847). Finally, He mentions that in the years 5 and 6 (the years Há' and Váv) on this night He was in the mountain fortress of Chihríq; there were only two persons in His presence in the year 5, and one in the year 6.[16] These dates fit perfectly with the previously mentioned chronology of the five years.

As we saw, the term "Morn of Eternity" refers primarily to the Báb as the Manifestation of the Primal Will, and secondarily to the afflictions and tests the Bábís had to undergo at the Shrine of Shaykh Ṭabarsí.[17] In fact the Báb is making a sociological prediction here: that the Morn of Eternity, the explicit and public revelation of the truth of the Báb in the year 5, would also be a period of brutal persecution for His followers. We can see the logical relation between the two aspects of the meaning of the "Morn of Eternity" when we consider that the public proclamation of the Báb as the Qá'im and the new Prophet led to the self-sacrifice and martyrdom of the "lights" of this Morn of Eternity. In this way, the waves of the supreme Light (the Báb) penetrated the inmost reality of the "Temples of Unity," or the Letters of the Living.

Truth as the Creative Word

The writings of the Báb emphasize the fundamental epistemological concept that the individual's understanding of reality is always determined by that person's epistemic perspective, and that perspective is determined by the existential, spiritual station and attributes of that individual. In other words, the objective characteristics and limits of the subject shape the object that is understood by that subject.

In the history of Western philosophy it was Kant who made this insight the core of his philosophical outlook. According to Kant, the empiricist theory of knowledge, which treats the human mind as a blank slate that reflects objective reality passively through sense perception, is inadequate. Kantian theory replaced that model with a conception of the mind as an active mental structure that imparts form to the chaotic manifold matter of perception, creating a particular perception and conception of the world. These mental structures, which create our understanding of reality, are the a priori forms that constitute the conditions of the possibility of experience and objectivity. The forms of intuition (space and time), as well as the categories of understanding, are the basic mechanisms of such a construction.[18]

Kantian theory thus differentiates between the *phenomenal* world of appearances, and the *noumenal* world of the things in themselves. The world that we can know is only the phenomenal world, and this world is given its particular appearance by the type of being that we are. The world of noumenal reality, in contrast, is beyond the reach of human reason or understanding, and all the mind's attempts to understand it must fail.[19]

Kantian theory was, in turn, historicized in the writings of German Idealists like Hegel, and was reinterpreted by many social theorists in the form of the sociology of knowledge. Both the original Kantian theory and the historicized sociology of knowledge, however, were trapped in some form of the relativistic dilemma: once knowledge is held to be a function of social or material conditions, "truth" (as classically understood) no longer has meaning.

The writings of the Báb offer a unique insight on this issue. While the Báb relates different epistemic perspectives to particular existential positions, He explains that the source of those existential positions is spiritual in nature. One of the most direct expositions of this issue is found in Panj Sha'n, in which He explains the name of God, the Most Near. He turns the topic of nearness to God into a discussion of the differing spiritual stations of people in their understanding of divine Truth. Clarifying a prevalent misconception about the Sufi notion of the "unity of existence" (*vaḥdatu'l-vujúd*), He explains that the noumenal reality of the world is not the Essence of God (for nothing else exists at the level of the Essence), but is rather the realm of the divine Action, divine attributes, Logos, and Primal Will:

> Bear thou witness . . . that verily God, glorified be He, hath ever been, and will ever exist without anything to exist with Him. He verily hath created all things by virtue of His Will (*Mashíyyah*), and hath created the Will by Itself, out of nothing else. . . . All things are created and affected by It.
>
> Then behold naught in the heavens, the earth, and that which lieth between them, save as the effects thereof. They all, verily, are fashioned by the Will and have proceeded from It, while It is verily created by Itself and abideth beneath Its Own Essence. It hath proceeded from God, Its Lord, and unto God, Its Fashioner, It shall return. . . .
>
> [T]hou must bear witness that the Will is in one sense all things and, in another, devoid of them all; in one respect It is before all things and, in another, devoid of them all; in one gaze It is above all things and, in another, beneath them all. For, verily, all those different directions have been created by the Will and generated through the modes of Its revelation. Therefore, It is more manifest to things than even their own reality, inasmuch as the first is a creature, created by It, the last is a creature created by It, the seen is a creature fashioned by It, and the hidden is a creature fashioned by It.[20]

Kantian noumenal reality, in the Báb's terms, pertains to the realm of the divine Word, the Primal Will. The Primal Will is the "true reality of things"; in one sense it is all things, while in another sense it transcends all things. Although the realm of the divine Essence itself utterly transcends human knowledge, human beings can nevertheless have an indirect relation to the noumenal realm through divine revelation. This revelation is manifested in various ages, in both the realms of cosmic creation and spiritual civilization, by one of the representatives of the Primal Will: "God, glorified and magnified be He," writes the Báb, "hath made all the pluralities to proceed from the Thrones of the Will, as He willeth. Even as thou dost witness that God hath caused all human generations to proceed from the First Wondrous Creation through a single drop of water. Thus, verily, God hath created all things by the Will. . . ."[21]

True reality, or the noumenal world, is manifested by the totality of the revelation that is manifested in each age. However, the perspectives through which human beings perceive and understand this revelation are limited by the individuals' own existential stations. Those stations in turn are determined by the revelation of the creative Word of God within the inmost reality of the individual:

> The Primal Will, once it is manifested in this world at the behest of God, speaketh of all things, and by virtue of its speaking thereof, all things are brought into existence. When He revealeth, "I am verily the Mirror of God," a mirror is created in which naught is seen save the Countenance of God. Therefore he [a person] would gaze upon the Bayán, and would always refer to these words, inasmuch as his inmost reality is verily created by this verse. He, therefore, would consider those who fail to believe in those words to be of a lower spiritual station. And he is correct at his own level of existence.
>
> Likewise, when He revealeth, "I am verily the first to bow down before God," there would be one whose inmost reality is created in the image of those words. Thus, he would adduce proofs from the Bayán in that manner and gazeth upon him who is above him as he doeth, on account of his inability to comprehend the higher station. For verily his inmost reality is generated beneath the station of the higher one.[22]

According to the Báb, this difference in existential stations, corresponding to the dominance of a particular divine Word, or verse, in the heart of the individual, is the objective basis of the differences of interpretation and the contention about the meaning of the Holy Scriptures that occur within a Dispensation. He continues:

> Thus these two would dispute: This one sayeth, "Thou art an extremist (*gh͟álí*)," and the other one sayeth, "Thou art intolerant (*qálí*)." This one adduceth evidence from a word of God, and that one reasoneth by another word of God. But I affirm unto them: Ye both are true and right, on the condition that thou not say unto him, "He is an extremist," and he not say unto thee, "Thou art intolerant." As to thee who art in the

lower station, thou verily art created by this verse, and thus thou wouldst not comprehend above it. As to thee who art in the highest station, thou art fashioned by that verse and thou canst understand the station beneath thine existence. . . . Thus, wert thou to acquire wisdom, thou wouldst not reject anyone because of his limitation, but must foster the growth of all in the palm of thy mercy. Shouldst thou succeed in elevating him to the realm of glory, great would be his blessings from thee; and should he fail to ascend to thy height, thou shouldst train him within his own rank of existence. For verily he too is a creation of thy Lord; God loveth him and he loveth God. . . ."[23]

This epistemological precept has far-reaching implications, especially for discourse and communication. Because the diverse perceptions of truth entertained by different minds are due to the varying reflections of the divine creative Word in their hearts, an approach of humility and tolerance is called for, as well as avoidance of conflict and contention. Although no one can comprehend the Truth in its absolute reality, there clearly is a hierarchy of spiritual stations and corresponding perspectives on truth. The attitude of those who occupy higher stations must be one of compassion and understanding toward those of lower stations. They must try to educate them and assist them to understand, but they must never forget the limits of their own understanding.

This epistemological doctrine should not be mistaken as a form of relativism, however, although it has some similarities to perspectivism, which holds truth to be related to the perspective or standpoint of the subject. Here, the constitution of the subject's standpoint is not due to some arbitrary material or social factor that is accidental to the noumenal reality. Instead, the perspective is constituted by a specific aspect of the self-disclosing act of the same creative noumenal reality. As we will see in the next chapter, the two extreme perspectives discussed by the Báb in the example above represent the twin aspects of the station of the Point, which reveal the ultimate structure of reality. Each of these perspectives thus unveils one aspect of the reality of being, while at the same time they differ hierarchically in the degree of disclosure they represent, within and between diverse, historically specific revelations of the Primal Will.

The Báb's epistemology is based on a metaphysics that defines the creative Word of God as the supreme noumenal reality of the world. It implies that recognition of the Word of God as revealed in each age is the ultimate state of truth-knowledge that is possible for human beings to attain. One can most directly approach noumenal reality through the sanctuary of the heart, which affords the only perspective from which an all-encompassing gaze of unity is possible. Within the sanctuary of the heart, from the perspective of unity, it becomes evident that there is no contradiction in the divine words, and that if there *seems* to be any contradiction, that perception is accountable to the limitations of the readers and their varying stations. In one of His tablets the Báb writes: "Beseech thou God to open, through His grace, the gate of the heart unto thee, inasmuch as, without the light of that sanctuary, man is unable to conceive of contrary attributes within one and the same thing."[24] And elsewhere He writes:

> Such conclusive truth hath been revealed through the gaze of the heart, and not that of intellect. For intellect conceives not save limited things. Verily, bound by the realm of limitations, men are unable to gaze upon things simultaneously in their manifold aspects. Thus it is perplexing for them to comprehend that lofty station. No one can recognize the truth of the Middle Way between the two extreme poles except after attaining unto the gate of the heart and beholding the realities of the worlds, visible and unseen.[25]

The Báb provides another example of a typical dispute over doctrine, in which different individuals with opposing, although equally absolutist, orientations adduce different passages to support their positions, unable to see that things have multiple aspects which are true simultaneously:

> For instance, in the Dispensation of the Furqán, ʻAlí affirmed, "I am the Ever-Living, the Imperishable." He whose inner reality is created through the influence of that gemstone would not hesitate to believe in these words and adduceth them as proof of his station. Still, there is also another who referreth to that outward fate which befell him [ʻAlí], which is known and manifest to all. He argueth, for example, that inasmuch as God hath revealed to Muḥammad, "Verily, Thou wilt die, and verily they will die,"[26] how can it be that the One Who hath said, "Verily, I Myself am but a servant amongst His servants," would not be subject to mortality? Thus this one calleth the other an extremist, and the other calleth this one intolerant.

> Thus, O ye two beloved ones of Mine! Contend not. . . . Thou art correct: He is verily the Ever-Living, the Imperishable; and thou art also right, thou who seest his shrine and bearest witness unto his death. However, thou must not be veiled by thy knowledge of his physical death. For, verily, the station in which it hath been affirmed, "I am the Ever-Living, the Imperishable," is different from this other mortal station. It is a station in which he is a mirror of God, his Lord; whereas the station that is subject to mortality is his created station, where he is subject to change, transformation, slaying, quickening, and resurrection. Both stations are praiseworthy and beloved within their own level of existence.[27]

The underlying principles of the Báb's epistemology are confirmed and further amplified by both Bahá'u'lláh and 'Abdu'l-Bahá. Bahá'u'lláh, in the Seven Valleys, describing the Valley of Unity—the perspective from which the wayfarer is able to see beyond the pluralities that cause conflict and difference and to "look on all things with the eye of oneness"—explains that "all the variations which the wayfarer in the stages of his journey beholdeth in the realms of being, proceed from his own vision."[28] Another treatment of this topic is found in 'Abdu'l-Bahá's commentary on the Tradition "I was a Hidden Treasure . . ."[29] An important portion of 'Abdu'l-Bahá's text is devoted to the debate between those who believe that the essences of things are pre-existent, and those who believe the essences are originated and created (the same issue the Báb uses as an example of differing perspectives). The views that 'Abdu'l-Bahá discusses are those of the Sufi followers of Ibn 'Arabí as opposed to the position advocated by Shaykh Aḥmad, who frequently criticized the Sufis for thinking that the essences of things—their archetypal kingdom, the realm of the "eternal intelligible forms"—are present in the Essence of God and thus are uncreated and pre-existent.

As Keven Brown has noted, the position articulated by 'Abdu'l-Bahá is not that the two opposite views are equally valid.[30] In fact, for 'Abdu'l-Bahá clearly Shaykh Aḥmad's arguments are more accurate. However, in a manner identical to that of the Báb, 'Abdu'l-Bahá explains that the positions and beliefs held by each of these two groups are perfect "in their own stations." In other words, the two positions reflect the epistemic perspectives of the two groups, and each position is valid relative to the spiritual station of that group. Like the Báb, 'Abdu'l-Bahá affirms that the difference between the positions of the two groups is a product of the difference of the revelation of the divine names in their hearts. Although all humans are manifestations of all the divine names and attributes, different names of God are predominantly manifested in different minds and thus difference of ideas occurs.[31]

In 'Abdu'l-Bahá's analysis, it becomes clear that, again, the perspective of unity and oneness is the approach closest to spiritual truth in its most complete form. Therefore, those who turn their hearts toward the totality of divine revelation will be enabled to behold reality in the sanctuary of the heart, in ways that transcend more limited perspectives. The supreme manifestation of this epistemic perspective of the heart is of course the Manifestation of God, Who is the embodiment of all the names and attributes of God, and for this reason His recognition is emphasized as the most important step on the path of search for truth. As we have seen, His station of servitude is subservient to His station of divinity. Thus the perfect epistemological stance unites the two stations of servitude and divinity with superiority given to that of divinity.

A glimpse of this perspective of unity is possible for people of high spiritual station, as we can see in 'Abdu'l-Bahá's resolution of the different names that are manifest within the contending groups described. Here 'Abdu'l-Bahá distinguishes among not two, but three positions. The third position is the perspective of the one who understands that both names are valid, each pertaining to a different aspect of reality, and who therefore sees no contradiction between the two names. For 'Abdu'l-Bahá, the third perspective is the most adequate one. This third perspective, however, is closer, but not identical, to Shaykh Aḥmad's position.[32]

According to 'Abdu'l-Bahá, within some mystics the divine attribute of sanctification and transcendence is dominant. Such people affirm the sanctification of God from any association with the creatures. This perspective corresponds to that of Shaykh Aḥmad, who rejects any form of pre-existence for the contingent realm. Yet within other mystics, the divine attribute of lordship and being the object of adoration is dominant. These people cannot conceive of God without the existence of His creatures. This position is the view of those Sufis who posit the essences of beings in the Essence of God. However, for 'Abdu'l-Bahá, there is a third possibility. For this third group, although the name of Sanctification has ascendancy in their being, the name of Lordship is also manifestly reflected in their reality, and they are therefore closer to the station of real truth. 'Abdu'l-Bahá explains that they affirm both the attributes of sanctification and lordship, each at its own appropriate level of reality. They recognize that God, at the level of the divine Essence, is sanctified above all else, and thus they understand that, at that level, only God is pre-existent and there are no "eternal intelligible forms." Yet they also affirm the lordship of God in the realm of the revelation of divine names and attributes. At this level—the level of divine Action—they recognize the world as pre-existent with the divine attributes, for here the existence of the divine attributes implies the existence of the created world.[33]

It is important to note that in this framework, the view that asserts the pre-existence of the essences of things at the level of the divine Essence is objectively false. Likewise, the view that denies the pre-existence of the realities of things at the level of the attributes and the divine Action is incorrect. Each of the two views is correct only when it is applied to its own appropriate aspect or level of reality. Thus we can see that this epistemology is not any sort of metaphysical relativism. Metaphysical truth in itself is not dependent on, or a product of, contingent and varying conditions, although it is reflected differently in different objects—including minds.

As was noted, in Kantian theory the categories of understanding only apply to the phenomenal realm of appearances and are incapable of describing the noumenal realm of the things in themselves. According to Kant, when we try to understand the unconditional realm of the noumena through the limited categories of understanding, we find ourselves in an epistemological impasse, the "antinomies of reason," where we can simultaneously affirm and deny the same proposition. While Kant tried to resolve these antinomies through non-theoretical means, including moral action and aesthetics, he proposed no epistemological solution to the problem.[34] In terms of the Báb's metaphysics and epistemology, we can see that Kant's antinomies are a product of the limited epistemic perspectives that correspond to the categories of what the Báb calls intellect, soul, and body. But by attaining the higher perspective of the heart one can transcend the oppositions of the limited station of intellect and arrive at a more comprehensive, holistic perspective. In fact, whenever the Báb addresses a complex metaphysical question, He normally begins by explaining that it is necessary to take this higher perspective in order to understand reality: one must traverse the path of unity, submerge oneself in the sea of the heart, journey in the realm of the divine names, and attain the stage of utter servitude in order to be able to discern the truth of things.

7
The Primal Will as the Unity of Subject and Object

IN THE BÁB'S METAPHYSICS, a central role belongs to the concept of the Primal Will of God. In this chapter, we investigate the concept of the Will, its relation to God, and the stages of divine creative Action. As we have seen, in the Báb's writings the Primal Will is also referred to by such terms as the "Point," the "Tree of the Will," the "Mystery," the "Word," and the "Remembrance." In the texts that will be discussed here the Báb speaks of the Primal Will as the "Point."

The Analytics of the Point

One of the most important facts about the Point is its dual station. In a sense, everything returns to this fundamental concept. In a key passage from the Persian Bayán, the Báb explains that one station speaks "from God," while the other speaks "from that which is other than God." The second is the station of servitude for the first station. The first station, He goes on to explain,

> is the station of His unknown and unknowable Essence, the Manifestation of His Divinity. Thus, all His revealed divine verses stream forth on behalf of God. . . . All else beyond this supreme Sign present within Him is His creation. . . .
>
> And within the inmost reality of all things there hath been, and will forever continue to be, a sign from God through which the unity of the Lord is celebrated. This sign, however, is a reflection of His Will present within it, through which naught is seen but God. However, within the

> Will, that supreme Sign is the Will Itself, the Supreme Mirror of God, which hath never referred, nor will it ever refer, to aught but God. . . . He is the possessor of two signs, that of God and that of creation, and through the latter he worshippeth God and boweth in adoration before Him. In like manner, all things adore their Beloved through the sign of Creation, though it hath never reached, nor will it ever reach, beyond its own sign from God, which is present within it and pointeth unto Him.[1]

Recognizing the limitations of all language in attempting to describe the Divinity, we can approach an understanding of the dual station of the Primal Will and its relationship to God using the philosophical concepts of *subject* and *object*. God, as the unknowable Essence, transcends the realm of both subject and object. God is the Supreme Subject without any Object. The station of the Primal Will, however, can be described as the unity of subject and object. The Primal Will is the Cause and the Ground of Itself, while all other phenomena are created by the causation of the Will, and the sign of God that is reflected in each being is actually a sign of the Will.

The Báb refers to the Will's stations of divinity and servitude as two "aspects" or "directions," the higher and the lower. The station of divinity, the higher direction, is the Will as the supreme Mirror of God; here nothing is seen in the Will except God. At this level there exists no mention of anything except God: the Will is the sheer revelation of the Absolute Unity of God, where there is no possibility of creation, differentiation, or diverse names or attributes. The Báb usually designates this station as the "Sea of Names" or the "Sea of the One True God." Those who tread the path of this Sea behold nothing else but God. The Báb does not call this the Sea of the *Essence* of God, because He emphasizes that the divinity of the Will is not identical with the Essence of God, but it is the aspect of unmitigated divine revelation in the heart of the Point.

The Will as object, however, represents something that is created, and there is now mention of the Will itself as that created reality. This is the aspect of the servitude of the Will, and is what the Báb refers to as the lower direction of the Will. The Báb usually calls this station the "Sea of Creation" or the "Sea of the First Creation." In this station, there is mention of the mirroring nature of the Will, or the "self" of the Will. It is through the relation of this lower station to the higher station of the Point that God is worshipped and adored by the Will.

Since the distinction between the Sea of Names and the Sea of Creation (that is, the Sea of the created beings) is so pervasive in the writings of the Báb, it is important to observe the basis of this distinction. As we have seen, to attain a high level of spiritual understanding one must fix one's attention on the inner reality of things and behold phenomenal reality as the manifestation of the spiritual realm. However, things can be regarded in two ways. They can be seen in terms of their own characteristics and essence, or as manifestations of their Supreme Origin and End. The example the Báb uses to illustrate this distinction is the mirror: one can focus either on what is reflected in the mirror or on the mirror itself.

These two views can be applied to any being. The only view that is acceptable to the Báb, however, is that which concerns God, the Primal Will, and the stages of divine Action; thus both views are acceptable when they are directed at the Point. One can focus on the *hidden* aspect of the Point, in which nothing is seen but God, or the *manifest* aspect of the Point, as the station of the Will, the Word, and the Primary Creation. Here both perspectives in fact point to the divine realm, although the latter aspect is subordinate to the former. Likewise, one can regard the first believer (the first Letter of the Living) in either of these two aspects: in his hidden aspect, which is the station of the Will, or in his manifest aspect, which is his own essence as a Letter of the Living. In the latter aspect, the first believer represents the second stage of divine creative Action, Determination. Thus, in a secondary way, both perspectives are acceptable with regard to all nineteen members of the Primal Unity. As for all other created things, however, only the first perspective is acceptable: in the realm of phenomenal reality, only the perspective which sees in things nothing but the revelation of the Will and its divine Action is a spiritual perspective. The view that sees phenomenal things in terms of their own contingent material essences is an ordinary perspective of limitation. In the Persian Bayán the Báb writes:

> In like manner, gaze upon all the Names and Attributes with His eyes. Thus, when a servant cometh to know, he seeth that none knoweth but Him, and when he obtaineth the power to accomplish something, he seeth that none is powerful but Him, for in each Dispensation, all who are guided by that Revelation are naught but the manifold modes of that Manifestation of God. Therefore wert thou to look at all the Revelations from the first, which was that of Adam, to infinity, thou wouldst not see

> anything endued with reality except through God, and wouldst fail to recognize the Manifestation of Divinity except through the Exalted Tree of His Revelation, which is naught but the Primal Will. This is the decree, for naught else is possible in this contingent world. . . .
>
> This is the fruit of the existence of all things [all humans], since all things depend upon the Primal Will for their existence, and naught is seen in everything but the revelation of God, in accordance with the degree of the reality of any entity which beareth the divine revelation.[2]

As we saw before, these two stations of the Will are the source of the two fundamental revelatory modes of divine verses and prayers. The divine verses issue from the higher direction of the Will, while the revelation of prayers comes from the lower direction. In Panj Sha'n, the Báb summarizes the concepts discussed so far and relates the two directions of the Will to differential stations of recognition by human beings:

> Inasmuch as the recognition of the Eternal and Unseen Essence hath been impossible . . . , He, therefore, hath enjoined all, from the beginning that hath no beginning to the end that hath no end, to recognize the Sun of Truth, Who is the Mirror of His Essence and the Primal Will, Who is the Throne of His Manifestation. He hath accepted the recognition of that Sun of Truth as the recognition of His own Reality. . . .
>
> God hath ordained two stations for the Sun of Truth: the unseen station, where naught is seen in the Will save God, and the manifest station, where naught is seen in It except the Primal Will. And He hath ordained the second station to be the creation of the first, and hath decreed the first station to be the world of Names and Attributes for those servants who traverse the Seas of Attributes and the Oceans of Glory, who move by virtue of God and repose by His grace, whose firstness is from God and whose lastness is through His grace . . . who behold the Hidden Unseen within the visible and manifest, even as other servants only see the Will within the manifest.
>
> Should one who traverseth the Sea of Names be present in the time of Him Whom God shall make manifest, and desire to be granted permission to ask Him questions, He would say: "Ask then God, thy Lord, that which thou willest, for verily We are ready to answer." And should He desire to grant him an answer, He would say: "Hearken then unto what shall be revealed unto thee from God, for verily there is none other God but Me, the best of those who are ready to answer." . . . This hath been and will continue to be the unseen station of the Sun of Truth and

> the higher direction of the Dawning-Place of the Sun of Eternity, while the numerous series of prayers and supplications are but a droplet of that Sea. . . .
>
> All, according to their capacity, are enjoined to love Him and recognize Him and traverse the path of the Seas of Names and Attributes. Should it be beyond their power, however, God hath ordained for Him a different station and a lesser course, which is to recognize His manifest station, known also as the Sun of Truth, the Primal Creation, the Primal Will, the Eternal Sun. . . . It is within this lesser station that after the utterance, "There is none other God but God," servitude and its association with the Manifestation of each divine Revelation have been mentioned. Should one fail to tread the path of that Sea, he must traverse the path of this alternative Sea.[3]

It should be pointed out that these two stations are the same stations that Bahá'u'lláh has identified as the higher and lower stations of recognition when He states, like the Báb, that the creative Word of God has created people in different ways, and that some traverse the path of the highest station of recognition while others tread a path beneath that. Giving an example of these two stations, Bahá'u'lláh says that one person beholds the unknowable and exalted Hidden Essence in the Temple of Manifestation, without any mention of connection or separation, whereas another considers the Temple of Manifestation as the Manifestation of God, and finds His ordinances and prohibitions the very ordinances of God. Bahá'u'lláh states that both these groups are acceptable to Him unless the advocates of the two positions engage in contention and dispute, in which case both are unacceptable.[4]

Although Bahá'u'lláh's statement is sometimes mistaken as an expression of a relativistic epistemology in which all positions are equally valid, the two positions He is speaking of are not just two contradictory statements, but expressions of the dual character of the Point. While the first station referred to is a higher station, the second is also an objective, although lower, direction of the Will. Both are acceptable because both are true, and each corresponds to a different aspect of the revelation of the divine Word. But of the two, the first is closer to the truth of the Will—as a mirror in which nothing is seen but God, a mirror in which the revelation of the Sun within the mirror, and not the mirror itself, is primary. However, Bahá'u'lláh's statement must not be taken as suggesting the divinity of Bahá'u'lláh. Both statements are references to the station of the Primal Will, although in the Point of the Will nothing must be seen but God.

This logic is the same that informs 'Abdu'l-Bahá's discussion of the two philosophical positions on the nature of the essences of things: both are correct when confined to their specific aspect. The most comprehensive truth is the recognition of the dual aspect of the Point, with priority given to the aspect of divinity. In other words, the very statement of Bahá'u'lláh that affirms the dual character of the Manifestation of God and acknowledges the validity of both aspects (with the priority of the first) is the perfect view that synthesizes the apparently opposing perspectives. This is exactly the third, overarching perspective that is emphasized by 'Abdu'l-Bahá. Yet we can see that these are all different expressions of the same analytics of the Point that is expounded in the writings of the Báb.

The fundamental dual character of the Point, which corresponds to its ontological station as both subject and object, is also frequently reflected in the Báb's analysis of the two declarative testimonies of faith. Since all modes of spiritual reality are reflections and revelations of the Point, the essence of faith is contained in the recognition of the Point. Given the dual character and station of the Point, the two expressions that constitute the declaration of faith describe the two aspects of the Will. In the Islamic Dispensation, these two declarative testimonies are represented by expressions like these: "I bear witness that there is none other God but God," and "I bear witness that Muḥammad is the Servant of God and His Apostle." In the Persian Bayán, the Báb states that these testimonies are renewed with each new Revelation:

> For example, at the time of the Revelation of the Apostle of God, were one to say, "There is none other God but God; Jesus is the Spirit of God," he would not have been considered a Muslim unless he added to "there is none other God but God" the testimony, "Muḥammad is the Apostle of God." In like manner, at the time of the manifestation of Him Whom God shall make manifest, the testimony, "There is none other God but God," will only be accepted if it is joined with the second testimony acknowledging Him [Whom God shall make manifest]. These two testimonies will indeed be the very testimony, "There is none other God but God," together with the further testimony concerning the Point of the Bayán; nevertheless, in that day, naught is acceptable save His manifestation.[5]

The Báb states that these words of God are alive and organic. They change and progress. They appear in new forms, and thus a traditionalistic, static approach to divine revelation has nothing to do with true faith. Only those who change the words of the second testimony to affirm the Manifestation for the current age will be accepted as recognizing Divine Unity.[6]

Because all reality, both physical and spiritual, derives ultimately from the two stations of the Point, the Báb devotes much of His writings to discussing how the modes of revelation relate to these two stations. As we have seen, of the four basic modes of revelation, the first two—divine verses and prayers—refer to the dual aspects of the Point, while the next two—commentaries/sermons and rational discourse—are derived from the first two modes, with commentaries being expositions about the divine verses, and rational arguments explaining the prayers. Rational arguments correspond to the station of the Gates and the learned who endeavour to understand divine Reality. But this mode of learning is a reflection of the mode of prayer, which is the servant's attempt to connect to the divine Reality. The mode of divine verses corresponds to the Sea of Names, that stage in which nothing is seen in the Will except God, and it is only the denizens of the Sea of Names who fully appreciate the divine verses as conclusive testimony.[7]

The dual structure of the Point, and its reflection in the two primary modes of revelation, is also reflected in the fact that the Báb sent His first believer, Mullá Ḥusayn, to proclaim the Báb's message bearing two of His works: the Qayyúmu'l-Asmá', which was revealed in the mode of divine verses, and the Hidden Treasured Epistle (Ṣaḥífiy-i-Ma<u>kh</u>zúnih), which was revealed in the mode of prayers.[8] The dual station of the Point is also the reason that the Qayyúmu'l-Asmá' speaks of the revelation of both the Qayyúmu'l-Asmá' and the Hidden Treasured Epistle as the Báb's conclusive proofs:

> We verily have sent down unto Thee, in addition to this Book, the Hidden Epistle, that the people may recite its supplications in the daytime and in the night season, and learn from its sublime verses the paths of their servitude to God, in the path of this Most Great Gate (Báb). This, verily, is a mighty testimony from God unto the truth of the Most Great Remembrance.
>
> Learn ye by heart that which ye can from this Snow-white Book, and that Crimson-coloured Epistle, for God hath, in very truth, guaranteed

> for those who learn the former by heart and recite from the latter, in the path of the Báb, a heavenly paradise.[9]

One of the most significant expressions of the dual structure of the Point is found in the Báb's discussion of the unity of the two stations of divinity and servitude within His own being. He frequently refers to the Tradition, "Servitude is a substance whose essence is divinity," and emphasizes Imám 'Alí's saying that his manifest aspect is the station of the imamate while his hidden reality is the Unknowable Hidden Essence. Additionally, the Báb often speaks about the appearance of the divine "fire" in the midst of "water," or the manifestation of fire within the "dust." All these statements ultimately signify the dual station of the Point.

Causation and Creation

In religious and metaphysical discourse, one usually finds that views on the relationship between God and creation are split between two opposing positions. These positions have sometimes been termed *monism* and *dualism*. In the first, monistic position, which Max Weber called *mysticism*, there is no separation between the world or the self and God; they are ultimately one reality and God is immanent in the world. In the second, dualistic position, which Weber termed *asceticism*, there is complete separation between the world and God: God utterly transcends all creation.[10]

The writings of the Báb, in contrast, represent a complex approach which does not correspond to either monism or dualism but in which the highest "mystic" orientation is combined with the most powerful expressions of "asceticism." With regard to the "mystic" aspect, the Báb's writings universally celebrate Divine Unity and attaining the sanctuary of the heart. The form of consciousness that He desires to create is one which sees the signs of God in all things, and in fact sees nothing but God. In the Commentary on the Súrih of Abundance, for example, the Báb explains that

> true belief in God is unattainable for anyone except at the time when the light of the Countenance of the Effulgent Source of Revelation is manifested in all His stations, tokens, movements, pauses, glances, allusions, testimonies, evidences, and signs.

> Even as his heart is a pure manifestation of the Unity of the Essence, and of the element of dust amidst the Fire of the Attributes, so too will his body be like his heart, a manifestation of Divine Unity. All the atoms of his body will, therefore, testify at all times unto the Unity of God and the Manifestations of God, even as his tongue testifieth.
>
> Should he attain unto such a station, his body would, as would his heart, manifest naught but the revelation of the Absolute, the manifestations of perfection, the evidences of the Essence, and the expressions of the Attributes. Thus would he become the ideal of the Transcendent World, the Universal Light, the Heavenly Mystery, the Bright Symbol, the Divine Sign, and the Universal Tree.[11]

Despite the all-embracing "mystic" orientation of His writings, the Báb equally emphasizes the absolute transcendence of God. The two concepts of immanence and transcendence are both integral aspects of the Báb's theology that are reconciled and unified in the concept of the Primal Will or the Point.

In the last chapter, we saw that for the Báb the Kantian realm of the noumena refers to the realm of the Primal Will and not the Essence of God. This same principle is operating in all the works of the Báb that deal with controversies and questions arising in various mystic and philosophical schools of Islamic culture. Of these issues, perhaps the most important in the history of Islamic philosophy is the question of the creation of the world by God. This issue has been the central point around which ideas concerning the unity of God, the divine attributes, the pre-existence or originated nature of the world, the distinction between the Necessary Existent and the contingent existent, the nature of divine causation, and the problem of emanation have been discussed and debated.

For example, philosophers have been divided on whether causation is rooted in origination or contingency. Is the need for an ultimate Cause of the world due to the originated nature (*ḥudúth*) of the world or its inherent contingency (*imkán*)? Those who find causation to be rooted in the originated nature of the effect argue for the originated nature of the world and reject the idea that the universe is pre-existent. In this approach, God creates the world and brings it into existence out of nothingness.[12] The alternative theory sees causation as rooted in the contingency of the effect. This approach sees the world as pre-existent and co-eternal with God, while it conceives of the world as caused by a necessary God by virtue of the world's inherent contingency. Contingency is defined in terms of the relationship of *essence* and *existence:* in contingent beings, essence is distinct from existence. Since, in everything other than God, essence is separate from existence, a cause is needed to join existence to essence. But God, Who is the unity of essence and existence, needs no cause: He is the Necessary Existent.[13]

Those who argue for the originated nature of the world usually believe that God is the Cause of all beings. At some moment, God, by His unconstrained Will, chose to create all beings and then brought every single one into existence.[14] Those who argue for the contingency of the world have usually defended some form of the thesis of emanation and mediation, meaning that God created one reality, and that reality—an intellect—caused another intellect, and so on, in a chain of causal mediations until a final celestial intellect caused the earth and its inhabitants to come into existence. Many Muslim philosophers spoke of the "tenth Intellect" as the direct cause of earthly creatures.[15] The crucial point here is that according to the first theory God is the direct cause of all pluralities, whereas in the second theory God can only be the cause of unity and not of plurality.

However, despite their differences, the opposing parties in these debates assume one point in common. They both believe that it is the Essence of God which is the cause and the creator of reality. It is this basic assumption that the Báb rejects. Because divine transcendence is absolute, the Essence of God cannot be the cause of the world:

> For that Essential Pre-existence which is not the cause of any thing, and beside Whom nothing is present, and at Whose rank none can ever be mentioned, is solely the Ancient Pre-existence of the Eternal Essence, which hath ever existed by virtue of His own Existence. Naught is mentioned besides Him, and no plurality whatsoever can be uttered in the absolute indivisible Unity of His Essence.
>
> Immeasurably exalted is God above the claim of the philosophers that the cause of the originated beings is the Pre-existence of the Essence, seeking thereby to connect God with the contingent realm, and desiring to demonstrate the presence of the eternal intelligible forms (*a'yáni'th-thábitah*), by virtue of the subtlety of the Indivisible, within His Essence. . . .

> Inasmuch as the Pre-existence of the Essence can never be associated with, or equal to, anything, and nothing is worthy of mention before His station, it is not possible, therefore, that He could be the source of plurality. For, the condition of causation is the mode of association, resemblance, and utterance in relation to the effect. This, however, is both impossible and forbidden in the realm of Utter Essence, which in turn is exalted beyond mention by any of His creatures. . . .
>
> The statement of the philosophers that the cause of the created beings is the Essence is erroneous because of the lack of association, the utter impossibility of change, and the precondition of the resemblance of the cause and the effect. The truth is that the Cause of beings is God's Handiwork, created by God Himself for Himself, and ordained to be the Cause of all His creation.[16]

It is thus, rather, the Primal Will which is both its own Cause and the Cause of created reality:

> Bear thou witness . . . that verily God, glorified be He, hath ever been, and will ever exist without anything to exist with Him. He verily hath created all things by virtue of His Will, and hath created the Will by Itself, out of nothing else. . . . All things are created and affected by It.
>
> Then behold naught in the heavens, the earth, and that which lieth between them, save as the effects thereof. They all, verily, are fashioned by the Will and have proceeded from It, while It is verily created by Itself and abideth beneath Its Own Essence. It hath proceeded from God, Its Lord, and unto God, Its Fashioner, It shall return.[17]

This same theme is one of the focal points of the Báb's Epistle of Justice: Root Principles (Ṣaḥífiy-i-'Adlíyyih). Exposing the incoherence of both traditional philosophical positions, which are equally dualistic, the Báb writes:

> The advocates of the doctrine of the unity of existence are joining partners with God by virtue of the testimony of the idea of existence itself. For the "unity" affirmed by them is derivative of the existence of duality; otherwise why would they deny the duality and affirm the unity? Likewise, those who advocate that the cause of the existence of the contingent beings is the Essence of God, and thus believe in some form of relation

> between the two, are disbelievers. For causation is dependent on the association with the effect, and relation is dependent on the existence of duality, whereas both conditions are utterly false.[18]

In the Commentary on the Súrih of Unity, interpreting Súrih 112 of the Qur'án, the Báb explains the phrase, "God begetteth not," in this way:

> Verily, God hath intended by these exalted words to sanctify His Essence utterly from any attribute of causation, refuting the views of those who have considered the Essence to be the Cause of all causes. For, verily, that Cause is His Handiwork, and that Handiwork is not preceeded by any cause, to such an extent that the tongue of His Favoured Ones repeatedly addressed this absence of causation by the Essence. Had it been the Essence that was also the Cause, this would have required association and resemblance. Yet, exalted and glorified then be God! He hath fashioned the Will from nothingness, through Itself, and ordained It to be the Cause of all that is other than It, with no descent of anything from His Essence unto the Will.[19]

We can see that the Báb defines causation as a relation between two beings, where the two parties are associated with each other and in some ways resemble one another. The Essence of God cannot be the cause of creation in this sense because nothing exists at the level of the Eternal Essence, let alone that such a thing could be related to, associated with, or resemble God. Rather than the Essence, it is the realm of the divine Action, the Primal Will, the Logos, and the Remembrance of God that is the supreme Cause of the created world.

One of the most important expressions of this principle in the writings of the Báb is found in His discussion of the thesis of the unity of existence and its twin correlate concepts—the eternal intelligible forms and the True Indivisible Being (*Basíṭu'l-Haqíqah*). Many Islamic philosophers and mystics advocated the unity of existence, arguing that the world is co-eternal with God, that it is thus uncreated, and that it is ultimately one with God. One of the most well-known arguments for this thesis is that the essences of things, their "eternal intelligible forms," are objects of divine Knowledge. Since there can be no knowledge without an object of knowledge, the eternal knowledge of God logically requires the pre-existence of these eternal intelligible forms in the Essence of God. Since the Essence of God is the True Indivisible Being, the realities of the world must be nothing other than the Essence of God. Therefore, the world of plurality is an appearance whose true existence is nothing but God.[20]

Earlier, Shaykh Aḥmad had addressed these very issues, emphasizing the transcendence of God. His various commentaries on the works of Mullá Ṣadrá are basically a refutation of the doctrine of the unity of existence; he finds the Sufis to be infidels who have subverted Islamic truth and principles. One of the most important discussions exemplifying Shaykh Aḥmad's standpoint is his refutation of Mullá Muḥammad Muḥsin-i-Fayḍ-i-Káshání's concept of the knowledge of God. Shaykh Aḥmad distinguishes two types of divine knowledge: that which pertains to the level of the divine Essence, and that which corresponds to the level of divine Action. God's knowledge at the level of His Essence is the same as the Essence itself. Such knowledge has no object of knowledge and is not dependent on the existence of the essences of things in the Essence of God. God's knowledge at the level of divine Action, in contrast, is associated with the objects of knowledge, and becomes the cause of the creation of the world. This second knowledge, however, is not eternal but originated and created.[21]

The Báb confirms the absolute transcendence of the Essence of God from the realm of creation, but although He endorses the basic point of Shaykh Aḥmad's position, He takes a more nuanced standpoint with regard to Sufism. While strongly condemning the vulgar forms of Sufism and their parallel philosophical expressions, the Báb notes that the true intention of some Sufis has not been entirely different from His own position. In the Persian Bayán, He writes:

> And this statement of the famous author who hath meant by "sea" the sea of the Will and not that of the Eternal Essence, testifieth unto this same truth: "The Sea is the Sea as it hath eternally existed, while those in the phenomenal world are naught but diverse waves and forms." They can be likened unto the very reflections and shadows appearing in mirrors that point toward the Sun, inasmuch as the level of the contingent world is naught but the realm of the mirrors; naught else is attainable.[22]

In other words, the Báb affirms that the concept of the eternal intelligible forms pertains to the realm of the Primal Will. Thus the True Indivisible Being is the divine Action, the Logos. However, both these concepts—the True Indivisible Being and the eternal intelligible forms—are false if they are attributed to the realm of the divine Essence. It is in this context that the Báb often categorically affirms that God's knowledge is the same as His existence. Just as the existence of God is not dependent on the existence of the creatures, the knowledge of the Essence is also absolutely independent from any form of existence of the world and its objects.

> Thus the station of association or pairing (*iqtirán*) and that which precedeth it merely pertain to the station of His Action (*Fi'l*) and His Manifestation, which is created. God, the Fashioner, created the Action through Action itself, and established it beneath His shadow. Indeed, all descriptions intended for the recognition of God describe its station; and the encompassing dominion of its Word is the encompassing dominion of God's Word. Nothing whatsoever 'neath His shade escapeth Him.[23]

One of the most direct discussions of this issue can be found in a tablet of the Báb to the poet Mírzá Sa'íd-i-Ardistání.[24] It answers three questions about the concept of the True Indivisible Being, the issue of pre-existence versus origination, and the Neoplatonic statement, "From the One proceedeth only One."[25] The doctrine of the True Indivisible Being (from the well-known assertion that "the True Indivisible Being is all things") assumes that the essences and realities of things—their archetypal forms, or the eternal intelligible forms—exist in an undifferentiated manner in the Essence of God. God is the True Indivisible Being and is one with the essence of all things. The Báb refutes this argument by showing that, logically, it reduces to absurdity:

> Concerning the doctrine of the True Indivisible Being, as mentioned by some philosophers as evidence for a common existence between the Absolute Being and utter nothingness: this is, undoubtedly and for many conclusive reasons, a false concept. . . . Among these reasons is the incontrovertible testimony of the intellect, that naught existeth besides the Essence of Eternity, and that He posesseth no attributes, of whatever different meaning, save His own Essence. . . .
>
> Thus, no recourse is there for one who claimeth the truth of the idea of the True Indivisible Being, except to assert one of two blatant errors: either the pre-existence of pluralities in the Essence of God, or the descent of the Essence into the rank of the dust. Both of these are impossible, nay,

> forbidden, inasmuch as there can never be any descent for the Essence of God, nor can any mention ever be uttered, other than of Him, at His level. He is God; all else are His creatures, and there can be no third between, or besides, them.[26]

The Báb explains that the source of such confusion is the logical error, a false analogy, on the part of the philosophers who have assumed divine knowledge to be similar to human knowledge:

> Verily, that which hath forced some philosophers to conceive of the presence of the eternal intelligible forms in the Essence of God, and the doctrine of the True Indivisible Being, was their desire to validate the concept of the knowledge of God, magnified be His station! For they stated that knowledge must needs have an object of knowledge, and hence the affirmation of divine knowledge indicateth the existence of pluralities within the Essence of God.
>
> Exalted be God, the Sovereign, the Just! Verily, their grievous sin is due to their use of analogy in their desire to comprehend the essential properties of the Essence at the level of the contingent beings. Exalted be God above such a notion! . . .
>
> Inasmuch as it is evident that His life is His Essence, since His life doth not rely on the existence of any living thing besides Him, then the same is true with regard to His knowledge. He, glorified be He, hath been omniscient from and throughout His immemorial eternity, without the existence of any object of knowledge.[27]

This same principle is evident in the Báb's discussion of origination versus pre-existence. Again, the Báb's most important concern is that what is taken by some of the philosophers to be the eternal Pre-existent is actually not the Essence of God but, rather, the Primal Will. The philosophical discussions of origination and pre-existence, and of contingency and necessity, are based on the assumption that the Pre-existent or the Necessary Existent is the cause of the originated or contingent world. Likewise, in these theories, both the existence and the attributes of that Pre-existent and Necessary Being are inferred from the characteristics of the contingent and originated world. Some philosophers have generated a long list of attributes for God through rational deductions. In the same manner, advocates of the thesis of origination assumed that the originated character of the world was preceded by the absolute pre-existence of God, concluding that the originated was caused by the Essence.

However, the Báb argues that the Pre-existent Being that is the cause of originated being is in fact itself an originated Reality—the Primal Will, which represents the absolute Pre-existence of God in the realm of creation. Our human understanding of these realities, however, remains confined to the created realm, and does not touch the absolutely transcendental Essence of God:

> Know thou, of a certainty, that the Pre-existence of the Eternal Essence hath ever been Himself, and His Eternity is naught but His Essence. Nothing existeth besides Him, much less that it could be capable of explaining His Pre-existence. . . . Therefore, any praise made by His creation, and any description comprehended by His servants, is the outcome of their limited creation and the attributes that their minds may invent within the created realm. . . .
>
> Verily, the Source of the originated is the Primal Creation, which God hath created for Itself, by Itself; no other mention can ever be made besides It. . . .[28]

Although the Primal Will is originated, it is not originated in time; thus it transcends the limitations of time. As the Báb has emphasized in so many instances, the revelation and effulgence of the Will has always existed without any beginning or end: "There should be no doubt," He writes, "that, before this Adam, there have been infinite worlds and endless Adams in God's creation, to a degree that none besides God can, or ever will, reckon."[29]

The absolute otherness of the Essence of God implies that, contrary to the claims of philosophers, the contingent world cannot be taken as a "proof" of God, of His existence, or of His attributes. All attributes predicated of God refer to the Primal Will. Reference to these attributes in the Holy Scriptures, the Báb explains, is solely due to the limitations of the people—and such reference is made only in order to correct even worse misconceptions. In the Epistle of Justice: Root Principles, He states:

> Know thou, O seeker, that, in the books they have penned, the philosophers have brought forth arguments for the existence of a Fashioner, even as the mystics have adduced proofs for His unity. But these books

> are all refuted by the testimony of the very proofs they contain, inasmuch as the latter are all contingent, and it is impossible for the proof of the divine Essence to be contingent. Nay, rather, should anyone fix his gaze upon the Point of Truth, pierce the veils, and unravel the allusions, he would know of a certainty that to provide any argument for the existence of the Incomparable One or any proof for His unity, other than God's own description, is a cardinal sin and a most grievous transgression. Verily, I find no proof for His existence and His unity save His own self.[30]

In His answer to Mírzá Sa'íd regarding the Neoplatonic statement, "From the One proceedeth only one," the Báb explains why the arguments of the mystic philosophers also fail. The traditional understanding of this statement in Islamic philosophy was the thesis of emanation. Like Plotinus, both Fárábí and Avicenna maintained that the Essence of God is the "One" and from such an Absolute Unity nothing could issue except unity. That second "one" is the created Intellect which, although one, is potentially many. Through its contemplation of God, another intellect comes into existence, its contemplation of itself gives rise to a celestial soul, and finally its contemplation of its relation to God causes the First Heaven.[31]

The Báb's interpretation of the statement is entirely different. Although He does confirm a kind of emanation concept, He makes it clear that it is inaccurate to assume that the creator "One" is the Essence of God. Rather, both the creator "One" and the created "one" refer to the Primal Will—the "Primal Utterance" of the divine creative Action:

> Concerning thy question about the meaning of the philosopher's saying, "From the One proceedeth only One": The statement is incorrect when the Cause is meant to be the Absolute Essence. For, verily, God hath been and will continue to be independent of all things, and nothing proceedeth from Him. His eternal praise is that He begetteth not, nor is He begotten.
>
> However, when the intention behind the statement is to refer to the Primal Utterance, which is created by God by Itself, for Itself, then verily it is the truth. . . .
>
> There is no doubt that the Eternal Essence hath ever been immeasurably exalted above any association with His creatures; how much less

> could It become the source out of which things proceed. Though the statement is discussed in philosophy, the truth is that it must refer to the grades of the creative Action itself.[32]

The divine Action, as one, creates the Will as one. This unity and diversity of the subject and object leads to the creation of the phenomenal world of plurality through the causation of the Will.

One of the reflections of this dual structure of the Point as the unity of subject and object is the mysterious assertion of the Báb, found in the introductory part of the Persian Bayán, that the Will, to Whom "belong all the most excellent names . . . is the First to believe in Him Whom God shall make manifest, and He is the First Who hath believed in Him Who hath been manifested."[33] The exalted station of the Will as the supreme Origin and End of reality means that only He can truly recognize Himself. The human being who is considered to be the first believer in the Manifestation is a mere shadow of the true First Believer. Mullá Ḥusayn, the first Letter of the Living, was the first human being to believe in the Báb, but in reality he was only a reflection of that transcendental First Believer, Who was the Báb Himself:

> It is for the Will, and through the manifestation of His own Self, that God hath fashioned, out of His Self, eighteen souls, ere the creation of all things, and He hath enshrined the sign of their recognition in the inmost reality of all things that all, from the depths of their essence, may bear witness that He is the Primal Unity and the Eternal, the Ever-Abiding. . . .
>
> Know thou that He is the Supreme Mirror of God out of Whose revelation is manifested the worldly Mirror, Which is naught but the Letters of the Living, and naught is seen in that Supreme Mirror of God but God.[34]

Thus the "worldly" first believers, the Letters of the Living, are mirrors of the Point in the world and are created out of the Point, Who is the First Believer in Himself. This subtle fact, however, is usually neglected and has led to some mistaken readings of the Báb's writings.[35]

In a visitation tablet for Mullá Ḥusayn, the Báb clearly states the same point, saying that in this Day of Resurrection He has made Himself known through His divine verses. He goes on to say that "the first to know Me was I Myself, the Lord of the letters of *'Aẓím* ('Alí), then it was the possessor of eight exalted and glorious letters (Mullá Ḥusayn), and subsequently I was recognized by the glorious Guides."[36] We find this idea repeated elsewhere in the Báb's writings as well. In the Epistle on the Proofs of the Prophethood of Muḥammad, the Báb explains that true knowledge of a being is not possible for one who is devoid of the perfections of that being—for example, whiteness can only be recognized through whiteness and not through redness. The truth of the Manifestation thus can be recognized only by the Manifestation Himself and not by any human being besides Him. Therefore, He concludes, at this supreme level of recognition it is the Prophet Who is His own First Believer, and, for the same reason, in the primordial Day of the Covenant, the first to recognize Him is none other than Himself.[37]

We can see that the Báb unites the absolute transcendence of God with an utterly "mystic" orientation. Disregarding the complex unity of these aspects in His theology, however, can lead to unwarranted reductions of the Báb's teachings as representing either a merely "mystic" or a merely "ascetic" orientation. Although the Báb speaks of the sanctuary of unity or the heart as a central category of His Revelation, He is not a mystic who would reduce God to the inward level of the phenomenal manifestations. Conversely, although He emphasizes the transcendence of the divine Essence, He is not opposed to mysticism, nor does He exclude the ecstatic moment of divine experience and love. The writings of the Báb, like those of Bahá'u'lláh, confirm that God is the divine Object of mystic devotion, while asserting that the realm of the unknowable Essence is above traditional conceptions of God. The traditional conception of God has always referred to the Primal Will, the Manifestations of God. All the yearnings of the mystics thus have always referred to the Revelation of the Primal Point, and all praise and description of God will continue to point to the Manifestations of God. Therefore, a true mystic orientation must be accompanied by a clear consciousness of the limits of human experience and mystic attainment, recognizing that the summit of the human spiritual journey is the recognition of the Manifestation of God in each age.

8
The Stages of Divine Creative Action

One of the most notable features of the writings of the Báb is their emphasis on the seven stages of divine Action through which all creation comes into being. As we have seen, the phenomenal world is the mirror of its supreme Origin, but more specifically it is a reflection of divine attributes and of the divine creative Action which unfolds through a sequence of stages comprising Will (*Mas͟híyyat*), Determination (*Irádih*), Destiny (*Qadar*), Decree (*Qaḍá*), Permission (*Id͟hn*), Term (*Ajal*), and Book (*Kitáb*).[1] Elaboration of these seven stages of creation thus is a major component of the Báb's metaphysics. In various writings, the Báb describes the details of the stages of creation in order to emphasize the spiritual orientation which is the goal of His Revelation. Indeed, this purpose forms the primary context of His discussion of these stages, and the all-encompassing perspective of unity differentiates His writing from other philosophical and theological discussions on the topic.

Reference to the seven stages of creation can be found in the Traditions attributed to the Imáms. The Báb sometimes refers to these Traditions, as in this passage: "Thus, the descent of the divine Command furnisheth seven stages. Hence the Imám said, 'Nothing can exist, whether on earth or in heaven, except through the seven stages of creation: Will, Determination, Destiny, Decree, Permission, Term, and Book. Whoso denieth the necessity of even one of these stages hath repudiated God's truth.'"[2] The first author who dealt with these stages extensively was S͟hayk͟h Aḥmad-i-Aḥsá'í, whose work, *S͟harḥu'l-Favá'id*, provides a systematic discussion of them.[3] The Báb confirms many of the categories S͟hayk͟h

Aḥmad uses in his discussions of the stages, but the Báb addresses the issue within the unique context of His perspective of unity. However, the Báb reinterprets these stages in completely novel ways: the seven stages also represent the stages of the perpetual renewal of divine revelation in new Dispensations. Thus, as we will see, the concept of the stages of divine Action becomes historical as well as metaphysical.

All the seven stages of divine creative Action are diverse manifestations of the Word of God. The various aspects of all beings are reflections of the divine Action, and, in this way, all the different modes of the reality of phenomena refer ultimately to their common Ground, the revelation of God, and the Primal Will. It is not hard to see why reference to the seven stages of creation occurs so frequently in the Báb's sermons. Most of His tablets begin with an introductory sermon that affirms the spiritual nature of reality, reminding people of the unseen realm, connecting the visible phenomena to transcendental spiritual realities, and demonstrating that all beings are manifestations of Divine Unity. For example, He writes:

> Glorified and exalted is He! Verily, He hath created the Will for the exis tence of matter, and Determination for the specification of materials, and Destiny for determining the shape of inmost realities, and Decree for the confirmation (*imḍá'*) of quintessences, and Permission, Term, and Book for completing the potentialities at the level of identities, that all may recognize, by the remembrance of those stages, the due rights of the Manifestations of His Sanctity and the Signs of His Unity in the kingdom of Names and Attributes, and may comprehend that which God hath destined for them of the knowledge of the Ends and Purposes, in the infinite realms of the substances, extending unto the station of dust.[4]

Will, Determination, and Destiny as Existence, Essence, and the Link

The most often-encountered explanation of the stages of divine creative Action in the writings of the Báb addresses the conditions for the possibility of the reality of any being. For anything to exist, it must have an essence. But the essence is not sufficient for the thing to be realized. In addition to essence it must also have existence. An imaginary horse with a hundred heads and ten wings, although it might be said to have an essence (which enables it to be conceptualized), nevertheless does not exist because the essence is not accompanied by existence. Nor, conversely, can there be existence without an existent entity.

Yet neither essence nor existence can lead to the realization of a thing unless they are united together, just as the birth of a child is dependent on three elements: a father, a mother, and their union. The first stage of the process of coming into being, the stage of Will, is the source of the thing's existence; the second stage, Determination, is the source of its essence; and the third, Destiny, of their coming together. In this way, the first three stages of creation constitute the minimum conditions for the reality of any being. The last four stages involve the descent of the first three into the phenomenal world:

> For, verily, when a thing is made mention of, it becometh invested with the station of existence, and it is impossible for the thing to exist except through the station of essence, which is the agent of the acceptance of existence. And the affirmation of duality requireth the affirmation of the link between the two. And by virtue of the realization of the link in the station of the trinity, it is necessary, according to wisdom, that four further stages be realized for the descent of the Command from the Unseen Realm to the manifest world. Thus the utterance of truth requireth the affirmation of the seven stages of causation at all levels of existence.[5]

In the Báb's writings the seven stages of creation are frequently portrayed as the three plus the four stages. In the following passage, we can see that the twin aspects of divinity and servitude are fundamental to the constitution of all beings:

> The reality of all beings save God dependeth on two aspects (*jihat*). The first is the existential aspect (*jihat-i-vujúdí*) which indicateth the divine effulgence, while the second is the essential aspect (*jihat-i-máhíyyatí*), which indicateth servitude and the acceptance of that effulgence. Through the realization of both these aspects, the link of Destiny, which is the connection between these two aspects, will become manifest. And after the appearance of the three, the other four aspects are realized, for the descent of the three is impossible save through the appearance of the four. This is the reason for the seven stages of causation.[6]

Although the actualization of the possibility of a thing in the manifest world—its descent from the unseen realm to the seen realm—requires the elaboration of further details through the last four stages, all the seven stages ultimately depend upon the two primordial stages of Will and Determination. This concept is captured in the often-encountered assertion in the writings of the Báb and Bahá'u'lláh that "He doeth whatsoever He willeth and ordaineth what He pleaseth." In this statement, the words for "willeth" and "pleaseth" are the same as the first two stages of creation, Will and Determination.

The centrality of Will and Determination, as well as their union, in the creation of the universe, can be expressed figuratively as well. Bahá'u'lláh identifies the Will as the "father," Determination as the "mother," and Destiny as the product of their union: "Verily, His Will is the father of the universe, while His Determination, the mother of the children of Adam. Destiny is indeed the station of the scheme of things as ordained by God, the Fashioner of heaven, while Decree is His conclusive and mighty Command."[7] In this passage, Bahá'u'lláh presents Will and Determination not only as the first two revelations of the divine creative Action, but He also identifies them as the real meaning of the figures "Adam" and "Eve." The same point is also made by the Báb, Who often explains the Qur'ánic references to the story of Adam and Eve as symbolizing the stages of divine creative Action, for example: "The Primal Adam is the Will, Who is the Primal Utterance, manifested in the primal realm of contingency. His consort is Determination, which is the resolution regarding the Primal Utterance. . . ."[8]

The writings of the Báb explain the stages of divine creative Action in many other symbolic ways as well, but they are all parallel to the definition of Will and Determination as the agents of existence and essence. In a passage discussing the stages of creation, the Báb speaks of Will, Determination, and their union, in terms of matter and form: "For, verily, a thing hath specific aspects: the aspect of matter, the aspect of form, and the aspect of combination. When these three aspects descend, they become seven. . . . Verily, the Merciful hath alluded to these seven aspects as Seven Seas, and they are the words of God. Nothing can come into being in the heaven of receiving matter and the earth of received form save through these seven stages."[9] Occasionally in His writings the Báb describes the first stages of divine creative Action in terms of causation, equating Will, Determination, and Destiny with cause, effect, and the causal relation.[10]

The Stages of Creation and the Grammar of Language

The fundamental principle in all the Báb's discussions of the seven stages of divine creative Action is the unity of all reality: all beings, in their own ways, celebrate the divine praise, reflect the divine attributes, and manifest the heavenly realm. The Báb discusses numerous phenomena in terms of this same underlying principle, which is reflected even in the way He approaches the topic of Arabic language and grammar. In one of His works, the Treatise on Grammar (Risálah fi'n-Naḥv), He addresses the education of children with reference to grammar, reading, and arithmetic, stating that the children of the faithful should not be deprived of the delights of the new paradise that is made available to their parents, and that they should learn the Arabic language in a way that is different from traditional ways.

In this new style of education, Arabic grammar is to be taught as a symbol of spiritual grammar: children are to learn the words as symbols of the Logos, the Word of God, so that from the very beginning they will perceive all of phenomenal reality as mirrors of spiritual values. He relates both language and arithmetic to the manifestation of the Point in the form of the Báb. Although it is not possible here to discuss all the details of the Báb's reinterpretation of language and arithmetic, one of its main elements is the reinterpretation of the three categories of verb, noun, and preposition. Arabic divides all words into these three categories. A verb (*fi'l*) refers to an event, or motion, in time. A noun (*ism*) refers to a thing and makes no reference to time. A preposition (*ḥarf*) has no independent and substantive meaning but functions as a link between nouns and verbs.

The Báb interprets "verb" as a reference to the first stage of divine Action, Will, which is the source of existence. It should be noted that the word for "verb" in Arabic is the same as the word for "action." But this verb is the essence of both motion and stillness. It transcends all words and yet is the source of them all. The noun symbolizes the second stage of divine Action, Determination, which is the source of the essences of things. The preposition represents the third stage, Destiny, which unites existence and essence: "Verily, the noun is the attribute of the thing as it is in its own station. . . . But the verb referreth to the movement of that thing, and is the source of both noun and preposition. The verb, in truth, is a motionless Creation that is not defined by stillness . . . and a moving Creation that is not defined by motion. . . . As to the preposition, it is that meaning which testifieth unto naught but the link."[11]

We can see that the verb, which refers to the movement of things in time, is the unity of opposites; it is the Primal Will, the Logos, and the source of all other words. This is also manifest in the fact that in Arabic, the root of all words is their verb form, the masculine third-person singular past tense. This root is both an event in the past and a primordial constant source of all diverse combinations. The preposition is the link of Destiny, which connects the essences of things (nouns) to the revelation of God or their existence (verb).

A similar point is made in another tablet the Báb wrote in answer to a number of questions including some concerning the rules of Arabic grammar. The Báb says that He has not studied the normal science of grammar, and that the questioner must concentrate on the spiritual reality of syntax. According to Arabic grammar, there are three possible ways of pronouncing the last letter of each noun. If the noun represents the station of the subject (*fá'il*), it is in the nominative case (*marfú'*), and thus its last letter is normally pronounced by the vowel sign, *u*. If the noun represents the station of the object (*maf'úl*), it is in the accusative case (*manṣúb*), and its last letter is normally pronounced by the vowel sign *a*. But if the noun is postfixed (*muḍáfun ilayh*), it is in the genitive case (*majrúr*), and its last letter is normally pronounced by the vowel sign *i*. However, the verb root is not subject to any of these three rules. The Báb describes the three noun possibilities as reflections of the three stages of divine creative Action. Thus the nominative form represents the station of Will and the divine name "the Creator"; the accusative form refers to the station of Determination, the station of receptivity, and the divine name "the Quickener"; while the postfixed (genitive) form of the noun stands for the station of Destiny, as the link of the duality, and the divine name "the Ever-Living." Finally the verb root represents the Hidden Name of God and the higher direction of the Primal Will, sanctified beyond any mention of plurality or creation.[12]

The most extensive of these discussions can be found in a work in which the Báb answers a question regarding the education of children. He emphasizes the necessity for students to show respect and gratitude to their teachers. He also asks teachers never to show anger and harshness to their young students. He tells them that if they do not strike children and refuse to hurt their gentle hearts, God will assuredly be gentle to them. Then the Báb explains for the teachers that Arabic grammar must be understood as an expression of the seven stages of divine Action. In Arabic grammar, the past tense of the verb has fourteen possible conjugated forms. The Báb explains these fourteen forms as the hidden and manifest revelations of the seven stages of divine Action. In addition He says that the past tense of the verb represents the first stage of divine Action, Will. The present tense of the verb represents the second stage, Determination. The future form, He adds, refers to the station of Destiny.[13]

Decree and the Problem of Alteration

One of the most enigmatic issues in relation to the divine creative Action is the problem of *badá'* or alteration in the divine Will. This concept is usually understood as the non-fulfillment of divine prophecy. The belief in "alteration" in this sense has been one of the main doctrines of Shí'ih Islam, particularly for adherents of Twelver Shí'ism—distinguishing it from Ismá'ílí Shí'ism—because the imamate of the seventh Imám was itself subject to "alteration." The sixth Imám, Ja'far as-Ṣádiq (d. 148/765), had appointed his son Ismá'íl to be the seventh Imám. But when Ismá'íl died during his father's lifetime, another son replaced him as the seventh Imám. The Ismá'ílí Shí'ih, however, still hold Ismá'íl to be the seventh Imám.[14]

In Shí'ih Traditions, the problem of alteration or *badá'* appears in the context of the stages of creation as a metaphysical issue. Various Traditions state that there can be alteration in the Will of God within the first three stages of divine Action, but not after the completion of the fourth stage, Decree. Thus the first four stages of creation have a particular significance. In this sense it is the first four stages that constitute the ultimate reality of things, because once these stages are realized, there can be no further alteration. For this same reason, the completion of the stage of Decree is described as the stage of *imḍá'*, or the stage of confirmation and signature. Discussing the stages of creation, the Báb writes that until the completion of the stage of Decree, "it is incumbent upon all contingent beings . . . to acknowledge that the law of alteration (*badá'*) may transpire, through the Will of God, sanctified and exalted is He. However, there is no alteration once the Decree hath been set."[15]

In order to understand this statement, we need to pay attention to the Arabic term for "thing" or object. As also noted by Shaykh Aḥmad, the word *shay'* (thing, object) is taken to be derived from the root *shá'a*, meaning "he willed it," which is also the root of the word *mashíyyat* (will).[16] The thing, in other words, is an event of the will. The world is thus conceived as an expression of a spiritual force—the divine Will.[17]

As I have discussed in *Logos and Civilization*, the Báb reinterprets the concept of *badá'* in significant ways.[18] The first of these new meanings of alteration is the change in divine revelation, or the principle of progressive revelation. In the Persian Bayán the Báb explains:

> However, God's alteration is immeasurably exalted above any association with the alteration of His creatures. For the creatures' alteration is due to their powerlessness, whereas God's alteration is the outcome of supreme power. Therefore, in each Revelation of the Will, His alteration is manifest. Should He, in former Dispensations, destine faith and paradise for the believers, in a new Revelation He may choose to subject all to the decree of alteration and judge them to be non-believers, to reveal His absolute might. . . .[19]

He goes on to explain that the concept of alteration is not relevant to the Essence of God; it only applies to the revelation of the divine Word. In this way, alteration becomes identical with the concept of abrogation (of previous Dispensations):

> Having understood the alteration of the Eternal Essence as the alteration of the Will, and His confirmation as the confirmation of the Will, thou must gaze upon the evident alterations in each Revelation, which have ever been and will continue forever to be like unto an infinite and tempestuous ocean. Thus, all who are associated with this Revelation have witnessed such manifestations in the ocean of the Will, even as it was manifest in the Furqán by the name "abrogation."[20]

In this sense, it remains a question why alteration is not possible after the fourth stage of creation. The answer given by the Báb relates to His interpretation of the four stages of creation as the four aspects of the reality of the Manifestation of God. As we already have seen, the Will pertains to the heart of the Manifestation of God, whereas the fourth stage, the stage of Decree, corresponds to His body. The abrogation of the former religion is possible as long as the new Manifestation is alive. After the passing of the Manifestation from the world, there can be no change in the divine ordinances until the coming of the next Manifestation. As the Báb explains:

> As to that which is mentioned in certain traditions that once a thing attaineth the stage of Decree no alteration will affect it, . . . by the stage of Decree, in the pillar of magnification, is intended the ascent of the Will. From the shining morn rising from out of the pillar of glorification, until His setting at the pillar of dust, He completeth His path unto His own Self. For example, during the life of the Apostle of God, the blessings of God rest upon Him, the very act of ordaining and the manifesting of alteration remaineth the very truth, till the time of His ascension; yet, thereafter, that which is made lawful by Him remaineth lawful till the Day of Resurrection, namely His Next Revelation in His Resurrection, while that which is forbidden by Him remaineth forbidden till His Next Revelation, His own Resurrection.[21]

A second reinterpretation of the concept of *badá'* in the writings of the Báb is related to the theological question of faith and works and the inscrutability of God's judgment. The Báb discusses the question of *badá'* as a dialectic of divine justice and mercy. One may be said to have recognized the true meaning of *badá'* if one realizes that even if one has worshipped God and faithfully observed all the divine commandments during one's life, it still remains within the prerogative of God to condemn that person to hell. This doctrine does not imply that God rewards or punishes capriciously or unjustly, but rather that the acceptance of all good works, or acts of human will, is utterly dependent on God's grace and mercy. The fact that a person continues to be considered among the believers is solely due to divine mercy; at any moment God could deprive this person of faith because of His justice. Conversely, one should not feel superior to people who are without faith because at any moment they may be turned into letters of paradise through divine mercy and grace. In all these cases, faith in divine *badá'* implies the need for a sense of humility and equality, as well as perpetual self-examination. Discussing the question of contentment and acquiescence, the Báb states: "For verily a servant can never advance or ascend to the truth except through witnessing divine alteration in all its modes and conditions. Therefore, should he be the doer of all good deeds, he would still be fearful of his Lord, that He might change them into misdeeds, whenever He desireth and however He pleaseth.[22]

Thus the affirmation of *badá'* is the affirmation of the twin principles of unconstrained divine sovereignty and human servitude.[23] *Badá'* is of exceptional significance because its acceptance embodies the recognition of God's absolute power and authority and thus is the highest sign of spiritual maturity.

A third new aspect of *badá'* relates to the concept of magnification (*takbír*), as the symbol of the completion of the four layers of the divine covenant that correspond to the four stages of divine creative Action. One's faith is complete and will not be subject to alteration or negation if one believes in all four supports or pillars of the covenant. The stage of Decree, in this sense, symbolizes the fourth pillar. But one's faith is always incomplete and subject to alteration if one has only accepted three layers of the covenant but has failed to recognize the fourth.[24] As we will see in the next chapters, these levels of the covenant are realized through the Primal Unity of the Bábí Dispensation. The affirmation of divine alteration or *badá'*, therefore, is an affirmation of the inalienable unity of all the elements of the divine covenant. Breaking the covenant, by rejecting any one of its levels, deprives one of faith because in doing so one has rejected the totality of the divine covenant.

Predestination or the Question of Destiny

One of the aspects of the seven stages of divine Action most often discussed by the Báb is the question of Destiny, or *Qadar*, that is, the relation between human freedom and divine predestination. Although the issue is raised directly at the level of human action, Destiny is actually a more general metaphysical principle and applies to any event in phenomenal reality.

In philosophical terms, the question of Destiny is related to the mystery of divine Action. Is God's creative Action determined by the divine unconstrained Will, or is it dictated by the essences of things as a logical necessity? Are human actions determined by the divine Will, or are they products of human freedom? How can divine knowledge, which knows every event in advance, be compatible with human agency? How can actions be created by God yet caused by human beings? Finally, how can the essence of a thing be created by God and yet its choices— which are themselves rooted in that created essence—be *free?*

Like other philosophical discourses, Islamic philosophy has seen many divergent positions advanced on these issues. Of direct relevance to this debate is the metaphysical question discussed in a previous chapter concerning the nature of the essences of things. Usually those who believe in the eternality of the essences define divine Action as a determined event dictated by the logical necessities of those eternal essences. This position is particularly encountered in authors who find the eternal forms present in the Essence of God. The followers of Ibn 'Arabí referred to this position as the unity of existence or *existential monism*.[25] In contrast, those who emphasize the created and originated nature of the essences usually advocate the absolute freedom and agency of divine Action, holding that there is only one real cause and that is God. This perspective defines human action as determined by the divine creative Action. The Muslim Ash'arites were among this group.[26] Shaykh Aḥmad also addressed these issues in various writings, emphasizing the reality of human freedom while arguing for the originated character of phenomenal reality.[27]

For the Báb, the fact that creation belongs to the realm of divine creative Action, and not to the Essence of God, has far-reaching implications for the metaphysical question of freedom. The Báb frequently speaks of the difficulty and complexity of the nature of Destiny; in many of the tablets in which He addresses the topic, He refers the reader to the Commentary on the Letter Há' (Tafsír-i-Há'). There He explains:

> Indeed, all who have endeavoured to explain the problem of Destiny have advocated either absolute divine determinism or human choice, and thus all the philosophers have confessed their powerlessness to explain the truth of this question. Indeed, this verily is the truth, inasmuch as the philosophers wanted to explain the divine truth, the Middle Path between absolute determinism and absolute freedom, by proofs of reason, which is, however, impossible. For, verily, reason, even in its utmost level of abstraction, is confined to understanding mere limited phenomena, which fail to guide humans unto the summit of the delight of their heart. Thus, he who abideth upon the throne of the kingdom of reason hath no recourse but to believe in either absolute determinism or absolute freedom.[28]

According to the Báb, when we are confronting the unconditional realm of infinity—in this case, the mystery of divine creation—we must approach the issue from the perspective of the heart, and with the eye of unity, for it is only with this orientation that we can understand that the oppositions which apply to the phenomenal realm (as in the two mutually contradictory philosophical positions discussed) do not apply in the unseen realm of higher reality. The Báb writes: "[T]hat which is beyond these two extremes, which is the Middle Path . . . can be comprehended by naught save the heart. God hath created the heart to understand His unity and transcendence, and it is through the heart that Divine Unity can be witnessed at the level of action."[29]

As the Báb mentions in the passage quoted earlier, usually the various theological schools have either affirmed human freedom at the expense of divine eternal creation, or advocated an absolute perpetual divine creation and determination at the expense of human agency. The Báb maintains that both these positions are inadequate and remote from the truth. The basic error in these traditional approaches is that they posit an absolute opposition between divine determination and phenomenal choice. Confirming the truth of a Shí'ih Tradition attributed to Imám Ṣádiq, the Báb explains that it is the simultaneous truth of both divine determination and human freedom which is the true "Middle Path." The stages of divine creative Action are a testimony to this truth: all things come into being through the conjunction of Will and Determination, existence and essence, the divine effulgence and the thing's receptivity, divine determination and free choice.

Thus, according to the Báb, God has created not only human beings but all things in such a way that freedom is inherent in their very nature: it is embedded in their reality as a part of the process of creation. God has created human beings with freedom and has enabled them to be shaped in time in accordance with their own decisions and choices—for which they are inevitably accountable.

But how is God's omniscience compatible with human freedom? The logical error (a false analogy) has always been to assume that God's knowledge is the same as, or comparable to, human knowledge. But in fact divine knowledge cannot be compared to human knowledge: God's knowledge is not an event in time, and it is not bound by the phenomenal, temporal logic of human knowledge. The divine knowledge of events before and after their occurrence is one and the same thing. It is thus a logical fallacy to deny human freedom on account of God's omniscience.

As the Báb makes clear, the relation of divine causation and knowledge to human action cannot be comprehended within the categories of human reason. Reason's attempts to apply the logic of phenomenal causation and knowledge to the realm of divine causation and knowledge are erroneous and futile. All human actions are supremely determined by divine Action, while they are simultaneously the product of human free will. At the level of divine creative Action, the first is the same as the last, and before is exactly the same as after.

The Báb frequently mentions the mystery of Destiny in the context of bearing witness to Divine Unity at the level of actions (*tawḥíd-i-af'ál*). According to Him, one must bear witness to Divine Unity at four levels: unity of essence, unity of attributes, unity of action, and unity of worship. The first act affirms the absolute transcendence of the divine Essence. The second emphasizes the unity of the divine attributes and the divine Essence, meaning that none can understand the divine attributes. The third pertains to the realm of divine Action. Here all events in the world, including human actions, are subject to absolute divine sovereignty. Finally, the fourth act implies that none can be worshipped except God. With respect to the third act, concerning the realm of divine Action, the Báb declares that "verily, the feet of all have slipped in their understanding of that Middle Path that streameth between the dual paths, the mystery of Destiny. It is through this station that the servants declare the unity of their Creator in the realm of actions." The Báb explains that the knowledge of the secret of Destiny is concealed from the people:

> Thus 'Alí, peace be upon Him, said: "Verily, Destiny is a mystery among the mysteries of God and a guarded fort among His preserved fortresses. It is veiled within the exalted veil of God, wrapped up away from the eyes of the creatures, sealed by the divine seal, and unreachable in the knowledge of God. Thus, God hath unburdened humans from its knowledge, and destined it to be exalted above their testimonies and the limits of their minds. . . . It is a bountiful, surging ocean, which belongeth solely to God, exalted be His name and glory! Its fathomless depths extend between the heavens and the earth, its width between the East and the West. It is dark as the dusky night, filled with whales and serpents. At one time it riseth and at another it falleth. In its depths there shineth a Sun. It behooveth none to fathom its mystery except the One, the Incomparable."[30]

But then the Báb explains the mystery of Destiny as follows:

> And the truth of this mystery is that none can behold the manifestation of the Action of God, as it befitteth Him, save through the very manifestation of the free choice of the things themselves. . . . Verily, at the time of action, the human being is the agent, who acteth by virtue of the Destiny-ordaining Action of the All-Knowing, the All-Informed. . . . Indeed, that free choice is bound to the existence of each thing, and naught is called into existence except through its free choice. Verily, at the primordial moment of choice, when God said unto the thing, "Am I not your Lord?" it would not have replied, "Yea," had it been deprived of freedom of choice.[31]

The Báb's interactive approach to human action is reflected in His reinterpretation of an Islamic Tradition which is usually taken as a definitive argument for total determinism. The Tradition says: "The wicked is wicked in the womb of his mother, and the just is just in the womb of his mother." The literal meaning of this Tradition seems to deny any sense of human freedom. But the Báb interprets this Tradition in a way that indicates an interaction between the divine effulgence and human choice:

> It is in the station of Destiny that pluralities appear, lights are distinguished from shadows, and essences are differentiated from attributes. It is by virtue of this station that the wicked becometh wicked on account of his free choice, and the just becometh just, through the grace of God, on account of his free choice. Thus Destiny is "the womb of the pure realm of contingency" and "the most great depth". . . . Verily, the reason for the manifestation of these distinctions in the station of Destiny is the very manifestation of freedom inasmuch as, verily, naught cometh into being in the world save through its own free choice. Though it is created free even in the station of the Will, its freedom is not reckoned by anyone except the Subtile, the All-Perceiving. The same is true with regard to the second station, for the aspect of the acceptance of good and evil is the third station, which cannot appear except after the union of the previous two stations [Will and Determination].[32]

In the Báb's interpretation of the Tradition, the "womb of his mother" is the station of Destiny, where freedom is manifested through the "marriage" of existence and essence. As noted before, all reality is the product of the union of Will and Determination, or, symbolically, "Adam" and "Eve." Together they create all the pluralities. Through that interaction, the faithful become differentiated from the faithless. Destiny is thus the realm of the conjunction of the divine effulgence and human receptivity and free choice. It is only at this station that freedom can manifest itself. In other words, the "womb of the mother" refers to the active choice of humans at the moment of the interaction of their existence and essence. The divine effulgence represents divine absolute determinism, and the essence of the thing represents its absolute freedom. It is however, only after the marriage of the two that the child of the Middle Path is created in the womb of the contingent world.

'Abdu'l-Bahá has also interpreted that same Tradition and has identified it as a reference to the realm of divine knowledge, a knowledge which neither precedes nor follows the reality of the things, for it is identical with their occurrence.[33] Thus divine omniscience does not contradict human agency and causal efficacy. Both divine determinism and human freedom are simultaneously true. The link between the two is the fact that God has created human beings with freedom. That divine determinism, therefore, is the very source which has made human freedom possible.

In the Tradition mentioned earlier, Imám 'Alí had described Destiny as "a bountiful, surging ocean, which belongeth solely to God, exalted be His name and glory! Its fathomless depths extend between the heavens and the earth, its width between the East and the West. It is dark as the dusky night, filled with whales and serpents. At one time it riseth and at another it falleth. In its depths there shineth a Sun. . . ." The Báb explains that this infinite ocean is more extended than the heaven of divine effulgence and the earth of receptive essences. It is the pure realm of contingency. It is "dark" because reason is unable to fathom its hidden mystery. However, in its depths shines the "sun" of the heart. It is through the perspective of the heart, seeing with the eye of God, that its truth can become manifest. "At one time it riseth"—that is, it is oriented toward the divine effulgence—"and at another it falleth"—that is, it is oriented toward the essence of the thing itself.[34] It is this surging and falling ocean that defines the reality of human action, the Middle Path between the two extremes.

The true Destiny of all things is the free choice of the good. All human beings are created capable of that choice, and the purpose of creation is the unity of that choice with the attainment of spiritual qualities and the recognition of God. In other words, when freedom is accompanied by the choice of the good, the end and purpose of creation—its true destiny—is realized. For humans to attain this destiny requires turning toward the divine effulgence and annihilating their own will in the Will of God. At that time their essences are as pure mirrors in which divine revelation is manifestly shining. That station is the station of the heart, the very station that makes possible the understanding of the secret of Destiny.[35]

9
The Epistle of Justice and the Root Principles of Religion

ALTHOUGH MANY WRITINGS OF THE BÁB discuss His metaphysics of the Primal Will, the Epistle of Justice: Root Principles (Ṣaḥífiy-i-'Adlíyyih) is entirely devoted to that topic and can thus be considered to exemplify the second stage of the Báb's writings. This chapter will briefly introduce the basic structure and discuss the content of this representative and important text.

At the beginning of the Epistle itself the Báb explains the occasion for its writing, indicating that it was set down in early 1262 (1846). Within the text, the Báb mentions a work titled Commentary on the Occultation Prayer (Sharḥ-i-Du'á'-i-Ghaybat), which we know was also written in the early to middle part of the first month (Muḥarram) of 1262.[1] Yet, the listing of the Báb's works in the Khuṭbiy-i-Dhikríyyih, written on Muḥarram 15, makes no mention of the Epistle of Justice. We can thus conclude that the Epistle of Justice was written after that date, most likely during the second half of Muḥarram 1262 (January 13–28, 1846). It was followed shortly thereafter by another, related work entitled the Epistle of Justice: Branches, which deals with the derivative, secondary laws of religion.

The Epistle of Justice represents three major transitions in the Báb's mission. First, the writing of this work is part of the gradual termination of the Báb's intentional withdrawal from communication with His followers which was initially to last for five years, and the beginning of the time when He answered the believers' questions more frequently. Second, although during this stage of His mission the Báb continues to present His true station in coded and ambiguous terms, He provides a consistent explication of His actual claim through a more direct elucidation of the meaning of His title, the Báb. Therefore, the Epistle of Justice, like many other works that belong to the second stage, emphasizes the meaning of the letter Há' and its equivalence with the word *Báb*. Finally, the Epistle of Justice represents a major step toward making the Báb's message accessible to all the people of Iran.

Until this point, the Báb had revealed all His major works in Arabic, the language of revelation in the Islamic Dispensation. The Epistle of Justice was the first major work He revealed in Persian. The first chapter, in which the Báb explains the context and purpose of the text, is one of the most difficult and enigmatic sections of the Epistle of Justice, and it requires some clarification.

The Báb begins by stating that by the time He returned to Shiraz from Mecca in mid-1261 (June 1845), the revelation of His true divine knowledge, through His books and epistles, had rendered the divine testimony complete and conclusive for all people. But after His return, during the time of His sorrow and isolation, He received many letters from learned individuals who indicated that the unlearned were unable to sufficiently grasp the knowledge contained in His Arabic writings.[2] But, He continues, "inasmuch as the divine Confirmation had not yet decreed the fulfillment of their wish for the revelation of Persian divine words in this lucid religion, all were referred to the First Learned One of the First Book." Mullá Ḥusayn, the Gate to the Gate, had been responsible for explaining the Báb's Arabic writings to other believers, and when the Báb withdrew from contact with His followers, He referred them to Mullá Ḥusayn to answer their questions as well.

Then the Báb makes a most enigmatic statement. He says: "Until the time when, by the leave of God, the dawning of the Sun of trysting shone forth, out of the horizon of darksome night, upon the letters Sín and Bá', in the sacred year 1262."[3] This unique time of "the most great celebration and the most mighty bounty," the Báb continues, coincided with the arrival of a letter written by "the most excellent amongst the noble ones and the most beloved of the people of the world," who confessed his utmost powerlessness and poverty and beseeched the Báb for guidance. The Báb then states that He has decided to fulfill the questioner's wish, "for the sake of the Truth, that all the people of the world, whether learned or not, may, by virtue of His Servant, vibrate out of the vibration of the

Morn of Eternity from the Sun of the Muḥammadan Primal Light, the blessings of God rest upon Him."[4]

A careful reading of these passages makes it clear that the Báb is speaking here about various stages of His Revelation in the terms of the Tradition of Truth. Thus during the first years of the Báb's Revelation (1260 and 1261)—which correspond to the introductory part of the Tradition, in which 'Alí refuses to grant Kumayl's request for an explanation of truth—the Báb does not reveal any work in Persian or fulfill the believers' requests. Instead He designates Mullá Ḥusayn to answer their questions. Then the year 1262 arrives, the time of the first public revelation of truth in the Tradition. In this year the "Sun of trysting" shines forth upon the "letters Sín and Bá,'" or the "veils of glory." The word "veils" (*subuḥát*) begins with Sín and Bá', which numerically equal 62. Thus the first public reflection of truth, in the form of the revelation of this work, that is, "Pierc[ing] the veils of glory," is taking place in 1262.[5]

The Title of the Text

The topic of the Epistle of Justice is the root principles of religion and their distinction from the derivative laws. But, one may wonder, why would a book on the root principles of religion be titled the Epistle of *Justice?*

The concept of justice plays a fundamental role throughout the writings of the Báb. The word *'adlíyyih,* in the title of the Epistle of Justice, can be translated variously as "justice," "the just," and "adherents of divine justice." And indeed, the references to justice in the Báb's writings imply a complex of interrelated meanings. First, the idea of justice refers to the reality of true Islam. The Báb often calls the Imáms the "Imáms of Justice" (*A'immatu'l-'adl*). The term *'adlíyyih* also refers to the distinct theological doctrine that elevates divine justice to the rank of a root principle of the Faith, and which is the distinguishing mark of Shí'ih Islam. The Epistle of Justice thus is a discourse on the root principles of true Islam.

But the reference to justice in the Epistle of Justice implies many other layers of meaning as well. One of its primary implications is the Báb's station as the Qá'im. According to numerous Islamic Traditions, in an idea that constitutes the heart of Shí'ih millenarianism, the advent of the Qá'im will initiate an age of justice in the world after it has undergone a period of oppression and injustice. These words of the Báb, then, are the words of justice, and His Revelation is nothing less than that long-awaited advent of true justice in the world.

The arrival of the Qá'im was expected to take place shortly before the Day of Judgment. The Qur'án contains vivid descriptions of divine justice on that fateful Day, when the straight path of God would be outstretched and the divine Balance would separate the wicked from the righteous. The gates of heaven and hell would be thrown open to all humanity and each soul would receive the just reward of its actions. The Báb's references to Himself in the Qayyúmu'l-Asmá' and other writings as the "Straight Path," the "Balance," the "Word of God," and the like, can be seen as signifying that He Himself is the manifestation of that promised divine justice in the world, the One whose Revelation and whose Word separate the damned from the blessed, and create the paradise of divine knowledge for the righteous and the hell of remoteness for the wicked.

However, the term "justice" in the title of the Epistle is most directly an affirmation of the doctrine of Destiny. As we saw in the previous chapter, Destiny as the third stage of divine creative Action represents the realm of pure contingency, where the basic preconditions for the reality of things are fulfilled. As we also saw, Destiny is characterized by the conjunction and linking of existence and essence, divine effulgence and human free choice, or divine Action and human receptive acceptance. This point is crucial for reading the Epistle of Justice. The Báb identifies the root principles of religion with the stages of divine creative Action—primarily the triad of Will, Determination, and Destiny. The comprehension of the mystery of Destiny, however, as has been said, is possible only if one has attained the elevated perspective of the sanctuary of the heart, has transcended the realm of limitations, and has discerned the supreme Origin of all things as the unifying principle within all phenomenal reality. The Epistle of Justice, then, is actually a discourse on the sanctuary of the heart and an exposition of Divine Unity. The principle of justice becomes identical with the principle of Divine Unity, the sanctuary of unity, and the perspective of the heart.

Thus the question of justice becomes the question of the necessity of divine guidance. Human beings are created to recognize the Divine Unity, but as it is impossible for the creatures to do so at the level of the Essence, Divine Unity must be manifested in the phenomenal world in ways that are accessible to human comprehension. Divine justice then requires the presence of divine guidance in the world so that people will have access to divine knowledge. Thus the various layers of divine mediation and guidance are the various levels of the root principles of religion. The doctrine of justice then becomes an affirmation of the truth of the agents of that guidance—the Manifestation of God, the vicegerents of the Prophet (the Imáms), and the mediators between the vicegerent and the people (the Gates).

But the most important meaning of "justice" is the station of the Báb Himself. The three letters of the word *Báb* symbolize the three stages of divine Action, which are the true fulfillment of divine justice. The Báb's name, 'Alí, is another expression of these three stations. In fact, the root principle of religion is none other than recognition of the Báb, Who appeared as the Gate to the Imám even though His station of gatehood contained the truth of all the layers of divine manifestation. The Epistle of Justice is in fact a subtle commentary on the word *Báb,* which is the same as the mystery of the letter Há'. In this sense, the Epistle of Justice should be seen as inseparable from three other writings of the Báb that discuss the letter Há': the Commentary on the Letter Há' (Tafsír-i-Há'), the Commentary on the Mystery of Há' (Tafsír-i-Sirr-i-Há'), and the Interpretation of the Letter Há' (Commentary on the Occultation Prayer).

The Structure of the Text and the Word "Báb"

Before addressing the substantive content of the Epistle of Justice, it is necessary to consider its structure and order. The text is about forty pages long in its printed format and consists of five chapters. Each chapter is called a *báb,* meaning a gate as well as a chapter.

The connection mentioned between the Epistle of Justice and the Báb's three other works on the letter Há' is directly relevant to the structure of the Epistle of Justice. As we know, five is a significant number, the numerical equivalent of Há', the first letter of *Huva* (He), which signifies the transcendental realm of Divine Unity. Since the Epistle of Justice is a discourse on the root principles of religion, and since these root principles all derive from the principle of the unity of God, the text is divided into five chapters. At the same time, each of these chapters is a *báb,* or gate, of Divine Unity. Taken together, these five chapters constitute the word *Báb*. This identity of symbols already conveys the fundamental substantive thesis of the text: the root principle of religion is the recognition of

Divine Unity, and that is the same as recognition of the Manifestation of Divine Unity in the world—the Báb. The identification of the letter Há' and the word *Báb* is made within the text itself. In the third chapter we find:

> They [the nobles], through the assistance bestowed upon them by the chiefs, all lead the people unto the divine grace, both in the realms of Creation and Revelation. As to their distinguishing sign, these nobles are the devoted ones who are associated with that supreme Word that is the lightest word in the realm of utterance. Nay, rather, the number of the letter Há', which is the inner secret of all the letters and the mystery of Divine Unity, is the number of that "good word," which is naught but the very revelation of the letter Há' in the realm of the letters.[6]

Here the Báb says that the "lightest" Word is the same as the Qur'ánic "good word" which is likened to the goodly tree and the Word of divine revelation. Its number is that of the letter Há'.[7] That the word in question is *Báb* becomes even clearer when we see that in another passage the Báb says: "No word is revealed in the Book of God, in terms of the simplicity of its letters, that is lighter than the word *Báb*. This is a guiding evidence of the inner secret of this Cause."[8] As is evident there, He finds *Báb,* as the lightest word, to be the inner secret of the letter Há', the secret of Divine Unity, and "the inner secret of this Cause." In order to better understand these connections, we need to consider the Báb's more extensive explanation of this "lightest word" in the Commentary on the Letter Há':

> Verily, the letter Há' is the essence of all the letters and the utmost remembrance of servitude for the Best Beloved. In the realm of the letters, verily it referreth to the Letter of the Crimson Elixir, which purifieth all the words, tokens, signs, and allusions. By virtue of this letter, Divine Unity is affirmed and the realm of pluralities is negated. Verily, those endued with true understanding recognize the truth of all the worlds through the symbolism of this letter, for that which is there cannot be known except through that which is here.
>
> The letter Há' is the number of that word which is the lightest Word revealed by God in the Qur'án. That letter is identical with that Word in all its outward manifestations and inward meanings. For, verily, the root principle of letters is the point, and when the point unfoldeth, it appeareth as the letter Alif (*A*), and when the letter Alif submitteth unto its Lord,

> it becometh the letter Bá' (*B*), which is the same as the very letter of Alif, and thus the point is set beneath the letter Bá'. Verily that Word is naught but the upright Alif between the two Bá's. That referreth to the Cause of God between the Twin Names. . . . Thus God hath not ordained for this Word, unlike the other words, any half, third, or fourth measure, for it is the Manifestation of the everlasting Light, and naught proceedeth from it.[9]

In this passage, the Báb explains that *Báb* represents the inner and outer truth of Divine Unity (divinity and servitude). The word consists of the most simple letters—an Alif (*A*) between two Bá's (*B*'s). The "upright Alif" refers to the creative divine Command, the divine Cause which is manifested through the Twin Names, "'Alí" and "Muḥammad." Alif is written as a vertical line, while Bá is written as a horizontal line with a point beneath it. The Báb is indicating that the horizontal nature of the Bá as well as the presence of the point beneath it symbolize the station of servitude. Additionally, the stations of vicegerency and prophethood are united in the Báb, Who is the upright Alif, the Qá'im, and Who also appears in the station of gatehood. Since the Báb is the Manifestation of Divine Unity, and since nothing else proceeds out of the divine Essence, the word *Báb* also represents an indivisible unity.

It should be noted here that *Báb* is defined in the passage above as the totality of the stages of the creative divine effulgence. In other words, the Báb represents the various stages of divine Action, from the point to the Alif to the Bá'. As we shall see, this is the same as the root principles of religion in the Epistle of Justice. The essential idea being conveyed is that the entire structure of the root principles is embodied in the being of the Báb Himself. The same concept is emphasized in other ways in the Interpretation of the Letter Há', which discusses the fundamental verities of religion, including the doctrines of the divine Essence, Names, Attributes, and Action, through an interpretation of the divine name *Huva* (He). The Há (*H*) in *Huva* refers to the Hidden Mystery of God. *Huva* is equal to 11, and the Báb's name, 'Alí, is equal to 110. Thus it is that the letter Há' (or 5) is the "inner secret" of 11. Therefore, the word *Báb* is the twin Alifs, the Twin Ones—referring to the Báb's dual station of divinity and servitude, the *A'lá* (the Most Exalted) and the *Adná* (the Lowest, or "even closer"). We can see how what is being described corresponds to the station of the Point. Discussing the five stations of divine

Action and revelation in the world, the Báb writes: "The fifth station testifieth unto God in the mirror of the Letter Há', and it is the Word that consisteth of the Twin Alifs. It is by virtue of the first Alif that it soareth unto the supreme cloud of the Essence, the station of 'There is none other God than *Him,*' while through the other Alif it descendeth unto the heaven of vicegerency, the station of 'He is the Most Great *'Alí.*'"[10]

A New Approach to the Root Principles

The five root principles of religion in Shí'ih theology are usually enumerated as Divine Unity, prophethood, the imamate, divine justice, and the Day of Resurrection. It should be noted that the usual Shí'ih conception of the root principles as the five pillars of the Faith is different from the five pillars of Sunní Islam. Shí'ih Islam distinguishes the root principles, which are the articles of faith, from the derivative laws or the main ordinances and laws of the religion. Sunní Islam, in contrast, defines the root principles as a series of deeds which begins with the act of testifying to the articles of faith, and continues with specific laws of Islam—prayer, fasting, alms, and pilgrimage. In other words, what for Sunnís is the first root principle of the Faith is equivalent to the Shí'ih root principles, whereas the other Sunní root principles are defined by the Shí'ih as derivative laws. The Sunní act of testifying, however, does not contain the two principles of divine justice and the imamate, which are distinctively Shí'ih.

Since the Epistle of Justice concerns the fundamental principles of the Faith and contains five chapters, one might expect these chapters to be devoted to discussion of the five root principles of Shí'ih Islam. That expectation, however, is not confirmed by the Báb's text; the chapters are organized in accordance with an entirely different logic, and the five Shí'ih root principles are replaced by a very different system.

The first chapter or gate is titled "On the Remembrance of God, Exalted Be His Name and Glory" and is an introductory chapter which praises God and discusses the context of the revelation of the text. The second chapter, "On the Exposition of This, that the Balance is Dependent on the Command of God . . . ," deals with the methodology of the discourse on the root principles of religion, or what can be called the root of the root principles. The third, "On the Recognition of God and the Recognition of His Chosen Ones, as Ordained by the Command of God . . . ," contains the discussion of the root principles of religion. The fourth chapter, "On the Day of Return to God . . . ," concerns the Day of Resurrection, which is treated as a principle derived from the root principles, but not a root principle by itself. The fifth chapter, "On the Prayer of Devotion unto God . . ." is a prayer testifying to the root principles discussed in the preceding chapters.

Because the Epistle of Justice was written during the period when the Báb was proclaiming His true station in veiled and symbolic language, it discusses the root principles in a unique manner, using traditional Shí'ih categories but in a way that revolutionizes them. The immediate background context of the work is the Shaykhí discourse about the root principles of religion. In various writings, Shaykh Aḥmad and his disciple Siyyid Káẓim had appeared to emphasize a new conception of the root principles, one which consisted of four principles: Divine Unity, prophethood, the imamate, and gatehood. This discussion remains largely implicit in their writings, although it is unmistakable.[11] The Báb makes the principle explicit and fundamentally transforms it.

Although a chapter of the Epistle of Justice is devoted to a discussion of the Day of Resurrection, the Báb makes it clear that this principle is not one of the root principles. Rather, it is derived from them: "O questioner! Know thou that the root principle of religion is the recognition of that seven ordained in the Tradition, while the principles regarding the Day of Resurrection and Return unto God are inscribed beneath its shadow. Nay, rather, these seven stages of recognition are the truth of the seven holy heavens and the very principle of return to God in the next world."[12] In this passage, the Báb is saying that the Day of Resurrection should be understood in a new manner, in which heaven and hell are the states of recognition or non-recognition of God. Although in the Epistle of Justice the Báb discusses this novel and revolutionary idea in the context of the Shaykhí approach to the concept of Resurrection, the birth of the new principle is unmistakable. As we will see, this principle will be elaborated in detail in the third stage of the Báb's writings.

The passage also indicates that the root principles of religion are now being defined as the seven stages of the recognition of God. Yet, although we are presented with seven categories of recognition as the root principles—an approach which is compatible with the normal fourfold definition of the principles of the covenant—the Báb's discourse on these principles is characterized by many turns and complexities. More specifically, He identifies the meta-principle from which the root principles are derived. That meta-principle is the revelation of the divine Command, divine Cause, and divine Will in His own being and words. And He makes it clear that all these stages of recognition are realized within and through His own reality. Thus all the root principles of religion return to the recognition of the Báb, or the "mystery of the letter Há'."

The second chapter of the Epistle of Justice is devoted to the discussion of that meta-principle of the root principles; thus the second chapter is even more important than the third chapter because it unveils the foundation on which the root principles are constructed, a foundation which defines the eternal basis of faith. The third chapter discusses the manifestation of that meta-principle in the Dispensation of Islam. While the Báb discusses the root principles in the terms of the Islamic Dispensation, His emphasis on the meta-principle unmistakably points to the expressions of the root principles in His own Dispensation.

The Root of the Root Principles

In the second chapter of the Epistle of Justice, the Báb begins with the meta-principle of the root principles of religion, discussing the divine Balance or Standard (*Qisṭás*) and defining it as the Will of God and His Command. This methodical discussion of the Balance fulfills two functions. First, it establishes that God's Will is the sovereign source of authority to determine what constitutes the root principles of faith. Moreover, that Will is not static: as human capacities evolve, the divine Will determines the root principles in new forms in each age. The Báb explains that what was the root principle in one Dispensation, or stage of spiritual evolution, becomes a derivative principle in the following Dispensation.[13] Although He does not discuss the doctrine of progressive revelation as such here, the presence of its spirit is unmistakable, although couched in veiled terms. But because He discloses His own truth in accordance with the evolving capacity of His audience, that message, implicit in the Epistle of Justice, will become explicit in the later stages of His writings.

This takes us to the second function of the Báb's discourse on the concept of the Balance. Here He is speaking of the measure or standard by means of which the truth of His own authority can be conclusively determined. In other words, the second chapter is simultaneously a discourse on the nature of the conclusive testimony and proof of the truth of the Báb's Revelation. Understanding this chapter of the Epistle of Justice is dependent on comprehending the inner unity of these two functions. If the meta-principle of the root principles is the Will of God, then the discourse on the root principles must hinge on recognition of the representative of that Will, the Manifestation and bearer of the divine Revelation. To know the supreme Standard that determines the root principles depends on recognizing the Báb as the Speaking Book, the Manifestation of God in this age, for it is the words of the Báb, as the embodiment of the divine Cause, that now define the root principles. Thus, prior to any discussion of the root principles of religion, the methodology by which one can recognize the Word of God, the Remembrance of God, and the divine Balance must be established.

The unity of these two functions defines the form and the content of the second chapter of the Epistle of Justice. This meta-discourse concentrates on the changing character of the capacities of humanity and, consequently, the changing character of the conclusive testimony of the truth of the Manifestation of God. The essence of this discussion is that humanity has now arrived at the beginning of a new age: human spiritual culture has evolved from the stage of the "body" through that of "soul," to that of "intellect," and has arrived at the stage of the "heart." Humanity is now ready to receive a revelation based on the sanctuary of unity. This fact has far-reaching consequences for the root principles of religion, as well as for the testimony of the truth of the Báb's cause. The first of these topics is discussed in the third chapter of the Epistle of Justice, and we can now clearly see why such a discussion cannot be the same as traditional definitions of the root principles.

The discussion of the second topic, the testimony that vindicates the Báb's truth, is carried out in the second chapter. The Báb explains this issue in terms of the evolution of human spiritual receptivity from more physical and concrete, lower levels ("body") to the highest spiritual level ("heart"). The nature of what constitutes vindicating testimony or proof parallels this development. In this Day, the conclusive testimony of the new Prophet is no longer physical miracles and prodigious signs, as in the past, but solely the transcendent glory of the revelation of divine truth in the form of divine words and verses. It is the immaterial mystic wisdom of heavenly truth, expressed in the body of words, that constitutes the supreme testimony of God in the Day of the Báb.

The Báb explains that the seed of religion was conceived in the Dispensation of Adam. But as the capacities of the people have progressed, so has the religion of God. By the time of the Báb, the people had developed rationally and had become prepared to receive the effulgence of the sanctuary of unity; but without the divine effulgence they were lost in infinite contentions and disputes. It was at this time that, by virtue of divine mercy, God sent the Báb to reveal the sanctuary of the heart, the mystery of true religion, and to bring unity to the chaos of conflicting opinions.[14]

Since humanity has become ready to receive divine revelation at a higher, more spiritual level, the signs of vindication are correspondingly more spiritual:

> Just as the root principles of religion and its faithful people have progressed beyond the physical realm, the divine signs have also infinitely advanced beyond the limited physical realm. Thus, it is supremely necessary that the testimony of that Servant should belong to the realm that surpasseth the world of intellect, which is naught but the stations of true recognition and transcendent unity. Yet, inasmuch as the acknowledgement of such an exalted Cause is difficult for most people, He hath brought these mighty stations to the level of the body of words, in such wise that none hath the power to produce the like thereof, so that the divine testimony would be as conclusive to all beings as the Day-Star shining in the zenith of heaven.[15]

In this new age, the Báb explains, physical miracles are no longer the conclusive testimony of the Prophet; those who ask for miracles are merely testifying to the immaturity of their own spiritual level. It was because the revelation of divine verses is the most conclusive and incontrovertible evidence of divine power that the Qur'án was the most conclusive evidence of Muḥammad's truth, and for the same reason throughout the Qur'án it is stated that should all men join together to attempt to produce verses like those of the Qur'án, they would be unable to do so. In the Dispensation of Islam, He continues, it took twenty-three years for the Qur'án to be revealed by an Arab Prophet, but in the

Dispensation of the Báb in a few days an equivalent amount of divine verses has been produced by a Persian Prophet untutored in the conventional learning of His time.[16]

The Báb's discourse on the conclusive testimony of God is a call to the people to realize their latent spiritual capacities, to attain the sanctuary of the heart, and to behold the Supreme Origin of all phenomenal reality in the Primal Will of God. Because this is the age of the sanctuary of the heart, the testimony of God now takes the form nearest to that supreme Origin: the direct revelation of God, the revelation of divine verses the reality of which is the heart of the Primal Will. This point is emphasized in all the later writings of the Báb.

But the Báb is also invested with other modes of divine revelation, each of which constitutes another conclusive testimony. He now speaks of three of these signs: the revelation of prayers, sermons, and rational arguments. The Báb identifies all these forms with His own Revelation, while attesting that each of these modes was the testimony of the truth of different sacred beings in the Dispensation of Islam. Divine verses proved the truth of Muḥammad; prayers were frequently cited as the proof of the Imáms; while sermons and rational arguments were taken as the signs of true knowledge.[17] The fact that all these modes are united in the Revelation of the Báb reflects His unique station. Although all these points clearly explain His true station, the Epistle of Justice—apparently for the sake of wisdom—emphasizes the Báb's servitude as compared to the prophethood of Muḥammad or the vicegerency of the Imáms. But no perceptive reader can fail to discern the sovereignty that is shining through that servitude.

Discussing the prophecies concerning His Revelation, the Báb refers to a Tradition attributed to Imám 'Alí, announcing the glad tidings of the dawning of the moon in the east. Here, once again the Báb is disclosing the true station of His own Revelation.[18] The east of course is the dawning place of the sun, not the moon. But in the Revelation of the Báb, the moon will shine forth from the east. Just as His name unites the "sun" of prophethood (Muḥammad) and the "moon" of vicegerency ('Alí), in His Revelation these two stations are joined together. In other words, this is the stage in which servitude and divinity are united in the sanctuary of the heart.

The Root Principle and Destiny

The third chapter of the Epistle of Justice, the longest section of the book, is devoted to a substantive discussion of the root principles of religion. Since this is the age of the sanctuary of the heart, the root principle of faith in this age is also an affirmation of spiritual knowledge in the sanctuary of unity. Although this principle is explained in terms of its diverse manifestations, its essence is described in the first paragraph of the chapter:

> Know thou that the essence of religion is the knowledge of God. The perfection of this knowledge is belief in His unity. The perfection of this belief is the negation of all names and attributes before His sanctified Essence. And the perfection of this negation is to immerse oneself with certain knowledge in the Ocean of oneness and to witness one's attainment to its bounty. And the truth underlying all these stages is the Sign of God alone, whereby the existence of the Lord of might and glory is recognized and known with certitude.[19]

In that paragraph, the Báb summarizes the essence of His discourse on the root principles. There is in reality only one root principle and that is the recognition of God, the recognition of Divine Unity. But as direct recognition of God is impossible, that recognition is actually recognition of the fact that an absolute separation exists between God and the creatures. Thus recognition of God is really recognition of God's grace as the divine Reality that connects the creatures to the divine realm. This grace is, first, the Primal Utterance of God—the Primal Will, the supreme Origin and End of all things—and, second, the revelation of the Primal Will within each being. Recognition of the Manifestation of the Primal Will and beholding reality with the eye of the heart in the sanctuary of unity constitute recognition of God. Consequently, recognition of the Báb as the supreme Mirror of God and the Repository of divine grace is the root principle of religion. The remainder of the chapter is amplification of this opening paragraph. Although the root principle is one, its manifestations are seven in number; the chapter thus is a discussion of the seven root principles as seven stages of the recognition of spiritual truth.

Understanding the Báb's analysis of the root principles in the Epistle of Justice is dependent on comprehending a fundamental point. The third chapter of the Epistle of Justice is in fact a discussion of two topics:

one is an analysis of the seven stages of divine creative Action, and the other is an exposition of the seven stations comprising the hierarchy of the divine covenant in Islam, extending from God to the Prophet Muḥammad, Imám ʻAlí, the eleven other Imáms and Fáṭimih, the Gates or Pillars, the chiefs, and ending with the nobles. The heart of the third chapter is the identity of these two discussions, for both chains of spiritual concepts symbolize the same manifestations of Divine Unity.

Although the Báb's root principle of religion is the recognition of God, a major portion of the first and third chapters of the Epistle of Justice is devoted to affirming the impossibility of recognizing God directly. Nor is it possible, He says, "to fabricate any name or attribute for the Essence of God, and unto none is given any proof for, or path to, His recognition. The proof of His Essence hath always been, and will ever be, His Essence, and it is impossible for the contingent to be considered His proof."[20] This paradox leaves us in the apparent impasse that, on the one hand, the root principle of religion is recognition of God and, on the other hand, recognition of God is impossible. The resolution of this foundational antinomy is presented as the seven stages of divine creative Action, as well as the hierarchy of the covenant in the Islamic Dispensation. The divine creative Action, in the form of the seven stages of creation, and the Primal Will out of which those stages proceed, become the focus of that recognition which constitutes the root principle of religion. The seven ranks of the divine covenant in the Dispensation of Islam are the cosmic expressions of the seven stages of creation. Recognition of God thus is actually the recognition of divine Action and Causation, and that in turn is the recognition of the seven categories of spiritual hierarchy.

We can now understand the following statement in the Epistle of Justice: "Know thou that the root principle of the recognition of the modes of the causation of divine Action consisteth of seven stages, whose acknowledgement is the binding duty of all. True recognition is not complete without the recognition of all of these stages, and the recognition of the first is not accepted save through the recognition of the last."[21] Although in the Islamic Dispensation the primary manifestation of these seven stages of divine creative Action was the fourteen Sacred Souls—corresponding to the visible and unseen aspects of the stages—here recognition of the seven ranks of spiritual hierarchy becomes another, secondary expression of the recognition of the same chain of divine causation.[22]

The root principle of religion is thus the recognition of God through the recognition of the Primal Will, and because of the connection between the Primal Will and the divine Action, the root principle involves the process of divine causation and creation. As that process is the realm where the divine effulgence interacts with the free choice and receptivity of the things themselves, the root principle is actually identical with the mystery of Destiny—a mystery that can be grasped only in the sanctuary of unity through the perspective of the heart.[23]

The Seven Modes of Recognition

After the Báb explains that the root principle, the recognition of Divine Unity, is realized through the recognition of the modes of causation in the seven stages of divine creative Action, He discusses those seven modes of recognition by explaining a famous Shí'ih Tradition, the Tradition of Jábir. The Báb writes:

> This is the original tradition: ". . . O Jábir! Knowest thou what is recognition? Recognition is first the affirmation of Divine Unity, second the recognition of the Meanings, third the recognition of the Gates, fourth the recognition of the Imám, fifth the recognition of the Pillars, sixth the recognition of the chiefs and seventh the recognition of the nobles. . . . O Jábir! Give heed unto the affirmation of Divine Unity and recognition of the Meanings. As to the affirmation of Divine Unity, it consisteth of the recognition of the Eternal Unseen God. . . . As to the Meanings, We are His Meanings, and His Manifestation amongst you. He hath fashioned us from the light of His Essence, and hath conferred upon Us the affairs of His servants. Thus We do, by His leave, what We will, and when We will, it is God Who hath willed. . . ."[24]

This Tradition is frequently mentioned in the writings of Shaykh Aḥmad, and a version of it is partly quoted by Bahá'u'lláh in Epistle to the Son of the Wolf.[25] In the interpretation given by the Báb, He first identifies each of these seven forms of recognition with the recognition of one of the seven stages of divine Action. Then He interprets the stages of recognition as referring to God, Muḥammad, Imám 'Alí, the eleven Imáms and Fáṭimih, the four Gates, the chiefs, and the nobles. The terminology used here requires some explanation. Although in this Tradition the third stage is called the stage of the Gates, it refers to the station of 'Alí only, not the Gates to the Imáms. And while the fourth stage is that of the Imám, here that refers to the eleven other Imáms and Fáṭimih.[26] The fifth stage, that of the Pillars, indicates the former Prophets. Four of these were the pillars of prophethood: Noah, Abraham, Moses, and Jesus. Yet pillars exist in all ages. In the Dispensation of Islam, four prophets were the vehicles of divine grace on behalf of the Qá'im: Jesus, Khiḍr, Elijah, and Idrís. These are the four Gates indicated here. Finally the chiefs and the nobles are those who convey the divine grace from the Qá'im, through the Gates, to other people. The nobles receive guidance through the chiefs.

The third chapter discusses these seven stages in some detail, with the most extensive discussion devoted to the first two stages. Not only are the first two stages particularly emphasized by the Tradition itself, but they also represent the two most fundamental elements of faith: bearing witness to the unity of God and to the prophethood of Muḥammad. As we have seen before, these two elements actually represent the twin stations of the Point.

In similar Traditions, the first stage, which deals with the recognition of Divine Unity and God's transcendence, is called *Bayán* (Exposition). In a Tradition quoted by Shaykh Aḥmad and by Bahá'u'lláh, we read:

> "O Jábir! Give heed unto the Bayán (Exposition) and the Ma'ání (Significances)." He—peace be upon him—added: "As to the Bayán, it consisteth in thy recognition of God—glorified be He—as the One Who hath no equal, and in thy adoration of Him, and in thy refusal to join partners with Him. As to the Ma'ání, We are its meaning, and its side, and its hand, and its tongue, and its cause, and its command, and its knowledge, and its right. If We wish for something, it is God Who wisheth it, and He desireth that which We desire."[27]

Thus recognition of God is the inner mystery of *Bayán*, whereas recognition of Muḥammad is its manifest meaning. Recognition of God takes place through recognition of the Manifestation of God. In discussing the stage of *Bayán*, the Báb refers to the four stations of testifying to Divine Unity—unity of Essence, unity of Attributes, unity of Action, and unity of worship.

The second stage of recognition, that of the Meanings or Significances, involves the recognition of the station of Muḥammad. But in fact, within the Báb's discussion of the second stage, He speaks of the *seven* stations of Muḥammad. This paradox is a key element for understanding the message of the Epistle of Justice: all seven stages of divine Action, and all seven stages of spiritual hierarchy, are reflections of the reality of Muḥammad as the Manifestation of the Primal Will. Just as all seven stages were present in the first stage, crystallized in the four modes of Divine Unity, all seven stages are also present in the reality of Muḥammad. That is why true recognition of the Manifestation is the recognition of all the stages.

The seven stations of Muḥammad are the seven stations of the Point—a clear reference to the Primal Will. The first station of the Point is the Point of the supreme beginning, the second is the Point of contingency, the third is the Point of separation, the fourth is the Point of connection, the fifth is the Point of truth, the sixth is the Point of the centre of adoration, and the last is the Point of the visible world. These seven stations embrace all the levels of reality from the supreme station of the Primal Will to the physical body of Muḥammad.[28] We can see how closely the different levels of this Point correspond to the stages of divine creative Action and the layers of spiritual hierarchy.[29] And, in fact, the Báb's description of these seven levels of the Point correlates exactly with His description of the seven stages in general.

Resurrection and Purification

Chapter 4 of the Epistle of Justice addresses the Day of Resurrection. Although the Báb does not consider the doctrine of resurrection to be a separate root principle, He indicates that it is directly related to the seven root principles. His discussion of the issue is short and is expressed in terms of Islamic symbols and Shaykhí concepts. Yet, despite the veiled language of His analysis, a completely new interpretation of the concepts of heaven and hell is evident in this chapter. While the Báb denies the position of those who reject the possibility of resurrection in physical form, He makes it clear that He is not speaking here either of the traditional Islamic conceptions of physical resurrection, or of the Shaykhí idea of the resurrection of the essential or archetypal body. Instead, He unfolds two new principles. The first is that the true meaning of heaven is the recognition of the root principles of faith, while true hell is deprivation of that recognition. He asserts that those who are endued with understanding can see paradise and all its rewards in this world.[30]

The second principle adduced by the Báb is that resurrection applies to all levels of reality. The real question is not whether the resurrection is physical or spiritual. Instead the question concerns the precise meaning of "resurrection," and that meaning can be better understood when we remember that all things, within their own stations, are subject to resurrection; thus every being, whether physical or spiritual, also has its own heaven and hell. While the Báb does not elaborate on the issue here—referring to it simply as the inner truth of Shaykh Aḥmad's position—it is not difficult to see the revolutionary import of His approach to the concept, which He explains in detail in His later writings. In the Epistle of Justice He announces: "Nay, rather, he (Shaykh Aḥmad) affirmeth the return of all things, by virtue of an inspiration from the knowledge that hath encompassed the Book of God: heart in its own station, intellect in its own station, soul in its own station, and body, together with its three dimensions, in its own station."[31]

The Báb also discusses the subject of resurrection in another tablet, the Commentary on the Occultation Prayer (Sharḥ-i-Du'á'-i-Ghaybat), which was written shortly before the Epistle of Justice. In that work, although He appears to confirm Shaykh Aḥmad's version of the doctrine of physical resurrection, He rejects the Shaykh's concept of two twin bodies (two *jism*s and two *jasad*s) and their connection with a world called *Húrqalyá*. Again, what the Báb is presenting is something completely new: all created things are resurrected on the Day of Resurrection.[32]

The last chapter of the Epistle of Justice is a prayer for purification. The Báb states that all the principles elaborated in the previous four chapters are reaffirmed in that prayer. The topic of purification of the heart and true devotion is directly related to the entire discussion of the Epistle of Justice, for it is only through such purification of the heart that true recognition of truth can take place. This connection, again, becomes clearer in the Báb's later writings.

The Epistle of Justice affirms that the seven types of recognition that constitute the root principles of religion need to be crystallized and manifested in the observance of divine ordinances and laws. The text, however, does not deal with the specifics of derivative laws—with the two notable exceptions of the command to "act in regard to the people of paradise in accordance with affection and mercy," and the duty to treat women "in the utmost manner of love."[33] These two ordinances occupy a prominent position in the writings of the Báb, a fact that is evident in this text. But although the Báb does not address here the details of the derivative laws, He discusses something more fundamental: the moral and spiritual motives for performing actions. Purification of motive and detachment from all but God become the mediating principle which links the discourse on the root principles of faith to that of the derivative and secondary laws and ordinances.

The later writings of the Báb make it clear that the purification He speaks of in the Epistle of Justice is the same as attaining the sanctuary of the heart and fixing one's gaze on the Supreme Source of all the root principles of the Faith. One who achieves such purity and devotion will be able to recognize the new Manifestation of God together with the new root principles as well as the derivative laws. According to the Epistle of Justice, humanity has arrived at a new stage of spiritual development. The seven types of recognition of God, as the root principles of religion, which are the same as the five stations of the letter Há', refer to the reality of the Báb, Who is proclaiming the commencement of the sanctuary of unity and the revelation of the inner essence of the divine Mystery.

III
The Primal Point and Progressive Revelation

10
Resurrection and Historical Consciousness

IN PART 1 WE SAW that the interpretive logic of the Báb was essentially a logic of unity, interpreting all the statements in the Holy Scriptures as pointing toward a unified reality—the Primal Will—as the Origin and Cause of all things. In part 2 we discussed the pivotal role of the concept of the Primal Will in the Báb's metaphysics and cosmology, which defined the entire universe as the effects and manifestations of the Primal Will's divine creative Action. In part 3 we will examine the same dynamic of unity as it applies in the realm of history, civilization, and religious culture. This chapter will focus on historical consciousness in the third stage of the writings of the Báb.

The New Language of the Third Stage

The Báb's imprisonment in Mákú marks the most important turning point in His mission, and the beginning of the third stage of His writings. It is during the Mákú period that He begins to declare His true station openly, announcing that not only is He the promised Qá'im but also a new Manifestation of God. While in the first two stages of His writings the full nature of His Revelation was concealed, this third and last stage sees the explicit proclamation of a new religious Dispensation and the abrogation of the laws of Islam.

It is also in this third stage that the Báb begins to employ a completely new set of terms and concepts as vehicles of that Revelation. Terms like "the Primal Point," "the Letters of the Living," "the Tree of the Will," "He Whom God shall make manifest," the "Bayán," "All Things," and "the

Primal Unity" all come into use during this period and constitute the new language of the new religion. Even the terms and concepts used by the Báb in His previous writings become transformed within the new conceptual framework of this stage. Terms like "Gate," "Day of Resurrection," "Destiny," and "root principles" are now used in senses that were only latent or implicit in the early writings.

The explicit character of the writings of the third stage of the Báb's Revelation gives these texts an epistemological and hermeneutical priority over the writings of the two earlier stages. The Báb Himself establishes this priority, stipulating that the earlier writings should be understood in terms of the later writings, in a holistic approach. For example, discussing the term *Bayán* as the designation for the totality of His writings, He says:

> Say! Gain ye certitude in that which God hath revealed in the Bayán, for understanding the Bayán is dependent on understanding the totality of its revelation from beginning to end. For that which was revealed first is based upon the Qur'ánic laws; only later were the true measures of the Dispensation of the Bayán manifested. Neither be ye shrouded from the later writings by the earlier writings, nor fix your eyes merely on the later writings and ignore the earlier ones. . . . Yet, the later the revelation of the writings, the more manifest is the divine intention therein. Verily, all the Bayán is the Word of the Point of Truth.[1]

Two of the new concepts that are distinctive of the third stage need to be noted. During the first two stages, the Báb had referred to His first believers as *Sábiqún,* those who "have preceded in faith." This term is rooted in Islamic concepts referring to the eminent early followers of Muḥammad. The Báb's writings in the third stage, however, use the term *Ḥurúf-i-Ḥayy,* or Letters of the Living, to designate the first believers in the Báb. The other major term characteristic of this stage is *Man Yuẓhiruhu'lláh,* He Whom God shall make manifest, referring to the Promised One Who would come after the Báb. In fact, the most visible sign of the third-stage style of writing is the presence of this term, which is absent from the Báb's earlier writings.

The use of the term "He Whom God shall make manifest" in the Báb's later works, however, is crucial for understanding all His writings. The Báb is not simply referring to another Revelation to come after Him, in the same way that all the prophets of the past foretold the future advent of a Promised One. The issue is much more complex. In fact all the writings of the Báb that openly declare His true station as a divine Revelator also emphasize the centrality of Him Whom God shall make manifest. Even the Báb's discourse on His own station is defined in terms of the station of Him Whom God shall make manifest. Instead of rare, obscure, and hidden allusions to this Figure, we find in the Báb's later writings numerous unambiguous discussions about Him. So definitive is this feature that the Báb states that the covenant of the Promised One precedes His own: "Bear Thou witness that, through this Book, I have covenanted with all created things concerning the mission of Him Whom Thou shalt make manifest, ere the covenant concerning Mine own Mission had been established."[2] The subordination of His own covenant to the covenant of the Promised One is a powerful expression of inseparability of the Báb's twin stations as an independent Prophet and as the Herald of the Revelation of Bahá'u'lláh. That imminent Revelation is already present within the germ of the Báb's Dispensation, which is why the identification of the Báb's station and Dispensation is carried out through the identification of the Promised One and His Dispensation. These twin roles constitute the explicit foundation of all the Báb's later writings.

Yet another implication of the Báb's focus on the coming Dispensation is the central importance of the doctrine of progressive revelation. The Báb's later writings unfold a completely new sense of religious history, the relation of the religions to one another, and the dynamics of culture and society. This vision is further elucidated in the writings of Bahá'u'lláh, notably the Kitáb-i-Íqán (The Book of Certitude). For that reason, it is not surprising that the Kitáb-i-Íqán has been considered as the completion of the Persian Bayán.[3]

Destiny as the Principle of Manifestation

One of the most important expressions of the theological revolution initiated by the Báb is the reinterpretation of the concept of Destiny that is expounded in His later writings. We have already discussed the historicization of the idea of alteration (*badá'*) in the Persian Bayán, where alteration was defined as the abrogation of the former Dispensation and the initiation of new laws and principles. In terms of the process of divine creative Action, however, alteration is the renewal of the first three stages of creation—Will, Determination, and Destiny. We have seen the significance of the idea of Destiny in the earlier writings of the Báb as the third stage of that creative process, linking Will and Determination, or divine revelation and the receptivity of the things themselves, and reconciling determinism and freedom. But if the earlier writings of the Báb emphasized the doctrine of Destiny at the level of cosmic creation, His later writings extend this concept to the realm of scriptural revelation and cultural dynamics. The Báb defines the various religions as products of the interaction between the divine effulgence and the receptivities of human beings. These receptivities, however, change in time and advance in accordance with the development of social and cultural dynamics. The progressive receptive capacities of human beings in the march of history are accompanied by progressive revelations of the Primal Will. As this process of human spiritual evolution has no end, there can be no end for divine revelation, and there can be neither a final religion nor any one total revelation of spiritual truth. Discussing the unity of the endless divine Revelations, the Báb identifies this historical approach with the true meaning of the Mystery of Destiny, or the doctrine of the Middle Path:

> Should one traverse this sea, he would behold that there is no power nor strength except in God. He would recognize the concepts of God's absolute determinism (*jabr*) and human absolute freedom (*tafvíḍ*) as both barred from the truth. . . . He would identify, in each age, the Manifestation of "He doeth what He willeth, and He ordaineth what He pleaseth," and acknowledge Him upon His declaration. . . . Thus he boweth down before the Manifestation of "He shall not be asked of His doings, while all are questioned at His behest" upon His declaration. He shall not be veiled or separated from Him even to the extent of the separation between the letters *B* and *E*. For he can see that whatsoever is manifested in each Revelation is also manifested in His Word, and thus he fixeth his gaze upon the Essence of the Cause, and not on the multifarious tokens of each Revelation.[4]

This passage touches on many complex topics. A main point to note in it, however, is the Báb's distinction between divine revelation—the reality of the Primal Will—and the specific laws and symbols of religion, which are dependent on the conditions of humanity in the particular age in which that revelation appears. Because each religion is a product of the interaction between the supreme Source of religion—which is the common reality of all the Prophets—and the specific conditions of culture and society in each age, one should fix one's eyes on divine revelation itself in order to recognize the truth of the new Manifestation beyond the diversity of religious forms.[5]

It is this historicization of the "arc of descent" at the level of civilization that explains the fascinating new turns in the Báb's interpretation of the stages of divine creative Action. This insight is expressed in His identification of the stages of creation with the seven sacred figures responsible for the unfolding of Islamic civilization, and with His own being in the present. In other words, the stages of divine creative Action refer to the manifestations of the divine covenant in each age. The most striking symbol of this identity is evident in the name of the Báb Himself. We have seen that the Báb usually characterizes the seven stages of divine creative Action in terms of three and four. The literal fulfillment of these seven stages is reflected in His name, ʻAlí-Muḥammad (3 + 4). In various writings, He refers to His name as the unity of the "triangle" and the "square," or the trinity and quaternity, for instance: "Verily the Essence of the letters of the triangle preceding the square is the Manifestation of His Self in the kingdoms of heaven and earth, and whatever lieth between them."[6]

The Doctrine of Manifestation

The Báb's dynamic and historical approach offers the key that resolves what have been puzzling difficulties in attempts to understand religion, culture, and society. First, the Báb defines religion in a way that transcends the limited categories of both the fundamentalist/traditionalist and postmodern concepts of religion. The fundamentalist/traditionalist approach ignores the historical aspect of religion and conceives of religion as static. The consequence of this view is a fossilization of the historically specific laws and doctrines of the particular Dispensation, elevating them to the status of eternal and unchangeable laws, and turning religion into an obstacle to social development and a justification for violence. The postmodern approach ignores any reference to the divine aspect of religion and reduces religion to a function of human cultural categories and practices. The result of this relativistic view is that revelation becomes irrelevant and conflicting interpretations become incommensurable; religion then no longer has any moral force or arbiting role in society.

The one-sidedness of both the fundamentalist/traditionalist and postmodern conceptions of religion is rooted in the assumption that divine revelation is static. The fundamentalist sees their own religion to be final and denies the possibility of a further revelation. The postmodernist, who sees religion as the existing practices and traditional ideas of the people, recognizes change only in the human interpretation of revelation, but fails to see revelation itself as a dynamic and progressive force. Hence, the postmodern consciousness sees no need for the adherents of the earlier religions to accept any subsequent expression of divine Will that might appear in the world.

In the writings of the Báb, as we have seen, religion is characterized as the product of the interaction between the divine effulgence and the current stage of human spiritual and social development. In addition, both these elements are regarded as dynamic and historically specific entities. In this view, if all the religions represent the progressive revelations of the same Primal Will, then all the religions are valid and true because they are in fact one and the same reality. The sanctuary of unity is realized, in its most complex expression, in the principle of the unity of all the Prophets and the religions.

At the collective level, in the context of humanity's unfolding spiritual journey as a whole, the doctrine of Destiny becomes the doctrine of manifestation and the principle of progressive revelation. Just as the stages of divine Action mediated between the realms of divinity and contingency, the doctrine of manifestation synthesizes the absolute transcendence of God and the human longing for knowledge of the unseen realm of Divinity. As the Primal Will reveals Itself in each age in accordance with the conditions of the time and the spiritual aptitudes of humanity, the dynamics of divine Action in this context are expressed in the cycles of endless, successive divine revelations appearing in history. The principle of manifestation, therefore, is the general root principle of religion. In the Seven Proofs, the Báb explains:

> Thou hast asked concerning the fundamentals of religion and its ordinances: Know thou that first and foremost in religion is the knowledge of God. This attaineth its consummation in the recognition of His divine unity, which in turn reacheth its fulfillment in acclaiming that

> His hallowed and exalted Sanctuary, the Seat of His transcendent majesty, is sanctified from all attributes. And know thou that in this world of being the knowledge of God can never be attained save through the knowledge of Him Who is the Dayspring of divine Reality.[7]

Although the Primal Will, the "Dayspring of divine Reality," is the common reality of all the Manifestations of God, each Prophet appears with a different name, bringing different laws and teachings to advance the progress of spiritual culture and civilization: "The process of His creation hath had no beginning and can have no end," the Báb writes, "otherwise it would necessitate the cessation of His celestial grace. God hath raised up Prophets and revealed Books as numerous as the creatures of the world, and will continue to do so to everlasting."[8] The Báb likens the Primal Will to the sun:

> Were the risings of the sun to continue till the end that hath no end, yet there hath not been nor ever will be more than one sun; and were its settings to endure for evermore, still there hath not been nor ever will be more than one sun. It is this Primal Will which appeareth resplendent in every Prophet and speaketh forth in every revealed Book. It knoweth no beginning, inasmuch as the First deriveth its firstness from It; and knoweth no end, for the Last oweth its lastness unto It.[9]

The principle of progressive revelation is central to almost all the major later works of the Báb. Like the Seven Proofs and the Persian Bayán, Panj Sha'n, His last major work, begins with an exposition of this concept:

> [A]ll that hath ever dawned and set is verily the same sun. In like manner, the One Who is manifest in all the Messengers that have ever been sent or will ever be sent, is the same Will. Give heed then unto the recognition of that Will in all Its Revelations. This is thy recognition of thy Lord, and thy certitude in thy Fashioner. There is no beginning and no end for that divine Creation, for He traverseth from the beginning that hath no beginning to the end that hath no end.[10]

Beyond Hegelian Dialectics

In order to better understand the doctrine of progressive revelation, it is instructive to compare it with the work of the main representative of historical consciousness in Western philosophy, Hegel. Hegel's philosophy represented a turning point in Western philosophy precisely because he emphasized the dynamic nature of reality as a dialectical process. In his approach to the study of religion, Hegel applied his dialectical model to the realm of religious history as well. Dialectical method sees reality as the unity of opposites. Each side of this unity contains its opposite within itself. The true totality is realized when the opposition of the two sides is cancelled and they are united in a higher totality.

Hegel conceived of religious history as a dialectical process comprising three stages. In the first stage, worship of the Absolute Reality takes the form of the veneration of natural phenomena. The second stage is the worship of the Absolute as God, a spirit that is conceptualized as the creator of the universe but which is entirely opposed to material nature. Hegel, however, found both these approaches to religion inadequate. He posited as the final stage in his sequence what he termed "Christianity," in which God and the world become identical, and the believer finds God to be immanent in the world. Hegel's pantheistic interpretation of Christianity was based on the doctrine of God-manhood, or incarnation—the belief that in Christ God has become flesh. Thus human beings and God, or nature and Creator, are perceived as one and the same reality. For Hegel the apparent merging of opposites in this stage represents the consummation of the dialectical unfolding of religious truth, and is explicated as the attainment of divine self-consciousness.[11]

Although the Báb does not address the works of Hegel, His writings address virtually the same questions Hegel grappled with. Hegel's philosophy of religious development advocates a thesis of historical consciousness and change, and it attempts to transcend the opposition between the spiritual and the natural realms. Both of these issues are addressed by the Báb. However, unlike Hegel, who terminates historical dynamics in the final resolution of the dialectic, the Báb sees no end for the dynamics of religious truth. Even the truth represented by the Revelation of the Báb, in the inception of the age of the sanctuary of the heart, is still partial and relative to the receptivity of human beings in the current stage of spiritual development. The writings of the Báb thus introduce a truly historical consciousness, one which avoids the static thesis of the end of history.

Hegelian theory achieves its positive orientation to nature by dissolving God into the level of phenomenal beings. But for the Báb such a pantheistic conception is not an advanced consciousness, and the Hegelian dialectic is typical of the tendency of human beings to take the categories that pertain to their own reality and then elevate them to descriptions of the Essence of God. This attitude is comparable to that of an ant who defines God as a reality whose antennae stretch to infinity. According to the Báb, any claim to rationally understand the Absolute Mystery is a sign of imprisonment within one's self. Although the perspective of the heart transcends the limited categories of intellect, this perspective is never suggested as a means of understanding the Essence of God but, rather, the revelation of God at the level of the phenomenal world.

The main problem with the Hegelian construct is that Hegel, like some of the Sufi writers, confounds the Essence of God with the realm of divine Action. The conception of God that Hegel speaks of—a God that was first conceived as the creator of the world and then discovered to be the same as the world—refers, in the Báb's terms, to the twin stations of the Point or the Primal Will, where the unity of opposites is realized. This realm, however, is neither the unity of the world with the Essence of God, nor a static final point of civilization. Instead, it represents the dynamic principle of progressive revelation. Nor is this station confined to Christ; it is the reality of all the Manifestations of God. Christ was the Manifestation of the Primal Will in the world at a particular stage of humanity's spiritual development.

Therefore, Hegelian philosophy, at best, can be viewed as a somewhat crude affirmation of the principle of manifestation, and the thesis of the identity of God and human in Christ as an inadequate expression of this general doctrine. The Manifestations of God do represent the revelation of God in the phenomenal world. But unlike Hegelian theory, which takes this fact as evidence for the end of history and of religious progression, the Báb defines this principle as progressive revelation, and as the resolution of the existential paradox of human reality. The Báb affirms the principle of manifestation in order to announce not the end of spiritual dialectics but the perpetual renewal of divine revelation. The metaphysical truth that the doctrine of the trinity attempts to explain, thus, has nothing to do with the Essence of God. Rather, it is an affirmation of the triad of Will, Determination, and Destiny, or the Manifestation of God in the world.[12]

Worship as Paradise

If the writings of the Báb affirm the principle of historicity through an analysis of the divine aspect of the Point, they also expound the same truth through a reinterpretation of its other aspect, that is, servitude and worship. The two aspects of the Point are present in the reality of all created beings as the aspects of divine revelation and the thing's own station of servitude. But all former categories undergo a transformation within the sanctuary of the heart, and the idea of worship is no exception. The ultimate meaning and the supreme end of phenomenal reality is worship of God. In typical approaches to the idea of worship, fear of punishment and desire for reward are the main motivations, but in the Báb's writings these are inferior reasons as they are focused on something other than God. Worship of God must be an end in itself. It still entails reward, but in a new way. True worship, as the Báb explains, is the most exalted station human beings can attain: it is a mode of consciousness and feeling in which one is aware of being related to the entire universe by virtue of concentrating on the Supreme Origin of all reality. This kind of worship is the realization of the inner truth and reality of one's own being, as well as union with the Divine Beloved. As such, it constitutes the realization of the potentialities of one's own essential reality and the attainment of the state of paradise for human beings.

Worship, therefore, is an absolutely mystical state of being, a spiritual orientation in which one perceives in every thing nothing but the divine names and attributes. Worship, in other words, is a relation of true love, in which the lover, the Beloved, and the love become one and the same. All the concepts of heavenly reward revolve around this supreme state of servitude, a servitude whose inner reality is divinity:

> Verily, the most sublime station of reward, and the most exalted position of divine summons, is naught but the state of the servant's turning toward his Lord with utter devotion. For verily God will ever shed upon thee and through thee the splendours of His revelation. . . .
>
> By thy Lord! Shouldst thou taste the joy of that ecstatic station, thou wouldst never part with it, even shouldst thou be torn asunder. For should one truly testify, "There is none other God but God," he would taste the sweet delight of the revelation of everlasting glory, would be illumined by the dawning light of the Sun of Divine Unity, and would be exalted

above all the contingent beings through the radiant Countenance of the Sovereign Source of Revelation.[13]

God cannot be worshipped for any reason other than His own intrinsic Beauty, for at that station, nothing else even exists. The Báb extends this principle to the recognition of Him Whom God shall make manifest, stating that one must recognize the Promised One out of the intrinsic worth of His reality and not due to any social and material reasons external to Him. Again, this recognition constitutes the true paradise of human beings:

> For were I to find Him alone, in His transcendent unity, I would unhesitatingly bow down before Him, solely on account of His intrinsic supreme worth, inasmuch as that kneeling is naught but adoration for Thee in Thy oneness, for there is none other God but Thee.
>
> In like manner, should I find that all on earth prostrate themselves before Him, this would in no wise increase the awe of His majesty in my heart. . . . For recognizing Him by Him, and through the testimony of His own Self, is paradise, the like of which hath not been created in Thy Knowledge. And were I to be swayed by anything, then I would have not believed in Thy Unity as it beseemeth Thee, nor acknowledged Him as it befitteth Him.[14]

In this elevated state of worship, the worshipper is completely oblivious to the consequences of the rapturous expression of love. Thus the Báb frequently says that true worship is performed by the servant even if the consequence of the deed is punishment rather than reward. In the Persian Bayán, He writes:

> Worship thou God in such wise that if thy worship lead thee to the fire, no alteration in thine adoration would be produced, and so likewise if thy recompense should be paradise. Thus and thus alone should be the worship which befitteth the one True God. Shouldst thou worship Him because of fear, this would be unseemly in the sanctified Court of His presence, and could not be regarded as an act by thee dedicated to the Oneness of His Being. Or if thy gaze should be on paradise, and thou shouldst worship Him while cherishing such a hope, thou wouldst make God's creation a partner with Him, notwithstanding the fact that paradise is desired by men.

> Fire and paradise both bow down and prostrate themselves before God. That which is worthy of His Essence is to worship Him for His sake, without fear of fire, or hope of paradise.
>
> Although when true worship is offered, the worshipper is delivered from the fire, and entereth the paradise of God's good-pleasure, yet such should not be the motive of his act.[15]

Thus, the Báb says, the mark that distinguishes true testifying to the unity of worship is the continuous awareness of the possibility of alteration—the recognition that it is only by virtue of divine grace and mercy that the act of worship is recompensed by the reward of heaven, and that at any moment divine justice may alter this decision and replace it by the punishment of hell. Yet, for the servant in such a state of devotion, this knowledge would not have the slightest effect on the worship. Just as testifying to the unity of divine Action was exemplified in the consciousness of Destiny, testifying to the unity of worship is crystallized in the ever-present consciousness of the possibility of alteration.[16] The prayers of the Báb are imbued with this same consciousness; for example, He writes: "By Thy Glory! I testify in Thy presence that, verily, wert Thou to torment me for my mention of Thy Self, throughout the eternity of Thy glory, by all that is in Thy power of seizure and vengeance, violence and wrath, Thou must assuredly be praised in Thine action and obeyed in Thy judgment, for I would truly deserve it."[17]

Worship through the Self-Description of God

But how can we say that paradise is the state of union with God, and the remembrance and mention of the Beloved, if the divine Essence cannot be described by the contingent constructs of the human mind? The solution to this paradox is the self-description of God. Humans worship God through God's own description of Himself. This self-representation, of course, could only be a description of the revelation of God within the world. One expression of this divine self-description is the inner reality of the created being—the aspect of divine effulgence which is manifested at the level of that being. True worship thus is the realization of the truth of one's own self and finding God present within one's own heart—experiencing the reality of being made "in the image" of God. In the

Commentary on the Tradition of Truth, the Báb writes that because no access is possible to God Himself,

> Therefore it is necessary, according to true wisdom, that the Pre-existent God describe Himself to His creatures, that they may recognize their Creator and that, out of the grace of the Pre-existent, the contingent beings may attain their supreme End.
>
> This divine self-description is itself a created being. It is unlike any other description, the sign of "He is the One Who hath no equal,"[18] and the truth of the servant, his true being. Whoso hath recognized it hath recognized his Lord. . . .
>
> This description is denoted as the "soul" or "self," and that he who hath known himself hath known his Lord. At other times, it is expressed as the "heart," which is a description of the Divinity, by the Divinity, and is the essence of Servitude. It is the Sign of God shown by Him in the world and within the souls of men, that it may be revealed unto them that verily He is the Truth.
>
> Behold with the eye of thy heart. Verily thy truth, the truth of thy being, is the divinity of thy Lord revealed unto thee and through thee. Thou art He Himself, and He is thou thyself, except that indeed thou art that thou art, and He is that He is.[19]

Devotion to God, therefore, requires transcending all the particular characteristics of one's self and directing one's gaze toward the divine revelation within: this is the sanctuary of unity or the heart.

True worship, in the station of the heart, requires the negation of all names and attributes from the Essence of God. According to the Báb, one worships God when there is no reference to one's own limited essence, no consciousness of the act of worship itself, and no allusion to that through which worship is made. The distinctions between the worshipper, the Object of worship, the act of worship, and the means of worship must all disappear. The presence of any other thing in the consciousness of the worshipper is tantamount to idolatry:

> At the level of the contingent world, true worship is realized for those who worship God through Him and submerge themselves in the Sea of Absolute Unity. For in that Sea, the worshipper and the words of worship are annihilated, and thus there remaineth naught for the worshipper but

> the very revelation of God and the pure Countenance of the Beloved. . . . He who worshippeth God through any one but Him, by gazing at his own self as the Worshipper and at God as the Object of his worship, hath joined partners with God and hath never worshipped Him.[20]

As we have seen, a being consists of two aspects, the aspect of divine revelation and the aspect of its own self. According to the Báb, the revelation of God within is the sign of God through which God describes Himself to each being. One therefore must forget one's own individual essence, characteristics, and identity in order to be able to see within one's own reality only the Countenance of the Beloved.

The other aspect of divine revelation, and the supreme form of the divine Self-description, of course, is the Primal Utterance, the Primal Remembrance, and the Primal Word of God—the Primal Will, the common truth of all the Manifestations of God. In The Epistle of Justice, the Báb explains that only through the self-description of God in the Sacred Scriptures can one worship God: "After the coming into existence of all beings, God revealed His own Self in the world of creation by virtue of the contingent signs. It is incumbent upon all to worship His holy Essence, alone and by Himself, as none other God is there but Him, by virtue of the description that He hath revealed in the Qur'án."[21] This self-description of God is manifested in a historically specific way: true worship, therefore, is only possible through the recognition of, and devotion to, the most recent Manifestation of the divine self-description in the world, and by reciting the words revealed by Him.

We can see that, like the concept of manifestation, the Báb's discourse on worship is an affirmation of progressive revelation. His emphasis on the inseparable dual character of the divine self-description, as both the Manifestation of God and human inner self-realization, combines a mystic orientation with a most complex historical consciousness. In this way, the truth of the inner reality of the human soul is a reflection of the Primal Will, which is in turn the Manifestation of God in the realm of contingency.

Hegel's notion of alienation was taken even further by the Young Hegelian Ludwig Feuerbach. Unlike Hegel, who thought that the world was an alienated objectification of God and called for overcoming that alienation by finding God immanent within the world, Feuerbach argued that the very idea of God is the essence of the alienation of human nature from human beings. He maintained that God is an illusion created by projecting human characteristics onto the heavens and alienating humans from their own perfections. Feuerbach considered worship to be just another display of human degradation in which the abject human begs God to return to him some of his human characteristics.[22]

Feuerbach's devastating critique of the traditional approach to God and worship was effective because the traditional approach defined God anthropomorphically, as an exaggerated version of a man. Such an idea of God, however, was limited to the human realm and could not describe a real God. Feuerbach was correct that the conception of God he was critiquing is only an extension of human characteristics. In the Báb's theology, however, the idea of a perfect human being is not an illusion: it reflects the station of the Manifestation of God in the realm of human history. Reference to His superhuman virtues thus is not a reference to what pertains to God, but rather to the revelation of God, in the inner reality of human beings and the Manifestation of the Primal Will. In this view, the act of worship is not a process of alienation by projecting human virtues onto God and then begging the imaginary God for various rewards. Instead, true worship is carried out by turning toward the inner reality of one's own being as the ever-present divine sign within, negating all attributes from the Essence of God, and affirming universal love of all reality as the mirror of Divine Unity. Such love is itself the ultimate paradise and the affirmation of one's own true reality.

Resurrection as Historical Consciousness

One of the most important expressions of historical consciousness in the writings of the Báb is His novel interpretation of the Day of Resurrection. Traditionally, in both Christianity and Islam, the doctrines of resurrection and the Day of Judgment have been used to refute historical consciousness and to support a thesis of the "end of history"—the world and history itself were expected simply come to an end. This belief was usually accompanied by the doctrine of the finality of one's own religion, which held that revelation itself had come to an end with this "final" message for humanity. Although some Ismá'ílí groups spoke of the advent of the seventh Imám as the Day of Resurrection, that resurrection was only applicable to the advent of the Qá'im, and they still maintained the finality of the Islamic Revelation.[23] In addition, they usually understood the Day of Resurrection as a time when all things would be permitted and there would no longer be any laws.

The Báb reinterprets the doctrine of resurrection not as the end of history but as the substance of history itself. Resurrection is described not as a single, final event but a recurring, cyclic, and progressive process linking all past, present, and future divine Revelations. Each resurrection is characterized by the abrogation of the former laws and ordinances and the inception of new ones, corresponding to the specific social needs of humanity in the emerging age.

The concept of progressive revelation transforms all the traditional categories and confers upon them new meanings. Not only is the doctrine of finality replaced by the doctrine of infinite sequential divine Revelations, but the very idea of the Day of Resurrection, traditionally a static notion, itself becomes an affirmation of the dynamic nature of spiritual reality. As we saw in the discussion of the Epistle of Justice, the Báb identified the root principle of religion in terms of the concept of manifestation and defined the doctrine of resurrection as a derivative principle. This same logic appears within His later writings: the Persian Bayán begins with a discussion of the doctrine of manifestation and divine testimony, but then it addresses the Day of Resurrection and its symbolic signs. According to the Báb, resurrection is another expression of the doctrine of manifestation and progressive revelation.

More specifically, the Báb explains that each spiritual Dispensation has its own life history, with a beginning and an end. The end of each Dispensation is its own Day of Resurrection. This end is a "resurrection" because it is also the inception of the next Dispensation, when the religion itself is recreated through the revelation dispensed by a new Manifestation of God. Thus the Day of Resurrection is the period when the new Manifestation of God is present on earth. In the Persian Bayán the Báb writes:

> The substance of this chapter is this, that what is intended by the Day of Resurrection is the Day of the appearance of the Tree of divine Reality. . . . that from the time of the appearance of Him Who is the Tree of divine Reality, at whatever period and under whatever name, until the moment of His disappearance, is the Day of Resurrection.
>
> For example, from the inception of the mission of Jesus—may peace be upon Him—till the day of His ascension was the Resurrection of Moses. . . . And from the moment when the Tree of the Bayán appeared

> until it disappeareth is the Resurrection of the Apostle of God, as is divinely foretold in the Qur'án; the beginning of which was when two hours and eleven minutes had passed on the eve of the fifth of Jamádíyu'l-Avval, 1260 A.H., which is the year 1270 of the Declaration of the Mission of Muḥammad. This was the beginning of the Day of Resurrection of the Qur'án, and until the disappearance of the Tree of divine Reality is the Resurrection of the Qur'án.[24]

The unity of divine revelation as both the inner reality of all things and the Manifestation of God is also the basis of the Báb's reinterpretation of the concepts of heaven and hell. Paradise is the highest state of perfection and self-actualization that can be attained by a being within its own station. Hell is the state of deprivation of that perfect actualization. Thus not only human beings but all other created things have their own "heaven" and "hell." This new definition has far-reaching implications for the attitude the believer should take toward all things, including the natural world, but extending to all aspects of human culture. Human beings are invested with the unique responsibility to ensure, to the limits of their power, that all created things achieve their paradise. While, in the Bible, human beings—because they are created in the image of God—stand in a relation of "dominion" over the rest of God's creatures, this relation is now characterized by the Báb as one of responsibility for their development and refinement.[25] The principle is frequently expressed in the later writings of the Báb. In the Persian Bayán, for example, we find:

> [W]hoever possesseth power over anything must elevate it to its uttermost perfection that it not be deprived of its own paradise. For example, the paradise of a sheet of paper on which a few excellent lines are inscribed is that it be refined with patterns of gold illumination, adornment, and excellence that are customary for the most exalted parchment scrolls. Then the possessor of that paper hath elevated it to its utmost degree of glory. Should he know of a higher degree of refinement and fail to manifest it upon that paper, he would deprive it of its paradise, and he would be held accountable, for why hast thou, despite the possession of the means, withheld the effusion of grace and favour?[26]

As we have seen, the ultimate state of perfection for human beings is attaining union with God and beholding the Countenance of the Beloved within their own being, and the state of true worship is the essence of paradise. That paradise is union with the revelation of the Primal Will that reflects itself in the world as the Manifestation of God:

> Man's highest station, however, is attained through faith in God in every Dispensation and by acceptance of what hath been revealed by Him, and not through learning; inasmuch as in every nation there are learned men who are versed in divers sciences. Nor is it attainable through wealth; for it is similarly evident that among the various classes in every nation there are those possessed of riches. Likewise are other transitory things.
>
> True knowledge, therefore, is the knowledge of God, and this is none other than the recognition of His Manifestation in each Dispensation.[27]

Recognition of the Manifestation of God, attainment of which constitutes the attainment of paradise, is also the culmination of true self-recognition. In the following passage, the Báb explains "resurrection" as the day in which the "tree" of the previous Dispensation becomes perfected and its "fruits" are harvested:

> The stage of perfection of everything is reached when its resurrection occurreth. The perfection of the religion of Islám was consummated at the beginning of this Revelation; and from the rise of this Revelation until its setting, the fruits of the Tree of Islám, whatever they are, will become apparent. . . . even as the Revelation of the Qá'im . . . is exactly like unto the Revelation of the Apostle of God Himself [Muḥammad]. He appeareth not, save for the purpose of gathering the fruits of Islám from the Qur'ánic verses which He [Muḥammad] hath sown in the hearts of men. The fruits of Islám cannot be gathered except through allegiance unto Him [the Qá'im] and by believing in Him.[28]

Various writings of the Báb, including a significant portion of the Persian Bayán, explain the meaning of the signs of the Day of Resurrection. But even though it is only in the third stage of the Báb's writings that the meaning of the Day of Resurrection is explicitly disclosed, His earlier writings also indicate that the Day of Resurrection has arrived in the Revelation of the Báb itself. We saw direct references to this fact in the Epistle of Justice, concerning the doctrine of the Day of Judgment. But it should be remembered that even the opening chapter of the Qayyúmu'l-Asmá', the very first revelation of the Báb as He made His declaration to

Mullá Ḥusayn, ends by saying, "We verily have moved the mountains upon the earth, and the stars upon the Throne, by the power of the one true God, around the Fire which burneth in the centre of Water, as ordained by this Remembrance"—an unmistakable statement that the signs of the Day of Resurrection have been fulfilled on that historic night.[29]

11
History and the Perspective of Unity

In the last stage of the Báb's writings, many concepts that had been expressed in His earlier writings in allusive, symbolic, or coded language are now openly expounded in the most unequivocal and direct manner. It is also in this, the final stage of His Revelation, that the full import of the foundational principle of the heart, or the sanctuary of unity, becomes unveiled. This chapter will discuss the ultimate expression of the principle of the heart in the later writings of the Báb, particularly the Persian Bayán, the Mother Book of the Bábí Dispensation.

Dating the Persian Bayán

Some confusion exists about the dating of the text of the Persian Bayán. There is no doubt that the vast majority of this work was revealed in Mákú. Much evidence within the text itself testifies to that fact. Yet there are reasons to believe that the last sections of the book were revealed in Chihríq. Denis MacEoin, however, has offered a theory that the Persian Bayán was revealed throughout the nine months of the Báb's imprisonment in Mákú. He suggests that on each day of this period the Báb wrote one of the chapters, and he bases this theory on the Báb's statement, in the book, that He revealed three commentaries on the Qur'án. MacEoin argues that since nine commentaries on the Qur'án were revealed in Mákú,[1] and the reference to three commentaries is found in the third unity of the Persian Bayán (3:16), it is reasonable that, in a parallel manner, each day a different chapter of the Persian Bayán was revealed.[2]

The facts, however, do not support this argument. The Báb's reference to three commentaries in the Persian Bayán is not to the three He revealed in Mákú, but to commentaries that were revealed in earlier years, before the Báb had disclosed His station as a new Prophet. This is what the Báb actually says in the Persian Bayán:

> Even should He [Whom God shall make manifest] choose not to reveal Himself or make Himself known unto anyone, the Bayán that He ordaineth would be like unto a Sun amongst the stars. This is the time when all people are wrapped in their own veils, even as when the Point of the Bayán wrote three commentaries on the Qur'án: two commentaries in the mode of [divine] verses, complete to the end, and a commentary on the Súrih of the Cow in the mode of educational discourse. Indeed, all the commentaries written by the interpreters of the Qur'án from the inception of its revelation until its abrogation cannot equal even one letter of His commentaries.[3]

Here, "two commentaries in the mode of [divine] verses" refers to the Qayyúmu'l-Asmá' and another commentary on the Súrih of the Cow that, as the Báb has said, was revealed in the mode of divine verses but was stolen on the journey to Mecca.[4]

In any case, it seems possible that the last few sections of the Persian Bayán were written after the Báb's transfer to Chihríq. In gate 12 of the eighth unity, the Báb discusses the duty regarding *maḥall-i-ḍarb* (the place of striking). This may refer to the time in Tabriz when the Báb was subjected to the bastinado after His examination by the divines. Yet it is also possible that here *maḥall-i-ḍarb* refers to Shiraz, where He was struck by the governor of Fars. If we accept the former interpretation, we must conclude that the final parts of the Persian and Arabic Bayán were revealed in Chihríq. In the same section, the Báb specifies that the duty only applies to those who reside within a distance of sixty-six *farsakhs* (approximately four hundred kilometres) from the place of striking and who have reached the age of twenty-nine. The fact that the Báb Himself was twenty-nine years old when that indignation was inflicted on Him in Tabriz supports the first interpretation. However, Parviz Moini has argued that since 66 is the numerical value of *Alláh,* the specification of "twenty-nine years" refers to the fact that 29 + 66 = 95, which is equivalent to the words "for God" (*lilláh*). Yet the fact that 29 and 66 together make 95 can also be viewed as a further support of the first interpretation—namely, the number 29 was not chosen simply because it happens to be the difference between 95 and 66, but rather because it refers to the age of the Báb at the time.[5]

It is usually assumed that the Arabic Bayán was written and completed before the Persian Bayán. But in the Persian Bayán we find a reference to the commandment regarding the use of silk "in the Arabic version" (4:18), which refers to the Arabic Bayán's law giving permission to wear silk (6:9). The Arabic Bayán contains eleven full unities, whereas the Persian Bayán ends with gate 10 of the ninth unity. However, it seems that the sections of the Arabic Bayán that are not matched in the Persian Bayán (gate 11 of the ninth unity to the end of the eleventh unity) were written after the Persian Bayán was completed. In the Arabic Bayán's gate 10 of the eighth unity, the Báb speaks of the revelation of the Bayán up to this particular chapter, and then says that the revelation of the Arabic Bayán will be continued "by Myself" until a full eleven unities are completed and that, at a future time, its revelation will be continued until it comprises a full nineteen unities. "But fix your gaze on that which God hath revealed. Indeed, this is what hath hitherto been revealed, and I myself shall manifest eleven (Alif and Yá'). And should it then be His will, ye shall witness what is equivalent to the number of all things (*kullu shay'*) [361 gates or nineteen unities]."[6]

That sentence makes a number of things clear. First, when He was writing that specific chapter, He had already completed as much of the Persian Bayán as He intended to write, otherwise it would not make sense to refer to the revelation of the Bayán up to that gate as a turning point. Second, evidently the Báb had no intention at that time to complete either the Persian Bayán or the Arabic Bayán by Himself. Instead, He intended to write only a few more chapters of the Arabic Bayán, making it eleven unities. The rest of the Bayán, therefore, was to be revealed, as the Báb intimates, by Him Whom God shall make manifest.

The Meaning of "Bayán"

As we saw in the discussion of the Epistle of Justice, the Tradition of Jábir, like the Tradition of Truth, is central to the early writings of the Báb. But while the Epistle of Justice uses the terms of the Tradition of Jábir to define the root principles of religion, the inner truth of that Tradition is explained in writings that were set down only after the Báb's exile to Mákú. The subtle connection between the Báb's writings in the third stage and those in the earlier stages is directly visible in one of the most important concepts found in the Tradition of Jábir, the concept of *Bayán*.

In the Epistle of Justice, the root principle of religion was presented as a single fundamental precept that is manifested through seven specific principles. That fundamental precept was the recognition of God, which is the first of the seven types of recognition mentioned in the Tradition of Jábir. However, alternative Traditions of Jábir speak of the first principle as *Bayán* (Exposition). The Tradition of Jábir defines *Bayán* as the essence of the six other forms of recognition, which are termed the Meanings, Gates, Imám, Pillars, Chiefs, and Nobles. All these forms of recognition are manifestations of the recognition of God, namely, *Bayán*. That recognition represents the perspective of the heart in the sanctuary of Divine Unity. It is the root principle of all religion as seen with the eye of God.

The choice of this particular Tradition by the Báb as a vehicle to express the truth of His Revelation is significant, for it is in the third stage of His writings that He explicitly uses the term *Bayán* to refer to all His writings as a whole, in addition to the two specific works with that title. The entire Revelation of the Báb, as the "Bayán," therefore, is the disclosure of the hidden truth of the Logos, the divine Revelation in the sanctuary of the heart.

The idea of *Bayán* is first mentioned in the Qur'án, where it is said: "The God of Mercy hath taught the Qur'án, hath created man, and taught him *Bayán* [translated "articulate speech"]."[7] These verses have long puzzled Muslims: the chronology, beginning with the revelation of the Qur'án, then the creation of man, then teaching him *Bayán,* is enigmatic given the meanings traditionally assigned to these terms. In the theology and symbolism of the Báb's writings, however, these terms acquire new meanings. *Bayán* (exposition) signifies the Revelation of the Báb, which unveils the hidden truth of the Qur'án. "Man" here signifies the "Perfect Human Being"—the Manifestation of God, Who is the Manifestation of the Logos.[8] *Qur'án* means "recitation" or "the recited Word." Obviously, the Word as recited is the outward sign of the inner meanings. The inner meaning of that Word is the *Bayán*. Thus, it is through the Báb that the inner truth of the Logos is disclosed.

The Persian Bayán directly explains the word *al-Bayán* and interprets it as a reference to the fundamental truth of all the divine Revelations. First the Báb explains that all the writings of the Báb are the "Bayán," although the term applies differentially to the various modes of revelation: "[W]hatever is revealed by the Point hath been designated as the Bayán," He writes, "However, this name referreth in its primal reality to the divine verses, and in its secondary reality to prayers, third to commentaries, fourth to educational forms, and fifth to the Persian words. Yet, this exalted appellation solely denoteth the divine verses to the exclusion of all others."[9] Since *Bayán* is primarily the revelatory mode of divine verses, it directly refers to divine revelation in the sanctuary of unity. *Bayán*, as the root principle of religion, is now unveiled through the principle of the heart.

According to the Báb, *al-Bayán*[10] is a reference to the foundational concept of "for God" (*lilláh*):

> Thus it is permissible that some may bear the name 'Abdu'l-Bayán (servant of the Bayán), inasmuch as the name "God" (*Alláh*) is derived from the substance of the Bayán, and the first Who called Himself by the name *Bayán* was God, glorified and exalted be He, as He hath revealed, "I verily am God, there is none other God but Me, the One, the Bayán." Indeed the entire mystery of the Bayán is manifest in its name, for the numerical value of the word *al-Bayán* together with its integrative from of unity equalleth the numerical value of the words, "for God" (*lilláh*), rendering the word *Bayán* a mirror for the Point of the Bayán, Which in turn is the supreme Mirror of the words, "for God," as well as a mirror for Him Whom God shall make manifest, inasmuch as He is the supreme Mirror of the words, "for God."[11]

Al-Bayán, which is equal to 94, together with integrative form, or 1, equals 95, which is the numerical value of the words "for God." *Bayán* thus symbolically affirms the essence of the entire Revelation of the Báb because it mirrors or represents the phrase "for God," which in turn represents the Point of the Bayán as well as Him Whom God shall make manifest.

The Sanctuary of Unity and Progressive Revelation

As we have seen, the Báb interprets verses of the Qur'án as well as Traditions such as the Tradition of Truth and Tradition of Jábir, among others, as referring symbolically to His own Revelation. But is such an interpretation simply a statement about Himself? In fact, His interpretations are designed as a vehicle for presenting a far more complex truth.

In His interpretation of the Tradition of Truth, the Báb identified the various statements in the Tradition as the stages of His own Revelation. But, as He notes, the message of the Tradition of Truth concerns the piercing of the veils and the shining forth of the Countenance of Beauty—in other words, the realm where the inner mystery of reality is revealed, that is, the disclosure of the inner truth of all the divine Revelations and of human reality. In the Báb's terms, therefore, this Tradition refers to the inception of the age of the heart, to the direct experience of beholding the Countenance of the Beloved in the sanctuary of unity. That is why this particular Tradition is identified with the Báb's Revelation, as His Revelation is the essence and truth of all the Revelations. The Revelation of the Báb is the age of the *Bayán,* the age of the exposition of heretofore hidden meanings. The writings of the Báb—the Bayán—reveal the hidden truth of all the Holy Books of the past. But the understanding of this hidden truth is possible only if one regards reality from the sanctuary of unity with the eye of the heart, which is in reality the eye of God.

The essence of this perspective, the sanctuary of unity, is the foundational fact that the supreme sacred Reality is the Primal Will. In the sanctuary of unity, one focuses on that Primal Will as the sun which is one and the same sun even though it shines at different times from different horizons upon different mirrors. At this level, spiritual understanding transcends the realm of the specific appearance of each religion and beholds all reality through the supreme Origin of religion, which is one. The heart of this approach thus is an understanding of the progressive revelation of God in human history. But those who are imprisoned in the lower, concrete perspectives of limitation and conflict do not discern the Source of their religion, the Primal Will, and instead fix their attention on the historically specific expressions of that Will in the form of particular religious symbols and practices. As a result, they are unable to recognize the same spirit of the Primal Will when He appears in a new form. The consequence of the perspective of limitation is conflict between people who are similarly limited in their comprehension—all affirming their own religion and denouncing other faiths, and all finding their own religion to be the last and ultimate expression of divine truth.

In interpreting the Qur'ánic verse concerning *Bayán* (as well as numerous other verses and Traditions) as a reference to His own Revelation, the Báb affirms that His Revelation is just one specific expression of the Primal Will: the Báb Himself is the same as all the Prophets of the past and of the future. He asks people to see Him not just as another Prophet but as all the Prophets, the Manifestation of the First and the Last, Who will return again as Him Whom God shall make manifest. He desires to create a spiritual community that will not cling to the "Silent Book"—the Holy Scripture—and defy its Revealer, Who is the "Speaking Book." In other words, the Báb must be recognized by virtue of the inner truth of His reality—the station of the Primal Will. Recognition of the Báb implies recognition of His identity with all the past and future Manifestations of God. If one rejects any of the Manifestations of God before or after Him, one has not really recognized the Báb.

The entire Persian Bayán, like all the Báb's other later writings, consistently stresses this principle. In the first chapter, the Báb states that recognition of the unity of God

> is dependent on the recognition of the Point of the Bayán. . . . Whoso believeth with certainty that He is the Point of the Qur'án manifested in His latter Resurrection, and the Point of the Bayán in His first Revelation, and that He is the Primal Will Who existeth in Himself, the Self-Subsisting, while all things are created through His behest and exist through Him, is numbered among those whose inmost reality testifieth unto the unity of his Lord.[12]

Although the root principle of religion is the declarative statement of Divine Unity, the true root principle is the recognition of the *reality* of Divine Unity. The declaration itself is just a shadow of the real Word, which is the truth of the Primal Will, the Word of God, and the true self-description of God. The words of the declarative statement become the emblem of true faith only because the Primal Will has spoken them. When the Primal Will, as the new Manifestation of God, speaks the same truth in a different way, that new utterance becomes the symbol of the root principle.

We can now better understand the discourse of the Báb on the root principles in the Epistle of Justice. In that text He first said that the nature of the root principle of religion revolves around the Will of God. The real root of all is the recognition of the Will of God in whatever manner that Will appears. In the first chapter of the Persian Bayán, discussing the declarative statement of Divine Unity, the Báb affirms this same point more explicitly:

> This is a Word [the declarative statement of the unity of God, whose reality is the Manifestation Himself] that hath verily glorified, exalted, magnified, sanctified, and praised His Lord in the daytime and in the night season. Gaze not upon this Word except as thou beholdest the sun in the heaven, and perceive not him who believeth in Him save as thou lookest at the mirror. . . . All things return unto, and by, this Indivisible One Being. During the next Resurrection, this Indivisible One Being is naught but the very being of Him Whom God shall make manifest. . . .
>
> Amongst the followers of the Qur'án today is he who beareth witness unto this Word, which is the essence of all faith. Without doubt, he uttereth this Word solely by virtue of its previous affirmation by Muḥammad, the Apostle of God, the blessings of God rest upon Him. For the True Sun of this supreme Word hath been shining in His heart, and it is a mere shadow thereof that is manifest in those who utter that Word today. Therefore, all expressions of this Word must now revert to the next Revelation of Muḥammad, which is the manifestation of the Point of the Bayán rather than His first Revelation.[13]

The Báb shows that the essence of the declarative testimony of the unity of God is recognition of the Command and Will of God; that Will is the reality that makes each of the diverse, historically specific expressions of this principle authoritative and binding. The Word as it is spoken by the Manifestation is the supreme testimony of God to Himself, and His self-description. The Word, then, is the very being of the Manifestation of God as the Logos, the Word of God. In the next Revelation, although the appearance of this Word may change, its true meaning remains the same. But if one rejects the new Manifestation and fails to testify to the new expression of that Word, one is in fact rejecting the very Word that one thinks one is affirming.

The earlier writings of the Báb discussed this principle as the mystery of Destiny. In both the Commentary on the Letter Há' and the Commentary on the Mystery of the Letter Há', the Báb writes that true spiritual journey is dependent on taking the perspective of the heart, which is characterized by two paradoxical features: all things are mirrors of the same reality, the Primal Will, but in the hierarchy of spiritual reality, the Will reveals itself in each thing according to the thing's own limited station. Thus the truth that is understood by the human mind is but a shadow of the truth accessible to the Manifestation of God.

Hence the Qur'án, as the true meaning of the revealed Word of God, is the same as the Bayán, and both are the same as the Gospel, and all are the same as any of the other Holy Scriptures. The eye of the heart recognizes the Word of God in whatever tangible words it appears. One who takes the perspective of unity recognizes the Manifestation of God, the Word of God, whatever physical body He appears in, whatever name He takes, and whatever form of Scripture and laws He brings.[14]

The Return of the Point and the Letters of the Living

The perspective of the heart disclosed the true reality of divine revelation as the common reality of all the Manifestations of God, affirmed as the principle of progressive revelation. The Persian Bayán identifies this same principle as the key for understanding religious symbols and sacred history. The first gate, as we saw, expresses the outlines of this concept as the universal truth of all the religions. The remaining eighteen gates elaborate upon the principle articulated in the first gate.

In the principle of the unity of the Manifestations of God as revelations of the Primal Will, each Manifestation of God is the return of all the others in the past. At the beginning of the Seven Proofs, the Báb concisely explains:

> In the time of the First Manifestation the Primal Will appeared in Adam; in the day of Noah It became known in Noah; in the day of Abraham in Him; and so in the day of Moses; the day of Jesus; the day of Muḥammad, the Apostle of God; the day of the "Point of the Bayán"; the day of Him Whom God shall make manifest; and the day of the One Who will appear after Him Whom God shall make manifest. Hence the inner meaning of the words uttered by the Apostle of God, "I am all the Prophets," inasmuch as what shineth resplendent in each one of Them hath been and will ever remain the one and the same sun.[15]

But in the Persian Bayán this principle of return is manifested in a particular form that constitutes one of the most important symbols of the Bábí Dispensation. The Báb claims that all the sacred figures of the Islamic Dispensation have returned to the world through the sacred figures of His own religion. The first of those sacred figures is of course the Báb. As the Point, He is the source of all the others. The other sacred figures are called the *Letters* of the Living because letters are the immediate manifestations of the Point. They are the Letters of the *Living* because they were the first to attain life in the new Dispensation. The Arabic word for "the Living" (*Ḥayy*) is numerically equal to 18, which was the number of Letters of the Living. These souls, together with the Báb, comprise nineteen sacred figures.

While the first gate of the Persian Bayán emphasized the common reality of all the Manifestations of the Primal Will, with the Báb as the return of Muḥammad in the station of the Point of the Qur'án, as well as the return of all other Manifestations of God, the subsequent eighteen gates address the return of the other Islamic sacred figures through the Báb's eighteen Letters of the Living. The principle of the return of the Letters of the Living derives from the principle of the return of the Point of the Qur'án in the form of the Point of the Bayán. In the second gate the Báb explains: "The substance of this gate is that Muḥammad, the blessings of God rest upon Him, and the Manifestations of His Self have all returned to this world and were the first amongst the servants who stood in the presence of God in this Day of Resurrection, acknowledged His unity, and proclaimed the verses of His Báb unto all humankind."[16]

The second gate, thus, discusses the station of the Letters of the Living in general and affirms the general principle of their return. This gate also emphasizes that Muḥammad as the Apostle of God—that is, in the station of servitude of the Point of the Qur'án—has returned through the first Letter of the Living, Mullá Ḥusayn (whose name is Muḥammad Ḥusayn). The gates that follow are usually short and state the return of a specific sacred figure in the form of one of the Letters of the Living. For example, the third states, "On this, that 'Alí, peace be upon Him, hath returned to the world, together with all of his faithful believers, and all who believed in the one other than him. He is, after the letter Sín [referring to Mullá Ḥusayn], the second to believe in the Point."

In the second gate, the Báb explains the return of the sacred figures as the Letters of the Living:

> As for the Most Excellent Names, God hath singled out, in this Dispensation, their names as the eighteen Letters of the Living. For they consist of fourteen sacred Souls, and the Hidden, Well-Guarded Name, Whose four letters are referred to by various names including the Four Gates, the Lights of the Throne, the Bearers of creation, provision, death, and life. All of these formed the name of the Living One, for these are the names that are nearest to God; the others are guided by their clear and significant actions, for God began the creation of the Bayán through them, and it is to them that the creation of the Bayán will again return.[17]

This statement demonstrates the complex meanings associated with the term "Letters of the Living." "Living" (*Ḥayy*) is one of the main names of God. The Letters of the Living, as sacred figures, are the manifestations of divine names and attributes. While the Báb is the supreme Mirror of God, the Letters of the Living are the supreme "worldly" Mirrors of God, and the first mirrors of the Báb. But "Living" also alludes to the arrival of the Day of Resurrection, on which the dead are quickened; the Letters of the Living are the first to attain life or be "resurrected" on that Day. They are also called the Letters of the Living because all the other letters receive their own life through them. As the first creation of the Báb, they are brought forth out of nothing, through their own selves, and all others are subsequently created through them. They recognized the Báb by themselves, and through no one else; the Bábí community comes into being through them as they teach others and spread the new Cause. The Letters of the Living also are the fulfillment of the Qur'ánic verse which describes God by the two names "the Ever-Living" (*Qayyúm*) and "the Self-Subsisting" (*Ḥayy*). As we have seen, the Báb Himself is the Manifestation of the name "the Self-Subsisting," the Reality that exists by Its own causation and on which all else depend for their existence. The Letters of the Living, then, are the manifestations of the name "the Ever-Living."

One immediately notes that, contrary to what one might expect, here the return of Muḥammad is not the Báb but rather the first Letter of the Living. The key to this puzzle lies in the dual station of the Point as elaborated in the later writings of the Báb. We have discussed this concept in connection with the Primal Will or the Point as the unity of subject and object: the Point can be regarded in terms of its station of divinity or its station of servitude. The station of servitude is the same as the station of the prophethood of the Apostle of God. In the Dispensation of Islam, however, a differentiation was made between the two stations of the Point—the Point of the Qur'án and Muḥammad as the Apostle of God. It was only when Muḥammad was the recipient of the words of God that He was speaking as the Point of the Qur'án, in the station of divinity, and was revealing divine verses. Therefore, in the Islamic Dispensation we have Muḥammad as the Point of the Qur'án, whose return in the Bábí Dispensation is the Báb (the Point of the Bayán), and Muḥammad as the Apostle of God, whose return is represented by the first Letter of the Living.

Since the Bábí Dispensation is the age of the heart and the sanctuary of unity, the Báb appears as the Point of the Bayán in the station of divinity, and the revelation of divine words is unceasing in His station. And since He manifests the station of the divinity of the Point, all the other divine stations, including all the names attributed to God, remain beneath His shadow and are manifested in the Letters of the Living as reflections. Thus, although the Báb Himself is in reality His own First Believer, He is not described by that station. Instead, this aspect of His reality is described through the reflection of that station in a "worldly Mirror," the first Letter of the Living. The station of the Prophet, similarly, is ascribed to the first Letter of the Living although he himself is not a Prophet but is rather a reflection of that station (and normally would be a successor or vicegerent of the Prophet). In other words, in the Revelation of the Báb, the station of Muḥammad as the Apostle of God returns as the first believer, Mullá Ḥusayn.

At the beginning of the Bayán, the Báb explains that He is the supreme Mirror of God, while the Letters of the Living are created by Him as the "worldly Mirrors." The hearts of all the believers are invested with the signs of their names:

> He is the First, yet not defined as such, and He is the Last, but not described as such. He is the Seen, and not praised as such, and He is Hidden, and not recognized as such. . . .
>
> He is the First to believe in Him Whom God shall make manifest, and He is the First Who hath believed in Him Who hath been manifested. . . .
>
> It is for the Will, and through the manifestation of His own Self, that God hath fashioned, out of His Self, eighteen souls, ere the creation of all

things, and He hath enshrined the sign of their recognition in the inmost reality of all things that all, from the depths of their essence, may bear witness that He is the Primal Unity and the Eternal, the Ever-Abiding. . . .

Know thou that He is the Supreme Mirror of God out of Whose revelation is manifested the worldly Mirror, Which is naught but the Letters of the Living, and naught is seen in that Supreme Mirror of God but God.[18]

In the fifteenth gate of the Bayán, the Báb deals with the same question in yet another way. There He refers to the return of the Twelfth Imám, the Qá'im, as one of the Letters of the Living. Yet we know that the Báb Himself is the Qá'im. This paradox is exactly like the previous one. The Báb explains that since His Revelation is the Revelation of the Point in the station of divinity, and since all other stations are created by Him and are reflections and descriptions of His own station, He, as the First and the Last, is all things, and therefore, He is Muḥammad, the Qá'im, and all the other sacred figures as well. Yet although all those stations are present within His own reality, it is at the level of the Letters of the Living that these stations are realized as independent realities. The Báb as the Primal Point remains in His transcendent station, where no other Letter of the Living is present, yet He also can be described in terms of those other names. We see here another expression of the truth of His title as the "Gate": He is the Gate and yet He is not defined by it, He is the Imám and yet not described by it, He is the Apostle and yet not praised by it.[19]

In an important but subtle way, the discussion of the Point and the Letters of the Living links the Persian Bayán, as the Mother Book of the Báb's Dispensation, to the Qayyúmu'l-Asmá'. In the Persian Bayán the Letters of the Living are described as the first to have knelt before the throne of God. The Báb writes:

Let there be be no doubt that man's glory is in testifying unto God's unity, in recognizing Him, acknowledging His justice, obeying Him, and seeking His good pleasure. It is, however, certain that these sacred souls have attained, before anyone else, unto that which is the quintessence of all excellence and glory. . . . Further, there can be no doubt that they were the first Lights who bowed down before God, accepted the verses He hath revealed unto His Báb, and proclaimed them to the world. . . . They are the lights which in the past have eternally prostrated

> themselves and will prostrate themselves eternally in the future, before the celestial throne. . . .
>
> In each Dispensation, they are called by different names amongst the people, and in each Revelation, their individual names are also changed. Yet, the names of their inmost realities, which refer unto God, and are manifest in their hearts.[20]

We can see that here the Báb is actually alluding to the story of Joseph and to the Qayyúmu'l-Asmá'. Recall that the Qur'ánic account begins with Joseph's description of his dream about eleven stars, and the sun and the moon bowing down before him. As the Báb had written in the Qayyúmu'l-Asmá', Joseph is Ḥusayn, and the rest of the figures are the sacred figures of Islam:

> Verily, the Most Gracious God hath unmistakably intended [by reference to Joseph], naught but Ḥusayn. . . . God hath verily shown Ḥusayn, within the Sanctuary of His Heart, and above the Throne, that the Sun, the Moon, and the Stars have manifestly knelt before Him, in adoration of the One True God. . . .
>
> Verily the stars of the Throne in the Book of God have bowed down in very truth for the martyrdom of Ḥusayn, and they were indeed, according to the Mother Book, eleven in number. . . .
>
> God hath verily intended by the sun, Fáṭimih; by the moon, Muḥammad; and by the stars, the true Imáms.[21]

In this way, we can see, the truth of the Qayyúmu'l-Asmá' becomes manifest in the Persian Bayán. The station of Joseph symbolizes the divinity of the Point, the station of the sheer revelation of God and of absolute Divine Unity. The martyrdom of Ḥusayn also symbolizes the same station; thus the Báb is Joseph and Ḥusayn, and will return as Ḥusayn (that is, Bahá'u'lláh) in His next Revelation. The Letters of the Living are those holy souls who in each Dispensation have knelt before God by kneeling before the divinity of the Point. The fourteen immaculate souls of Islam, together with the four manifestations of the Most Great Name of God, the four Gates, are the Letters of the Living.

Finally, it should be pointed out that the discussion of the return of Muḥammad and the Imáms through the Letters of the Living also affirms the fulfillment of the most important sign of the advent of the Qá'im. The

Shí'ih Traditions maintain that Muḥammad and the Imáms will return to this world when the Qá'im arises, a time that is to be followed by the Day of Resurrection.[22] Yet, as we have seen, not only are the Báb and His Letters of the Living the return of the sacred figures of Islam, but those same Islamic figures, in their own day, were themselves the return of the holy souls of all the Scriptures before them. The inception of Islam (like the birth of each of the religions preceding it) was also the Day of Resurrection, and the same cycle of return and resurrection will continue without end.

The Origin of the Cause

The writings of the Báb called upon people to regard the spiritual realm with the eye of the heart, to perceive the unity of truth beyond the diversity of religions and their symbols, in the Primal Will Who reappears in human history according to the exigencies of each age. The most frequent expression of this summit of spiritual recognition is the Báb's counsel to fix one's gaze on "the Origin of the Cause." All the Revelations derive their legitimacy and binding power from the fact that they are expressions of the divine Will. Consciousness of the Origin and the Source of religion is intended to prevent people from clinging to former expressions of the Will and rejecting the living embodiment of the Will itself. The principle of progressive revelation involves recognizing all the Manifestations of God because of their ultimate unity, but it is the Manifestation of the Age Who embodies the legitimacy and truth of all the Revelations. Hence, according to the Báb, recognition of the new Manifestation of God is a duty of all human beings.

This fundamental principle is discussed in many ways in the Persian Bayán and all the later writings of the Báb. In fact there is hardly a gate of the Bayán that does not directly address the issue. One of the vehicles for its exposition is the Báb's reinterpretation of commercial metaphors in relation to the divine covenant. Like Muḥammad, the Báb was engaged in commerce. As is well known, the Qur'án frequently uses commercial metaphors to convey spiritual truth: faith and good deeds are represented as a loan extended by the faithful to God and a good investment that is repaid by God with high interest. God is portrayed as the divine Merchant Who keeps an account of all things in His Preserved Book, weighs the deeds of the people in the unerring Balance on the Day of Resurrection, and rewards all with fairness and justice. The Báb reinterprets these metaphors to convey the principle of historical consciousness.

The historicization of the commercial metaphors takes many different forms. For example, in gate 3 of the seventh unity of the Bayán, the Báb discusses the necessity of repaying one's debts, but He goes beyond the social level of this obligation to explicate its ultimate spiritual philosophy and purpose:

> The fruit of this ordinance is this, that the divine words of glorification, celebration of praise, sanctification, exaltation of unity, and magnification, and all the other parts of religion are tokens that are bestowed as a bounty from the Supreme Truth unto His created beings. Therefore, upon His revelation, it is incumbent upon all to return this bounteous loan unto Him, from the lofty word of the declaration of Divine Unity to the last token of limitation. Were one to repay at once, upon the revelation, his debt, nothing would be reduced from his possessions; rather, he would be acknowledged in both the world and within himself.[23]

Each Dispensation of divine revelation, with all its root principles and derivative laws, is thus a loan that is bestowed by the Primal Will on human beings. This loan has a fixed term: it is extended for the duration of the particular Dispensation. At the moment that Dispensation ends, the loan comes due and must be repaid. At this time the former religion, along with its symbols, is no longer intended to be kept by the believers but is to be returned to God for this is the Day of Resurrection when everything returns to God. Yet, paradoxically, repaying this loan will not render anyone poorer for doing so. The abrogation of the previous religion is simultaneously its exaltation and fulfillment, as it appears renewed in the form of a fresh Revelation. Repayment is thus actually a means of gaining true riches: the new wealth is attaining the good pleasure of God and recognition of His new Manifestation.

The words of divine praise mentioned in the statement quoted above ("glorification, celebration of praise, sanctification, exaltation of unity, and magnification") ultimately refer to the Revelation of the Manifestation of God and His Letters of the Living. It is this Revelation that creates the inner reality of the believers. Thus when the Sun of Truth dawns in a new Day, the human mirrors must turn to the Sun in its new location. The images of the previous dawning of the Sun perish unless they are renewed by the new illumination of the Sun. By repaying that loan to the new Manifestation, that is, by recognizing His new Revelation, the believers honour the divine covenant.

Another expression of this transformation of commercial metaphors is the Báb's discussion, in the Persian Bayán, of buying and selling. In gate 18 of the fifth unity, He affirms that transactions are valid if there is mutual consent among the two parties. Again, He goes beyond the social law and states that the purpose of this law is that "haply in the Day of the Revelation of God, the buying of the sign of the Sun of Truth and selling of all that is besides Him will occur by virtue of His good pleasure and the consent of their own souls."[24] The renewal of the divine covenant in each new Dispensation means that people must attain the good pleasure of God by "buying" from God the sign of His Revelation, and casting off any attachment to anything but faith in the new Manifestation.

Yet another form of the commercial imagery concerns the exchange of gifts. In this divine economy, every Revelation is a gift that is presented to the Manifestation:

> The substance of this gate is that in each Dispensation, the Writings of the Manifestation of Truth are a gift from God for Himself toward His next Revelation, which is the manifestation of His being in a subsequent Resurrection. . . . In like manner, all that is contained in the Bayán, of various beloved modes, is a gift from the Point of the Bayán unto Him Whom God shall make manifest, Who is the very next Revelation of the Point of the Bayán. And this supreme glory and pride would suffice all, should He accept a person or any thing through the honour of association with Himself. . . .
>
> How utterly remote is the man who severeth his relation with Him and forsaketh the chance of being a true gift. Thus, today, should the believers in the Qur'án desire to present the gift of the Apostle of God, the blessings of God rest upon Him, they should one and all recognize the Bayán, otherwise they would sever themselves from the attribute of glory and sublimity.[25]

This concept is based on the identity of the Primal Will as one and the same reality manifested in different Revelations. In each Revelation the Manifestation of God covenants with the company of His faithful to recognize Him upon His return on the Day of Resurrection. That covenant is the essence of each Revelation. In gate 16 of the sixth unity of the Persian Bayán, the Báb writes that "The Lord of the universe hath never raised up a prophet nor hath He sent down a Book unless He hath established His covenant with all men, calling for their acceptance of the next Revelation and of the next Book; inasmuch as the outpourings of His bounty are ceaseless and without limit."[26]

We can see, then, why the Báb begins the Persian Bayán with a discussion of the beginning and return of revelation. Divine revelation is binding solely because it has proceeded from the Primal Will, and it returns to the Will on the Day of Resurrection, which is simultaneously the beginning of the new Revelation. Therefore, although the former Dispensation is abrogated by the new one, the new Dispensation is, at the same time, the fulfillment and exaltation of the past Dispensation. Contrary to the normal conception held by the people, rejecting the new religion does not affirm the previous religion but prevents it from realizing its paradise and exaltation. Each Holy Book longs to be exalted through the next Book, which is nothing but itself manifest in a fuller way. The followers of any Book who reject the next Book are the cause of the grief of that Book and its Revealer. The Báb writes that

> the Bayán hath no goal but Him Whom God shall make manifest, inasmuch as none save Him hath ever elevated/abrogated, or will ever elevate/abrogate, this Book. Indeed, none but Him hath ever revealed, or will ever reveal, it. The Bayán and such as are believers therein yearn more ardently after Him than the yearning of any lover after his beloved. Even as the Qur'án and such souls as pertain unto it yearned after the Revelation of its Revealer, and never had any goal, nor will ever have any end, but Him. Today the Furqán bestoweth salutations upon those letters who uplifted it and caused it to enter in the Bayán, while it beseecheth its Revealer to torment those souls that have turned away from the Bayán, failing to give the Furqán its due measure. . . .
>
> For in the Day of the Revelation of Him Whom God shall make manifest, the Bayán will fix its eyes upon its believers while saying unto them: 'Is there any spirit related to me who would step forth in this Day to acknowledge Him Whom God shall make manifest, and thus be faithful to the covenant of his Lord that is established in me?' It would rejoice if its faithful believers recognize its Revealer, and would be saddened if its

> faithful believers cause its Revealer any grief. Thus, today, nothing is more afflicted with anguish than the Furqán. All recite it, yet they fail to receive its blessing, and attain naught but its torment, even as those who were reciting the Book of Alif in the day of the Revelation of the Furqán.[27]

Because of this paradoxical relation of abrogation and exaltation, the Báb has coined the term *irtifá‘* (meaning both removing and elevating) for the idea of abrogation. Each Revelation, in simultaneously abrogating and exalting the previous Dispensation, is the return of the previous Revelation in the station of its perfection. Thus we can see why the idea of maturation and perfection is central to the Báb's theology. Each thing's paradise is the state of self-actualization, maturation, and perfection of that thing within its own station. The Báb uses the metaphor of a tree to express the concept. Each Revelation is a seed that is planted in the hearts of the people. The tree must grow and achieve perfection. Perfection is the state of yielding fruit, when the faithful have become ready to attain the state of paradise, as a higher stage of spiritual development. The divine Cultivator Who planted the tree returns to gather the fruits, which are the first believers in the new Revelation. Thus the first fruit of the Tree of Islam is Mullá Ḥusayn, the first Letter of the Living. The Báb explains:

> The "day" of Resurrection, unlike the "night" of divine Revelation, resembleth the planting of a tree whose time of fruition is the Day of Resurrection, before which it hath not attained perfection. . . . From its transcendent Throne, the Tree of Truth watcheth over and beholdeth the tree that God hath planted in the hearts, spirits, souls, and bodies of all the people. As soon as He witnesseth the readiness of the Tree of the garden of Divine Unity for harvest, He reneweth His Revelation.[28]

The Báb also uses other organic metaphors to convey this principle. The religions are likened to different stages in the development of an individual person. This analogy implies that the new Revelation is both the past Revelation as well as a developmentally more mature stage of revelation. Although the adult is the same person who was once a child, the later stage is the realization of the earlier stage in a more fully actualized, mature form. And yet, the adult would no longer be identified in terms of the earlier stages of development, which are now outgrown.[29]

Another analogy used by the Báb to express the necessity to concentrate attention on the Origin of the Cause is the relation between the stars and the sun:

> The acts of Him Whom God shall make manifest are like unto the sun, while the deeds of men, provided they conform to the good pleasure of God, resemble the stars or the moon. . . . Thus, should the followers of the Bayán observe the precepts of Him Whom God shall make manifest at the time of His appearance, and regard themselves and their own works as stars reflecting the light of the sun, then they would reap the fruits of their existence; otherwise they would not deserve the appellation of "star."
>
> . . . . At night, all perceive they possess light from within, according to their own capacity. However, they are utterly oblivious that at the break of day their light shall fade away and be reduced to pure nothingness before the dazzling splendour of the sun.[30]

One of the most recurrent reflections of this principle in the writings of the Báb is found in the law of pilgrimage to the House of God. The Báb declares that it was He Himself, the Point of the Bayán and the very Point of the Qur'án, Who aforetime revealed the Qur'án and decreed the law of pilgrimage to be the circumambulation of a particular House. He explains that He revealed that law so the people would understand that when they must pay homage to a piece of dust because of its association to the Primal Will, how much more should they take an attitude of utter servitude and obedience toward the Primal Will Himself. However, the heedless people observe the mere outward tokens of divine revelation and disregard the Origin of the Cause. Although now the Point of the Qur'án Himself has appeared, all are still circling around the reflection of His former decree, while they have banished Him to the mountain prison of Mákú.

The dramatic expression of this cosmic paradox was the Báb's journey to Mecca. The true House of God is the Throne of the Manifestation, while all other things that are sacred derive their sacredness from the fact that the Manifestation has willed to associate them with Himself. Although the Báb was now present there in Mecca in person, all were clinging to images of His reality while rejecting the very Revealer of the words that made pilgrimage binding:

> Thou beholdest how vast is the number of people who go to Mecca each year on pilgrimage and engage in circumambulation, while He, through the potency of Whose Word the Ka'bah [the sanctuary in Mecca] hath become the object of adoration, is forsaken in this mountain. He is none other but the Apostle of God Himself, inasmuch as the Revelation of God may be likened to the sun. No matter how innumerable its risings, there is but one sun, and upon it depends the life of all things.[31]

The sanctity of the Ka'bah, He writes, is not due to its intrinsic qualities but rather to the Command of God:

> The substance of this gate is that there hath never been, nor will ever be, a material dwelling-place for God, but that during each Revelation of the Will, it is the earth that He hath attributed to Himself that hath become His House and the seat around which the angels of heaven and the people of the earth revolve. Nay, rather, all circle round His Command which is manifested in that realm of dust. If this sanctity were intrinsic to the dust itself, there would have been no change in the House of God in the past, and likewise no change in the future. Though it is evident to those endued with an understanding heart that the dust-House of God resembleth the Command, and that the Command is like unto the sun: should there be infinite change in the location of the House, it would remain one and the same House. . . .
>
> But the command to exalt the House intendeth naught but that through it they should discern signs and recognize that this House is the House of Divine Unity, and thus exalt that Supreme House accordingly through glorification, exaltation of divine unity, sanctification of praise, and magnification. Thus, they must fix their gaze upon the Manifestations of that latter House, so that at the time of the Revelation of Him Whom God shall make manifest they shall not be veiled from the One Who is the Source of the sanctity of that House. . . .
>
> Had the people circled around the House of Truth, the command concerning pilgrimage to the House would not have been enjoined. Inasmuch as they have failed to do so, the necks of the creatures have been shackled with the sovereign decree in order that they should circle around the dust which is attributed to Him and that they may comprehend their limits and in the Day of His Revelation not remain veiled from Him.[32]

The physical House of God that is the object of reverence is a but a sign of the real House of God, the Manifestation of God, around Whom all must revolve. This House of Divine Unity, of devotion to the Manifestation, is made out of the four words of divine praise. If the people had recognized that true spiritual House of God, and had concentrated their attention on the Origin of the Cause, the law of pilgrimage—of bowing down before the earthly symbol—would not have been necessary. The law of pilgrimage, the Báb explains, was required in order to educate the people to humble themselves before the Primal Will and to recognize Him Whom God shall make manifest on the day He appears.

12

Community and the Primal Unity

THROUGHOUT THE WRITINGS OF THE BÁB, we have seen the implications of the principle of beholding all reality with the eye of unity. Every aspect of reality, from nature to society and history, becomes an embodiment of the logic of unity. The Báb's writings and laws are structured in such a way that both their content and their form also express the same principle. The dialectic of form and content is so fundamental to the Báb's writings that one cannot adequately understand the one without the other. The Persian Bayán, the "Mother Book" of the Báb's Dispensation, is no exception to this rule. Since it is the Mother Book, the Bayán's symbolism of form should also be expected to directly represent the essence of the Báb's teachings—the principle of the heart.

That the Báb considered the Persian Bayán to be His Mother Book is evident in His statement, in the first gate of the text, describing the revelation of the Persian Bayán as the inception of the re-creation of all things:

> For the very beginning of the creation of all things is occurring at this time, a Friday, through the utterance of God. The Lord of Majesty hath fashioned this new and wondrous creation by virtue of His own Command, and He hath made it to abide beneath His shadow until such time as He will deign to return it. For it is beyond any doubt that it is God Who hath brought this creation into being and it is He Who afterwards will cause it to return.[1]

In this chapter we will examine the application of the principle of unity to the realm of the spiritual community through an analysis of the dialectic of form and content in the Persian Bayán.

From the Primal Unity to "All Things"

According to various writings of the Báb, all numbers proceed from 1, and 1 proceeds from the absolute One that transcends the limits of numbers. That absolute One is the Point; thus all proceed from the Point. Likewise, all words are expressions of the first letter of the alphabet, Alif (a vertical line), which proceeds from the written point. The most important implication of this idea is the principle of the unity of all things. All things proceed from the Primal Unity, which in turn proceeds from the Point. All things thus should be regarded as manifestations, reflections, and mirrors of the Point. We enter the realm of truth when we see in all things nothing but the Point.

This principle is the central theme of all the Báb's later writings. As we have seen, the Báb is the Point of the Will and the Primal Point Who has appeared to prepare humanity for the coming of Him Whom God shall make manifest. He is also the One, the unity that transcends the realm of numbers. Out of the revelation of His own being, the first believers, the Letters of the Living, are created, and the rest of the new spiritual community proceeds from them. Thus, "all things" (*kullu shay'*) signifies the new spiritual community which comes into being out of the unity of the Báb and His Letters of the Living.

The structure described above is not only a fundamental theological principle in all the Báb's later writings, it is literally the formal structure of both the Persian Bayán and the Arabic Bayán. In order to understand how this is so, first we need to pay attention to some important symbolism that is created in the Persian Bayán.

The word for "one" or "unity" in Arabic is *váḥid*. Throughout the writings of the Báb, one or unity is represented by its numerical equivalent, 19. The Báb and His eighteen Letters of the Living comprise the Primal Unity of nineteen figures. This Primal Unity gives rise to "all things"—a term that is particularly important. The numerical value of "all things" (*kullu shay'*) is 361, which is 19 multiplied by 19. In other words, all things literally are manifestations of the Primal Unity, and each unit of the Primal Unity is itself the source of a complete unity. The Báb makes this symbolic structure the organizing scheme of the Bábí community, in terms of successive units of "all things." The Bábí (solar) calendar is also divided in a similar way, with each year consisting of 361 days, in addition to 4 (5, in leap years) intercalary days which represent the letter Há', out of which all days come into existence.

As the Báb explains, He has created the Bayán in accordance with "all things," so the Bayán consists of nineteen unities (sections), and each unity consists of nineteen gates (chapters). In the first gate of the Bayán, He explains: "God hath organized the creation of all things in accordance with the number of all things, by virtue of the commandments which have been revealed from the Court of His holiness and have shone forth out of the Day-Star of His grace, that all things may attain perfection through the remembrance of all things within all things, in preparation for the manifestation of the next Resurrection."[2]

Thus the Persian Bayán, as "all things," has been revealed so that all things—the new spiritual community—will "attain perfection," that is, will become ready to recognize the next Manifestation. This perfection is achieved by remembering "all things," namely the 361 gates of the Bayán, the nineteen manifestations of Divine Unity (the Primal Point) that are manifest in the Bayán, within all things—in other words, within all reality and within all the days of the year throughout the duration of the Bábí Dispensation (which lasted nineteen years). The purpose of the Persian Bayán is that, through it, all shall perceive within all things nothing but divine revelation, and behold no power or strength in anything but the Primal Will which is manifest in the entire spiritual community. The universalization of the perspective of the heart, and a true understanding of the principle of progressive revelation, fixing one's gaze on the Origin of the Cause, and beholding all believers as stars before the Sun of Truth, is the ultimate end and purpose of the Persian Bayán.

Finally, the use of "gate," designating the chapters of the Persian Bayán, is also crucial in this symbolic formal structure. Each unity of the Bayán with its nineteen gates is also symbolically a way that leads to paradise, that is, each chapter of the book leads to the "paradise" of the Bábí Dispensation, which, as we have seen, is the Resurrection of the Bábí Faith in the advent of Him Whom God shall make manifest. "All things" simultaneously denotes the days of the year; the Báb equates each gate to one day. Every day is to be devoted to the remembrance of one of the chapters of the Persian Bayán, so that all things will become prepared to recognize the next Manifestation by remembering the Primal Will that is manifest in all those gates. In the Arabic Bayán this point is made even more explicitly, as each day becomes a gate to enlightenment, and each month (of nineteen days) a period for reflection on the truth of one of the letters of the Primal Unity:

> Verily the Bayán is Our conclusive testimony unto all things. . . . We, verily, have ordained the gates [chapters] of this religion to be according to the number of all things, even as He arranged the numbers within the year. Unto each day belongeth a gate, that all things may thereby enter His exalted paradise and thus, within each unity [nineteen gates/days], by virtue of the mention of a single Letter of the Primal Letters, become "for God," the Lord of the heavens, the Lord of the earth, the Lord of all things, the Lord of the seen and unseen, the Lord of creation. . . .[3]

Since each chapter is a gate leading to the recognition of Him Whom God shall make manifest, the gates of the Bayán are embodied in the first 361 individuals to recognize the Promised One. Those persons become the gates to paradise, and all others enter heaven through them. All those gates also are reflections of the first nineteen gates of the next Revelation, that is, the Promised One together with His Letters of the Living:

> Should exalted souls, to the number of all things (361), turn unto Him, the fruit of all things would be manifested before Him. Well is it with him who is gathered in the day of Resurrection before God, who is accepted by Him as one of the gates [chapters] of all things [the Bayán], inasmuch as he is that exalted soul unto whom shall return all who have believed in the Bayán, through their fulfillment of the commandment of that very gate. Therefore, hasten ye unto this lofty bounty: hasten ye, hasten ye, hasten ye, and hasten ye. For God is the Most Swift in Reckoning.[4]

Symbolically all the gates of the Bayán are also reflections of the supreme Gate of God, the Báb, and just as the Báb represents the difference between fire (*nár*) and light (*núr*)—differentiating between those who accept and those who reject him—the Persian Bayán and each of its divisions also play this role as a "gate" in the sense of being the standard by which all are judged and which determines their reward as either paradise or perdition.[5]

A further point should be noted about the Primal Unity. The Primal Unity—the Báb and His Letters of the Living—is the perfect manifestation of the attributes of God as the First and the Last; it is described as such at the beginning of the Arabic Bayán.[6] But in a secondary sense, the First is the Báb, and the Last is the final Letter of the Living, Quddús. In the Arabic Bayán, the Báb speaks of Quddús as the realization of the Last—the return of the Islamic station of gatehood, or the station of magnification (*takbír*). Quddús is thus a mirror of the First—the Báb—and indeed Quddús's own name, Muḥammad-'Alí, is the mirror image of the Báb's name, 'Alí-Muḥammad. Then the Báb calls Quddús the reality that is above eight unities of mirrors. Elsewhere, the Báb refers to Quddús as the one around whom eight unities revolve.[7] This concept of "eight unities" has complex meanings, some of which I have discussed elsewhere.[8] Here I will only mention another possible aspect of this enigmatic characterization of Quddús.

The Báb describes the Primal Unity as consisting of the First and the Last. The First is of course the Báb, representing *Huva* (He), equal to 11. The remaining eight Letters represent the station of Quddús as the Last. Since the "all things" of the Bábí community (19 x 19 = 361)—each member of which is a "mirror"—can also be considered as reflections of the First and the Last, the first eleven unities (11 x 19 = 209) are created through the Báb and the remaining eight (8 x 19 = 152) through Quddús. Quddús is thus above "eight unities of mirrors" or the one around whom eight unities revolve. And 152 mirrors thus fall beneath the station of Quddús. According to the Qur'án, eight angels will carry the Throne of God on the Day of Judgment. Quddús in this sense represents the station of magnification and gatehood, which "carries the throne of God," that is, the Báb or the Point of glorification.

The Structure of the Persian Bayán

As the Persian Bayán is organized in terms of "all things," it should theoretically consist of nineteen unities. In actuality, however, the Báb only completed nine unities of the book; the ninth unity ends with gate 10. The first unity is devoted to a discussion of the Primal Will, the Báb, and His Letters of the Living, affirming the Primal Unity and its perpetual return in all the divine Revelations. All the other unities of the Persian Bayán are beneath the shadow of this first unity.

The topic of the Primal Will is immediately followed by the question of conclusive proof or testimony. The first and most conclusive testimony of the Manifestation of God is His own Being, and the highest form of recognition is recognition of the Manifestation through His own Self. Various gates of the Persian Bayán explain that reliance on other forms of testimony is a mark of spiritual immaturity:

> Be aware that each Revelation, which is the Revelation of God, is unlike any manifestation of the creatures. Likewise, the testimony of God is a conclusive proof, the like of which all the dwellers on earth will ever be powerless to produce. Until the divine Dispensation advanceth in such wise that the people can recognize the Revelation through the Essence of Truth. At that time, the very dawning of the light of that Sun of Truth testifieth by itself unto His Revelation. It is then that "Recognize God through God" is realized. For until the present, all that hath been manifested is "Recognize God through His testimony." Here, the intention is not that "Recognize God through God" is an inconclusive testimony. Do not, therefore, be veiled from the Origin of the Cause. Nay, rather, the Dispensation advanceth to such an extent that those who glorify God in the Concourse on High will recognize their Beloved in each Revelation through Himself. Indeed, they would recognize the testimony through Him, rather than Him through the testimony. Know thou that the recognition of God in the station of "Recognize God through God" will not be affirmed save through "Recognize the Letters of the Primal Unity."[9]

The first unity of the Persian Bayán affirms that the supreme testimony of God is the being of the Manifestation and His Letters of the Living. The next level of testimony is the words He reveals. Hence the second unity of the Bayán discusses the nature of divine testimony, the binding character of the divine words, the Persian Bayán itself, the fulfillment of the Day of Resurrection through the Revelation of the Báb, and the realization of paradise in the very words of the Bayán. The nineteen gates of this second unity are organized around this theme, and the logic of this unity can be seen in the way these chapters are titled. The first is "On the recognition of testimony and proof"; in it the Báb identifies His writings as the conclusive testimony. The next specifies Him Whom God shall make manifest and the Báb as the ultimate authority with regard to the meaning of the Báb's writings: "On this, that none can encompass the knowledge of that which God hath revealed in the Bayán, except him whom God willeth." The third gate further explains the designation of the Bayán as "all things," and is titled "On the exposition of the Bayán, which verily encompasseth the truth of all things." Gate 4 further elaborates on the previous gate by explaining "the letters of the sublime paradise and that which is other than them."

The fifth gate explains the real meaning and end of all that is in the Bayán. It is titled "On this, that any virtuous name God hath verily revealed in the Bayán referreth, in its primary truth, to Him Whom God shall make manifest, while any evil name that God revealed therein intendeth, in its primary truth, him who will be, in His Day, the letter of negation." The sixth gate proclaims the Bayán to "constitute the unerring Balance from God until the Day of Him Whom God shall make manifest. He who followeth it is registered as light, and he who deviateth from it is recorded as fire." The next twelve gates are devoted to discussion of the Day of Resurrection and its signs. The Bayán is identified as paradise, and the believers as the inmates of heaven and light. The last gate of this unity refers to the Bayán as "a present from God unto Him Whom God shall make manifest."

The subsequent unities of the Persian Bayán are devoted to analyzing the characteristics and duties of the spiritual community in relation to the Primal Unity and the writings of the Báb. In other words, if the first unity addresses the ultimate Origin of the spiritual community, and the second unity discusses the creative Word through which that spiritual community comes into being, then the rest of the Persian Bayán deals with the attributes that befit human beings as mirrors of the Bayán and the Primal Unity. The link between the first unity (dealing with the Primal Unity) and the subsequent unities (the laws pertaining to all things) is the principle, outlined in the second unity, of the creativity of the divine Word: the Primal Unity creates all other realities through the Word revealed by the Primal Point. The Bayán—like all the Báb's writings in general and the Persian Bayán in particular—is the unity that encompasses all things and which brings all things to life through the creative divine Word.

The Standard of Search

The first gate of the second unity of the Persian Bayán discusses the testimony that demonstrates the truth of the Manifestation of God. According to the Báb, one must behold the Manifestation with the eye of God, with the eye of the heart, and with the eye of unity. One must fix one's gaze on the supreme Origin of the Cause and not on outward manifestations of the Primal Will. The standard of the Manifestation of God is His own being and His writings, which are inimitable, more powerful and excellent than any physical miracle. The Manifestation as the Speaking Book and His revealed writings as the Silent Book together are the mightiest expression of the love, beauty, and power of God, and nothing else can even be mentioned at their level.

Taking the perspective of the heart, therefore, is the proper method of embarking on the search for religious truth, the spiritual journey that leads to the recognition of the Point. The wrong method is to cling to the outward or token signs as the standard of truth, to regard rejection of the new Prophet by the supporters of former religions as evidence against Him, to forget the Balance and Testimony, and to take human interpretations of the tokens of previous Revelations as the precondition for accepting the new Manifestation of God. As the Báb frequently emphasizes, the tragic irony is that although the believers of the former religion were longing for the their Beloved One to appear, when He did appear they universally condemned him:

> Likewise in the manifestation of the Point of the Bayán, the people stood up at the mention of His Name and fervently implored His advent night and day, and if they dreamt of Him they gloried in their dreams; yet now that He hath revealed Himself, invested with the mightiest testimony, whereby their own religion is vindicated, and despite the incalculable number of people who yearningly anticipate His coming, they are resting comfortably in their homes, after having hearkened to His verses; while He at this moment is confined in the mountain of Mákú, lonely and forsaken.[10]

Frequently the outward tokens of the former religion become a veil hindering people from recognizing the Revealer of those tokens, and the abrogation of the former laws has always been used as the justification for rejecting the new Manifestation. This is the case, He explains, because people neglect the Origin of the Cause:

> There are people who every night until morning busy themselves with the worship of God, and even at present when the Day-Star of Truth is nearing its zenith in the heaven of its Revelation, they have not yet left their prayer-rugs. If any one of them ever heard the wondrous verses of God recited unto him, he would exclaim: "Why dost thou keep me back from offering my prayers?" O thou who are wrapt in veils! If thou makest mention of God, wherefore sufferest thou thyself to be shut out from Him Who hath kindled the light of worship in thy heart? If He had not previously revealed the injunction: "Verily, make ye mention of God," what would have prompted thee to offer devotion unto God, and whereunto wouldst thou turn in prayer? . . .
>
> . . . Thy purpose in performing thy deeds is that God may graciously accept them; and divine acceptance can in no wise be achieved except through the acceptance of Him Who is the Exponent of His Revelation.[11]

Sometimes the believers' interpretation of statements in the former Scriptures leads to the rejection of the Manifestation of God. The Jews rejected Jesus based on their interpretation of the Torah; the Christians rejected Muḥammad on account of their understanding of the Gospel; and, the Muslims rejected the Báb based on their interpretations of the Qur'án and the Traditions. But the Holy Scriptures contain complex and hidden meanings that are not always accessible to ordinary humans—including religious leaders and scholars. Therefore, nothing other than the testimony specified by God can be the grounds for accepting or rejecting the new Manifestation. No statement in any of the Holy Texts can be used as a standard for judging the new Manifestation because the believers cannot be certain they have understood the true meaning of that statement. It is partly for this reason that the second gate of the second unity immediately identifies Him Whom God shall make manifest, His successors, and then the Báb as the only ones who truly understand the meaning of the Bayán:

> The substance of this gate is that none shall encompass that which God hath revealed in the Bayán except Him Whom God shall make manifest, or the One Who is taught such knowledge by Him, as well as the

> Exalted Tree from which the Bayán hath emerged. For should all the oceans in the heavens and on the earth turn into ink, all the beings into pens, and all the souls into those who inscribe, they would be incapable of interpreting even a single letter of the Bayán, inasmuch as God hath destined neither a beginning nor an end for any letter thereof.[12]

Other gates of the second unity emphasize that the true meaning of all that is contained in the Bayán is Him Whom God shall make manifest; thus no one can cling to any statement in that Book as evidence with which to refute Him. In gate 1 of the sixth unity the Báb again warns His followers that, regardless of their station and knowledge, they should realize that their own understanding of the Bayán is only a shadow of its true meaning, understanding of which belongs only to the Promised One, and He cautions them not to use the words of the Bayán to reject its true Revealer. Making the same point in the Kitábu'l-Asmá', He writes: "Say! Verily the Revealer of the Bayán knoweth its beginning and end, which is none other than Him Whom God shall make manifest. As to all else besides Him, these know naught save that which He hath taught them."[13] And in His tablet to Mullá Báqir the Báb emphasizes that the Promised One should be recognized by Himself, and that nothing in the Bayán, not even the Primal Unity itself, should be used as an argument against Him:

> Beware, beware lest, in the days of His Revelation, the Váḥid of the Bayán shut thee not out as by a veil from Him, inasmuch as this Váḥid is but a creature in His sight. And beware, beware that the words sent down in the Bayán shut thee not out as by a veil from Him, inasmuch as these are His own words in His former Manifestation. He is the Sun of Truth, the Face of Unity, the Countenance of Lordship, the Inmost Reality of Divinity, and the Self of Eternity.[14]

In gate 1 of the second unity, the Báb speaks in the voice of God about the binding and sufficient character of the divine words. The Word of God is the source of the legitimacy of all religious phenomena, and now He Himself has appeared in the world:

> O My creatures! All that ye perform, throughout your lives, with utmost striving and endeavour, is for the sake of attaining My good pleasure. If ye observe the derivative precepts, ye do so solely because I have

revealed them in the Book; if ye recognize the Imáms of guidance, or seek My nearness through visiting their shrines, this is merely because their names have been alluded to in the Qur'án; if ye acknowledge the prophethood of Muḥammad, the Apostle of God, the blessings of God rest upon Him, it is only because He was sent as a Messenger by Me; if ye circle round the Ka'bah, it is merely because I have called it My House; and if ye magnify the Qur'án, that is solely because it is My Word. . . .

. . . But today is the Day of My own Revelation, appearing by My Self.[15]

The Persian Bayán and All Things

We can now better understand why the Persian Bayán is identified as "all things." The form and the title of the book, as "all things," express the supreme philosophical truth of the perspective of unity. The Persian Bayán represents the creative Word of the Primal Will, which calls all things into existence. In other words, it contains all things, and out of this "all things" all creatures derive their existence. The key concept here is the qualitative difference between the Word of God and the words of created beings. The words of ordinary humans at best describe a limited aspect of reality, whereas the Word of God *creates* reality. It is this creative nature of the Word of God which makes it the binding testimony of the Manifestation of God, and it is this unique feature of the Holy Scripture that renders it the most powerful miracle of all. The Báb explains:

> No power besides God can achieve this, inasmuch as that which is uttered by God out of the Tree of Truth would instantly create, by itself, the inmost reality of the said thing. . . . For the Word of God is the utter Truth, and whatever is mentioned by it acquireth reality at once, that it may provide further evidence of this truth, which is His utter Truth. . . . Unless one fixeth his gaze upon the inmost reality of all things, . . . he will not arrive at the true realization of "Verily, the Word of God is the truth," since it is through the very utterance of the Word that the entity acquireth truth in its inmost reality.[16]

The fact that all things are brought into being by the revelation of the Primal Unity through the creative Word, the Bayán, means that a true believer will perceive in all things one and the same reality: that is, the supreme Origin of all things which is the common truth of all the Manifestations of God. The unity of the Manifestations is now expressed in the unity of all things. More specifically, the dual station of the Point, its divinity and servitude, is the source of all beings, and the diverse aspects of the Point are reflected in the diversity of the spiritual community. For that reason, the regulating principle of that community should be tolerance and love. Additionally, the perspective of unity affords the insight that everything in the Bayán is also a reference to Him Whom God shall make manifest: if all reality is the diverse manifestations of the Primal Will, then the Bayán, which is the description of the inner truth of all things, is ultimately a description of Him Whom God shall make manifest.

The idea that the spiritual community is a mirror of the diverse aspects of the Primal Point, created by its stations of divinity and servitude, is a major theme in all the later writings of the Báb. In Panj Sha'n, applying this principle to the hierarchy of spiritual understanding, the Báb writes:

> For instance, shouldst thou desire to comprehend the diverse modes of the Will, thou must behold the creation of all things; and shouldst thou wish to understand the names of all things, thou must gaze, in each Revelation, upon the Book sent down by God upon the Throne of the Will. For instance, thou beholdest all things in the Dispensation of the Furqán, from Muḥammad Himself, Who is seen in the words, "I am verily God; none other God is there but Me, the Lord of the worlds," to the last insignificant atom of dust, manifest in the words "I, myself, am but the first to worship Him." The same is true in all Revelations.[17]

Here the Báb is speaking of how the dual stations of the Point bring into existence all things. Then, as before, He relates this to the issue of difference and dispute within the religious community, and resolves the cause of conflict through the perspective of unity.[18]

The most dramatic expression of this truth is the Báb's assertion that all reality and all things are present in the opening phrase of the Persian Bayán. The background of this statement is the Islamic Tradition which states that all truth is contained in the Qur'án, all that is contained in the Qur'án is present within its first súrih, all that is present in that súrih is contained in its opening phrase, "In the name of God" (*Bismilláh*), and all that is contained in that phrase is present in its first letter, Bá'.[19]

The Báb explains that the opening phrase of the Qur'án, "In the name of God, the Most Gracious, the Most Merciful," has been renewed in the Dispensation of the Báb as the opening phrase of the Persian Bayán, "In the name of God, the Most Exalted, the Most Holy." All that is contained in the Bayán is a reflection of the first unity, and all that is in the first unity is a reflection of the first gate of the first unity, and all that is in the first gate is in the opening letters of the Bayán.

The key to understanding the Islamic Tradition as well as the Báb's assertions is the fact that the opening phrases of both the Qur'án and the Bayán (Persian as well as Arabic) consist of nineteen letters, symbolizing the Primal Unity. Just as the first unity of the Persian Bayán was a discussion of the Primal Unity and how all things proceed from it, the opening phrase expresses the same concept in a condensed manner. Since the reality of all things derives from the revelation of the Primal Unity, all things are present in the opening phrase. The first of those nineteen letters is Bá', symbolizing the station of the Point. Bá' stands for the Most Great Name of God, *Bahá*, according to the Tradition of Imám Ṣádiq that "The letter Bá' is *Bahá'u'lláh*."[20] The Báb identifies various Letters of the Living as corresponding letters of the opening phrase of the Persian Bayán, for example, designating Mullá Ḥusayn as the letter Sín, the second letter of *Bismilláh*.

The Persian Bayán symbolically represents this truth in many other ways. A number of its consecutive chapters discuss the progressive condensation of the entire truth of the Bayán into smaller and smaller expressions.[21]

The Bayán and the Four Levels of the Covenant

The opening phrases of the Qur'án and the Persian Bayán contain all spiritual truth because these phrases represent the Primal Unity of their Dispensations. Both phrases consist of four words (and thus "all things," 19, 4, and 1 are symbolically equivalent). The Primal Unity consists of four levels of reality—the four levels of the covenant. In the Dispensation of Islam, the first word (*bism*, in the name of) corresponds to the station of the Point of the Qur'án, representing the recognition of God. The second word (*Alláh*, God) represents the station of the prophethood of the Apostle of God. The third word (*ar-Raḥmán*, the Most Gracious) stands for the station of the twelve Imáms and Fáṭimih, and the fourth word (*ar-Raḥím,* the Most Merciful) refers to the station of the four Gates, the four Pillars, the four Angels, the true Shí'ih and the four Prophets of the past who mediate between the Imám and the believers—all figures that return as the Primal Unity of the Báb's Dispensation.

The symbolic identity of 19, 4, and 1 emphasizes the indivisible nature of the divine covenant and its levels of recognition. True recognition of God is manifested through recognition of the entire Primal Unity. The Letters of the Living are to be recognized because they are mirrors in which nothing can be seen but the Point. Although the reflection in the mirror (that is, the Point), not the mirror itself, is the object to which one should turn, the recognition of the Point is inseparable from the recognition of all the other three levels of the covenant.

These four levels of the Primal Unity correspond to the four existential levels of spiritual reality distinguished by the Báb: heart, intellect or spirit, soul, and body—where the last should be understood primarily as the essential or inner body, not a material body. The station of the Point is the station of the heart; the station of prophethood is the station of the intellect/spirit; the station of guardianship is the station of the soul; and the station of gatehood is the station of the body. These in turn are symbolized by the stations of fire (the Point), air (the Prophet), water (the Imáms), and earth (the Gates). This identity is often found expressed in many different ways in both the early and later writings of the Báb. In the Persian Bayán, for example, we find:

> [T]he first land wherein the very body of Him Whom God shall make manifest appeareth [His birthplace], hath always been, and will ever be, the Sacred Temple. . . . The purpose of this ordinance is this, that when a piece of earth is enobled by virtue of its association with His body, it attaineth such an exalted station that it becometh the place of pilgrimage through the act of circumambulation around His House; then how much more exalted would be the soil of the essential bodies that point unto His magnificence, and the soil of the souls that refer unto His unity, and the soil of the spirits that hint at His praise, and the soil of the hearts that mirror His glorification. For in the foremost station of the heart, the fire of love shineth forth; and in the second, the air of guardianship ascendeth; and in the third, the water of unity surgeth; and in the fourth, the dust of existence is elevated.[22]

This statement already points to another important principle of the Bayán. Because human beings are temples of divine reality, all the levels of reality are present within them: they also possess the four levels of heart, spirit/intellect, soul, and body as reflections of the reality of the Primal Unity. Therefore, the human heart is a sign and testimony of the heart of the Primal Unity, the Point. Likewise, the essential body is a mirror of the essential body of the Primal Unity, which signifies the Gates. For example, in discussing the necessity of practicing cleanliness and refinement with regard to one's body and appearance, the Báb states:

> All these rules are ordained for this purpose: that haply, in the Day of Resurrection, naught shall be seen in the appearance and the inner reality of any soul save the love of God. Then those who are endued with true understanding of the meaning of symbols may realize that when God is not content with aught but love in relation to the accidental body, then how much more true would be His desire with regard to the essential bodies, souls, spirits, and the hearts, which are the seat of the revelation of the Primal Unity.[23]

Within the Primal Unity, the four levels are the various levels of the Logos or divine praise. Four stations of divine praise are distinguished in the writings of the Báb. These are usually designated "glorification" (*tasbíḥ*), "celebration of praise" (*taḥmíd*), "exaltation of Divine Unity" (*Tawḥíd* or *Tahlíl*), and "magnification" (*takbír*). The choice of these particular words is significant: they constitute the essence of the levels of the covenant. The station of the heart, which belongs to the Point, is the station of the glorification of God. It affirms the sanctity of God beyond any description and refers to the divinity of the Point, where all names and attributes are negated. The station of the intellect or spirit represents the celebration of praise, which is the station of Muḥammad, the Apostle of God. The expression of this station is "Praise be to God." The word *Muḥammad* is derived from the word *ḥamd* (praise). The station of the soul is the station of the exaltation of Divine Unity, which is realized in the Imáms. In the Qayyúmu'l-Asmá' and other works, the Báb extensively states that the twelve Imáms are the letters of the exaltation of Divine Unity ("There is none other God but God," which consists of twelve Arabic letters).[24] Finally, the station of the essential body is the station of the magnification of God, which is realized in the four Gates.

In the words of magnification, "God is Most Great," the word for "Most Great" (*Akbar*) consists of four letters. In addition, as the Báb has said, the four Gates are the letters of "the Hidden, Well-Guarded Name, Whose four letters are referred to by various names including the Four Gates, the Lights of the Throne, the Bearers of creation, provision, death, and life."[25] Since the Báb appeared as the Gate, the unity of the Point and the Dust, "magnification" refers to His station of gatehood as the reflection of the Most Great Name of God.[26]

In the Commentary on "All Food," the Báb relates these four words of praise to the four stations of heart, intellect, soul, and body, and identifies them as the rivers of paradise mentioned in the Qur'án:

> At the initial manifestation, associated with the arc of descent, the first pillar of the Sacred House is established. At this station it is incumbent upon the servant to make his remembrance of God that of glorification (*tasbíḥ*), as God, exalted and glorified be He, hath said, "Their cry therein is 'Glorified art Thou, O Lord, my God.'"[27]
>
> Wert thou to recline upon that sublime seat, and repose on that lofty throne, thou wouldst partake of the crystal, incorruptible water, by chanting that which God hath taught thee: "Glorified art Thou, O Lord, My God." For verily this is the food that God hath sent down unto the people of this sublime station.
>
> When thou descendest from that sublime world unto the world of intellect, thou wouldst find that therein God hath assigned thy food to be His remembrance through the word of praise (*taḥmíd*). Unto this referreth the statement of God, exalted and glorified be He, immediately following the word of glorification, "Glorify the praise of thy Lord."[28] Drink thou then of the fresh pure milk "whose taste changeth not" during the hours of thy night-season and daytime.[29]
>
> When thou descendest from this station unto that of the soul—by which is meant the divine soul—thou wouldst see that therein God hath destined thy drink to be the wine "delicious to those who quaff it."[30] Make thou the food that God hath allowed unto thee the remembrance of the exaltation of Divine Unity (*Tawḥíd*): "There is none other God but God."
>
> When thou descendest from that station unto the station of thy body, thou wouldst witness that therein God hath allotted thy food to be that which is revealed by Him of the word of magnification (*takbír*), through

> His name, the Most Merciful. That pure honey is lawful unto thee, as a token of God's grace, and is a sustenance from God unto those who have recognized Him and His verses, who observe His laws for His sake.[31]

It is important to note that, in the above passage, the Báb identifies the station of magnification with the name "the Most Merciful." At first this may seem enigmatic because the word of magnification is "God is Most Great." However, the Persian Bayán makes this point easily understandable. Since the station of magnification is the station of the Gates, it represents the fourth word of the opening phrase of the Qur'án, which is "the Most Merciful." Here, what is explicated in the Persian Bayán can be seen to have been expressed in a concealed way in the earlier writings.

In the Persian Bayán the Báb explains that human hearts, spirits, souls, and bodies consist of the words of God relating to creation, provision, slaying, and quickening, which call them into existence. All the actions performed by the faithful are in fact actions of the Primal Unity:

> The substance of this gate is that all things return to man, and he is fashioned by four divine words: the word of creation, which is the truth of his heart; the word of provision, which is the truth of his spirit; the word of death, which is the truth of his soul; and the word of life, which is the truth of his body. And these are all attributed to the nineteen Souls who are the Gates of paradise, for whatsoever creation, provision, death, and life that occurreth doeth so by virtue of the appearance of these Manifestations. . . . For example, should one of the people of the Bayán offer a flower to a faithful believer, this deed is naught but the very action of the Letters of Unity, for the soul that offereth is the burgeoning of that Unity, and he doeth this solely for the sake of obeying them. Thus naught is seen in this deed but the Action of God.[32]

These four realms of the Primal Unity and their corresponding words of divine praise manifest themselves in the four modes of revelation. Through the four modes of revelation, which are the four rivers of paradise, the hearts, spirits, souls, and bodies of the faithful are created. As noted earlier, the fact that all of these four modes of revelation were revealed directly by the Báb has far-reaching implications. Most importantly, the four levels of the divine covenant were realized within the Báb's lifetime, and no one other than the Báb could reveal verses or have binding authority until the appearance of Him Whom God shall make manifest. Thus, literally, all the stations of the Primal Unity were realized within the Báb Himself.

We can now see how the entire spiritual community is defined by the Báb as the reflection of the Primal Unity, which in turn reflects the supreme Origin of all, the Primal Will. An exploration of all the aspects of the complex symbolic structure of the Persian Bayán would be beyond the scope of this study, but a glimpse of the mutual relations of many of these symbols is afforded by this concise statement from that work:

> It behooveth those who point to unity of Essence, unity of Attributes, unity of Actions, and unity of Worship; to creation, sustenance, death, and life; to glorification, celebration of praise, exaltation of divine unity, and magnification; to fire, air, water, and earth; to heart, spirit, soul, and body; and to snow-white light, green light, yellow light, and crimson light, to behold all beneath the shadow of the Letters of "In the name of God, the Most Exalted, the Most Holy."[33]

13
Ethics and Laws in the Bayán

THE SAME FUNDAMENTAL UNIFIC PRINCIPLE that we have seen expressed in the Báb's approach to the interpretation of Holy Scriptures, in His metaphysics of the universe, in His concept of progressive revelation, and in His epistemic perspective of unity also informs His laws and moral teachings. The laws and ordinances of the Báb, however, represent a somewhat paradoxical structure. As we shall see, this paradoxical structure corresponds to the Báb's twin stations as an independent Manifestation of God and the Herald of another imminent Revelation. In the first station, He creates laws to order the behaviour of the community of believers during His Dispensation, but in the second station He fashions laws to concentrate His followers' attention on the Revelation to come. Many of the laws of the first type were later reaffirmed and retained by Bahá'u'lláh in the Kitáb-i-Aqdas. Many of those laws of the second type, however, were ostensibly severe, and all of them were abrogated by Bahá'u'lláh.

The apparent severity and harshness of those laws of the second type, and their apparent inconsistency, even incongruity, with the rest of the Báb's teachings, has long been a topic of puzzlement and speculation. A literal reading of the severe laws has led some scholars and commentators to arrive at a variety of negative conclusions about the Báb and His intentions. I suggest, however, that the literalistic approach to understanding these laws obscures their real meaning. To discover that meaning it is necessary to consider the severe laws in the context of the totality of the Báb's writings, and in terms of the interpretive principles that we have been exploring in this book. Such an approach yields a reading of these laws that is startlingly different from the conclusions arrived at by applying the literalistic approach.

Before discussing the philosophical premises of the Báb's laws, a series of seven laws that belong to the early stage of His writings should be noted. These laws are mentioned in a work entitled Seven Attributes (Khaṣá'l-i-Sab'ih), and they were set down during the period before the Báb abrogated the Islamic laws. The Báb enjoins seven practices, as follows:

1 Carrying around one's neck the sacred circle (holy writings arranged in the form of a circle and carried for protection)
2 Abstaining from smoking tobacco
3 Drinking tea with the utmost purity and refinement
4 Adding to the *adhán* section of the Islamic obligatory prayer the testimony, "I verily bear witness that 'Alí before Nabíl is the Gate of the Remnant of God"
5 Performing one's prayer prostrations on a piece of clay containing dust from Imám Ḥusayn's shrine, so that both forehead and nose touch it
6 Reciting the Báb's Grand Visitation Tablet on Friday and the other holy nights
7 Wearing a ring of white agate bearing the words, "There is none other God but God, Muḥammad is the Apostle of God, 'Alí is the Guardian of God, 273."[1]

The observance of these seven laws by the followers of the Báb served to markedly distinguish the Bábí community from Muslim society, and that fact occasioned the persecution of three believers, including Quddús. We can already see here that an important function of these early laws is symbolic: they serve as forms of communicating a message. In the fourth law, the words "'Alí before Nabíl" only make sense if we read them symbolically: "Nabíl" is numerically equal to "Muḥammad"; thus the phrase means "'Alí-Muḥammad." We can see the symbolic significance of "Ḥusayn" in the ritual in which dust from Imám Ḥusayn's shrine is made the focus of the act of prayer: when engaging in prayer one is worshipping God through "Ḥusayn." In the seventh law, the number 273 is clearly a symbol: it is numerically equal to "'Alí-Muḥammad is the Gate of God." The prohibition on the smoking of tobacco was a major feature that set the Bábís apart from Muslims socially, especially distancing them from the Shaykhí leader Karím Khán-i-Kirmání, who was known as an excessive smoker. The symbolic role that is evident in these early ordinances becomes predominant in the Báb's later laws.

Action as Spiritual Journey

All the writings of the Báb stress the inseparability of spiritual or mystical knowledge, on the one hand, and action in accordance with the divine precepts, on the other. This principle distinguishes the Báb's Revelation from both the legalistic approach to religion and the mystic total disregard of religious laws.[2] The principle is abundantly evident in the Persian Bayán, but it is not only in the Persian Bayán that the mystic character of action is emphasized. One of the Báb's earlier texts, On the Virtuous Journey II (Fí's-Sulúk II), is entirely devoted to this principle. There are actually two works by the Báb that bear the title "On the Virtuous Journey." One is a shorter text, written before the declaration of His mission, called On the Virtuous Journey I (Fí's-Sulúk I). Here we will not address the complex content of this work, but it should be noted that it defines the essence of both religion and the spiritual journey as the realization of divine love. This divine love can only be realized when one attains the four manifestations of love, which are the four pillars of the covenant: the unity of God, prophethood, the imamate, and gatehood or the Shí'ih. These four levels are inseparable from each other and can be considered as expressions of God's love for His creation, as well as the creation's love for its Creator. In this tablet the Báb also associates these four levels with the heart, intellect, soul, and body.[3] The other tablet, On the Virtuous Journey II, was written after the declaration of the Báb, in honour of Abú Ṭálibi'l-Ḥusaynávi,[4] and responds to his question concerning the reward of good deeds on the Day of Resurrection.

The word *sulúk* has two different meanings: "mode of conduct" and "spiritual journey." The heart of this tablet is the unity and harmony of these two meanings. Thus Fí's-Sulúk is a treatise on ethics and laws which defines action as a process of attaining union with God. A true action is one that is oriented to spiritual truth, while a true spiritual journey is inseparable from action in accordance with the precepts of God. For this reason I have translated *sulúk* as "virtuous journey."

The Báb begins this text by taking the categories posed by the questioner and transforming them. Although the questioner wished to know about the external rewards that could be expected on the Day of Resurrection in recompense for good deeds, the Báb explains that true reward is not external or physical, but rather an inner mystical state of nearness to God. The goal of one's actions should not be winning an external reward, but attaining divine good pleasure and love. True paradise is not a state of physical pleasure in the next world; it is the realization of divine revelation within one's heart. Consequently the question of *sulúk* as conduct is actually of *sulúk* as spiritual journey. The Báb tells him:

> Thou hast implored to receive an answer concerning the concepts of true reward, the reality of punishment, and the light of rapture. . . .
>
> . . . For verily, before God and before those who behold paradise in this earthly life, every moment is the very Day of Resurrection. Shouldst thou purify thy vision, and cleanse thy sight, thou wouldst assuredly witness that verily the Balance hath been appointed within thine own soul; paradise hath been brought nigh unto thee on thy right hand; hell hath been made to blaze on thy left; the Maidens with large and lustrous eyes, abiding in their lofty chambers of heaven, have been established upon their thrones; and the essence of the infidels hath been tormented in their terrible stations. . . .
>
> Wert thou to desire in thy heart the performance of a good deed, God would assuredly reward thee within thy soul. Then, in the life to come, the result of that which God hath immediately conferred upon thee will be revealed unto thee. For God, verily, is the Omniscient, the Omnipotent, and the Swift in Reckoning.[5]

Then the Báb begins His discussion of action as a mystical process by positing a universal maxim of moral behaviour:

> Be thou for God and for His creatures even as God hath been for God Himself and for His creatures. Just as God hath verily created thee out of nothing, in like manner must thou adore Him in utter devotion, for the sake of His Countenance, without desire for reward or fear of punishment. Act likewise in all conditions and with regard to all matters and phenomena.
>
> Shouldst thou unlock this gate to thy heart, thou wouldst assuredly be adorned with the virtues of the All-Merciful. Then, were all the people to wrong thee, thou wouldst forgive them and, indeed, do good unto them,

> even as God, glorified be He, provideth, through His grace, for those who have ungratefully repudiated Him. Thus, apply the same maxim with regard to all phenomena and matters.[6]

This universal imperative is the essence of the Báb's philosophy of ethics, and all His other discussions are extensions and amplifications of it. We should note that the Báb defines this maxim as the universal principle of action that human beings are to employ not only in their dealings with other humans, but "in all conditions and with regard to all matters and phenomena." This universal imperative is also a deeply spiritual principle, one which renders human conduct a mirror of divine action.

The Báb's moral imperative has an obvious similarity to the categorical imperative of Kantian philosophy, yet in many important respects it transcends the Kantian formulation. The Kantian formal theory of ethics rejected utilitarian ethical philosophy, which held that the intrinsic reward was a state of happiness and pleasure, and which therefore defined the morality of acts in terms of the calculation of their consequences.[7] Kant argued, however, that the morality of an act can be judged independently from such a calculation of consequences. He asserted that the "good will" is morally good in itself, and thus He defined moral action as action motivated by good will, derivable from the very form of the action, generalized as the categorical imperative: one should act in a such way that one's act can serve as a universal rule of behaviour for all people. More specifically, one should treat other human beings as ends in themselves and not as mere instruments for the attainment of one's own ends.[8] The essence of the Kantian categorical imperative is that action should not merely be a means of achieving one's own desires. Moral action requires a universal concern for all human beings as members of the "kingdom of ends"; they cannot be reduced to mere instruments or conditions.

The Báb's universal imperative includes the positive elements of Kantian theory, that is, one should act without regard for one's own desires and without expectation of external rewards or benefits. But the Báb also defines this principle in a way that links morality to the spiritual journey: one should act in the same way that God acts with regard to all things. No act of God is motivated by any expectation of benefit for Himself: He is the supreme All-Merciful One Who showers His favours and bounties upon all—even those who reject Him—regardless of their actions. Human beings, the Báb is saying, should act that way toward others as well. No action should be motivated by anything other than the intrinsic spiritual pleasure of performing the good deed itself. The same principle must govern human acts of worship offered to God. One should relate to God in the same way that God relates to Himself. Just as all things are non-existent at the level of God (and thus the divine self-description is not motivated by receiving anything besides God), humans should worship God as if nothing else even exists before God, let alone that it could become a reason for worship. The spirit animating one's prayer should be that of utter detachment, love, and the intrinsic beauty of the divine Countenance.

Despite the similarity between the Báb's moral imperative and that of Kantian philosophy, there are significant differences between the two. First, Kantian philosophy excludes non-humans from the kingdom of ends, and thus natural phenomena have no moral rights. In contrast, the Báb's imperative applies to all phenomena. Second, for the Báb, morality is the mystic process of attaining divine good pleasure. This implies that recognition of the Manifestation of God is inseparable from moral action. Third, this mystic orientation is dictated by the logic of universal love. Kantian theory dismisses the significance of love as the basis of moral action.[9] In the writings of the Báb, however, morality is defined as a type of action that is oriented to beholding the Countenance of the Beloved within one's heart and within all beings.

The Báb's universal moral imperative is at the same time the principle of contentment with divine good pleasure and radiant acquiescence before the decrees of the divine Will. Since all actions must be performed for the sake of God, they all should be a gift offered to God. This gift, however, will be accepted by God only if it is offered in the spirit of utter selflessness and servitude. The Báb reaffirms His universal imperative in this poetic form:

> Behold thou that, verily, all things are contained within the treasuries of God. Verily, God, glorified be He, shall never accept from anyone a gift that existeth in the treasuries of His dominion. Present then unto God that which hath never existed in the treasuries of His majesty, which is naught but powerlessness and its modes. God verily accepteth the deeds of all things through such a gift.

> This is the greatest of all gifts, according to God's religion, to Him. Inasmuch as there is no trace of poverty before God, He, exalted is He, loveth poverty, even as thou lovest to find a jewel or Elixir, for thou possesseth them not.[10]

The only thing that God does not already possess, and which human beings can thus offer to Him as a gift, is their own powerlessness and poverty.

The substantive topic of On the Virtuous Journey II, thus, is contentment with divine good pleasure, which the Báb defines as the wellspring of ethics. The rest of the tablet is devoted to an exposition of the types of *riḍá'*, or radiant acquiescence to the good pleasure of God:

> Be thou contented, in utter acquiescence and at all times, with the Decree of thy Lord, first in thy soul, and then in thine outward manifestation. Thou wouldst attain the utmost state of contentment with the good pleasure of God when thou art pleased with misery even as thou wouldst be with glory, with poverty as with wealth, with exertion as with tranquility, and with sorrow as with joy, in the states of thy soul and the outward condition that God hath destined for thee.
>
> Verily, all the knowledge of ethics streameth forth out of the wellspring of this crystal, living water. For, verily, there are infinite stations and endless modes in thy life. Thus, shouldst thou desire thy Lord, thou must be pleased with the will of God in all thy circumstances and modes. Verily, I shine upon thee the light of the day-star of radiant acquiescence (*riḍá'*), which would enable thee to dispense with all besides Him in the path of God.[11]

Then the Báb discusses the modality of contentment in relation to all the layers of reality. First, one must be content with divine Action. This is the secret of *badá'* or alteration, when one realizes that one's existence is due to divine mercy and grace, and that one's utter contingency implies the constant possibility of immediate non-existence. As the Báb has explained in His other works, such a possibility is inseparable from the essence of contingent beings. The only reason that one exists is divine grace and bounty—not divine justice.[12]

Next is contentment with the laws and commandments revealed by the Manifestation of God. Since at this time the Báb had not yet abrogated the laws of Islam, He states that all have the "duty to be acquiescent to the truth and ordinances (*aḥkám*) of Muḥammad, the Apostle of God, and to be submissive unto Him in all that He hath performed within the religion of God, all that He hath enjoined, as well as all that He hath forbidden."[13] Making sure that the mystic orientation of contentment with the good pleasure of God will not become an excuse for disregard of the laws, the Báb strongly rejects those Sufis who question the absolutely binding nature of divine revelation. According to the Báb, "Wert thou even to conceive in thine heart, regarding any matter, other than that which He hath ordained unto all men in the Book, thou wouldst fail to reach, in the realm of good character and virtue, the lofty station of the people who are faithful to the covenant."[14]

After contentment with God and the Manifestation of God is contentment with others: "Thus the state of contentment is also incumbent upon thee in thy relations with people."[15] The Báb begins with the necessity of contentment within the spiritual community and declares that the right of the faithful is derived from the right of God. Then He emphasizes the right of parents, a precept that is repeated often in His works:

> After the right of thy faithful brothers, it is thy duty to submit in acquiescence unto thy parents, even though they should wrong thee. Utter no word of contempt to them, and repulse them not.[16] Obey their wishes before they ask thee. For verily thine obedience to them is more beloved in My sight than thy heart's delight in refreshing, cool ice on a burning hot day.
>
> Were either of them, for any reason, to be wrathful to thee, thou must reveal, in return, thy satisfaction even with their wrath, that no sorrow, even to the extent of a mustard seed, may ever cross their heart from thee. Verily the command of thy parents is mightier, in the sight of God, than all good deeds, unless it calleth thee to sin against the Lord. Seek thou their satisfaction with thee, for their pleasure is naught but the good pleasure of the Lord, exalted be His sanctity.[17]

Next, at the level of contentment with others, comes contentment with one's own self. Here the Báb calls for complete harmony between the inward and outward aspects of the human reality. One must respect both aspects in order to attain a harmonious unity:

> As for thine own self, it is thy duty to be pleased in thine inner heart (*sirr*) with thine outward action or expression (*'aláníyah*). The reverse is also thy duty. Should thine inner heart desire to pray at night, and thine outward action fail to manifest its wish, then thou wouldst not be numbered amongst those who are content with their inner heart.
>
> Likewise, wert thou to desire for thine outer expression one of the delightful favours of this earthly life, and thine inner heart deny such a desire, thou wouldst not be recorded in the Book of God amongst those who willingly resign themselves unto His Decree.[18]

Having discussed the various levels of contentment, the Báb adds that the highest form of contentment in this day is contentment with the testimony that God has assigned for demonstrating the truth of His Manifestation. Thus the summit of contentment is contentment with the revelation of divine verses as the supreme proof of the truth of the Báb:

> However, in this Day, radiant acquiescence, in all its forms, is confirmed for the one who is content with the revelation of verses by God, without the slightest desire for any other proof besides them. Were any man to be adorned with all spiritual virtues in utmost contentment in all the worlds, and yet assert in this Day that his heart is not utterly satisfied with the revelation of verses in the absence of witnessing miracles, then all his acquiescence would be brought to naught in the Book of God, and no other mode of resignation would be of any profit to him.[19]

The rest of the tablet deals with the station of the Báb and the fact that true reward is the recognition of God and His covenant; instead of seeking external rewards, one should seek the paradise within. Because the inner human reality is a sign of the stages of divine Action, the spiritual journey toward recognition of the Manifestation of God is both the true reward and the attainment of self-realization. One's heart is the reflection of the pure divine revelation before which there can be no mention of reward, whereas one's intellect is the reflection of the station of prophethood, which is the first station of the realization of intrinsic reward. The other spiritual stations are reflections of this intrinsic reward at their respective levels of phenomenal reality. The supreme reward, however, is the station of absolute unity of the inner and outer beings, where the self is utterly annihilated in the divine Will, and "thou must not even allude, save by His leave, and then that allusion would be reckoned in the Book of God as equal to the obligatory prayer, for the fragrances of thine inner heart would accord with thy manifest prayers"—where all human actions are naught but the very Action of God.[20] This true reward is the station of the unity of servitude and divinity, realized in the very being of the Báb Himself, invested with the revelation of divine verses as His conclusive testimony.[21]

The Báb concludes His discourse with the statement: "For verily thou wouldst attain the summit of excellence in divine knowledge when thou yearnest for naught but God, and fearest naught but thy transgression. Shouldst thou act according to this lofty path, thou verily wouldst abide in security."[22]

Six Principles of Spiritual Action

Since the Persian Bayán is the Mother Book of the Bábí Dispensation, it should be no surprise that the Báb's most extensive discussion of the philosophy of moral and spiritual action is to be found in that text. A detailed discussion of all the elements of the Báb's approach to ethics and law would be a book in itself, so here we will investigate only six of the general principles of moral and spiritual action in the Persian Bayán: the mystic character of action, the concept of "for God," refinement and perfection, the prohibition on causing grief, the spiritualization of life, and spiritual linguistics.

The Mystic Character of Action

The distinctive feature of the Revelation of the Báb—the divine summons in the sanctuary of the heart—constitutes the core of the Báb's diverse discussions of laws and ordinances. There is virtually no exception to this rule. The Persian Bayán is structured around this fundamental principle, decreeing laws and ordinances only after presenting the fundamental principles of faith which those laws represent. The first and second unities of the Persian Bayán, as we have seen, expound the spiritual principles that underlie all the laws that are mentioned in subsequent unities. Yet the most striking feature of the Persian Bayán's approach to laws is that while a particular ordinance itself is mentioned in the short opening paragraph of its corresponding gate, the substance of the gate is devoted to an explanation of the philosophical meaning and purpose of that ordinance.

Among religious texts, normally laws are least likely to be couched in highly figurative language. Although laws are certainly subject to differences of interpretation as to their exact meaning, the normal assumption is that laws are intended to be taken as more literal than symbolic since their purpose is to regulate concrete practices and actions and to provide the pattern and standard of behaviour that, over time, structures the particular society. The Báb's laws, uniquely, were not intended to structure a society over any significant period of time because His Dispensation was soon to be abrogated by Him Whom God shall make manifest. For this reason, many of the normal assumptions that accompany the concept of law do not apply to the laws of the Báb. Knowing that His laws would soon be superseded by those of the Promised One, the Báb was free to use the "genre" of legislation for other, symbolic purposes.

It is therefore extremely significant that all the chapters of the Persian Bayán define their respective laws as symbolic in nature. The Báb repeatedly stresses that the most important aspect of the law is the recognition of its spiritual meaning and the fulfillment of its purpose. Otherwise, obeying the law without obeying its real message is of no value. Every one of the laws of the Báb is *dalíl*—a symbol, a metaphor, a guide, a reference and a proof, of something spiritual and transcendental. The purpose behind these laws and rituals is that the faithful will engage in *istidlál* (from *dalíl*)—the act of inferring the true spiritual meaning of the symbolic law, deriving the real import of the metaphorical ordinance, and vindicating the truth that is represented by the behavioural sign. Thus the Báb frequently speaks of the necessity of the act of *istidlál*. But, then, for the Báb, the entire universe is a *dalíl*, or symbol of the Primal Will, and a sign of the divine Action that is enshrined in the heart of every being. His laws and rituals are consciously created to lead His followers to the realization of the perspective of unity in all aspects of their lives so that their lives become pure mirrors reflecting the inner reality of all things, and to prepare them, above all, to recognize the Promised One upon His advent.

The ordinances of the Báb are thus essentially mystical processes: as we saw in relation to Fi's-Sulúk II, the conduct of life and behavioural expressions are simultaneously a process of spiritual journey. The laws cannot be separated from their spiritual ends, just as the recognition of the divine truth is inalienable from observing the command of the Manifestation. Discussing the law of pilgrimage, for example, the Báb states:

> This is the fruit of pilgrimage, that they may arise to fulfill His Command, that haply in the Day of His Revelation, by the aid of such an approach, they will ascend toward Him. Alas! For the Dispensation of the Qur'án no such fruit is harvested, inasmuch as while seventy-thousand souls circle round that House, at this very time the supreme Source of the sanctity of the House resideth within the mount of Mákú, yet except for one soul, none is present before Him! It is evident that the fruit is not yet gathered. In truth, it was befitting that, at the time of revelation, all the faithful believers in the Qur'án, who by virtue of His Command revolve so frequently around a mere piece of dust, revolve infinite times and until the end that hath no end, around the Command of His own Self.[23]

Therefore, spiritual knowledge (*'ilm*), and observance of laws (*'amal*) are both necessary aspects of the same reality. That is why, as we have seen before, one should recognize that even the affirmation of Divine Unity by the believer is a mere shadow of the same word of affirmation that is revealed by the Primal Will, and thus its sole purpose is the recognition of the new Manifestation of God. In the words of the Báb, "This is the essence of all knowledge and faith, could anyone but behold, gather the fruit of his existence, and attain utter death before each Revelation, even as all are now dead before the command of His previous Revelation."[24]

As we will see in more detail, the various laws of the Persian Bayán are symbols of the spiritual journey. For example, the Báb's obligatory prayer consists of nineteen *rak'ah* units (prostrations). He describes these nineteen units as a journey from the realm of the body to that of the heart, a journey that realizes the signs of the Primal Unity within one's being. This spiritual journey can be depicted as traversing the arc of ascent, which consists of the stages of body, soul, spirit/intellect, and heart. This arc of ascent is the mirror image of the arc of descent, which can be represented as the first four stages of divine creative Action: Will, Determination, Destiny, and Decree.

The station of the body signifies the "refined" body, which is the spiritual representation of the material body, or the inner spiritual nature of the physical body. The station of soul represents the struggle of the human soul which, having transcended the realm of selfish desires, is transformed into a will "for God" and exerts effort to attain God's good pleasure. The station of spirit or intellect denotes the realization of the perfections of the soul, through understanding spiritual realities. At this stage the soul is united with celestial spiritual realities. The heart is the station of the pure revelation of God within, a reflection of the realm of the Primal Will at the human level. The attainment of the station of the heart permits one to transcend the realm of limitations and oppositions and to behold all things in their station of unity.[25]

As we have seen before, in the writings of the Báb these four stages of the spiritual journey correspond to the other symbolic series in fours: the four colours, the four elements, the four words of divine praise, the four rivers of paradise, the four stages of creative Action, the four layers of the covenant, the four modes of revelation, the four levels of the unity of God, and many others. In this sense the spiritual journey embraces all reality, physical and celestial, in one all-encompassing symbolic structure.

"For the Sake of God"

The Báb's most direct discussion of the philosophy of ethical action in the Persian Bayán is found in His explanations of the concept of *lilláh*, which means "for God," abiding by the will of God, or acting for the sake of God, and which refers to the inner motivation of action. The Persian Bayán repeatedly commands that all actions must be performed "for God." This motive of action is the same as contentment with divine good pleasure and attaining true annihilation of self before God. As we saw in the Báb's universal imperative, one must be for God and for the creatures of God just as God is for God (for Himself), and for His creatures. The perspective of unity renders the meaning of these two principles one and the same: an action that is truly for God is simultaneously an action for the creatures. All deeds are acceptable if they are performed to attain the good pleasure of God. In the gate entitled "On the motive of action," the Báb creates a symbolic law to convey this principle:

> The substance of this gate is that no behaviour turneth into a real action unless it is performed for the sake of God. It is for this reason that it is enjoined upon all those who perform any act to utter these words at

> the time of their action: "Verily, I do this for God, the Lord of the heavens and earth, the Lord of all that is seen and unseen, the Lord of creation." Should he recite them in his heart, his action would be rewarded as a result.[26]

As the Báb explains in the same gate, this principle applies to all actions whether testifying to Divine Unity or performing a mundane action such as eating food. This principle is expressed in the Báb's frequent discussion of the meaning of heaven in the Persian Bayán: the very performance of a deed that is truly done for God is the instant attainment of the pleasure of paradise. Furthermore, the Báb emphasizes that the true act is the end of the act itself: a good deed is its own intrinsic reward. Thus He writes, "Before those who bear witness to the unity of God, there is no paradise more exalted than the very act of observing the ordinances of God."[27] The opposite is also true: "For those who commit a grievous act, no fire hath ever been, nor will ever be, more tormenting than their very own action, even as for the faithful no paradise hath ever been, nor will ever be, more mighty than their own recognition and faith."[28]

As the Báb explains in the Persian Bayán, all people believe that their actions are for the sake of God. But for the Báb the concept of "for God" is not merely a subjective phenomenon. Instead, it is an objective state of affairs. It is only through the realization of a pure heart that the subjective and objective meanings of "for God" coincide. An act is for God when it is truly ordained and desired by God. Thus one is acting for God when one is attaining the good pleasure of God—and that of course always means the good pleasure of the Manifestation of God for the age. "For God" thus presupposes the recognition of the Manifestation for the age and obedience to His commandments. In the gate discussing the motivation of action, the Báb instructs the believers to recite, inwardly or outwardly, a verse expressing the orientation that acts are "for God." Then He says:

> However, no act will become for God unless the one who performeth the act recognizeth the Tree of Truth. . . . It is not appropriate that anyone perform an act for someone, unless he doeth it for the sake of God, and it will not be for God, unless it is for the sake of the Revelation of that time. . . .
>
> In like manner, the people who are now acting in accordance with the Bayán, and recite this verse, should they, in the day of the Revelation of

> Him Whom God shall make manifest, perform action for Him, they act for the sake of God, otherwise their action will come to naught, as if they had not done anything.[29]

Here the Báb is affirming what Bahá'u'lláh states at the beginning of the Kitáb-i-Aqdas, that the goodness of deeds is inseparable from the recognition of the Manifestation of God.[30] In explaining this logic, the Báb says that since the new Manifestation is the previous Manifestation Himself, any act that is not done for the new Manifestation is not done for the previous Manifestation either:

> The secret of this mystery is this, that from the Day of Adam, the One Who was followed by the faithful was none other than the Apostle of God, and all the revealed Books naught but the very Qur'án that was sent down unto Him. This meaneth that, in truth, they have been veiled from the previous Revelation and His Book inasmuch as they have failed to recognize Him as the same previous Manifestation Who is now manifested in the next Revelation.[31]

One of the most extensive discussions of action for God is carried out in gate 7 of the sixth unity of the Persian Bayán, in connection with the law of marriage. According to the Báb, marriage becomes lawful if both parties utter a sentence vowing that their action is "for God": "Verily I abide by the will of God [I am for God], the Lord of the heavens, the Lord of the earth, the Lord of all things, the Lord of that which is visible and that which is unseen, the Lord of all the worlds." In this law, the Báb fixes the limit of the dowry at ninety-five *mithqáls* of gold. He explains that 95 is the numerical value of "for God" (*lilláh*): "The law of marriage is ordained thus that all may abide beneath the bounty of God's grace and mercy, and fix their eyes upon that which is the basis of the lawfulness of marriage, which is naught but the words "for God," that haply in the Day of the Revelation of Him Whom God shall make manifest they will not deviate from the supreme Mirror of these words, the One Who testifieth unto God."[32]

We can see that the Báb not only historicizes the concept of "for God," but He also defines moral action as inseparable from the recognition of the Manifestation of God. This conception of moral action and recognition (or faith and works) as inseparable from each other also rejects any opposition between mystical insight and observance of religious laws.

We have noted the resemblance of the Báb's universal imperative (to act for God and for His creatures as God acts for Himself and for His creatures) to the Kantian categorical imperative. The Báb's emphasis on action for God has affinities with Kantian theory because it emphasizes purity of motive, universality of action, and detachment from selfish desires. Yet, as we have seen, the Báb's universal imperative differs from the Kantian formulation in being objective as well as subjective, spiritual as well as moral, and historically specific as well as universal.

In the history of modern Western philosophy, Kantianism was opposed by the school of utilitarianism. Where Kantian theory explained morality in terms of the formal properties of action, as categorical imperatives, utilitarianism defined morality in terms of the calculation of consequences leading to the maximization of happiness. In fact, in the Báb's writings the two opposing categories represented by utilitarian and Kantian theories are joined together. The philosophy of morality embodied in the Báb's writings could even be considered a spiritualized utilitarianism. Discussing the inward remembrance of God, the Báb says that one should reckon the consequences of one's action, and that such insight is the source of all moral knowledge. This calculation of consequences must take into account action in both the physical and spiritual dimensions: one should ascertain not only the outward amount of wealth, but also the inner health and dignity of one's soul. This calculation must be geared toward not only one's own happiness (both inner and outer) but also the happiness of all others. Thus utilitarianism becomes inseparable from the universal imperatives, and from concern for inner serenity:

> [T]he essence of all knowledge is the knowledge of good character and traits. Man must act in conformity with them, that by virtue of such knowledge of ethics he shall neither witness any grief in his soul, nor inflict sorrow upon any other soul. All the reasons for ordaining righteousness, abstinence, and other attributes return to this principle. For example, should one be afflicted with poverty but choose contentment and patience, his self-esteem would remain intact, and he would not be grieved, and therefore when the days of his need would have passed, he would not experience any abasement. On the other hand, should he show his poverty he would, at best, receive assistance from someone, which would remove that which is grieving him, but when he beholdeth

himself, the assistance received would never equal the abasement brought about for him. Regard, in like manner, all the good traits and attributes in all stations.[33]

Perfection and Refinement

If action is a process of spiritual journey, and if it is performed for God and to attain God's good pleasure, then every single action must be a means of realizing the potentialities of things and the beautification and refinement of the world. This principle is one of the main criteria of an acceptable action in the Persian Bayán. In the writings of the Báb, the two concepts of perfection and refinement are inseparable from each other. The principle of perfection refers to the duty of all human beings to exert their utmost efforts to realize the potentialities of all things in the world. This duty is based on the idea that heaven and hell apply to all beings and that a thing's state of perfection is its paradise. Humans, however, are required by the Báb to ensure that all phenomena achieve their perfection because "[n]o created thing shall ever attain its paradise unless it appeareth in its highest prescribed degree of perfection."[34] Thus, in whatever activity the Bábís are engaged, whether in the realm of industry or art, they must perform that work in the best possible manner and realize the utmost perfection in all things.

We can see, in the spiritualized utilitarianism of the Báb, as well as in His universal imperatives, that one should take into account not only the interests of human beings, but the interests of all created things because the realm of nature is endowed with moral rights as well as spiritual significance. The spiritual distinction of human beings is realized not by dominating nature, but by fulfilling their duty to facilitate its attainment to perfection, as its "paradise." Again, the logic of the sanctuary of unity is visible in this approach to ethics.[35]

It is in this connection that the Báb consistently emphasizes the idea of purification. All levels of reality, from the material body to the human heart, must be purified.[36] Natural resources must be preserved in the utmost purity. The Arabic Bayán prohibits the commodification of the natural elements of fire, air, water, and earth.[37] The Báb turns the idea of the purity of water into the protection of the environment. In the Persian Bayán He writes: "Nothing is more beloved before God than to keep water in a state of the utmost purity, to such an extent that if a believer should become aware that the glass of water he holdeth in his hand hath passed through any impure parts of the earth, he would be grieved."[38] In other words, it is implicitly necessary that all streams, lakes, and seas through which the water passes be clean.

An extended discussion of this principle can be found in one of the later writings of the Báb, The Book of Divine Names (Kitábu'l-Asmá'). In discussing the name of God, the Most Perfect (*Atqan*), the Báb commands people to reflect the perfection of God's handiwork in their own. Speaking in the mode of divine verses, He says:

> Say! We verily have perfected Our handiwork in the creation of the heavens, earth, whatever lieth between them, and in all things; will ye not then behold? . . . Perfect ye then your own handiwork in all that ye produce with your hands working through the handiwork of God. Then would this indeed be a handiwork of God, the Help in Peril, the Self-Subsisting. Waste ye not that which God createth with your hands through your handiwork; rather, make manifest in them the perfection of industry or craft, be it a large and mass product or a small and retail one. For verily one who perfecteth his handiwork indeed attaineth certitude in the perfection of the handiwork of God within his own being.[39]

By striving for perfection in art and industry, human beings manifest the divine perfection within themselves, and in this way, human action becomes a divine action. In discussing the same name of God, this time in the mode of prayer, the Báb writes:

> O my God! Thy handiwork hath always been complete, all-encompassing, perfect, and unfailing, and it will always continue to be perfect, unfailing, complete, and all-encompassing. . . . Thou hast commanded Thy servants, from the beginning that hath no beginning, till the end that hath no end, to produce handiwork with the utmost perfection, for this is verily the reflection of the perfection of Thy handiwork. . . . Educate then, O my God, the people of the Bayán in such wise that no product may be found amongst them but that the very utmost perfection of industry shall be manifest therein. . . . For verily Thou hast desired, by this law, to build the earth anew by virtue of Thy glorious handiwork through the hands of Thy servants.[40]

The requirement to realize the perfection of all things is simultaneously the requirement to refine and beautify all things. Emphasizing the importance of this law, the Báb writes in the Persian Bayán:

> For, in this religion no other command is as rigorously enjoined as the duty of refinement, and it is forbidden that one bring any object into being in a state of imperfection when one hath the power to manifest it in full perfection.
>
> For example, should one build an edifice and fail to elevate it to the utmost state of perfection possible for it, there would be no moment in the life of that edifice when angels would not beseech God to torment him; nay, rather, all the atoms of that edifice would do the same. For each thing, within its own station, yearneth to attain unto the utmost height of excellence in its own level. Thus, should a man who is capable not realize and respond to the yearning of his capability, he will be held accountable therefor. . . .
>
> It is ordained in this religion to design the doors of each place to allow a tall man to enter through them without bending his head. It behooveth them, each day, to build all the places in the utmost manner of exaltation possible at that time, so that haply in the Day of the Revelation of God, nothing that causeth grief may be witnessed in His kingdom.[41]

The requirement of perfection and refinement is also applied to the calligraphy used to copy the writings of the Báb. The Báb makes it clear that He wants His community to be the embodiment of perfection in all things. Furthermore, He defines beautification and excellence in art as the means of the spiritualization of the world and the propagation of the Cause of the Bayán:

> Thus, just as today the letters of the Gospel are distinguished amongst other communities in the art of ornament, the believers in the Bayán should likewise reflect in their handiwork naught but perfection within the limits of each endeavour, in such wise that a faithful believer in the Bayán in the East of the earth should be beloved in his station on account of his beauty and the beauty of all that he possesseth. And this is the most mighty path for attracting the people of other religions to the true Cause of the all-merciful God. However, these are all binding to the

extent that one possesseth the means to do so, not to inflict pain on oneself toward perfecting things.[42]

We can see that the ordinance regarding the perfection and beautification of all things is fundamental to the sanctuary of the heart: physical beauty is a sign of spiritual beauty. Refinement and beautification thus become the mediating point that links the physical to the spiritual. The kingdom of the Báb is thus an aesthetic as well as a spiritual kingdom.[43]

The principle of perfection and refinement is the basis of a number of ordinances of the Persian Bayán that emphasize the necessity of physical cleanliness and the beautification of one's own body. Gate 3 of the sixth unity ordains that a bathhouse must be built in any place of human habitation. Gate 6 of the eighth unity ordains beautifying oneself and bathing at least every four days. The Báb directs His followers to look into the mirror to manifest and observe the divine beauty that is conferred upon them, and to remember that they should not veil their primordial inner beauty by failing to recognize the Manifestation of God. The Báb emphasizes the cleaning and beautification of one's clothing, and states that it is better to change one's clothes at least with each bathing as well. He shows His strong disapproval of dirty and malodorous clothing, and affirms that nothing abhorrent or distasteful should be seen in His kingdom. In gate 7 of the ninth unity the Báb prohibits the smoking of tobacco, and in the next gate He prohibits the use of opium and intoxicants. Gate 10 of the ninth unity ordains the purification of all things, including the purification of one's heart, spirit, soul, and body. The believer must extend such purification to all things, so that all things become the mirror of the love of God.

Gate 12 of the fifth unity applies the rule of refinement even to the body in death. Since the physical body has been the throne of the spiritual reality, it should be treated with the utmost refinement and dignity. Gate 9 of the sixth unity abrogates the Islamic prohibition on the wearing of silk and on the use of silver and gold utensils. Gate 14 of the fifth unity discusses the various means of physical and spiritual purification, stating, "Nothing is more dearly beloved in the Bayán than purity, refinement, and cleanliness . . . and in the Dispensation of the Bayán, God wisheth not to witness amongst humans that which is other than joy and radiance, and He desireth that all appear in utmost spiritual and physical purity, that their own souls be not repulsed, how much less the souls of others."[44]

Since it is incumbent to manifest refinement and perfection in art, industry, and socioeconomic development, we can see in these discussions a clear stance emerging on the question of modernity and modernization. In fact the Báb directly addresses the issue of modernization in His writings on the perfection and beautification of all things. At a time when relations with Western "infidels" and any learning from Western culture and industry were being vehemently rejected by the Muslim clergy, the Báb praised the industry of Europeans and urged His followers to learn from its positive elements. The Báb in fact expresses benevolence toward Europeans (referred to as the "people of the Gospel") on account of their industrial and scientific advancements, and He takes this perfection as a manifestation of the inner perfection of human reality. At the same time, He shows His loving-kindness by beseeching God to spiritually revive the Europeans by bringing them into His Faith:

> Verily, whenever I have gazed upon the diversity of Thy creation upon the earth, I have seen none to resemble the people of Gospel in the creativity of their handiwork and the wonders of their products. Indeed, My heart is saddened for them, O My God, for it is not befitting Thy bounty that Thou wouldst allow such a people to be veiled from attaining Thy presence. Raise up, then, amongst them, O My God, one who shall bring them into Thy Faith inasmuch as they follow Thy path and seek Thy way.[45]

Later, discussing the same name of God, using the mode of rational arguments, the Báb tells His followers to "perfect then all your handiwork and industries, and seek to learn [in that regard] from the letters of the Gospel."[46] The positive appreciation of the printing industry expressed in gate 7 of the eighth unity is another expression of the same logic.

The Persian Bayán and other later writings of the Báb also call for perfection in social development. The Báb praises the West's material development but calls for an all-encompassing perfection in which the inner divine sign manifests itself not only in technical creativity but also in moral and spiritual perfection. The West's technological and industrial perfection must be extended to all dimensions of life, so that all things are treated with respect and dignity, and all become mirrors of the Divine Unity. Material development, however, must be accessible to all the people and not be a privilege of the rich and the powerful. In addition, all these forms of material advancement must be the means of spiritualization and not ends in themselves. Thus, they must be accompanied by inner perfection and the realization of divine beauty in all physical and spiritual aspects of life. The discussion in the Persian Bayán about the post and the media of communication expresses the Báb's attitude toward material advancement and modernization: material progress must be accompanied by social justice as well as spiritual progress and recognition of the Manifestation of God:

> It behooveth the sovereign of the kingdom wherein lieth the Sacred House of God—indeed, it behooveth all kings—to establish offices in every part of their territories to disseminate the news and correspondence within that land from one end to the other. In the West, such a system is organized in the utmost excellence, whereby the current news, which otherwise can take several months to arrive, is received within a short time. However, it is befitting that the king make this accessible to all, that all can be informed of the news swiftly. For He Whom God shall make manifest will assuredly be manifested, and should the means of receiving news and books be prevalent amongst all, the servants of God will attain the blessing of guidance more speedily. Were one to hear the news of the Revelation earlier—to the extent of an infinitesimal part (a ninth of a ninth of a tenth of a tenth) of a moment—become aware of His appearance, and recognize Him, it would be better for him than to be the possessor of all that is on earth and offer it in the path of God.
>
> It is for this reason that such an ordinance is decreed, that haply in the Day of the Revelation of that Most Mighty Day-Star, the means to facilitate the attainment of the glory of guidance for His servants will be prepared. However, until such a system is made universal, its benefit will not reach those servants of the kingdom unless there come a time when it will be accessible to all the people. Although today the kings have their own special couriers, this is fruitless, for the poor are deprived of such a service.[47]

The Prohibition on Causing Grief

As we have seen, the laws and ordinances of the Persian Bayán are oriented to realizing the divine Presence, are to be performed for the sake of God, and are to be concerned with the beautification and perfection of all things, so that one's labour becomes a means of manifesting the inner sign of divine revelation in the outward phenomenal world. All these objectives are based on the universal imperative of the sanctuary of the heart, in which all creatures are seen as sacred mirrors of divine attributes. This same foundational principle informs one of the most central ordinances of the Persian Bayán, the categorical prohibition on causing sadness and grief to anyone. In fact, together with the principle of perfection and refinement, the prohibition on causing grief is the most often emphasized among the ordinances of the Bayán.

One of the most dramatic expressions of this law is the Báb's ordinance concerning the duty to reply to communications and questions:

> It is enjoined in this Revelation that should anyone receive a letter from someone, it is his duty to reply, by his own hand or that of another on his behalf; indeed, any delay is abhorred. In like manner, should one ask a question, it is incumbent upon the person asked, to give a guiding answer, that haply in the Day of the Revelation of God no one may be shut out as by a veil from Him. Hence, the question revealed by God, "Am I not your Lord?" requireth all to answer, "Yea." Thus, the duty to reply is enjoined for this purpose, although its influence will last until the very last atom (*dharr*) of existence. . . .[48]

This ordinance is by itself a clear expression of the norm of reciprocity, care, responsibility, and kindness that is emphasized in the Persian Bayán. However, we can understand the true significance of this law when we consider the Báb's explanation of the philosophy and purpose of the ordinance. The duty of responding is intended to remind people to say "yea" to the call of God in all the realms of the divine covenant, and to recognize Him Whom God shall make manifest.

The Báb then extends the duty of responding, to the degree that all must be attentive to the tacit call of all things, whether person or thing, including their inner states:

> He is a man endued with vision who answereth the call of God in all worlds and stations, whether in writing, through utterance, or action, which is the most mighty means of response. And it is by virtue of the blessings accruing from the act of answering of such a soul that all are enjoined to respond to each other. So much so, that if an infant cry, it is a duty to respond to him through appropriate means. Likewise, should

> one's condition silently call upon others, it is the duty of men of discernment to answer his call. In like manner, should one's place of residence call for an answer, or any other manifestation discernible to men of vision, it is binding upon them to reply, that at no time anyone should witness that which would cause him grief.[49]

The universal love of the Báb for all beings is clearly visible in this passage. The Báb gives the example of an infant because an infant represents the utmost state of powerlessness. One must respond to the call of all people, but especially the powerless, and one must go beyond the overtly expressed and respond, through action, to unexpressed needs. This same point is made elsewhere: the Báb defines the most exalted persons as those who lovingly reply to a call or need even before the request is made, addressing the voice of the inner reality.[50]

The prohibition on causing grief is so central that the Báb ordains a punishment for any act that causes sorrow. Gate 18 of the seventh unity states that "he who knowingly causeth grief to any soul must pay a fine of nineteen *mithqáls* of gold, should it be in his power to do so." Then the Báb declares that God has forbidden anyone to inflict sorrow upon any soul. This rule is also extended to the spiritual community, so that causing grief to any member of the community is like causing grief to the Letters of the Living, and inflicting sadness upon the Letters of the Living is like causing grief to the Primal Point. The Báb asks His followers not only to refrain from saddening people but to seek actively to bring them joy and happiness. This injunction is even more important; He states, in relation to women:

> Therefore, in the Bayán there is no act of obedience that ensureth greater nearness to God than bringing joy to the hearts of the faithful, even as naught yieldeth more remoteness than causing them grief. This law is doubly binding in dealing with the possessors of circles (women), whether in causing them joy or grief. However, man must always be watchful that even if he fail to bring joy to a human being, at least he should refrain from causing him grief.[51]

In the same chapter the Báb categorically prohibits restricting the movements of any person or detaining them against their will—which of course is one extreme expression of the act of causing grief. Various similar ordinances that prohibit forcing people to do things against their will, mutilating the human body, and any kind of killing—are all laws that abrogate some of the harsh practices found in Islamic tradition, such as taking slaves in war, cutting off the hand as punishment for theft, and stoning to death as punishment for adultery.

As we have seen, the Persian Bayán advocates a form of spiritual utilitarianism, where the essence of ethics is the prevention of sorrow caused to anyone: "Man must act in conformity with" the knowledge of good character and traits, "that by virtue of such knowledge of ethics he shall neither witness any grief in his soul, nor inflict sorrow upon any other soul."[52] In the Kitábu'l-Asmá', interpreting the name of God, the Most Peaceful (*Aslam*) the Báb singles out gentleness toward all things as the most exalted deed. He prohibits rage and wrath and commands the Bábís to act, in all the material and spiritual aspects of life, with the utmost consideration and courtesy, so that no one will be saddened by them.[53] Elsewhere in the Kitábu'l-Asmá' the Báb instructs His followers to be the essence of love and care for others:

> Be lovingly watchful of one another and thus improve your affairs. Should ye find amongst you one who is afflicted with grief, remove his sorrow by any means in your power, and should ye find one stricken with poverty, enrich him to the extent of your ability. If ye find in your midst one who is abased, exalt him to the extent ye can, and if ye find one who is veiled by ignorance, educate him to the degree of your capacity. Should ye find amongst yourselves one who is single, help him to marry, in accordance with the divine law, to the limits of your ability, and should ye find one who is in distress, bring him tranquility by any means in your power.... Gaze upon others with the same eyes with which ye gaze upon your own selves.... If ye find in your midst one who is hungry, send him, in truth and to the extent of your power, food in such a way that his heart will not be saddened, and if ye find one who has no clothes, provide him with clothes in the most dignified manner, to the extent possible for you. Look then not at your selves and your possessions, but rather look at God, Who hath created you and conferred upon you from His kingdom that which is your lot.[54]

One of the most powerful expressions of this deep concern of the Báb regarding the causing of grief is His discussion, in the Persian Bayán, of pilgrimage and the House of God, recounted in the context of the Báb's own experiences on the way to Mecca:

> Guard yourselves, that ye may not in any way be the cause of sadness to another soul, inasmuch as the hearts of the faithful are nearer to God than the House made out of clay. . . .
>
> However, nothing is more important in the path of pilgrimage than adornment with virtuous conduct, so that should he be in the company of another, neither he himself nor his companion should have cause for sadness. I have observed (on the way to Mecca) acts which, in the sight of God, are of the vilest kind, sufficient to undo the good that results from the act of pilgrimage. These were the quarrels among the pilgrims! For quarrels are forbidden at all times and under any condition, and the ways of the faithful have never been, nor will ever be, aught but forbearance, patience, shame, and tranquility. Verily, the House of God hath no need of such people![55]

The general prohibition on causing grief and discomfort to others is reflected in several other laws of the Persian Bayán. Gate 3 of the sixth unity calls for change in the way buildings are built so that no one will experience inconvenience; doors are to be designed "to allow a tall man to enter through them without bending his head."[56] Gate 3 of the seventh unity emphasizes the believer's duty to repay loans. Gate 6 of the seventh unity prohibits carrying weapons and means of coercion, or appearing in frightening outfits in public, so as to avoid causing alarm: "The substance of this gate is that things which may cause a soul to become frightened by another are not beloved before God. . . . It behooveth the servant to be ever watchful that nothing he doeth can cause fear to any soul, that haply in the Day of Resurrection all shall abide in the temple of humanity with all its befitting characteristics."[57]

Gate 11 of the sixth unity prohibits the physical punishment of young children and discourages treating them in a humiliating or disrespectful way:

> The substance of this gate is that God never wisheth that any soul should be saddened, how much less that he should be afflicted with harm. Thus, He hath prohibited all from punishing a child who hath not yet reached the age five, save by words, and He hath prohibited causing him

> any grief. And after reaching the age of five, more than five light strikes, not to the flesh but to a protecting cover, is not permitted, and should not be inflicted in a disrespectful and discourteous manner, as is customary in these days.[58]

In the same gate, the Báb commands adults to allow children to have toys and engage in play. He asks adults to treat children with dignity and for that reason He states that, in school, children should be seated on chairs.

Gate 16 of the sixth unity discusses a number of other ordinances that are intended to prevent sorrow being caused to anyone. Unnecessary travel is discouraged because of the difficulties of travel at that time (elsewhere the Báb exempts from pilgrimage those who are separated by sea from Shiraz, because of the difficulties of the voyage). In that same gate, the Báb prohibits forcing anyone to do anything, coercing anyone to leave their home, afflicting anyone during a journey, compelling anyone to move while travelling, and entering anyone's house without permission. This ordinance even applies to the treatment of animals, which at that time were used for transport in commercial and personal travel: "Should, at a stopping place, any hardship or pain be inflicted upon an animal, the latter would beseech God to torment its owner. It is always necessary to consider the limits of the capacity of animals, in such wise that after the entrance of its owner into the Bayán, it would not be forced to carry a load unless it is less than the limits of its capacity, otherwise, the profit he may gain thereby would be of no benefit to him."[59] The Báb continues to emphasize the necessity of helping travellers who are weak, assisting those who are on foot and offering them transportation. He mentions that giving a ride, even if only one step, to a traveller who is walking, for the sake of the good pleasure of God, merits the reward of a full pilgrimage.

Gate 18 of the sixth unity prohibits opening and reading another's mail or book without permission. Gate 11 of the seventh unity prohibits the use of pulpits, and recommends, for the sake of dignity, the use of chairs and dais for teachers and pupils. Finally, gate 14 of the seventh unity prohibits confession and seeking forgiveness from anyone but God and His Manifestation.

The Spiritualization of Life

The logic of the spiritualization of the world and of all human life defines a most important principle that governs the ordinances of the Persian Bayán. Since all creatures are mirrors of the divine Reality, and all things are reflections of the Primal Unity, the Báb wishes to turn all aspects of human life into explicit symbols of their supreme Origin. Thus every law becomes a symbol that points to its transcendental meaning. Yet the Báb is not content with merely creating these symbols; He actively interprets and unravels their meaning as well, constantly reminding His followers not to be veiled from the meanings of the symbols by the symbols themselves.

According to the Báb, all reality metaphorically sings the praises of Divine Unity. He writes: "Thou art the One before Whom bow down in adoration all that are in Thy heaven and on Thy earth, Who art worshipped by all who inhabit the kingdom of Thy revelation and creation, each in accordance with its own reality: lightning shineth when it sanctifieth Thee, light flasheth when it praiseth Thee, water falleth when it beareth witness unto Thy unity, and snow filleth the air and earth when it magnifieth Thee."[60] The Persian Bayán testifies that all the laws of the Bayán are intended to be symbols of the spiritual principle of Divine Unity. Thus the Báb asks His followers to pay attention to the inner meaning of these symbols, all of which point in the same spiritual direction: "[A]ll the laws of the Bayán have been revealed on the basis of the recognition of God and divine mysteries. Should one gaze [upon them] from the beginning to the end, he would observe that the same crystal water of Divine Unity streameth forth in all of them in the same manner."[61]

These symbols deal with the beautification and refinement of phenomenal reality. They call for fixing one's attention on God, they link the physical to the spiritual, they unite the community of the believers around a common truth, and they bring together nature and culture. Almost all the ordinances of the Persian Bayán follow this same logic. Thus every moment of human existence is marked by spiritual symbols.

The moments of birth and death represent the beginning and end of this symbolic journey in the material world. Gate 15 of the fifth unity associates these two moments with rituals that are filled with symbolic meanings. At the time of birth, five *takbírs* (the phrase of magnification, "God is Most Great") are to be recited, each followed by the recitation nineteen times of a particular verse avowing faith in God, certitude regarding God, quickening by God, death by God, and contentment with God. For honouring the dead there are six *takbír*s, each followed by the recitation, nineteen times, of verses about worshipping God, kneeling before God, submitting to God, remembering God, and offering thanks to God. Not only is the name of God (the *takbír*) mentioned on both occasions, but these occasions are also defined in terms of the revelation of God through the symbolism of 5 (Há') and 6 (Váv)—*Huva* (He), through the Primal Unity (nineteen times). In the same gate the Báb explains that the numbers 5 and 6 mark the moments of birth and death, so that all should know that they all have proceeded from the Primal Will and will all return to Him. As the Báb emphasizes, the purpose of this ritual is that all should be prepared to return to God on the Day of Resurrection and be reborn in the new Faith.

It is not only the moments of birth and death that are signs of spiritual meanings. The Báb turns the entire concept of time into a process of spiritualization. Time becomes literally filled with God. This process is most evident in the new calendar introduced in the Persian Bayán. In the first paragraph of the gate dealing with the calendar, the Báb explains the symbolic meaning of His new organization of time. The year of 361 days is equal to "all things" and represents various gates of the Persian Bayán, so that all the people, in the space of each year, will traverse the path of the Primal Unity that is symbolized by the nineteen months of the year:

> The substance of this gate is that the Lord of the universe hath fashioned all types of years by His behest, and hath ordained that from the inception of the Bayán, each year should equal the numerical value of the words "all things" (*kullu shay'*) [19 x 19 = 361], to consist of nineteen months, where each month equalleth nineteen days, that from the moment of the rising of the sun in the vernal equinox—corresponding to the first sign of the Zodiac, the sign of Aries—till the end of its voyage at the end of winter—corresponding to the last sign of the Zodiac, the sign of Pisces—all beings may traverse through all the nineteen stages of the Letters of Unity.[62]

Then the Báb explains that these nineteen months correspond to the four words of the opening phrase of the Persian Bayán. The nineteen months are divided into units of three, four, six, and six, corresponding to the number of letters in each of those four words. The first three months represent the fire of God; the next four, the air of eternity; the following six, the water of Divine Unity; and the last six, the sacred realm of the earth:

> Thus, He hath destined each day to be the springtime of one of His laws, that the inmates of this paradise may partake of divine delights in the utmost joy possible within the realm of creation. Therefore, during the first three months—the months of glorification—the fire of the hearts of existent beings is kindled. During the next four months—the months of the celebration of praise—the spirits of the contingent beings are created, during which time they are provided for. In the subsequent six months—the months of the exaltation of unity—God causeth the beings to expire, not as a physical death, but the death of negation and life in affirmation. Finally, in the last six months— which are the months of magnification—the Lord of the universe, glorified and exalted be He, quickeneth those souls who have died to the love of anyone other than Him and have remained steadfast in His love.[63]

These four divisions, in turn, correspond to the four layers of the divine covenant, the four words of divine praise, and the four creative names of God.

The first month, the month of Bahá, has special significance, as the month of the Point, while all other months, the months of the Letters of the Living, are created from this pivotal month:

> The first month is the month of the Point, and the months belonging to the Letters of the Living revolve around it. Among all the months, the month of the Point resembleth the sun, while all other months resemble mirrors which reflect the radiant lights of that supreme month, in such wise that naught is seen in them but that month. God hath called that month the month of Bahá (Splendour, Glory), meaning that therein lieth the splendour and glory of all months, and He hath singled it out for Him Whom God shall make manifest. Each of its days is related by God to one of the Letters of Unity.[64]

The first day of the year, the day of Naw Rúz, is the Day of Him Whom God shall make manifest—the day of Bahá, of the month of Bahá. This day is the source and the excellence of all days.

All the other aspects of life—one's body, religious deeds, and social relations—are similarly represented as symbols or tokens of spiritual reality. Only a brief reference to a few examples can be made here. The period in which the religious duty of fasting is binding is between the ages of eleven and forty-two. These numbers correspond to the words *Huva* (He) and *balí* (*balá*) or "yea," respectively, signifying the acceptance of the divine covenant.[65] Various laws of the Bayán deal with the human body, turning it into a symbol of divine attributes. We have already seen how in the Persian Bayán cleanliness and beautification is emphasized as a means of spiritualizing the material body. The Báb even allows the believers to have a tattoo on their bodies: since the heart is the seat of the love of God, the Báb states that it is permitted that the phrase "O Thou My God" (*Alláhumma*), for males, and "the Most Gracious" (*ar-Raḥmán*), for females, be inscribed on their chests, in the most beautiful of calligraphy.[66]

The Báb speaks of males and females symbolically as the possessors of "temples" (*hayákil*; singular, *haykal*) and "circles," respectively. "Temple," here, refers to the pentagram or five-pointed star, which abstractly resembles a human figure with a head, two arms and two legs.[67] Gate 10 of the fifth unity discusses the ordinance that males should carry with them a temple and females a circle. Both temples and circles are made of complex symbols, and the believers are allowed to inscribe within them various verses of the writings of the Báb and to seek protection and the realization of the truth of those divine names in their lives.

Some short works of the Báb are even written in this pentagram form. The temple consists of five lines which create six chambers. As the Báb explains, the "manifest" part is 5 and the "inner" part is 6.[68] These numbers, again, refer to the two letters of *Huva* (He); the temple therefore refers to God and His Manifestation. The Báb allows the faithful to write on the five lines and in the six chambers whatever they wish of the writings of the Báb so that the divine words, reflected in the symbolic form of the human temple, will affect the souls of the people, making them the embodiments of divine attributes.

The circle that women are to carry consists of six concentric circles which create five units of space between the six lines. Thus the circle mirrors the temple but with the manifest and inner aspects reversed. This also symbolizes the unity of men and women— although appearing in different forms, they are essentially the same and refer to the same reality (both are 11, manifestations of divine attributes). Each concentric circle is to be divided into nineteen units, making the circle consist of ninety-five chambers which stand for *lilláh* (for God).

The circle symbolizes the Sun of Truth while the temple refers to the Manifestation of God. We can see that the reason the Báb calls men "possessors of the temple" is not simply the fact that they are to carry this sign. Since the temple is ultimately a reference to the Manifestation and since the revelation of this divine Temple is enshrined in the hearts of all men, men are called "possessors of the temple." Since the circle stands for the Sun of Truth (again, the Manifestation of God), and the revelation of this Supreme Sun is the very heart of women, they are the possessors of the circle. The ritual law, then, is an affirmation of the exalted and spiritual character of all human beings. In this symbolism, both males and females are reflections of the Primal Will, and both together make up the divine name *Huva*, referring to the fact that they all proceed from God and return to Him.

Another earlier work of the Báb, the Commentary on the Súrih of Praise, gives more detailed instructions for the construction of a different form of circle, one consisting of seven concentric circles, with a square in the centre of the seventh circle. The Súrih of Praise is the one held by the Traditions to contain all the truth of the Qur'án in its seven verses, and all that is in the súrih within the four words of its opening phrase. The Báb interprets this súrih in manifold and complex ways as a reference to His own truth, the secret of the "seven," who has appeared as the unity of all the four levels of the divine covenant, as well as the station of the Gate and the reflection of the Most Great Name of God that consists of four names or letters. These and other complex meanings of the Súrih of Praise are then symbolized in the form of the seven concentric circles which contain within themselves the four sides of the square.[69]

From what we have seen so far of the overall symbolic nature and logic of the Báb's writings, we should be reluctant to fall into the simplistic mistake of ascribing the use of these symbols of temple and circle to a mere literalistic talismanic and magical logic, especially in light of the Báb's approach to prayer and His thorough rejection of any magical orientation in worship. While the Báb affirms the efficacy and creativity of the divine names, He makes it abundantly clear that the primary intention of these symbols is to facilitate constant awareness of their symbolic meanings. Both the temple and the circle refer symbolically to the Manifestation of God and the supreme reality of all beings. The believers are enjoined to carry these symbols so that the consciousness of the meanings of the symbols will infuse their lives with spiritual awareness, and above all so that they will recognize the Promised One. Ultimately it is intended that by the year 5/6 of the Revelation of Him Whom God shall make manifest all the Bábís will recognize Him. As the Báb explains: "This is the purpose of their revelation, that haply at the time of the manifestation of that Sun of Eternity and the Ancient Countenance, all people may attain such heights that the possessors of temples would be wholly devoted to Him within five (Há'), and the possessors of the circle would do likewise within six (Váv)."[70]

The same symbolism is reflected in many other ordinances of the Báb. As we have seen, the relations of commerce, exchange, correspondence, and conversation are represented as reflections of the reciprocity of the divine covenant and the recognition of the new Manifestation of God. A further example is the four types of greeting ordained by the Báb. Women are to say, "God is the Most Glorious" (*Alláhu Abhá*), and are to be greeted in return by "God is the Most Beautiful" (*Alláhu Ajmal*). Men greet one another by saying, "God is the Most Great" (*Alláhu Akbar*), which is to be returned with the greeting, "God is the Most Mighty" (*Alláhu A'ẓam*). All these greetings express the fact that any human praise of Him Whom God shall make manifest is incapable of describing Him.

In general, the Persian Bayán affirms that no action is acceptable unless it is performed for God, and therefore it ordains that before embarking on any action the believer should recite, outwardly or inwardly, a verse which testifies to this motivation for performing the action.[71] The same logic applies to prayers and devotional acts. Laws are ordained governing various occasions to remember God in ways that all symbolize spiritual meanings. Fasting is interpreted as the duty to abstain from anything but the love of the Primal Unity and Him Whom God shall make manifest. Although abstaining from eating, drinking, and intercourse is included, refraining from contention, injustice, and rejection of the Manifestation of God is far more important:

> The substance of this gate is that before fasting thou must comprehend God's purpose thereof, regarding that which is the fruit of the fast. . . . The purpose of fasting is to fast from anyone who is not godly. . . .

> When fasting, it behooveth the one who fasteth to take heed lest he be veiled from the good pleasure of God, so that, during his fast, should the Tree of Truth shine forth, and command the breaking of the fast, he would unhesitatingly obey. . . . Guard thyself from drinking; eating; intercourse; contention, even in words; injustice, even to the slightest extent; and pronouncing judgment against God. Be especially careful with regard to the last three prohibitions inasmuch as, from the inception of the Revelation till the commencement of the next Revelation, whosoever pronounceth judgment against the Point hath pronounced judgment against God, which rendereth his fasting null.[72]

The Báb's obligatory prayer consists of nineteen *rak'ah* units (prostrations). The Báb explains these nineteen units as a journey in the love of the Primal Unity. Like the nineteen letters of the opening phrase of the Bayán, these nineteen *rak'ahs* correspond to the four stations of testifying to the Divine Unity: unity of essence, attributes, actions, and worship. The point to which one should turn when reciting the prayer is Him Whom God shall make manifest, Who is the supreme focus and purpose of all acts of devotion.[73] For that reason the obligatory prayer is to begin at noon because the noontime or zenith of the physical sun is the symbol of the Primal Point, Who is the zenith of the spiritual Sun.[74]

Various other, equally symbolic, acts of devotion are prescribed by the Persian Bayán as well. Gate 8 of the fifth unity ordains that every day the believer is to recite at least nineteen verses—in other words, one page—of the Bayán, to remember the Primal Unity. Gate 14 of the eighth unity states that each day the believer must recite seven hundred verses of the Bayán, or if unable to do so, must mention God seven hundred times by saying, "God is Most Manifest" (*Alláhu Aẓhar*). The number of repetitions, the Báb explains, signifies the letter Dhá', which is equal to 700. Dhá', in turn, is an abbreviation of the word *alladhí,* which symbolizes the fifth level of Divine Unity, as affirmed in the statement, "there is none other God but Him in Whom (*alladhí*) all believe."

Gate 17 of the seventh unity commands the believers to recite a particular verse on Fridays, the day of rest, while facing the sun. The Báb explains that the sun is a symbol of the Sun of Truth—Him Whom God shall make manifest—and that through this turning of their physical bodies they are to remember to turn their hearts to the Primal Will. In the

Kitábu'l-Asmá' a particular recitation is also enjoined to be said once a month while facing the moon.[75]

Gate 17 of the fifth unity prescribes that on each of the nineteen days of each month one is to recite a particular name of God ninety-five times. On the first day of the month it is "God is the Most Glorious" (*Alláhu Abhá*), while on the last day of the month it is "God is the Most Ancient" (*Alláhu Aqdam*). Here again, ninety-five symbolizes "for God," and through this practice, each day of the month becomes a celebration of one of the Letters of the Primal Unity. Gate 8 of the seventh unity states that within each month one is to write "nineteen times nineteen" names of God, as one chooses, to remind oneself that "all things" are created by the Primal Point, and to see nothing in anyone but the revelation of the power of Him Whom God shall make manifest.

One of the most complex symbols in the writings of the Báb is His law of inheritance, which is discussed in the Persian Bayán only in general terms. The Báb specifies that the seven categories of people who are to inherit from the deceased represent the seven letters of the word of affirmation "but God" (*illa'lláh*) in the declarative testimony of Divine Unity. Other aspects of the symbolic structure of the inheritance law are unveiled in the Arabic Bayán and the Tablet of Nineteen Temples.[76]

Spiritual Linguistics

The final foundational principle of action in the Persian Bayán can be termed a new spiritual linguistics. All the other principles come together in this principle. Action must be oriented to perfection and beauty: it must reflect divine attributes, it should be a process of attaining the paradise of divine good pleasure, it must bring happiness to the world, and it must spiritualize reality.

The Báb crystallizes all these principles by outlining a new approach to language. Language concerns the names of things and their relations, but it also inescapably communicates the speaker's attitude about those things, an attitude that is determined by the speaker's perspective. Words, then, can be the means of exalting the human condition by expressing love, unity, and the spiritual direction of reality, or alternatively they can be the vehicle of alienation, hatred, and violence. To complete the spiritual transformation of the world, the realm of language must also be transformed so that all things refer to the names and attributes of God.

This goal is precisely the concern of many gates of the Persian Bayán, and is a central principle in all the Báb's later writings. In gate 4 of the fifth unity, the Báb addresses the question of names and naming. He states that He wants to spiritualize the realm of language to such an extent that all words become the names and attributes of God:

> For the divine Cycle advanceth in stages, until such Revelation when all things will be called by the names of God, such that no name will be assigned to anything unless it resembleth one of the names of God, glorified and exalted is He, like *Ḥalím* (Forbearing), which is a food but resembleth a name of God, lauded and magnified be He. . . . For in the Day of the Revelation of the Sun of Truth, should people attain the utmost limit of perfection, they shall not call anything except by a name that is like one of the names of God, glorified and exalted be He. And if such a level of perfection be not attained, it will assuredly happen in the subsequent Revelation.
>
> This will occur gradually and in stages, until all heaven, earth, and that which lieth between them, will be filled with the names of God. . . . Well is it with the people of that age who call nothing but by a name of God. That age is worthy to be praised as the beginning of the worlds of paradise![77]

The significance of the Báb's approach to language cannot be overestimated. The Báb intends that all beings should reflect their inner truth, the revelation of God enshrined within them; thus He transforms even the names of the things, so that thereby the world will become filled with the names of God. If the truth of all beings is the revelation of God within them, and if this is the sanctuary of the heart, then this spiritual linguistics links the inner reality of things directly with their appearance and their names. The harmony of inner and outer is realized in this construction of paradise in the phenomenal world. One could even say that this is a return to the mythical original language that was taught by God to Adam. In both cases, the names of things disclose the truth of things, which is nothing other than the names and attributes of God.

Once again, it is a question of symbolism, not a literalistic magic. The actual essence of the things in themselves of course is inaccessible to human knowledge. The significance of the phenomenal names of things lies in the fact that names are the symbolic representations used by human beings in language. Thus it is through the existence of these new names of things within human consciousness that the spiritual transformation is effected.

In gate 9 of the fifth unity, the Báb declares that any name of any thing must be seen as the embodiment of various names of God. In other words, each letter of a name should be seen as the abbreviation of one of the names of God. According to the Báb, people are allowed to conceive of ordinary things in this way because this is the age in which all things are to achieve their perfection and realize their true nature. Thus, to be identified by a name of God is the paradise of each thing. In this way, one sees nothing in reality except God:

> The substance of this gate is that inasmuch as nothing possesseth reality except through the grace of God, glorified and exalted be He, and that a day is destined for each thing to attain unto its utmost perfection, when all its potentialities shall be manifestly realized, and it is only then that it is worthy to be called by a name of God, within its own limit, and not the limit of that which is above it; and inasmuch as God hath commanded the people of the Bayán to elevate all things to their uttermost limit of perfection, He hath granted them permission to call everything, through the letters of their names, by the names of God, lauded and magnified is He, that none may see in anything aught save the Countenance of the Revelation of the Will, in Whom naught is seen but God.[78]

To illustrate this concept, the Báb gives an example of the lowest level of things—a stone—showing that even an apparently worthless piece of earth is the embodiment of exalted divine names. This is the way all things should be called, conceived, and treated: "For example, the lowest rank in the mineral kingdom is that of the stone [*sang*, consisting of the letters *SNG*]. Then in its letter Sín (*S*) naught would be seen but the All-Glorious (*Subbúḥ*); in its letter Nún (*N*), Light (*Núr*); and in the letter Káf (*K*, that is, *G*), the All-Bountiful (*Karím*) . . . that naught may be seen in anything except Him Whom God shall make manifest, Who is the Source of the names and attributes of God. . . ."[79] The principle expressed here is the one that Bahá'u'lláh alludes to at the end of the Seven Valleys when He interprets each of the letters comprising the word *gunji<u>sh</u>k* (sparrow) as referring to a mystical meaning: "on every plane, to every letter a meaning is allotted which relateth to that plane. Indeed, the wayfarer findeth a secret in every name, a mystery in every letter."[80]

Reading the Book of Divine Names

Understanding this mystical, symbolic principle, expressed as a foundational feature of the Persian Bayán, can clarify a difficult and often misinterpreted aspect of the later writings of the Báb. We know that the Báb gave many of His believers titles after the names of God. These names were intended to direct their attention to the Lord of those names so that people would not be veiled from Him Whom God would make manifest. Various later writings of the Báb, like Panj Sha'n and the Kitábu'l-Asmá', contain lengthy sermons in which various names of God appear in multiple derivative forms, many of which are not used in the Arabic language. However, the Báb derives these new forms in a systematic way and as forms that are potentially possible, although not realized, in Arabic. He derives many new names from the names of God such as *Bahá, Aḥad, Iláh, Váḥid, Jalál, Jamál,* and many others. In praising these names, the Báb creates alternative structural patterns (such as: I verily am God . . . ; Say! Glorified art Thou, O God Who . . . ; Exalted be God . . . ; In the name of God . . . ; By God . . . ; O thou My God . . . ; God hath verily witnessed that . . .) which are repeated for the description of the various derived names of God. These sermons are difficult to translate, but they possess a beautiful and magnetic, rhythmic energy. Their meaning, however, has remained enigmatic for various commentators.

We can see that the Báb's principle of spiritual linguistics is one of the main inspirations for these works. In fact, the Báb is alluding to these same practices, in discussing the spiritualization of language, when He mentions in the Persian Bayán: "For the divine Cycle advanceth in stages, until such Revelation when all things will be called by the names of God, such that no name will be assigned to anything unless it resembleth one of the names of God, glorified and exalted is He. . . . It is thus that in this Revelation of the Bayán many such structures shall emerge. . . ."[81]

In other words, the multiplication of the names of God is a part of the spiritualization of all names, so that the world will become filled with God and with Him Whom God shall make manifest. This becomes much clearer when we attend to the fact that such a spiritualization is the essential purpose and message of those writings. The pre-eminent example of this principle is the Book of Divine Names (Kitábu'l-Asmá'), the longest book revealed by the Báb. This volume was written during the period when the Báb was imprisoned in Mákú and Chihríq. It consists of 361 sections, each of which is divided into four parts, each part of which is written in a different mode of revelation—divine verses, prayers, commentaries, and rational arguments. As in the Bayán, the number 361 signifies "all things" and the days of the year. The Báb takes the names of various people and turns them into names of God, and thus makes the world and time filled with God. The supreme purpose of this spiritualization of the world is the preparation of all names for the coming of the Lord of Names, Him Whom God shall make manifest.

The extraordinary complexity of the Book of Divine Names has yet to be appreciated by scholars. MacEoin, for example describes it as a text "of little direct value to the student of Bábí doctrine (but perhaps much interest to the psychologist of religious inspiration). . . ."[82] But we can apply the fundamental principles and themes that we have observed throughout the writings of the Báb to gain some insight into just what relationship this text has to the Báb's teachings.

In this work the Báb takes human names and attributes, elevates them to the rank of the names of God, and deduces the type of life that is required by the true meaning of those names. The name "the Most Perfect" was mentioned earlier in addressing efficiency and creativity in industry and art. The Báb defines God as the Most Perfect Fashioner, Who has created His handiwork in the most perfect manner by enshrining within all His creatures the sign of His own revelation. Accordingly, those who engage in crafts are asked to realize that inner sign in the world by exerting their utmost effort to execute their craftsmanship in the most perfect and beautiful manner. Reference was also made to another name of God that is discussed in the Book of Divine Names, that is, "the Cultivator." The Báb describes God as the mighty Cultivator. Farmers, then, are reflections of divine names just as kings are manifestations of the divine name, the King. The Báb makes it evident that He wants everyone to treat all people, regardless of their social position, with the utmost dignity and love, because all are one and the same; all are mirrors of divine names. Likewise, men and women are representatives of this divine cultivation. Thus they both should be dignified and united in love. God as the Mighty Cultivator plants in the heart of the believers the verses of His love. These seeds must instantly yield fruits.[83]

Seen in this perspective, the puzzling nature of the Kitábu'l-Asmá' and its relationship to the teachings of the Báb becomes understandable as the expression of the spiritual unity of all reality through a phenomenology of names that elevates those names to their Supreme Origin and End. Aside from its complex content, the entire text of the Kitábu'l-Asmá' represents the best and most explicit expression of the Báb's doctrine, which is embodied in the laws of the Persian Bayán—the perspective of unity that transforms all of reality into mirrors reflecting the divine names, in every possible form, in all their glory.

14

The Law of the Sword and the Twin Revelations

No discussion of the laws and ethics of the Bayán can be complete without reference to two other key principles that are closely related to the six discussed in the previous chapter. The first of these two principles is the primacy of Him Whom God shall make manifest. The second is the paradoxical nature of the law of the sword in the Báb's writings. As we have seen, He Whom God shall make manifest is the most fundamental and pervasive theme of the entire Revelation of the Báb, especially as expressed in His later writings. There is virtually no law of the Persian Bayán which is not an affirmation of the Promised One, and indeed, all the principles discussed in the previous chapter exemplify the centrality of Him Whom God shall make manifest. For example, we saw that the Báb prohibits causing grief to any soul. As He has explained, the real purpose of this law is that no one should cause grief to Him Whom God shall make manifest. If the Bábís refrain from saddening anyone, they will not unknowingly cause grief to the Promised One. And although the Báb emphasizes the law of perfection and refinement, He reiterates that the purpose of this law is so that the eyes of Him Whom God shall make manifest will not witness anything unpleasant or distasteful in His kingdom.

The second key principle, the paradoxical nature of the law of the sword in the Báb's Revelation, is closely related to the first; in fact, we can only understand the meaning of the Báb's references to the law of the sword when we regard those references in light of the primacy of Him Whom God shall make manifest. The first principle, in other words, is the key that unlocks the meaning of the second principle.

When we read the laws of the Persian Bayán, we are confronted by a dilemma. On the one hand, those laws prescribe a spiritual attitude of all-encompassing love and compassion toward all beings. On the other hand, among those ordinances are a significant number of apparently severe laws, which ostensibly prescribe harsh measures against non-believers, similar to the Islamic "law of the sword," including holy war. The Bayán's gate 5 of the fifth unity ordains that all lands must be conquered by the Bayán and the property of unbelievers must be seized unless those unbelievers enter the Faith. Gate 6 specifies the distribution of the spoils of such a conquest: objects that are matchless belong to the Point, and the rest are to be used for propagating the Bayán, paying soldiers, building places of worship, and aiding the poor and the community. Gate 4 of the sixth unity extols the five lands that were the first to receive the Cause of the Báb—Fárs (Shiraz), Iraq, Azerbaijan, Khurásán, and Mázandarán. Since these lands represent the Letter Há', the five aspects of the human temple, the five layers of the name of the Báb, and the five levels of the affirmation of Divine Unity, God does not wish to behold anything in those lands except that which is most perfect and refined; thus it is not suitable for unbelievers to reside there. Gate 16 of the seventh unity orders Bábí rulers to expel all unbelievers from their lands except those who engage in wholesale trade that is useful to the believers. The same gate prohibits the Bábís from having unbelievers in their homes. Gate 6 of the sixth unity calls for the destruction of books other than those written by Bábís. Finally, gate 15 of the eighth unity ordains marriage among the faithful to bring into the world one who will sing the praise of God. Marriage with unbelievers is not permitted, and upon acceptance of the Faith by one spouse and its rejection by the other, the marriage becomes null, while the unbelieving spouse forfeits any claim to his or her property.

Two Approaches to the Laws of the Bayán

In general, two different approaches have been taken in interpreting these laws. The first way is the literal approach, represented by the followers of Yaḥyá Azal (the half-brother of Bahá'u'lláh) and a number of authors who take the writings of the Báb at face value, reading His ordinances as a straightforward code of laws that was intended to be enforced and to endure for a long time—which they generally assume to be about two thousand years. Browne and MacEoin have also taken this approach. Azal's followers maintained that the advent of the Promised One of the Bayán would only take place in the distant future and that the Báb intended His Dispensation to be just like others of the past, with a chain of successors or vicegerents whose writings would be binding on the Bábís. According to the Azalís, the Báb named Yaḥyá Azal as His vicegerent (*vaṣí*). In this approach, the severe laws are seen as an integral part of the Báb's Dispensation, revealed in order to be carried out literally.

This reading, however, is beset by numerous fundamental inadequacies, problems, and contradictions. To begin with, various texts of the Báb unequivocally disconfirm the premises of this interpretation. The Báb emphasizes the imminence of the advent of the Promised One, pointedly excludes the institution of vicegerency from His own Dispensation, decrees that there can be no other binding and authoritative writings after His own passing, defines His Revelation as a mere preparation for the Revelation of Him Whom God shall make manifest, and directs His followers to accept the Promised One without reference to anything or anyone other than His own being and verses. And, as we have seen, He gives many indications as to the identity of that Promised One. All these statements imply that the Báb did not consider His Revelation to be like previous Dispensations, with laws intended to be enforced for centuries, or even millennia, until the eventual appearance of the Promised One. On the contrary, He perceived His own mission as a preparation for the imminent coming of Him Whom God shall make manifest. As we shall see, this fact has critical, definitive implications for how we must interpret the "severe" laws of the Bayán.

It is important to note that the literal approach to reading the writings of the Báb is not an neutral, objective interpretive method as it is based on specific presuppositions which must be viewed as *theological* assumptions. The most important of these assumptions is the exclusion of the possibility that by "Him Whom God shall make manifest" the Báb could possibly be referring to Bahá'u'lláh.

The most salient question that arises, when we examine the Báb's writings on law, is how to interpret the evident contradiction between what are ostensibly harsh laws and the gentle spirit and compassionate philosophy of the Bayán. What are we to make of that seeming dissonance?

The simplest (though simplistic) conclusion is that the apparent contradiction is due to mere inconsistency and incoherence in the Báb's own statements. This conclusion has been favoured by those who take the literalist approach to the Báb's writings. But another and more context-conscious approach suggests that the literal reading of these laws is missing the point. In fact, the way we interpret the severe laws of the Bayán is directly dependent on our overall reading of the writings of the Báb and the context within which we view those laws.

The second approach to the writings of the Báb is that taken by Bahá'ís, beginning with Bahá'u'lláh. According to this approach, the key context in which we must regard the Báb's writings is their relation to and continuity with the writings of Bahá'u'lláh. Needless to say, this interpretive framework treats as factual that Bahá'u'lláh is the one indicated in the Báb's texts as Him Whom God shall make manifest. The fundamental purpose of the Báb's Revelation, as we have seen, was to prepare the people of His time so that they would be ready to accept the message of the Promised One—a message which the Báb regarded as the realization and fulfillment of His own Revelation. All of the Báb's writings thus were intended to prepare the way for, serve, and to underscore the authority of Bahá'u'lláh, and the fulfillment of the Báb's Revelation is expressed in the Revelation of Bahá'u'lláh. This point is crucial to understanding the meaning of the "severe" laws of the Bayán, for in this context even those harsh laws play a crucial role in setting the stage for Bahá'u'lláh's Revelation—specifically, for actions that Bahá'u'lláh would take in revealing His own laws for the new Dispensation by confirming, modifying, or abrogating the laws of the Báb.

In addition to the premise of the unity of the Twin Revelations, this second interpretive approach is shaped by several other crucial premises. Foremost among these is the proposition that the Báb was fully aware that His Dispensation would be very brief; His knowledge of this fact is an indispensable contextual key in understanding the intent of His laws. If the Báb knew His Dispensation would last but a few years, He would also have known that the laws He set down could never actually become the legal code of a society because they would soon be superseded by the laws of the Promised One and would be modified or abrogated as He chose. Hence the Báb was free to use the "genre" of legislation for a rhetorical purpose very different from the normal purpose of setting down laws but identical to the purpose that characterizes all the Báb's other writings.

Given the premise that the Báb knew His laws would soon be superseded, we must conclude that the Báb never intended the severe laws of the Bayán to be enforced literally, but, rather, He infused them with a symbolic purpose and function—to remind people that they were created to recognize the Manifestation of God, and to exalt the authority and primacy of the Promised One. He also used His laws to dislodge, in the minds of His followers, the symbolic foundations of the old traditional ways. In this regard Shoghi Effendi has written that the Bayán "should be regarded primarily as a eulogy of the Promised One rather than a code of laws and ordinances designed to be a permanent guide to future generations." He characterizes the Bayán as "[d]esignedly severe in the rules and regulations it imposed, revolutionizing in the principles it instilled," and "calculated to awaken from their age-long torpor the clergy and the people, and to administer a sudden and fatal blow to obsolete and corrupt institutions; it proclaimed, through its drastic provisions, the advent of the anticipated Day, the Day when 'the Summoner shall summon to a stern business,' when He will 'demolish whatever hath been before Him, even as the Apostle of God demolished the ways of those that preceded Him.'"[1]

The difference between the two interpretive approaches described above is fundamental and irreconcilable. Each leads to a radically different perception of the writings of the Báb. The Azalí approach makes the Revelation of the Báb into an intolerant, fanatical, brutal, and oppressive movement, one that would expel non-believers from Bábí lands, confiscate their property, annul marriages with them, destroy their books, and put them to the sword. The Bahá'í approach, in contrast, sees the writings of the Báb as laying the groundwork not for totalitarianism and oppression but for its opposite: for the eventual establishment of a society characterized by the unity of nations, fellowship of religions, equal rights of all people, and a compassionate, consultative, tolerant, democratic, moral world order as set forth in the writings of Bahá'u'lláh.

However, even without taking any position as to whether Bahá'u'lláh is the Promised One of the Báb, an objective and careful reading of the Báb's writings, with due attention to their logical implications, leads to the conclusion that the laws in question are not meant to be taken literally but instead perform a symbolic and profoundly transformative function.

The Imminent Advent of Him Whom God Shall Make Manifest

Because the relationship of the Báb's Revelation to that of Bahá'u'lláh is so crucial in interpreting the intent of the laws of the Bayán, before discussing that interpretation we will examine the case for the imminence of the advent of Him Whom God shall make manifest.

Unlike earlier Dispensations in which a future promised figure was mentioned occasionally and only by hints and allusions, the entirety of the Bayán is essentially a discourse on Him Whom God shall make manifest. The Báb always discusses His own Revelation and His own laws in the context of the Revelation of the Promised One. This unusual pattern is only understandable when we regard the Revelations of the Báb and Bahá'u'lláh as inseparable Twin Revelations, where the former had as its central purpose the preparation of the people for the latter. This unique structure also supports the thesis that the advent of Him Whom God shall make manifest was imminent.

Various writings of the Báb distinctly affirm this imminence and even indicate when the promised advent would occur. In the Arabic Bayán He says, "Rise ye all when ye hear the name of Him Whom We shall make manifest in the name of the Qá'im. Observe the difference between 'Qá'im' and 'Qayyúm,' then in the year nine ye shall attain unto all good."[2] In the Kitáb-i-Badí', Bahá'u'lláh refers to several passages in the writings of the Báb which all affirm that the completion and maturation of the Bayán would take place in the year 9 of the Revelation of the Báb.[3]

A further, exceedingly significant fact is that the Báb eliminated the institution of successorship, or vicegerency, from His Dispensation and stipulated that no one else's writings would be binding and authoritative after His own passing until the advent of Him Whom God shall make manifest. Nevertheless, He did name Yaḥyá Azal as the nominal leader after Himself, and Azal's followers maintained that the Báb actually made Azal His vicegerent. One of their arguments for this view was a statement made by the Báb in a tablet addressed to Azal, in which the Báb directs him to "manifest" the remaining eight "paths" of the Arabic Bayán if He Whom God shall make manifest is made manifest out of divine glory during Azal's days.[4] The Azalís take this to mean that the Báb authorized Azal to complete the unfinished text of the Arabic Bayán. However, since the Báb is affirming to Azal himself that the Promised One may appear in Azal's own lifetime, this statement actually argues for the imminent appearance of Him Whom God shall make manifest, which by definition eliminates the possibility of any vicegerency for Azal. It also proves that the typical arguments used by Azal's followers to reject the claim of Bahá'u'lláh—on the premise that the Promised One could not appear before the conquest of the world by the Bábís, the realization and enforcement of the laws of the Bayán, and the maturation of the tree of the Bayán in two thousand years—are all baseless.

Even if we assume that Azal was allowed to "manifest" the remaining eight unities, this could only happen if He Whom God shall make manifest had already appeared and had revealed those eight paths for Azal. In other words, Azal's authority is wholly conditioned on his acceptance of Bahá'u'lláh. This fact becomes clearer when we note these points: first, the Persian Bayán stipulates that from the setting of the Sun of Truth (the Báb) until the appearance of Him Whom God shall make manifest, no one else's writings will be binding; and second, the Arabic Bayán is written in the mode of divine verses, and the Báb states, for example, in the Kitábu'l-Asmá', that only the Point of Truth can reveal divine verses and that after the Báb no one will reveal divine verses except Him Whom God shall make manifest. In the Kitábu'l-Asmá', the Báb asks His followers to recognize and appreciate the station of these days of revelation for such days are more glorious than all things. He compares the days of His own Revelation to the twenty-three years of the Dispensation of Muḥammad; then He writes: "When the Cause scaleth the heights unto God, there shall not be any path for anyone to the words of God. Say! Deprive not yourselves of your share of the words of your Lord, and forget not your portion of the verses of your God."[5]

One of the texts used by Azal's followers to substantiate their thesis is the controversial book *Nuqṭatu'l-Káf,* attributed to Ḥájí Mírzá Jání Ká<u>sh</u>ání. This work, assumed to be an early Bábí text, describes Azal as the vicegerent of the Báb. However, its account of this issue is so contradictory and problematic that it certainly should open up many questions about the text itself. Referring to the Báb's tablet addressed to Azal, the author of *Nuqṭatu'l-Káf* states:

> And He [the Báb] also wrote a Will, and explicitly affirmed the vicegerency and successorship for him [Yaḥyá Azal], and ordained that he should write eight unities of the Bayán, and stated to him that when He Whom

> God shall make manifest was manifested by God with majesty in your time, abrogate the Bayán and enforce that with which I inspire your heart. . . . He meant by Him Whom God shall make manifest his holiness Azal himself and no one else, for there cannot be two points at the same time.[6]

Although the author of *Nuqṭatu'l-Káf* is misquoting the Báb (the tablet never tells Azal to abrogate the Bayán, but rather tells him that if God makes manifest the Promised One in Azal's time, Azal should manifest the eight paths), several issues are obvious from this statement. First, the author of *Nuqṭatu'l-Káf* fully realizes that the Bayán may become abrogated within a few years after the death of the Báb. Second, He Whom God shall make manifest may well appear during Azal's lifetime. Third, the notion of Azal's authority is self-contradictory since upon the appearance of the Promised One all must submit to Him. Azal's station, then, would depend on his acceptance or rejection of the new Manifestation.

In view of this last point, the proposition made by the author of *Nuqṭatu'l-Káf*—that by the Promised One is meant Azal himself—is strange indeed. Although this assertion clearly shows that the author of *Nuqṭatu'l-Káf* did not in fact believe that the appearance of the next Manifestation and the abrogation of the Bayán could not occur before two thousand years, the proposition itself is patently absurd since the Báb is discussing the advent of the Promised One during Azal's lifetime as a conditional point for Azal to take a certain action. But if Azal were the Promised One, then the statement would be meaningless: if you are you then do such and such, otherwise refrain from doing it! Additionally, in the preceding sentence in the tablet, the Báb orders Azal to obey Him Whom God shall make manifest; thus it would be doubly absurd to think Azal could be that person.

The statement in *Nuqṭatu'l-Káf* demonstrates the typical inconsistency of the Azalí objections to the claim of Bahá'u'lláh: on the one hand they quote various statements of the Báb to conclude that He Whom God shall make manifest cannot appear before two thousand years and therefore Bahá'u'lláh is not Him. On the other hand, they sometimes speak as though Azal is He Whom God shall make manifest!

However, manifesting the eight paths, as mentioned in the Báb's letter, may well refer to something completely different than completing the text of the Bayán. The Báb uses the word "paths" (*manáhij*) in two senses. One sense refers to the unities of the Bayán, and the other to the entire Bayán as the Path of God and His laws. The Báb's reference to manifesting the eight "paths" after the appearance of the Promised One may refer instead to making public or distributing the eight copies of the Bayán that the Báb had sent to Azal, commanding him to give them to eight individuals who are identified in the letter. The accuracy of this reading is supported by the Báb's statement, in that letter, that God has promised one of these eight paths to the Báb's mother. Obviously, this must refer to the copies of the Bayán sent to Azal for distribution at a time when Bahá'u'lláh would allow it.

Surprisingly, Azal did write a book that was supposed to complete the Bayán (titled *Mutammim-i-Bayán*), but it does not consist of supplying the eight unrevealed unities of the Arabic Bayán. Instead it attempts only to complete some of the remaining gates of the Persian Bayán (chapter 11 of the ninth unity to chapter 19 of the eleventh unity), which correspond to revealed gates in the Arabic Bayán. It seems that, unlike his followers, Azal himself did not take the reference to "manifesting eight paths" as signifying the revelation of the eight remaining unities of the Arabic Bayán.

In fact, the Azalí interpretation of the writings of the Báb completely contradicts the Báb's own unequivocal statements in the Persian Bayán that "from the time of the setting of the Sun [of the Báb] until the Rising of the Sun of Him Whom God shall make manifest, there will be no more binding Writings, and the Letters of the Living and all the believers in God and in the Bayán will be under their shadow [the Writings of the Point of the Bayán]."[7] This passage is most significant for understanding the covenant of the Báb. As we saw earlier, unlike the Islamic Dispensation in which the four layers of the covenant, and their four corresponding modes of revelation, were manifested over a period of more than a thousand years by a succession of different figures, the four layers of the Báb's covenant appeared simultaneously as the Primal Unity in the very first year of the Báb's Revelation, and all the modes of revelation were revealed by the Báb alone. This fact strongly suggests that the Báb's Dispensation was not destined to last beyond one generation. Regardless of the form that leadership of the Bábí community might take after the Báb had departed, the possibility for anyone to put forth authoritative writings before the coming of the Promised One is completely closed.

The elimination of the stations of vicegerency and prophethood from the Dispensation of the Báb is expressed unequivocally in gate 14 of the sixth unity of the Bayán; the Báb states that "regarding titles, in this Dispensation no one is called by the name vicegerent (*vaṣí*) or prophet (*nabí*)." Instead, He says, all should only be called "believers," until the day of Resurrection arrives, "when the Tree of Truth will choose to call anyone by any name He willeth," for only He Whom God shall make manifest would know who is a vicegerent and who is not. Any claim to vicegerency for Azal thus inherently violates the explicit text of the Persian Bayán.

The claim by Azal's supporters that the Báb conferred the title of vicegerent upon Azal is itself an outright falsehood. Nowhere in the works of the Báb is Azal called a vicegerent, and never did the Báb title any of His works the "Tablet of Vicegerency," as is sometimes claimed for the tablet discussed above. The Persian Bayán makes it unmistakably clear that after the Báb and the Letters of the Living, the only station open to anyone is that of mere believer, and the ability to confer vicegerency on anyone is reserved for Him Whom God shall make manifest.

In Panj Sha'n, the Báb speaks of the leadership of His community, after His own death, in terms of two figures. One He calls "Yaḥyá" and the other He calls by the enigmatic name, "Son of 'Alí" (that is, Ḥusayn). The former is the nominal leader, while the latter is the hidden one:

> This, verily, is that which We promised thee, ere the moment We answered thy call. Wait thou until nine will have elapsed from the time of the Bayán. Then exclaim: 'Blessed be God, the most excellent of Makers!' We also answered aforetime, that ere the year Ṭá' (9), it behooveth that two signs from the past, revealed by God in the Book, would be manifested in the year Váv (6). One of them is the prophet Yaḥyá (John), and the other is the Son of 'Alí, the true and exalted Imám.[8]

The Báb then tells 'Aẓím, the addressee of the tablet, that He has made one of these two figures known to him and that he should search the world to find and recognize the other. He asks 'Aẓím to obey the outward leader and to seek out the hidden leader, until the year 9, which would be the time of the advent of the Promised One. The same statement is found in another tablet in Panj Sha'n, again addressed to 'Aẓím, in which the Báb says that before the year 9, before the completion of the Primal Point in the womb of contingency, two Mirrors would reflect God: the prophet Yaḥyá (John) and Ḥusayn, the son of ʻAlí. He then says that God has made one known to ʻAẓím and orders him to search out the other among the Bábís.[9]

Bahá'u'lláh in one of His tablets testifies that He is the "Son of ʻAlí" mentioned in the Báb's statement in Panj Sha'n.[10] Bahá'u'lláh's given name, of course, was Ḥusayn-ʻAlí, and His identity was kept secret during the reign of Grand Vizier Mírzá Taqí Khán, Amír Kabír, who would have killed Bahá'u'lláh had he discovered the real station He held in the Bábí community. Both of the Báb's tablets to ʻAẓím clearly show that Yaḥyá Azal is the one who was already known to ʻAẓím—the tablets make extensive overt reference to Azal. In fact, as the two works make clear, the Báb is discussing Azal in the context of a reference by ʻAẓím to Azal's station.[11]

The identity of "Ḥusayn" becomes even clearer when we note that the Báb describes these two works as tablets for "the Brother of the Fruit (*Akhu'th-Thamarah*), 238." The "Fruit" referred to is Yaḥyá Azal, but 238 is equal to Ḥusayn-ʻAlí—that is, Bahá'u'lláh.[12] The tablets are described as pertaining to Yaḥyá's brother without mentioning the name openly. Regardless of the identity of these two leaders, it remains a categorical fact that any authority Azal might possess was limited to the period before the year 9, the time of preparation for the next Revelation, on the inception of which all the Bábís, regardless of their rank, were to seek out and recognize Him Whom God shall make manifest.[13]

Once again, however, the author of *Nuqṭatu'l-Káf* puts forth strange and inaccurate discussions of these statements by the Báb, falling into many inconsistencies in order to defend Azal's station. The Báb's statement in Panj Sha'n had referred to the two signs (Yaḥyá and Ḥusayn) appearing in the year 6. However, the author of *Nuqṭatu'l-Káf* identifies these signs as Dhabíḥ and Mullá Baṣír. Yet he says that they both appeared in "the year [A.H.] 67" and in the "year 7."[14] There are many obvious problems here. First, the Báb categorically describes the year 6, not 7, as the year of the appearance of the two signs. Second, the year 7 is actually the year A.H. 66, not 67 (the Bábí year 1 began with the declaration of the Báb in A.H. 1260, so the Bábí year 7 began in A.H. 1266). Third, the Báb identifies the two signs as Yaḥyá and Ḥusayn, and it is not clear what connection, if any, there is between them and the individuals Dhabíḥ and Baṣír.

However, the reason for such outright misquotation and inaccuracy seems to be the author of *Nuqṭatu'l-Káf*'s attempt to create internal consistency regarding his previous claim concerning Azal's supposed vicegerency. According to the author, the year 5 (corresponding to the fifth stage of the Tradition of Truth, and referring to the Morn of Eternity) is a reference to the appearance of Azal "in the earth of determination and shining forth." The author argues that in the year 4, corresponding to the fourth stage of the Tradition, the Báb was under Quddús, where the Báb was the *Dhikr* and Quddús was the Qá'im. But after the martyrdom of Quddús, the year 5 arrives, and the Báb becomes the Qá'im and Yaḥyá Azal becomes the Morn of Eternity who was to appear in the year 5.[15] We can see that since the year 5, and not 6, is specified as the year of the appearance of Yaḥyá Azal, he cannot also be the one who appears in the year 6. Furthermore, since the martyrdom of Quddús took place in May 1849, about two months after the end of the year 5 (and thus in the year 6), the author of *Nuqṭatu'l-Káf* has to postpone the year 6 to the year 7!

Yet the complete inaccuracy of applying the designation of the "Morn of Eternity" to Azal and the year 5 becomes clearer when we note that the same author speaks of the year 5 and the rise of the Morn of Eternity as events in two different years. First he twice mentions that Azal becomes the Morn of Eternity of the year 5 after the martyrdom of Quddús. This gives us the date May 1849, which is actually in the year 6 (only further proving why the reference to the Morn of Eternity has nothing to do with Yaḥyá Azal and, as noted, was a reference to the martyrdom of Mullá Ḥusayn). But then on the next page, the author explains that the year 5 begins with the Báb assuming the title of Qá'im by revealing a tablet addressed to 'Aẓím, in which He calls Himself the awaited Qá'im and orders the distribution of that tablet.[16] Although the author of *Nuqṭatu'l-Káf* seems to think that these events took place after the martyrdom of Quddús, we know that the revelation of this tablet, as well as the Báb's public declaration that He was the Qá'im, took place in the summer of A.D. 1848 (in the early part of the year 5), a year before the martyrdom of Quddús. All these inaccuracies and inconsistencies result from the author of *Nuqṭatu'l-Káf*'s insistence on identifying Yaḥyá Azal as the Morn of Eternity mentioned in the Tradition of Truth, as the vicegerent of the Báb, and as Him Whom God shall make manifest—claims which are all clearly baseless.

As mentioned earlier, although Azal was the nominal head of the community, his spiritual station was that of a "mirror," which merits praise by means of divine names (such as Eternal or *Azal*) only as long as it is turned toward the Sun of Truth; if it turns away, it becomes a letter of negation. It should be noted that it is in the very tablet to Azal discussed above, usually called the Will of the Báb to Azal (or mistakenly, the "Tablet of Vicegerency"), that the Báb makes the famous statement: "Verily I am He Who liveth in the Abhá realm of glory."[17] In addressing these words to Azal, the Báb was indicating to him that in the next Revelation, the Báb would appear as "Bahá" (Glory), and it would be toward Him that Azal must turn if he wanted to remain a letter of affirmation.

The Year 9

The year 9 passed, and when no one made any public claim to be Him Whom God shall make manifest, a number of prominent Bábís put forth claims that they were the awaited one.[18] Azal was forced to denounce them and called for them to be assassinated, particularly Dayyán (Mírzá Asadu'lláh-i-Khu'í). It was possible for so many Bábís to assert such claims only because the Báb had educated His followers to expect the coming of the Promised One imminently. The phenomenon of all those claims being made by various Bábís may be understood more as an affirmation of their longing to attain the presence of the Promised One than anything else. Dayyán himself later attained the presence of Bahá'u'lláh in Baghdad and recognized His station.[19] Since the Báb had said that Dayyán would be "the third Letter to believe in Him Whom God shall make manifest," it is not surprising that Dayyán would be convinced that the Promised One would appear during his lifetime.

One of those who were told by the Báb that they would attain the presence of Him Whom God shall make manifest was the Letter of the Living Mullá Báqir. In an important tablet addressed to him, the Báb tells him to "Count the numerical value of the letters of affirmation, including the *tashdíd* of the letter Lám, that haply thou mayest in eight years, in the day of His Revelation, attain unto His Presence."[20] If Mullá Báqir does not attain His presence at the beginning of the year, the Báb assures him, he will certainly do so at its end. "Know thou, however, of a certainty that His Cause is the Most Mighty (*A'ẓam*) above and beyond any Mighty (*'Aẓím*) Cause, and His Remembrance is the Most Great (*Akbar*), beyond any Great (*Kabír*) Remembrance."[21]

Within that passage, in at least four different ways the Báb alludes to the end of the year 8 and the beginning of the year 9 of His Revelation as the year of the Promised One's advent. First, He states that Mullá Báqir will attain His presence in the year 8 and by the beginning of the year 9. Second, when the Báb says, "Count the numerical value of the letters of affirmation, including the *ta<u>sh</u>díd* of the letter Lám" (referring to the phrase of affirmation in the declarative testimony of Divine Unity, which with the inclusion of the *ta<u>sh</u>díd* equals 8), the Báb is indicating that after eight years and by the beginning of the year 9 the Promised One will appear. It is important to remember that the two last months of 1268 and the two first months of 1269 correspond to the period when Bahá'u'lláh was imprisoned in the Síyáh-<u>Ch</u>ál dungeon in Tehran, where He received the revelation marking the beginning of the new divine Cause. Third, in the same statement, the Báb terms the Cause of Him Whom God shall make manifest *A'ẓam* in comparison to His own Cause, which is *'Aẓím*. The numerical difference between the two is 9, and this same difference is mentioned in other tablets as a reference to the timing of the Revelation of the Promised One. Finally, the Báb's statement is also a reference to the name of the Promised One. The value of the letters of affirmation including the *ta<u>sh</u>díd* (62 + 66 = 128) is equivalent to "Ḥusayn." Read in conjunction with the Báb's statement in Panj <u>Sh</u>a'n concerning the identity of the concealed Bábí leader, this tablet indicates that He Whom God shall make manifest is "Ḥusayn."

Despite the Báb's many references to the year 9 in connection with the appearance of the Promised One, MacEoin claims that those references were ambiguous and devoid of much significance for the early Bábís:

> But what of the "year nine" itself? There are clear references to it in some of the Báb's writings. In the Arabic *Bayán*, for example, he writes: "When you hear the mention of the one we shall manifest in the name of the Qá'im, anticipate the difference between *al-qá'im* and *al-qayyúm*. Then you shall attain to all good in the year nine." . . . One of the problems posed by the use of the terms [*sic*] *al-qayyúm* . . . in these passages is that it is not a normal eschatological term in <u>Sh</u>í'í literature and cannot readily be identified with an expected eschatological figure. Normally, in fact, the word occurs as a title of the divinity. . . . Nor is the

> numerical difference between *al-qá'im* and *al-qayyúm* of much help, since this may amount to 5, 9, or 14, depending on the value given to the third letter (either *yá'* or *hamza*) of *qá'im*.[22]

But these statements are not supported by facts. The claim that the difference between *Qá'im* and *Qayyúm* is not necessarily nine is incorrect. Even the statement MacEoin cites demonstrates that this difference refers to the year 9, a year in which people will "attain unto all good." Yet it is the Báb Himself Who has said, in reference to the same eschatological expectation, that the difference between *Qá'im* and *Qayyúm* is 9:

> Ere nine will have elapsed from the inception of this Cause, the realities of the created things will not be made manifest. All that thou hast as yet seen is but the stage from the moist germ until We clothed it with flesh. Be patient until thou beholdest a new creation. Say: Blessed, therefore, be God, the Most Excellent of Makers! I testify that the difference between the "Qá'im" and the "Qayyúm" is the number nine, which marketh the period when sanctified souls were consummated and established in their own stations. That is also the difference between "A'ẓam" and "'Aẓím."[23]

Here the Báb also definitively identifies the difference between *A'ẓam* and *'Aẓím* as nine. And in His work Lawḥ-i-Haykalu'd-Dín, the Bab explicitly describes the difference as nine *years*: "Ye shall assuredly find All Good in the numerical difference between *Qá'im* and *Qayyúm*, in nine years."[24]

There are other problems with MacEoin's assessment. First, he doubts that the Báb's words are related to the appearance of Him Whom God shall make manifest. But the statement itself clearly shows that it does indeed concern His appearance. The Báb's ordinance is better translated as follows: "Rise ye all when ye hear the name of Him Whom We shall make manifest in the name of the Qá'im. Observe the difference between *Qá'im* and *Qayyúm*, then in the year nine ye shall attain unto all good."[25] This law requires the believers to stand up at the mention of the name of "Him Whom We shall make manifest in the name of the Qá'im"—in other words, Him Whom God shall make manifest. His title is expressed in the first person plural because the Arabic Bayán uses the language of divine verses and thus God is directly speaking as "We"; and indeed this form occurs throughout that work in all references to Him Whom God shall make manifest. However, if there is any doubt that "He Whom We shall make manifest" is the same as "He Whom God shall make manifest," one need only consider the equivalent of this law in the Persian Bayán where the Báb commands all to rise when they hear the name of "Him Whom God shall make manifest in the name of the Qá'im."[26]

The fact that the passage in the Arabic Bayán relates to the coming of Him Whom God shall make manifest is made even clearer when we observe that in the Tablet to Mullá Báqir, the Báb speaks of attaining the presence of Him Whom God shall make manifest in the year 8 and by the beginning of the year 9. Furthermore, that tablet refers to the Revelation of the Promised One as *A'ẓam* in comparison to all others, which are *'Aẓím*. We already saw that in the other tablet the Báb equated the difference between *Qá'im* and *Qayyúm* to nine and identified both as the difference between *A'ẓam* and *'Aẓím*. This is yet further evidence why the *Qayyúm* mentioned in the passage about the year 9 refers to Him Whom God shall make manifest.

The Báb's statements regarding the year 9 speak of attaining the presence of God and attaining unto all good in that year. According to the Báb, in so many of His writings, both of these events refer to the advent of the Promised One. In the Persian Bayán, the Báb devotes a chapter to explaining this fact. Its title is "On this, that any reference, revealed by God, to meeting God or attaining the presence of the Lord intendeth naught but Him Whom God shall make manifest. For verily God, by virtue of His Essence, can never be seen."[27]

MacEoin's statement that *Qayyúm* is not a typical eschatological term in S̲h̲í'ih Islam needs to be critically examined. What is really relevant here of course is the meaning of the term *Qayyúm* to the Bábís, not what it meant in S̲h̲í'ih Islam. The term "He Whom God shall make manifest" may not have any eschatological meaning in S̲h̲í'ih Islam, but it was enormously meaningful to the Bábís. Knowing the meaning of S̲h̲í'ih terms is of course indispensable to understanding the context of Bábí documents, but to know what such terms meant to the Bábís it is necessary to examine them in the context of the writings of the Báb. The term *Qayyúm* is so central in the Báb's writings that it is hardly possible to find one of His works in which it is not emphasized. As we saw before, the Báb interprets the two names of God, *Qayyúm* and *Ḥayy*, as references to the stations of the Point and His Letters of the Living. That is why in His own Dispensation the Báb is both the Qá'im and the Qayyúm, and that is why the Qayyúmu'l-Asmá' is a reference to Joseph, Ḥusayn, and the Báb. In the larger sense, Joseph or the Qayyúm is the station of the Point, which appears in each Dispensation in a new form and with a new name. Thus He Whom God shall make manifest is also the Qayyúm relative to the previous (Bábí) Dispensation of the Qá'im. In fact what the Báb is saying is that although the term *Qá'im,* meaning "one who arises," is a description of the Báb, all these names are ultimately descriptions of the Promised One, Who is the Qayyúm. Thus whenever the word *Qá'im* is spoken, the Bábís are to symbolically demonstrate their allegiance to Him Whom God shall make manifest by standing up as well. The Báb is instructing the Bábís to be constantly attentive and ready to accept the Promised One. But it is in the year 9 that they can actually—not just symbolically—arise to follow Him.

MacEoin's own statement actually gives another clue to the correct understanding of the term *Qayyúm* when he notes that "normally, in fact, the word occurs as a title of the divinity." Indeed, it is precisely because *Qayyúm* was a well-known title of God among both Muslims and Bábís that we can understand the eschatological import of the term in the passage about the year 9. The most direct eschatological reference in the Qur'án is to the attainment of the presence of God on the Day of Resurrection. This in fact is why the Báb identifies the year 9 not only as the year in which people will attain unto all good, but also as the year when people will attain the presence of God.

Other evidence that *Qayyúm* did indeed have eschatological significance for the Bábís is contained in a statement by Mírzá Muḥammad 'Alí Zunúzí, surnamed Anis, who was martyred with the Báb. The statement is part of a work that describes Zunúzí's debate with a Shaykhí leader in Tabriz, and it is quoted a number of times by MacEoin.[28] Zunúzí tells us:

> Thus in the famous Tradition it is mentioned that the Qá'im, like Joseph, will engage in dissimulation. Just as Joseph did not unveil his true station, He also did not explicitly reveal His true station and the truth of some other matters. Thus He called Himself the Báb, which really meant the Gate to the City of Him Whom God shall make manifest, and the Remembrance, namely the Remembrance of that Object of Remembrance, and the Qá'im, namely the One Who riseth for that Qayyúm.[29]

This passage demonstrates that, even before the martyrdom of the Báb, among the Bábís themselves the relation of the Qá'im and the Qayyúm was perceived to be exactly the relation of the Báb and the Promised One of the Bayán.

The writings of the Báb also refer to the year 19 as the time when He Whom God shall make manifest would appear. This is no surprise, given the fact that in one of His tablets the Báb identifies the manifest aspect of the Most Great Name of God as 19, and the hidden aspect of that same name as *Bahá* and as 9: "The manifest name is *Váḥid*, and the Hidden Name is *Bahá* since it is equal to 9, while the former equalleth 19. The first is the Most Great Name in the hidden station. . . ."[30] While the concealed revelation of Bahá'u'lláh took place in the year 9 in the Síyáh-Chál, His public declaration took place in the year 19 (A.D. 1863) in the Riḍván Garden in Baghdad.

One of the references to the year 19 as the final date of the advent of Him Whom God shall make manifest can be found in the following statement in the Persian Bayán:

> As to the Revelation of Him Whom God shall make manifest, God knoweth the age at which He maketh Him to become manifest. However, from the inception of the Revelation till nineteen years (the number of unity), take heed and be watchful, inasmuch as each year the faith of the believers will be manifested through the affirmation of a different Letter, after which they will not be able to manifest the fruits of the past Revelation except through the next Revelation. Even as anyone who hath been associated with the early days of this Revelation would have witnessed that they refused to let the Manifestation of the fruit of 1270 years reveal Himself beyond the station of gatehood.[31]

This passage is important in many ways. Not only does it give the duration of the Dispensation of the Báb as nineteen years, but it also declares that each of the Letters of the Primal Unity symbolizes one of the years of that Dispensation. Thus the expression of faith within the Dispensation of the Bayán would become complete in nineteen years. Although in the first year of His Revelation the Báb revealed Himself as just one of the Gates—the last of the Primal Unity—He was in reality the manifestation of the Primal Point. The Bábís are urged to accept Him Whom God shall make manifest instantly so that He will not be forced to go through such a concealment of His true station.

The identity of the Primal Unity and the nineteen years of the Dispensation of the Báb is the essence of a complex and difficult tablet written in honour of Dayyán, called the Tablet of the Letters (Lawḥ-i-Ḥurúfát), or the Tablet of Nineteen Temples (Lawḥ-i-Hayákil-i-Váḥid).[32] While a detailed analysis of the nineteen temples referred to in the tablet is beyond the scope of this study, the relevant point with regard to the issue discussed here is that the Báb identifies these temples with His Primal Unity, but the last temple ends with the name *Huva'l-Mustaghíth*—the name of Him Whom God shall make manifest. Although the numerical value of that name is 2052, the Báb is alluding to the fact that in nineteen years, corresponding to the Primal Unity of His Dispensation, the year of *Mustagháth* will be realized and He Whom God shall make manifest will reveal Himself. The fact that this tablet was revealed for Dayyán, who was to become the third believer in Him Whom God shall make manifest, makes the meaning of the tablet even more evident. The Báb's identification of the year of *Mustagháth* (equalling 2001) and the name of the Promised One, *Huva'l-Mustaghíth*, with the nineteenth temple clearly shows that the Bábí cycle will be completed in nineteen years, corresponding to the nineteen temples. Besides the statements quoted from the Persian Bayán (where the Báb equated each letter of His Primal Unity with one year) and those in the Interpretation of the Letter Váv, in yet another tablet the Báb explicitly identifies His nineteen temples with nineteen years:

> As the Persian children say, the root principles of religion are five and its derivatives six. This indeed is thy Temple, manifest in the sign of the Most Great Name, whose outward aspect is 5 and its inward, 6. . . . Verily, We have sent forth unto thee the Temples of the Primal Unity [Nineteen Temples]. Though those who possess keen vision perceive all those stations to be present at the time of the Revelation, yet on account of the people's remoteness, I verily have ordained each station to be one year. . . .[33]

The Law of the Sword in the Writings of the Báb

Those who adopt an approach to the study of the Báb's writings based on the assumption that the religion of the Báb must be treated as disconnected from that of Bahá'u'lláh, and as intended by its founder to last for some two thousand years, take the laws of the Bayán as a straightforward code and read literally the Báb's references to the sword—particularly the law of holy war. One of those who has written extensively on this issue and takes this position, attempting to refute the Bahá'í approach, is Denis MacEoin. In various places MacEoin has argued that an offensive, and not merely a defensive, holy war was ordained by the Báb, and that the Bahá'í representation of the Báb and His message is inaccurate. MacEoin's views on this issue are summarized in his 1982 article, "The Babi Concept of Holy War." This article has been discussed by Muhammad Afnan and William Hatcher, who correct a number of its mistakes,[34] while MacEoin's treatment of the Ṭabarsí upheaval as evidence of Bábí insurrection against the Qájár state has been extensively criticized in Siyamak Zabihi-Moghaddam's work on the topic.[35] Here we will concentrate on some other aspects of the article, specifically the conception of holy war that is found in the laws of the Bayán.

The concept of holy war—jihad or *qitál* (meaning fighting and slaying)—waged against unbelievers for the spread and defence of the religion, has been subject to differing interpretations even within Islam. Several stages in the development of the concept can be identified in the Qur'án. At first, in Mecca, at a time when Muḥammad had no political power, there was no mention of holy war, and mild tolerance was the norm. Later, holy war was made a duty. In Súrih 9, the command is given to "slay the idolaters, wherever you find them," unless they repent, while Christians and Jews are to be fought against until they pay tribute willingly in a state of humiliation.[36]

Historically, until the nineteenth century, Islamic jurisprudence defined holy war as offensive (as well as defensive) war. Statements in the Súrih of the Cow such as verses 190–93, which say to fight against those who fight against you but "do not transgress the limits" became the basis of modern arguments that holy war is solely meant to be defensive, but these verses were classically interpreted as meaning that, in the conduct of a holy war, those among the enemy who do not take up the sword (in other words, the elderly, women, and children) should not be slain.

MacEoin claims that the doctrine of holy war—meant literally and as traditionally understood in its severest form within Islam—is present in both the Báb's earlier and later writings. To support his argument he refers to statements in the Qayyúmu'l-Asmá', the Báb's early work Ṣaḥífiy-i-Furú'-i-'Adlíyyih (The Epistle of Justice: Branches), and the Persian Bayán. From those statements he reaches the dire conclusion "that the Báb had, by the end of his short life, moved beyond even the harshest Islamic measures against unbelievers. A Bábí *jihad* was to be an ongoing process, each Bábí monarch striving to eliminate all traces of infidelity from his dominions and, ultimately, from the earth in order to establish a totalitarian Bábí state."[37]

The first problem with MacEoin's analysis is his use of the early writings of the Báb to infer a concept of holy war which is then superimposed upon the later writings. But the Báb has frequently stated that His earlier writings reaffirmed the Qur'ánic laws for rhetorical reasons of audience reception. We should thus not be surprised to find mention of the Islamic law of holy war in those earlier writings. The Báb has explained that the outward appearance of those early statements does not represent His own actual intent and that He did not express His real purpose openly in His early writings.[38] He attests that He reaffirmed the Islamic laws in the Qayyúmu'l-Asmá' out of mercy for the people, who were unprepared for the shock that would be caused by the disclosure of His true station as well as the new laws of His Dispensation:

> Consider the manifold favours vouchsafed by the Promised One, and the effusions of His bounty which have pervaded the concourse of the followers of Islám to enable them to attain unto salvation. Indeed observe how He Who representeth the origin of creation, He Who is the Exponent of the verse, "I, in very truth, am God," identified Himself as the Gate (Báb) for the advent of the promised Qá'im, a descendant of Muḥammad, and in His first Book enjoined the observance of the laws of the Qur'án, so that the people might not be seized with perturbation by reason of a new Book and a new Revelation and might regard His Faith as similar to their own, perchance they would not turn away from the Truth and ignore the thing for which they had been called into being.[39]

This vital fact, which is an indispensable key to understanding the meaning and intention of the Báb's early writings, means that neither the reference to holy war in the Qayyúmu'l-Asmá' nor that in the Ṣaḥífiy-i-Furú'-i-'Adlíyyih can be taken at face value. As we have seen, many of the traditional Islamic terms and concepts that are used in the Qayyúmu'l-Asmá'—such as the Day of Resurrection, life and death, hellfire and paradise, slaying and quickening, testifying before God, the Balance, and the like—undergo a radical symbolic transformation in the Persian Bayán. Why then should the references to holy war arbitrarily be treated differently and taken as literal rather than symbolic expressions, when the overall rule of the Báb's writings is transformation, symbolism, and metaphor? Furthermore, we cannot disregard the fact that the Báb has indicated that His very reason for introducing new ideas gradually was that the teachings He intended to inculcate were so very *different* from—indeed, opposite to—many of the traditional conceptions held by His Muslim audience that He could not breathe a word of them openly, especially at the beginning of His mission. In light of these facts, it seems illogical to assume that in this one case—holy war—He merely intended to confirm and perpetuate those same traditional ideas.

But the literal reading runs into serious interpretive problems on its own. On this reading of the Qayyúmu'l-Asmá', after the Day of Resurrection there would be no more unbelievers left on earth (because that Day is the end of history), so there would be no one left against whom to wage holy war. Additionally, we know that the Báb considered the very revelation of the Qayyúmu'l-Asmá' itself to be the Day of Resurrection. But even the Qayyúmu'l-Asmá' indicates that the Day of Resurrection has *already* taken place. The very first chapter speaks of the fulfillment of the signs of the Day of Resurrection, such as the movement of the mountains upon the earth and of the stars in heaven. In other words, even if we wanted to take the concept of holy war in the Qayyúmu'l-Asmá' literally, we must conclude that no holy war could actually take place.

Most of the references to holy war in the Qayyúmu'l-Asmá' appear in a few of the last chapters of the book. As we saw, the Qayyúmu'l-Asmá' interprets the story of the eventual victory and sovereignty of Joseph. The Báb interprets the references to Joseph's victory as God's promise to render the Báb's Cause victorious. In other words, in the language familiar to Muslims of His time, the Báb is affirming the necessity of rendering the divine Cause victorious.

MacEoin's strongest argument for his thesis comes from a passage of the Epistle of Justice: Branches, in which the Báb is discussing the typical derivative laws of Islam according to the categories prevalent among Shí'ih Muslims. Since the laws of holy war, obligatory prayer, alms, and the like, were affirmed in the Islamic Dispensation, the Báb reaffirms those same laws. But, commenting on a passage in that text, MacEoin claims it

> indicates that the Báb explicitly raised *jihad* to the rank of a sixth pillar of the faith. He then refers to the idea that, when God sent Muḥammad, it was with five swords, and that three of these would not be returned to their scabbards until war came to an end. This would not happen until the sun rose from the west. The first of these swords was that drawn against the pagan Arabs. . . . The second sword was that drawn against the Jews and Christians. . . . The third sword is that drawn against the peoples of the earth. . . .
>
> The Báb then goes on to say that after these three swords, there is that drawn against the "people of dissent". . . . The fifth sword is sheathed for the purpose of punishment. . . .[40]

While the passage paraphrased by MacEoin may seem to offer support for his argument, when read in the context of the totality of the Báb's writings, the passage actually demonstrates the opposite of MacEoin's thesis. As we can see, the Báb states that three "swords" that stand for holy war against non-believers will not be sheathed until the sun rises "from the west." In a number of places, including the Seven Proofs, the Báb explains that His reference to the rising of the sun from the west refers to His own rise from Shiraz (Fárs), because His Revelation occurred at the end of the Islamic Dispensation, which is the sunset (the "west") of Islam:

> However, all Traditions have been, and will continue to be, fulfilled. For example, the rising of the sun from the west intendeth not this apparent sun, for had it been such, it should have also occurred in the previous Revelations. Rather, it meaneth the rise of the Sun of Truth from the place of its setting. Witness that the dawning of the Sun of Truth took place in Mecca, and now it hath risen from the land of Fá' [Shiraz or Fárs] which is the setting-place of the Meccan Revelation. The true meaning is this, and not that which is understood literally.[41]

With this unequivocal explanation before us, we are suddenly facing an entirely different situation. The example just given dramatically demonstrates how the early writings of the Báb employ the language and concepts of Islamic law not to reiterate or confirm that system but to reverse its meanings and to introduce radically new ones. In the Epistle of Justice: Branches, instead of asserting that holy war would never come to an end (as MacEoin reads it—because its ending would be dependent on the impossible condition of the sun rising from the "west"), the Báb is saying that *holy war itself will come to an end* with the advent of the Báb in Shiraz! The duration of the law of the sword, then, is limited to the Islamic Dispensation. We can see that, contrary to the appearance of His severe laws, the Báb actually intended to abolish the law of the sword under all conditions. This reading is consistent with the rest of the writings of the Báb, which express nothing but universal love, compassion, and kindness to all beings.

Nevertheless, as we have seen, there also are some severe laws in the later writings of the Báb, even when He was abrogating the Islamic laws and initiating a new code. We have already listed the instances of the law of the sword that occur in the Persian Bayán. MacEoin concludes from these laws that the Báb intended to create a totalitarian state in which unbelievers would be deprived of rights. However, the Persian Bayán makes any legitimate holy war dependent on certain conditions. These conditions are critical to take into account, for their effect, once again, is to prohibit holy war altogether. A careful reading of the Persian Bayán leaves no doubt that the Báb fashions the severe laws only as a symbolic measure to remind the people of the necessity of recognizing the Promised One. But let us examine the issue more closely.

The first point to be emphasized is that the Persian Bayán restricts the duty (and the right) of enforcing all the severe laws to Bábí kings and rulers. This fact means that before any Bábí state, headed by a Bábí king, were to come into existence, and before the "exaltation" of the Bábí Cause takes place, *no Bábí is allowed to engage in any of those actions*. A close reading of MacEoin's article makes it clear that he is aware of this fact: in his description of the law of the sword in the Persian Bayán, he repeatedly refers to the duty of the *kings* to expel non-Bábís from their dominions, and says that a "Bábí jihad was to be an ongoing process, each Bábí monarch striving to eliminate all traces of infidelity from his dominions and, ultimately, from the earth in order to establish a totalitarian Bábí state."[42] The strict limitation of such warfare to Bábí kings and monarchs is very important to note: first, because it renders problematic

MacEoin's attempts to use such statements in the Bayán to argue that the conflicts in which the Bábís were engaged at the Shrine of Shaykh Ṭabarsí and other places were informed by such laws and thus were not merely defensive actions but also offensive (although his paper is inconsistent on this issue). While MacEoin attributes the allegedly offensive nature of these events to the laws of the Bayán, in fact the Bayán prohibits ordinary Bábís from undertaking any offensive measures; such measures could only be initiated legitimately by a king. If conflicts such as the siege at Shaykh Ṭabarsí could be characterized as having elements of offensive warfare on the part of the Bábís (which, as Zabihi-Moqaddam demonstrates, they did not), those conflicts would have to be regarded as being in direct violation of the laws of the Báb—not as examples of carrying out those laws.[43]

The main discussion of the law of the sword in the Persian Bayán is found in gate 5 of the fifth unity, where the Báb enjoins the Bábí kings to conquer various lands and to seize the property of non-believers. The Báb distinctly stipulates that "this law is confined to the sovereign Bábí kings and does not apply to everyone." Thus one cannot cite references to holy war in the early writings of the Báb, then mention the Persian Bayán's affirmation of the duty of the kings to engage in such warfare, and conclude that ordinary Bábís were expected to wage war against their rulers. Such a conclusion conflicts with both the early and the later writings of the Báb.

It must be kept in mind that the early laws of the Báb were superseded by the Persian Bayán. After the Persian Bayán was revealed, it alone was the authoritative standard of doctrine, and the Persian Bayán restricts the right to initiate holy war to future Bábí sovereigns. But even the early writings of the Báb contain a strict qualification and constraint on any attempt that might be made to initiate holy war: before undertaking any such action, it was necessary to obtain the Báb's permission. And the Báb never gave permission for any holy war or insurrection. The prerequisite set by the Báb ensures that conducting holy war is made dependent upon what was in reality an impossible condition.

Discussing gate 16 of the seventh unity of the Persian Bayán, MacEoin writes: "It is made a duty for every king who believes in the Bayán not to allow any unbeliever to live in his country, with the exception of traders, who bring benefits. This duty is also incumbent on all men."[44] MacEoin's paraphrase here is misleading, for it leaves the reader with the erroneous impression that the Báb is making the duty to expel non-believers binding upon all. The duty of ordinary believers, which is stated in that same chapter, is simply not to associate with unbelievers: "Should one be in the company of one [who is not a believer], such association would never be lawful unto him, for the precondition of fellowship is religious purity and naught else." But nowhere does the Báb say that holy war is a duty of ordinary believers.

In addition to limiting to the sovereign the right to initiate holy war, the Bayán sets in place two conditions that must be met before any Bábí king could ever do so. First, holy war is only allowed after the Bábí state has become triumphant and the Cause of the Báb has become "exalted." Before that, no severe law is permitted to be enforced. Discussing one of the instances of the law of the sword, the Báb states that the law can be implemented only after the exaltation of the Cause of the Báb. But the Báb has also said that the exaltation of the Promised One's Cause will precede the exaltation of His own Cause. In other words, the "exaltation of the Cause of the Báb" means the Revelation of the Promised One. Putting this law into effect is thus deferred until the advent of Him Whom God shall make manifest. Yet after His advent, the laws of the Bayán would no longer be binding, unless the Promised One chose to confirm them, and in this case He did not. The conditions set by the Báb make it clear that He made His law of the sword impossible to carry out. Thus we must conclude that in reality there is no law of the sword or holy war (as traditionally understood) in the Bábí Dispensation, and that the presence of such terms in the writings of the Báb has a symbolic and rhetorical function.

In fact MacEoin refers to the Báb's discussion in gate 15 of the eighth unity when MacEoin says that the Bábís "are not to marry" non-Bábís.[45] In this gate the Báb also says that should two people be married and one find that the other is a non-believer, then divorce is incumbent upon them, and the non-Bábí will have no claim on family property unless he or she returns to the religion. Here the Báb seems to affirm the traditional law of the sword. However, the Báb goes on to say: "But before the exaltation of the Cause of God in the Day of Him Whom God shall make manifest, it is allowed for Bábí males and females to marry non-believers, that haply they may return to the religion."[46]

In that passage, the Báb again delays the implementation of the severe law to the period after the advent of Him Whom God shall make manifest. Before that time—namely, during the entire Dispensation of the Báb—such severe laws, He indicates, are *not* to be enforced. The same gate of the Bayán generalizes this qualification to all other expressions of the law of the sword, for example:

> For the owner of all things is God, glorified be His name. And thus the non-believer is not permitted to own any property. And all that thou observest contained in the hands of the non-believers is not legitimate. Should there appear a mighty sovereign, he would deprive them of their breath, how much more of their property. This, however, is not to be observed before the exaltation of the Word of God. . . ."

We can see that in these passages the Báb is defining the exaltation of His own Cause and the rise of the Bábí state as equivalent to the Day of the Revelation of Him Whom God shall make manifest. By deferring the implementation of the law of the sword until after the end of His own Dispensation, the Báb set in place conditions that in fact prevented the severe laws of the Bayán from ever being put into practice. In doing so, He also set the stage for the eventual formal and complete abrogation of the law of the sword by Bahá'u'lláh.

The same deferral of severe laws occurs in the Arabic Bayán, in which the Báb postpones the prohibition on marriage with non-believers until after the exaltation of the Cause of Him Whom God shall make manifest. In the meantime, Bábís are free to marry whomever they wish, including non-believers, in order to further the exaltation of the Cause of the Báb.

When the Báb says that the Cause of Him Whom God shall make manifest will be exalted *before* His own Cause, this implies not only that, as demonstrated above, the law of the sword is actually forbidden in the Báb's Dispensation, but also that the Báb's own Dispensation would necessarily be very short—for it is only through the next Revelation that the Cause of the Báb will become exalted. This is exactly the doctrine of the Twin Revelations that is emphasized by the Bahá'í perspective. The passage on intermarriage in the Arabic Bayán is quoted by Bahá'u'lláh in the Kitáb-i-Aqdas as an argument for the imminent advent of the Promised One of the Bayán:

> And now consider what hath been revealed in yet another passage, that perchance ye may forsake your own concepts and set your faces toward God, the Lord of being. He [The Báb] hath said: "It is unlawful to enter into marriage save with a believer in the Bayán. Should only one party to a marriage embrace this Cause, his or her possessions will become unlawful to the other, until such time as the latter hath converted. This law, however, will only take effect after the exaltation of the Cause of Him Whom We shall manifest in truth, or of that which hath already been made manifest in justice. Ere this, ye are at liberty to enter into wedlock as ye wish, that haply by this means ye may exalt the Cause of God." . . .
>
> The Point of the Bayán hath explicitly made mention in this verse of the exaltation of My Cause before His own Cause; unto this will testify every just and understanding mind.[47]

Many of the laws of the Báb, and not only those concerned with the sword, are carefully designed in a way that testifies that the advent of Him Whom God shall make manifest was impending. This meaning, however, is sometimes communicated by omission and silence. An example of such a law is the most important ritual law of the Báb, the obligatory prayer. While the Báb enjoins the practice of daily obligatory prayer, consisting of nineteen *rak'ahs*, to be performed between one noon and the next, the Báb never revealed the words of the prayer itself, thus making the implementation of this law dependent on the arrival of the Promised One. Furthermore, the Báb identified the point toward which the worshipper should turn as the Promised One Himself.[48]

In addition to postponing the law of the sword to the time after the advent of Him Whom God shall make manifest, the Báb provides other qualifications that govern the implementation of the severe laws. One such condition is that the king may expel non-believers and seize their property only provided that no one will experience any grief in the process. "But this law is confined to the sovereign Bábí kings and does not apply to everyone," the Báb states. "Indeed, in the lands where the observance of this law may cause grief or harm to any soul, God hath not even permitted its mention. . . ."[49] Aside from the fact that non-believers would surely become saddened by such an action, it would inevitably lead to the suffering of some believers, thus violating the prohibition on causing suffering to anyone. In other words, the implementation of the law of the sword by the kings is made dependent on another impossible condition.

MacEoin discusses this chapter of the Bayán but pays no attention to the most important part of it. However, as the passage quoted above plainly indicates, the Persian Bayán not only prohibits causing grief to the believers, but it also forbids causing grief to non-believers. The kings are to do their best to bring people into the religion by methods that will not cause sadness.[50] This point is alluded to by MacEoin: "Elsewhere, the Báb asks how a king can drink water while there still remains on earth one person who is an unbeliever? Permission is given to conquer other countries in order to bring men into the faith, although, if possible, other means should be used to convert people, such as giving them the goods of the world."[51] In the same passage, the Báb explains this command to the kings (to use other means of converting people) by saying that God disapproves of inflicting the slightest grief on non-believers as well.[52]

As in the examples above, with regard to most of such laws the Báb ordains that the duty in question is to take effect only at the time of the Revelation of Him Whom God shall make manifest. And yet, again, this is an impossible condition, for the Báb repeatedly says in the Persian Bayán and in all His later writings that, upon the advent of Him Whom God shall make manifest, all the laws of the Bayán become null and void unless reaffirmed by the Promised One. In other words, the Báb legislates for the Dispensation of Bahá'u'lláh, knowing very well that none of that legislation will be binding when the specified time arrives. And, as we have seen, the severe laws He sets down are all conditioned so as to prevent them from being implemented. The only meaning these laws can have coherently, then, must be strategic and symbolic. They are all designed to dislodge and disrupt the traditional conceptions and to underscore for the Bábís their duty to be utterly obedient to Him Whom God shall make manifest.

It should also be noted that the Báb clearly outlines the proper method He intends His followers to use to promote the Cause of God during His own Dispensation. Just as the Bábís should marry non-believers for the sake of promoting the faith, "The path to guidance," He writes, "is one of love and compassion, not of force and coercion. This hath been God's method in the past, and shall continue to be in the future! He causeth him whom He pleaseth to enter the shadow of His Mercy."[53] And in Panj Sha'n the Báb states that in previous religions only the chosen ones accepted the Faith through inner choice and conviction, while the rest of the people confessed their faith out of force and coercion. That is why, He says, those who are born into a particular religion blindly accept it. Then He adds: "Therefore, it is forbidden in the Bayán for anyone to accept any religion save through evidence and proof, and testimony, and certitude."[54]

A further significant point is that the Persian Bayán does not even allow the use of violence or force for the punishment of criminal offences. In fact, the removal of the sword with regard to the punishment of crime is one of the most surprising aspects of the Persian Bayán. We saw that the Báb spoke of "five swords" in the Dispensation of Islam. The last two of these swords were related to punishing the people of "dissent" and those who commit crimes in society. But the Báb nullifies the first by forbidding the Bábís even to question one another's faith.[55] As to the second, as Muhammad Afnan has pointed out, only two kinds of punishment are allowed for transgression of the laws of the Bayán: one is a specified fine, and the other is the prohibition of intimate physical contact with one's spouse.[56] Throughout the Báb's legal code, neither imprisonment nor capital punishment is ordained. For example, in the Arabic Bayán, the punishment for intentional murder is the payment of eleven thousand *mithqáls* of gold to the victim's family, as well as nineteen years' deprivation of sharing a bed with one's wife.

Taking into account all the passages discussed above, a distinct pattern emerges which is entirely opposite to the "totalitarianism" MacEoin sees in the Bayán. We must conclude that although the Báb did not formally and explicitly abrogate holy war, He effectively eliminated it within His Dispensation. It would remain for Bahá'u'lláh to abolish it formally, and indeed the explicit abrogation of the law of the sword (with the exception of punishment for crime) was Bahá'u'lláh's first act in announcing His mission. "On the first day of His arrival in the garden designated the Riḍván," Bahá'u'lláh recounts, "the Tongue of Glory uttered three blessed verses," the first of which was "that in this Revelation the use of the sword is prohibited."[57]

The Perspective of Unity and the Realization of the Laws of the Bayán

The Báb's overarching purpose in all His writings was to prepare the Bábís for the imminent advent of Him Whom God shall make manifest—

Bahá'u'lláh—and His intention was not only to guide them to recognize Him, but also to ensure that Bahá'u'lláh would not suffer at the hands of the Bábís what the Báb had suffered at the hands of the Muslims. Many of the laws of the Persian Bayán express this aim: the Báb looks at His life and His sufferings and then ordains laws to prevent the same thing from happening to Bahá'u'lláh. In addition to those laws, the writings of the Báb eliminate any future excuse that might be used by the Bábís to justify rejecting Bahá'u'lláh. This last intention constitutes the most explicit, most frequently asserted, most emphasized, and most pervasive theme in all the writings of the Báb. And, in this regard, the mission of the Báb was a complete success. Within a short period of time after Bahá'u'lláh's public declaration of His station, the vast majority of the Bábí community had recognized Bahá'u'lláh—a transition unprecedented in sacred history.

Of course there are always allegorical and ambiguous statements in the former Scriptures that can be interpreted to contradict the new Revelation. The Báb's writings as well could not be free from such statements, for if He had identified all the characteristics of the next Revelation openly and unequivocally, there would have been no freedom and no test for the Bábí community. Thus although the Báb's writings emphasize the proximity of the advent of the Promised One in the year 9, some parts of His texts treat various ordinances as ordinary laws for the unspecified duration of His own Dispensation. Yet, as we saw, He also made it clear that the exaltation of His own Cause would only be carried out through the Revelation of Bahá'u'lláh. In other words, in accordance with the unific perspective that pervades the Báb's writings, the enactment of the laws of the Promised One would in fact constitute the realization of the laws of the Bayán, since despite the apparent differences, they are in reality one and the same.

The primacy of Him Whom God shall make manifest is nowhere more strikingly evident than in the Báb's exhortations, throughout His writings, that in evaluating the claim of the next Revelation, the Bábís should ignore any statement in the Bayán, as well as any statement made by any leader of the Bábí community that might seem to go against such a claim. Instead of measuring the Promised One's teachings and laws by their conformity to the Bayán, the Bábís are commanded to turn exclusively to the criterion and testimony that God has determined as the sole legitimate and supreme proof of the divine Manifestation—His divine verses. The Báb makes it unequivocally clear that neither any argument based on understandings of the statements in the Bayán, nor any decree of any Bábí leader, even the Letters of the Living, can be used as an excuse to reject the claim of the next Revelation.

Although the Báb removed any possible excuse for turning away from Bahá'u'lláh, He knew that, nevertheless, some Bábís would attempt to use their interpretations of the Bayán to argue against Him Whom God shall make manifest. The Báb even tells us what the Promised One's answer to such arguments would be:

> Methinks I visualize those who would, prompted by their own deluded conceptions, write to Him and ask Him questions about that which hath been revealed in the Bayán, and He would answer them with words not of His Own, but divinely inspired, saying: "Verily, verily, I am God; no God is there but Me. I have called into being all the created things, I have raised up divine Messengers in the past and have sent down Books unto Them. Take heed not to worship anyone but God, He Who is My Lord and your Lord. This indeed is the undoubted truth. However, alike shall it be to Me; if ye believe in Me, ye will provide good for your own souls, and if ye believe not in Me, nor in that which God hath revealed unto Me, ye will suffer yourselves to be shut out as by a veil. For verily I have been independent of you heretofore, and shall remain independent hereafter. Therefore it behooveth you, O creatures of God, to help your own selves and to believe in the Verses revealed by Me. . . ."[58]

To focus His followers' attention on the revelation of divine verses as the path to recognition of the Manifestation of God, the Báb makes one particular chapter of the Bayán the only one in the entire book that must be read by the believers every month. Its title is "On this, that he who adduceth any proof other than the Book of God and the verses of the Bayán, other than the powerlessness of all to produce their like, is veiled from any proof. He who recounteth any miracle, other than the verses, is veiled from any truth. He who claimeth to reveal divine verses should not be opposed by anyone. All must recite this gate once in every nineteen days, and ponder day and night upon that which is revealed therein."[59] In the substantive part of this chapter, the Báb says that the only way to recognize spiritual truth is to fix one's gaze on the Origin of the Cause and not on its derivative expressions as they appear in any

Dispensation—to look at God with the eye of God, using the method that is authorized by God, perceiving with the eye of the heart, independently and unaffected by either the approval or the rejection of anyone. He explains:

> Notwithstanding this impossibility, that none besides Him Whom God shall make manifest will be able to claim such a mighty Cause, it is enjoined in the Bayán that should anyone make a claim and verses be manifested from Him, no one should oppose Him, that haply no grief should assail that Sun of Truth. . . . His verses are, by themselves, sufficient proof of the radiant lights of the Sun of His Being, just as the powerlessness of all is the mighty evidence of the utter need and dependence of all upon Him. The reason for this command is that haply, in the Day of the Revelation of that supreme Truth, the feet of the people shall not falter upon the bridge, and that they shall not pronounce judgment against the Fashioner of their existence, adducing against Him the very shadow of His verse in their heart, and rendering naught, and at once, all their inmost realities and deeds, without even perceiving it.[60]

There is hardly any chapter of the Persian Bayán (or any other later writings of the Báb) in which such statements will not be found.

Conclusion: The Báb's Tablet to Mullá Báqir

It is befitting to end this study of the writings of the Báb with mention of the Báb's Tablet to the Letter of the Living, Mullá Báqir, a work which can be considered the Báb's mystical and theological will and testament for His followers. The tablet was also sent to Yaḥyá Dárábí (Vaḥíd), when he asked the same question posed by Mullá Báqir. On the importance of this tablet, the Báb writes in a letter addressed to Mírzá Aḥmad-i-Azghandí: "I have revealed a book on the exaltation of His mention. Ye all must possess it, for God hath not revealed any tablet more glorious than that. How can one be considered amongst those who eagerly await the Day of His revelation if he fail to possess a copy thereof?"[61]

Mullá Báqir had asked the Báb about Him Whom God shall make manifest and the signs of His revelation. The Báb responds that the very question is presumptuous:

How supremely exalted is the mention of Him about Whom thou hast inquired. Verily, exalted is He, immeasurably glorified, mighty, magnified, and sanctified above the comprehension of the hearts of His servants, of the spirits to bow down in adoration before Him, of the souls to celebrate His praise, and of the bodies to mention His supreme Glory. How supremely exalted is the One of Whom thou dost inquire, and how insignificant is thine essence! Doth it beseem the sun that lieth in the mirrors of His revelation, manifested through the Point of the Bayán, to question the Transcendent Sun before Whose Countenance, in the Day of His manifestation, all other suns bow down in adoration?

Hadst thou not been a letter of the Primal Unity, I would have ordained a punishment for thee, inasmuch as thou hast dared to inquire about thy God Who hath created thee.[62]

The Báb tells the Letter of the Living that if he wants even to conceive of mentioning Him Whom God shall make manifest, he must first recite five verses nineteen times, and then stand and recite certain words that affirm the glorification and sanctification of Him Whom God shall make manifest above any description and praise. Only then he can mention His name. In this recitation, the Letter of the Living is to attest that he should recognize Him Whom God shall make manifest by Himself and out of the intrinsic worth of His being and His verses, and not because of His acceptance by others. He should be known by Himself, and that perspective of the heart is the essence of paradise.[63]

Then the Báb says that he can now read the answer to his question:

I have written down in My mention of Him these gem-like words: "No allusion of Mine can allude unto Him, neither anything mentioned in the Bayán." Yea, By His glory! Those words are, before God, far mightier than all the deeds of worship of all who dwell on earth, inasmuch as the essence of all those deeds returneth unto the import of those same words. Therefore, recognize thou Him Whom God shall make manifest by the same testimony by which thou hast recognized God. For, exalted and glorified is He above the power of any one to reveal Him except Himself, or the description of any of His creatures. I Myself am but the first servant to believe in Him and in His signs, and to partake of the sweet savors of His words from the first-fruits of the Paradise of His knowledge.[64]

The Báb goes so far as to say that even if the Báb Himself and all the Letters of the Living were to reject Him Whom God shall make manifest, the believers should not allow themselves to be deprived of accepting Him. Nothing else and no one else matters. The Báb could not be more emphatic:

> Beware, beware lest, in the days of His Revelation, the Váḥid of the Bayán shut thee not out as by a veil from Him, inasmuch as this Váḥid is but a creature in His sight. And beware, beware that the words sent down in the Bayán shut thee not out as by a veil from Him, inasmuch as these are His own words in His former Manifestation. He is the Sun of Truth, the Face of Unity, the Countenance of Lordship, the Inmost Reality of Divinity, and the Self of Eternity. . . .[65]

Next the Báb tells Mullá Báqir that no good deed he might perform, and no words anyone, even the first Letter of the Living, might say can be a sufficient guarantee that he has attained the good pleasure of God. The only way to become assured of that is the direct testimony of Him Whom God shall make manifest, Who will confirm the divine good pleasure by accepting him as one of His believers.[66] "This," the Báb says, "is the true meaning of the utterance of God, "Say! God is all-sufficient unto all things, and nothing sufficeth save God, thy Lord, whether in the heavens or the earth, and whatever lieth between them. Verily, He hath power over all things.'"[67] If the Letter of the Living, or any other Bábí leader like Azal, with all his mighty titles and station, should reject Him Whom God shall make manifest, he would be denounced by the Báb as an unbeliever:

> By the righteousness of Him Whose power causeth the seed to germinate and Who breatheth the spirit of life into all things, were I to be assured that in the day of His Manifestation thou wilt deny Him, I would unhesitatingly disown thee and repudiate thy faith inasmuch as thou wert not created but to recognize Him. If, on the other hand, I be told that a Christian, who beareth no allegiance to My Faith, will believe in Him, the same will I regard as the apple of Mine eye, and accept as My believer. . . .[68]

Upon the revelation of Him Whom God shall make manifest, the Báb states, all distinctions are obliterated:

> In the day of the revelation of Him Whom God shall make manifest all that dwell on earth will be equal in His estimation. Whomsoever He ordaineth as a Prophet, he, verily, hath been a Prophet from the beginning that hath no beginning, and will thus remain until the end that hath no end, inasmuch as this is an act of God. And whosoever is made a Vicegerent by Him shall be a Vicegerent in all the worlds, for this is an act of God. For the will of God can in no wise be revealed except through His will, nor His wish be manifested save through His wish. He, verily, is the All-Conquering, the All-Powerful, the All-Highest; and He is the All-Victorious, the All-Exalted, the All-Sublime.
>
> Recognizing Him turneth the servant into a letter of affirmation, whilst being veiled from Him turneth him into a letter of negation.[69]

The Báb then discloses that Mullá Báqir will meet Him Whom God shall make manifest at the end of the year 8 and the beginning of the year 9.[70] The Báb concludes the tablet by addressing God and testifying these words, which distill the essence of all the writings of the Báb: "Bear Thou witness that, through this Book, I have covenanted with all created things concerning the mission of Him Whom Thou shalt make manifest, ere the covenant concerning Mine own mission had been established. Sufficient witness art Thou and they that have believed in Thy signs."[71]

The aim of this study has been to gain an understanding of the interrelationship of the writings of the Báb, expressed in the concept of the sanctuary of unity or the sanctuary of the heart, as reflected in the Báb's interpretation of Scripture, in His metaphysics of divine creative Action, and in His principle of progressive revelation. The same principle was found to be operative at the level of His laws and ordinances. The dual station of the Báb as both an independent Prophet and the Herald of the Revelation of Bahá'u'lláh is reflected in the uniquely metaphorical and symbolic character of the Báb's laws. Given the mediating station of the Báb between the Islamic Dispensation and the Bahá'í Revelation, the laws of the Báb sometimes employ the terminology and symbolism that was familiar to, and expected by, His audience, based on the culture and traditions of Islam. As the Qá'im, who was expected to come with the sword, the Báb uses the language of the sword, but in a way that radically inverts its meaning. He does so in order to transform and abrogate the tradition itself and to introduce an entirely different metaphysical and moral world view that affirms the sacredness and dignity of all created things and advocates a culture of refinement, compassion, and care for all beings—a standard of behaviour characterized by the universal maxim, "act toward others as God acts toward them."

But the ultimate expression of the sanctuary of unity is the principle of fixing one's gaze on the Origin of the Cause and turning toward the being and the verses of Him Whom God shall make manifest. Recognizing Him with the eye of the heart is the culmination of the entire Revelation of the Báb. In the sanctuary of unity, where all things are revealed in their essential oneness, the Twin Revelations of the Báb and Bahá'u'lláh are seen to be inseparable. It becomes evident that the spirit of all the writings of the Báb is exemplified and brought to fulfillment and fruition in Bahá'u'lláh's laws of the removal of the sword—laws which, like all the principles in Bahá'u'lláh's writings, seek not merely to achieve justice, equality, and an end to sectarian strife, but to lay the foundation for a new and global stage of human civilization imbued with the consciousness of the essential unity and wholeness of the human race.

NOTES

☆

INTRODUCTION

1 In this work, pronouns referring to God and to the Manifestations of God (the Primal Will) are capitalized. This style, initiated by Shoghi Effendi, serves to mark the distinct and unique ontological status of the Manifestation of God/Primal Will in Bábí and Bahá'í theology.

2 That campaign of cultural genocide continues today against the Bábís' spiritual heirs, the Bahá'ís.

3 Elsewhere, I have discussed the theology and world view of Bahá'u'lláh; see Saiedi, *Logos and Civilization.*

4 Browne, "Babis of Persia," p. 145, and Introduction to *Traveller's Narrative,* p. 407.

5 See Martin, "Mission of the Báb."

6 Along with earlier writers including Nicolas, Browne, Fáḍil Mázandarání, I<u>sh</u>ráq <u>Kh</u>ávarí, Badí'u'lláh Faríd, Muḥammad-'Alí Fayḍí, and Hasan Balyuzi, some authors who have written about the Báb include Muhammad Afnán, Nosratollah Mohammadhosseini, Parviz Moini, Denis MacEoin, Abbas Amanat, Todd Lawson, Vahid Ra'fati, Moojan Momen, Stephen Lambden, Ahang Rabbani, Abu'l-Qásim Afnán, Siyamak Zabihi-Moghaddam, Vahid Behmardi, Vahid Jacob Brown, Armin Eschraghi, Kavian Milani, William McCants, and Sepehr Manuchehri.

One of the first attempts to present a general introduction to the teachings of the Báb was the notorious *Ha<u>sh</u>t Bihi<u>sh</u>t* by Kirmání and Rúḥí. Ostensibly a presentation of the Báb's teachings, it was actually a polemic against the Bahá'í Faith. Yet even its representation of the writings and teachings of the Báb is highly unreliable—filled with contradictions, inaccuracies, misinterpretations, and outright fabrications.

7 For example, MacEoin opines at the end of his study on the works of the Báb: "There is little in this immense canon to interest or inspire the modern

reader. Bábí doctrine is of historical rather than human interest. . . ." (*Sources,* p. 102; see also p. 92).

8 Jamálu'd-Dín Afghání is an example of this position.

9 Weber, *Economy and Society* 1:24–25.

10 It is important to note that this abrogation applies only to the laws that prescribe external forms and social practices. The inner metaphysical truths and eternal principles do not change and constitute the core unity of the religions.

11 Feuerbach, *Essence of Christianity.*

12 Durkheim, *Elementary Forms.*

13 Freud, *Future of an Illusion.*

14 Comte, *The Positive Philosophy.*

15 See, for example, Edgerton, *Sick Societies.*

16 See Rawls, *Theory of Justice.*

17 See Heller, "Religious Foundations," part 1, p. 39; and part 2, pp. 51–52.

18 See Edgerton, *Sick Societies.*

19 For a more extensive scholarly discussion of this issue, see MacEoin, *From Shaykhism to Babism.* See also Lawson, "Qur'án Commentary"; Arjomand, *Shadow of God*; and Dabashi, *Authority in Islam.*

20 See, for example, Aḥsá'í, *Sharḥu'l-Favá'id.*

21 Nabíl-i-A'ẓam, *Dawn-Breakers,* pp. 59–61.

22 Consistent with the conventional treatment of books of Sacred Scripture, the titles of the Báb's works are given in roman type, unless a specific edition is referred to.

23 This is a reference to Qur'án 49:11.

24 The Báb, *Qayyúmu'l-Asmá'* (Súrih of *'Ulamá*), Iran National Bahá'í Archives (hereafter referred to as INBA) 3:5. Parts of this passage are in *Selections,* p. 44. Unless otherwise identified, all translations from the Báb's writings are provisional translations by the author.

25 The practice of dissimulation about one's religious beliefs in cases of danger was considered justified in Shí'ih Islam based on the Qur'ánic passage that exempts "those who are compelled while their hearts are firm in faith" from divine punishment for disavowing belief (16:106). See Momen, *Introduction to Shi'i Islam,* pp. 39, 183. The practice is even considered a praiseworthy duty: according to Imám Ṣádiq, one who does not believe in and practise *taqíyyih* is not a Shí'ih.

26 See, for example, Balyuzi, *The Báb;* Fayḍí, *Haḍrat-i-Nuqṭiy-i-Awlá;* Shoghi Effendi, *God Passes By;* 'Abdu'l-Bahá, *Traveler's Narrative;* Amanat, *Resurrection and Renewal;* Mohammadhosseini, *Haḍrat-i-Báb;* MacEoin, *Sources;* Nabíl-i-A'ẓam, *Dawn-Breakers;* Mázandarání, *Ẓuhúru'l-Ḥaqq,* vol. 3; Abu'l-Qásim Afnán, *'Ahd-i-A'lá;* Zabihi-Moghaddam, "Pírámún"; Browne, *Tarikh-i-Jadid.*

27 This declaration was apparently to a selective number of people while the Báb was in Mecca.

28 Kirmání, *Izháqu'l-Báṭil,* pp. 127–45.

29 The Báb, qtd. in Mázandarání, *Ẓuhúru'l-Ḥaqq* 3:280–81 and *Muḥáḍirát* 2:737.

30 The Báb, qtd. in Mázandarání, *Ẓuhúru'l-Ḥaqq* 3:280–81.

31 In addition to the Kitábu'l-Fihrist, another of these tablets can be found in INBA 91:1–4.

32 The Báb, Kitábu'l-Fihrist, pp. 2–3.

33 The Báb, Kitábu'l-Fihrist, p. 4.

34 MacEoin, *From Shaykhism to Babism,* p. 192.

35 There is some confusion about these two works as well as their relation to another text of the Báb, the Ṣaḥífiy-i-Raḍavíyyih. Following Nicolas, MacEoin (in *Sources for Early Bábí Doctrine and History*) calls Khuṭbiy-i-Dhikríyyih by the erroneous name "Risála-yi Dhahabiyya." However, "Dhahabiyya" (Dhahabíyyih) is actually the name of an entirely different work, one which MacEoin calls "Dhahabíyyah II." MacEoin also apparently thinks that the Ṣaḥífiy-i-Raḍavíyyih is the same as the Kitábu'l-Fihrist. He writes that "it is clear that *al-Ṣaḥífa al-Raḍawiyya* must, in fact, be . . . the *Kitáb al-fihrist*" (*Sources,* p. 207). His argument is that according to the Báb's description of the Ṣaḥífiy-i-Raḍavíyyih, it contains an account of the works stolen during the journey to Mecca. Such an account is found in the Kitábu'l-Fihrist; therefore the two works must be the same.

But the "Raḍawiyya" (Ṣaḥífiy-i-Raḍavíyyih), the book in which the Khuṭbiy-i-Dhikríyyih is found, is definitely not the Kitábu'l-Fihrist. The Ṣaḥífiy-i-Raḍavíyyih consists, as the Báb says, of fourteen chapters. The Kitábu'l-Fihrist, in contrast, is a short work without any divisions, and which certainly does not have fourteen chapters. The first chapter of the Raḍavíyyih is the Khuṭbiy-i-Dhikríyyih, in which the Báb lists the names of fourteen works (four books and ten epistles) written up to the date of the revelation of the Khuṭbiy-i-Dhikríyyih (Muḥarram 15, 1262). In that list He names the Raḍavíyyih as the tenth work, namely the sixth epistle listed after the four books. The book also begins by referring to itself as the sixth epistle. In chapter 11, entitled Khuṭbiy-i-Jiddah, the Báb does speak of the theft of tablets on the way to Mecca (which is also mentioned in the Kitábu'l-Fihrist). For more information, see Mohammadhosseini, *Haḍrat-i-Báb,* pp. 800–804.

36 The date of the Báb's arrival at Mákú is subject to scholarly dispute, and the dates suggested range from May to July.

37 The date of the Báb's departure from Mákú is also subject to dispute, with proposed dates ranging from January to April. The idea that the Báb left Mákú for Chihríq around January 1848 is assumed to be supported by a letter from Siyyid Ḥusayn to the Uncle of the Báb, stating that the Báb departed Mákú at the beginning of the year (see Abu'l-Qásim Afnán, *'Ahd-i-A'lá,*

pp. 337–38). However, this letter seems to have been misread and mistyped by Abu'l-Qásim Afnán. I thank Parviz Moini for bringing this point to my attention.

38 See also MacEoin, "Trial of the Báb"; and Amini, "Majlis-i-Munáẓiriy-i-Báb."

39 Sources differ on the number of persons in attendance. Shoghi Effendi writes that Bahá'u'lláh "entertained as His guests Quddús, Ṭáhirih, and the eighty-one disciples who had gathered on that occasion" (*God Passes By,* p. 68), which would be eight-four in all. I thank Dr. Nosratollah Mohammad-hosseini for calling this point to my attention.

40 Shoghi Effendi, *God Passes By,* p. 31.

41 Nabíl-A'ẓam, *Dawn-Breakers,* p. 296. For a comprehensive discussion of the life of Ṭáhirih, see Mohammadhosseini, *Haḍrat-i-Ṭáhirih.*

42 The martyrdom of the Báb took place in the thirty-second (lunar) year of His life. In Panj Sha'n He predicts this event in subtle ways, stating that in the beginning of His thirty-second (lunar) year of life He would attain true existence and the mention of God. See *Panj Sha'n,* p. 14.

43 Some of the Báb's works were translated into French by A. L. M. Nicolas, and E. G. Browne attempted, very inadequately, to translate some texts into English.

44 See Saiedi, *Logos and Civilization,* p. 243.

A SHORT CHRONOLOGICAL LIST OF THE BÁB'S WRITINGS

1 Rashtí, *Risálat as-Sulúk.*

2 The Báb, qtd. in Mázandarání, *Asráru'l-Áthár* 4:246.

3 Regarding the Kitábu'r-Rúḥ (Book of the Spirit), MacEoin speaks of a contradiction he cannot resolve concerning the dating of its revelation (whether it was revealed on the way to Mecca and Medina or on the return journey) because he claims there is a reference to the Kitábu'r-Rúḥ in the Báb's Ṣaḥífiy-i-Bayna'l-Ḥaramayn. Since the latter text was revealed in honour of Muḥíṭ-i-Kirmání between Mecca and Medina, that would mean that the Kitábu'r-Rúḥ had been revealed before the Báb arrived at Mecca. Yet the Báb Himself says that it was revealed on the return journey (*Sources,* p. 61, n. 76). However, there is actually no reference to the Kitábu'r-Rúḥ in the Ṣaḥífiy-i-Bayna'l-Ḥaramayn. Possibly the place where the Báb says that "Rúḥ," or the Holy Spirit—meaning Jesus—has revealed verses to Him (as is said in the Qur'án about Muḥammad) has been mistakenly read as a reference to the Kitábu'r-Rúḥ. The fact that the Kitábu'r-Rúḥ was revealed during the return journey is beyond doubt, not only because the Báb says so, but also because in the Kitábu'r-Rúḥ itself the Báb refers to events during the trip to Mecca including His meeting with Muḥíṭ-i-Kirmání and the declaration of His Cause to him (Kitábu'r-Rúḥ, p. 34).

4 The eighth Imám.
5 Nicolas, *Le Béyan Persan*, pp. xvii–xxv.
6 Mázandarání, *Ẓuhúru'l-Ḥaqq* 3:471. I would like to thank Siyamak Zabihi-Moghaddam for bringing this letter to my attention.
7 Mázandarání, *Ẓuhúru'l-Ḥaqq* 3:472.
8 The term *báb* (which in Arabic can mean "chapter" as well as "gate") is translated as "gate" in this book when referring to the chapters of the Bayán in order to retain the symbolic and mystical connotations that the Báb specifically assigns to the word in this context. At the beginning of the Persian Bayán, He explains that He has called each chapter a *báb* because it is a gate to paradise. He also explains that His work is "all things" (*kullu shay'*) and in all things nothing is seen except the revelation of the Point, the Báb.
9 Mehri Afnan, "Naẓarí bar Mundaraját," p. 28.

1 : THE MODE OF INTERPRETATION

1 One of the best listings of the interpretive works of the Báb can be found in Muhammad Afnan, "Sha'n-i-Tafsír."
2 The Commentary on the Súrih of the Cow has two independent parts. Part 1, which is a complete text, covers the first *juzv* (one-thirtieth) of the Qur'án which runs through verse 141 of the Súrih of the Cow. Both the beginning and the end date of the commentary's revelation are mentioned in the text itself. It was begun on the night of Siyyid Káẓim-i-Rashtí's death, at the end of A.H. 1259, and was finished at the end of 1260. Part 2 of the Commentary on the Súrih of the Cow was revealed after the declaration of the Báb. The copy in INBA deals with only two verses (142–43) of the Súrih of the Cow (INBA 69:377–410).
3 Nabíl-i-A'ẓam, *Dawn-Breakers*, p. 31.
4 In a number of His tablets including the Kitábu'l-Fihrist and Khuṭbiy-i-Jiddah (the Ṣaḥífiy-i-Raḍavíyyih) the Báb gives an account of the works that were stolen between Mecca and Medina. In this work, revealed in Jiddah, He lists among the names of the stolen works various commentaries including one on the Súrih of the Cow revealed in the language of divine verses (INBA 91:69–72). See also Mázandarání, *Ẓuhúru'l-Ḥaqq* 3:289; and MacEoin, *Sources*, p. 52.
5 Two tablets by the Báb are titled "Commentary on the Verse of Light" (Tafsír-i-Áyiy-i-Núr). The first, revealed in the first year of the Báb's ministry, is mentioned in the Kitábu'l-Fihrist. However, that work is not an interpretation of the Qur'án's Verse of Light but of another verse, "The Houses that God hath allowed to be erected," in the Súrih of Light. The Báb interprets the concepts of Houses of Worship and Remembrance as the sanctuary of the heart and His own being (INBA 14:495–98). The second work, Commentary on the Verse of Light II, which is specifically an interpretation of the Verse

of Light (Qur'án 24:35), was written much later in the mountain prisons. This fact is evident in the text in a passage where the Báb discusses the four earlier years of His Revelation and compares them to years 5 and 6. He explains why He appeared as the Báb, and the fact that the true meaning of that claim to gatehood is none other than being an independent Prophet (Collection, pp. 10–26).

6 See Muhammad Afnan, "Kúshishí," and Behmardi, "Muqaddami'í dar báriy-i-Sabk."

7 In various expressions of the typology of the modes of revelation, the Báb uses "sermon" and "interpretation" interchangeably. "Sermon" (*khuṭbih*) is repeatedly distinguished from prayer, divine verses, rational discourse, and Persian mode. In Panj Sha'n, the word "commentary" (*tafsír*) is distinguished from "sermon." However, in that instance commentaries are actually rational discourses. The reason, as we will see shortly, is that rational discourses are themselves actually commentaries on prayers.

8 See, for example, Sawyer, *Sacred Languages*.

9 The Báb, Persian Bayán 1:1.

10 The Báb, *Kitábu'l-Asmá',* INBA 29:384–85.

11 The Báb, *Ad'íyi-i-Haftigí,* INBA 58:92.

12 The Báb, *Ad'íyi-i-Haftigí,* INBA 58:89–90.

13 The Báb, "Tafsír-i-Kullu'ṭ-Ṭa'ám," Collection, pp. 220–21.

14 The Báb, "Fi's-Sulúk II," Collection, p. 452.

15 The Báb, "Fi's-Sulúk II," Collection, p. 461.

16 The Báb, *Tablet to Mírzá Sa'íd,* INBA 14:428.

17 The Báb, *Tablet to Mírzá Sa'íd,* INBA 14:430.

18 The Báb, Persian Bayán 3:17.

19 The Báb, Persian Bayán 3:16.

20 The Báb, Persian Bayán 3:16.

21 According to the Báb's own dating, at least seventeen of the nineteen parts definitely were revealed. In the published version of the book, twelve parts are present. The rest are yet to be located.

22 The Báb, Persian Bayán 4:1.

23 The Báb, Persian Bayán 2:15.

24 The Báb, *Kitábu'l-Asmá',* INBA 29:67. A similar structure is discussed elsewhere in the Báb's explanation of the two letters that constitute the imperative word of creation, "Be!" (*Kun*, consisting of the two letters *K* [Káf] and *N* [Nún]). According to the Báb, *K* represents the divine creation, while *N* refers to the essences of created things. Thus the Báb equates *K* with fire and air, where air is the moment of inclination toward fire. Likewise he equates *N* with water and earth, where water represents the reception of existence and earth sustains that reception. The Báb, *Tafsír-i-Bismilláh,* INBA 64:57.

25 The Báb, Persian Bayán 3:17.

26 The Báb, Persian Bayán, 2:14. Emphasis added.
27 See Jacob Vahid Brown, "Textual Resurrection."
28 Browne, Introduction to *New History*, pp. xii, xxvi, xxvii.
29 MacEoin, "Hierarchy, Authority, and Eschatology," p. 98.
30 MacEoin, *From Shaykhism to Babism*, p. 166.
31 The Báb, *Qayyúmu'l-Asmá'* (Súrih of *Ímán*), INBA 3:6; *Panj Sha'n*, pp. 388–95.
32 The Báb, *Tafsír-i-Súriy-i-Baqarih* II, INBA: 69:409.
33 For a discussion of the distinction between things in themselves and appearances, see Kant, *Critique of Pure Reason*.
34 See, for example, Jung, *Psychology and Alchemy*. One of the fundamental statements of medieval alchemy is the Hermetic text known as the Emerald Tablet of Hermes Trismegistus (translated into Latin from medieval Arabic manuscripts), which begins its explanation of the creation of all things through the One Thing by stating: "What is below is like what is above, and what is above is like what is below, to perform the miracles of the One Thing."
35 The Báb, *Tafsír-i-Súriy-i-Kawthar*, INBA 53:169.
36 For a good analysis of the relation between truth and hermeneutics, see Gadamer, *Truth and Method*.
37 These works are all unique yet organically related and inspired by the same principle. Lack of attention to this hermeneutical principle has led various authors to see qualitative breaks between various interpretive texts of the Báb. See, for example, the treatment of the Qayyúmu'l-Asmá' and Commentary on the Súrih of the Cow in Lawson's "Interpretation as Revelation."
38 The Ḥurúfíyyih school was founded by Faḍlu'lláh Astarábádí (died A.D. 1384); the Nuqṭavíyyih school by Maḥmúd Pasíkhání (died A.D. 1427/8).
39 See, for example, the Báb, Persian Bayán 5:3, 4, 9.
40 MacEoin, *Rituals*, p. 19.
41 MacEoin, *Rituals*, p. 77, n. 100.
42 MacEoin, *Rituals*, p. 19.
43 See also Behmardi, "Ṣaḥífiy-i-Bayna'l-Ḥaramayn."
44 The Báb, Ṣaḥífiy-i-Bayna'l-Ḥaramayn, p. 6.
45 The Báb, Ṣaḥífiy-i-Bayna'l-Ḥaramayn, p. 13.
46 The Báb, Ṣaḥífiy-i-Bayna'l-Ḥaramayn, pp. 27–36.
47 The Báb, *Panj Sha'n*, pp. 405–47; Persian Bayán 5:10.
48 MacEoin may have confounded the sign of Solomon's Seal, a hexagram consisting of two triangles, with the Bábí pentagram temple. But they are entirely different. The Bábí pentagram, as the Báb explains, consists of five lines constituting six chambers. Solomon's Seal consists of six lines and seven chambers. Shaykh Aḥmad frequently discussed the meaning of Solomon's Seal, identifying it with the interaction of the divine and the worldly.
49 The Báb, "Tafsír-i-Kullu'ṭ-Ṭa'ám," Collection, p. 223.
50 The Báb, *Tafsír-i-Súriy-i-Kawthar*, INBA 53:98.

51 The Báb, "Fi's-Sulúk II," Collection, p. 461.

52 The Báb, Tafsír-i-Súriy-i-Kaw<u>th</u>ar, INBA 53:98.

53 The Báb, Tafsír-i-Súriy-i-Kaw<u>th</u>ar, INBA 53:174. The quotation cites Qur'án 47:15.

54 The Báb, Tafsír-i-Súriy-i-Va'l-'Aṣr, INBA 14:111.

55 The Báb, Tafsír-i-Súriy-i-Va'l-'Aṣr, INBA 14:115.

56 The Báb, Persian Bayán 1:1.

57 The Báb, "Tafsír-i-Kullu'ṭ-Ṭa'ám," Collection, p. 224.

58 The Báb, Tafsír-i-Ḥadíth-i-Man 'Arafa Nafsah faqad 'Arafa Rabba, INBA 14:474–78.

59 The Báb, Tafsír-i-Sirr-i-Há', INBA 86:151–52.

60 The Báb, Persian Bayán 2:2.

61 The Báb, Selections, p. 106 (Persian Bayán 2:7).

62 The Báb, Tablet to Mírzá Sa'íd, INBA 14:439.

2 : THE DIVINE CHEMISTRY OF FIRE, WATER, AIR, AND EARTH

1 See, for example, Coleridge, "Aids to Reflection," p. 31.

2 See, for example, Zeller, History of Greek Philosophy.

3 The Báb, Qayyúmu'l-Asmá' (Súrih of Mulk), INBA 3:4.

4 Qur'án 11:7.

5 Qur'án 108:1–3.

6 Qur'án 47:15.

7 Qur'án 21:30.

8 The Báb, Tafsír-i-Súriy-i-Kawthar, INBA 53:175.

9 See also Bahá'u'lláh, Kitáb-i-Íqán, pp. 139–40.

10 The quotation is from Imám Riḍá'. The Báb, Tafsír-i-Súriy-i-Kaw<u>th</u>ar, INBA 53:175.

11 The Báb, Tafsír-i-Súriy-i-Kaw<u>th</u>ar, INBA 53:179.

12 The Báb, Tafsír-i-Súriy-i-Kaw<u>th</u>ar, INBA 53:180.

13 The Báb, Tafsír-i-Súriy-i-Kaw<u>th</u>ar, INBA 53:180.

14 The Báb, Tafsír-i-Súriy-i-Kaw<u>th</u>ar, INBA 53:181.

15 The Báb, Tafsír-i-Súriy-i-Kaw<u>th</u>ar, INBA 53:181.

16 The Báb, Tafsír-i-Súriy-i-Kaw<u>th</u>ar, INBA 53:181.

17 The Báb, Tafsír-i-Súriy-i-Kaw<u>th</u>ar, INBA 53:181–82.

18 The Báb, Tafsír-i-Súriy-i-Kaw<u>th</u>ar, INBA 53:187.

19 The Báb, Tafsír-i-Súriy-i-Kaw<u>th</u>ar, INBA 53:188.

20 The Báb, Tafsír-i-Súriy-i-Kaw<u>th</u>ar, INBA 53:188.

21 The Báb, Tafsír-i-Súriy-i-Kaw<u>th</u>ar, INBA 53:181.

22 For example, Qayyúmu'l-Asmá', INBA 3:165.

23 The Báb, Persian Bayán 5:3.

24 The Báb, Tafsír-i-Súriy-i-Kaw<u>th</u>ar, INBA 53:175.

25 The Báb, *Qayyúmu'l-Asmá'* (Súrih of *Ḥúríyyih*), INBA 3:53.
26 The Báb, *Qayyúmu'l-Asmá'* (Súrih of *Mulk*), INBA 3:3.
27 The Báb, *Selections,* p. 54 (*Qayyúmu'l-Asmá'* [Súrih of *Ḥúríyyih*], INBA 3:51–52).
28 The Báb, "Tafsír-i-Kullu'ṭ-Ṭa'ám," Collection, pp. 220–21.
29 The Báb, *Qayyúmu'l-Asmá'* (Súrih of *Kitáb*), INBA 3:76.
30 For a general discussion of the Sinaic mystery, see Lambden, "Sinaic Mysteries."
31 The Báb, "Tafsír-i-Kullu'ṭ-Ṭa'ám," Collection, pp. 227–28.
32 Qur'án 21:69.
33 The Báb, *Tafsír-i-Ḥadíth-i-Ḥaqíqat,* INBA 53:32–33.
34 The Báb, Persian Bayán 2:6. Part of this passage is in *Selections,* p. 102.
35 The Báb, *Dalá'il-Sab'ih,* pp. 58–59.
36 The Báb, *Qayyúmu'l-Asmá'* (Súrih of *Ra'd*), INBA 3:137.
37 The Báb, *Tafsír-i-Bismilláh,* INBA 64:37.
38 The Báb, "Tafsír-i-Kullu'ṭ-Ṭa'ám," Collection, pp. 221–22.
39 The Báb, *Tafsír-i-Súriy-i-Kawthar,* INBA 53:174–75.
40 The Báb, *Sharḥ-i-Asmá'u'lláh,* INBA 98:19–20.
41 The Báb, Persian Bayán 4:3.
42 The Báb, *Kitábu'l-Asmá',* INBA 29:383–86.
43 The Báb, "Tafsír-i-Kullu'ṭ-Ṭa'ám." Collection, pp. 221–22.
44 The Báb, Persian Bayán 5:1.

3 : THE REMEMBRANCE, THE GATE, AND THE DUST

1 See, for example, Mohammadhosseini, *Haḍrat-i-Báb,* pp. 190–92.
2 MacEoin, "Hierarchy, Authority, and Eschatology," p. 98.
3 MacEoin, *Sources,* p. 57.
4 MacEoin, "Hierarchy, Authority, and Eschatology," p. 98.
5 Lawson, "The Term 'Remembrance.'"
6 Amanat, *Resurrection and Renewal,* pp. 174, 199.
7 MacEoin, *Sources,* pp. 57, 69; and "Early Shaykhí Reactions," pp. 16–20.
8 See, for example, Lawson, "Interpretation as Revelation," p. 230, n. 19.
9 Qtd. in Momen, *Introduction to Shi'i Islam,* p. 169.
10 For a list of the signs expected to accompany the advent of the Qá'im see Momen, *Introduction to Shi'i Islam,* 166–70.
11 Majlisí, *Biḥáru'l-Anvár* 13:1125, 1106, 1124.
12 Majlisí, *Biḥáru'l-Anvár* 13:1122.
13 Majlisí, *Biḥáru'l-Anvár* 13:1080.
14 Majlisí, *Biḥáru'l-Anvár* 13:1103.
15 Majlisí, *Biḥáru'l-Anvár* 13:1133.
16 Rev. 6:4.

17 Rev. 9:15.
18 Rev. 19:11–16.
19 See Momen, "Trial of Mullá 'Alí Basṭámí."
20 Kirmání, *Izháqu'l-Báṭil,* pp. 127–45.
21 Aḥsá'í, *Sharḥu'z-Zíyárat* 1:200–207.
22 Qtd. in Momen, *Introduction to Shi'i Islam,* p. 164.
23 See, for example, *Qayyúmu'l-Asmá'* (Súrih of *Ra'd*), INBA 3:226; (Súrih of *Anvár*) INBA 3:46; (Súrih of *Sábiqín*) INBA 3:229; (Súrih of *Qadr*) INBA 3:40.
24 This concept of "normal discourse" is after Kuhn's notion of "normal science" (see *Structure of Scientific Revolutions*).
25 The Báb, *Selections,* p. 119 (*Dalá'il-i-Sab'ih,* p. 29).
26 The appellation "Qurratu'l-'Ayn" (Solace of My Eyes) in this text always refers to the Báb Himself and is not related to Ṭáhirih, who was also known by that title.
27 The Báb, *Selections,* p. 53 (*Qayyúmu'l-Asmá'* [Súrih of *Qarábah*], INBA 3:50).
28 The Báb, *Risáliy-i-Ithbát-i-Nubuvvat-i-Kháṣṣih,* INBA 14:391–92.
29 The Báb, *Tafsír-i-Súriy-i-Kawthar,* INBA 53:188–89.
30 The Báb, Tablet to Mullá Aḥmad, Collection, p. 556.
31 The Báb, Persian Bayán 8:18.
32 The Báb, Collection, pp. 16–18.
33 For an informative discussion of this issue, see Lawson, "The Term 'Remembrance.'"
34 The Báb, *Tablet to Mírzá Sa'íd,* INBA 14:436–37.
35 The Báb, *Tafsír-i-Ḥadíth-i-Man 'Arafa Nafsah faqad 'Arafa Rabba,* INBA 14:476.
36 John 1:1; Qur'án 3:45.
37 The Báb, *Selections,* p. 41 (*Qayyúmu'l-Asmá'* [Súrih of *Mulk*], INBA 3:3).
38 The Báb, *Selections,* p. 45 (*Qayyúmu'l-Asmá'* [Súrih of *Ímán*], INBA 3:7–8). This statement is also a reference to Qur'án 3:31–34.
39 The Báb, *Selections,* p. 53 (*Qayyúmu'l-Asmá'* [Súrih of *Ḥúríyyih*], INBA 3:51).
40 The Báb, *Selections,* p. 44 (*Qayyúmu'l-Asmá'* [Súrih of *Ímán*], INBA 3:6–7).
41 The Báb, *Selections,* p. 50 (*Qayyúmu'l-Asmá'* [Súrih of *Qadr*], INBA 3:41).
42 The Báb, *Qayyúmu'l-Asmá'* (Súrih of *Kitáb*), INBA 3:76.
43 Exod. 3:4.
44 The Báb, "Tafsír-i-Kullu'ṭ-Ṭa'ám," Collection, pp. 227–28.
45 The Báb, *Tafsír-i-Súriy-i-Kawthar,* INBA 53:181.
46 The Báb, Persian Bayán 1:15.
47 Qur'án 57:3.
48 See, for example, the Báb, *Tafsír-i-Súriy-i-Kawthar,* INBA 53:99.
49 Qur'án 42:51.
50 Qur'án 43:3.

51 The Báb, *Qayyúmu'l-Asmá'* (Súrih of *Mulk*), INBA 3:3.
52 The Báb, *Qayyúmu'l-Asmá'* (Súrih of *Ishárih*), INBA 3:62.
53 The Báb, *Qayyúmu'l-Asmá'* (Súrih of *Ḥujjah*), INBA 3:86.
54 See, for example, the Báb, *Tafsír-i-Súriy-i-Va'l-'Aṣr,* INBA 14:165.
55 In this regard, Imám 'Alí's Sermon of the Twin Gulfs (*Tutunjíyyih*) and the frequent references in the writings of the Báb to it and its content are particularly important. See Lawson, "Coincidentia Oppositorum."
56 The Báb, Collection, pp. 16–18.
57 The Báb, *Tafsír-i-Súriy-i-Kawthar,* INBA 53:179.
58 The Báb, *Tafsír-i-Súriy-i-Kawthar,* INBA 53:179–80.
59 Jung, *Aion,* pp. 220–21.
60 See, for example, the Báb, *Tafsír-i-Súriy-i-Kawthar,* INBA 53:169; *Tafsír-i-Bismilláh,* INBA 64:53–54, 79–80; *Sharḥ-i-'Ilmi'l-Ḥurúf,* INBA 67:203–204; *Risáliy-i-Ithbát-i-Nubuvvat-i-Kháṣṣih,* INBA 14:387–92.
61 The Báb, *Tafsír-i-Súriy-i-Va'l-'Aṣr,* INBA 14:172–173; *Risáliy-i-Ithbát-i-Nubuvvat-i-Kháṣṣih,* INBA 14:387–92.
62 The Báb, INBA 14:215–216.
63 The Báb's discussions concerning the Most Great Name are also an interpretation of the Islamic sign of the Most Great Name whose design is attributed to Imám 'Alí. This sign consists of eight motifs: a pentagram or "temple" (five-pointed star), a sign consisting of vertical lines or Alifs, the letter Mím, a square ladder, four vertical lines or Alifs, the letter Há' (equal to 5), the reverse of the letter Váv (equal to 6), and a final pentagram "temple." The identity of the "first" and the "last" is a reference to the reality of the Temple—the Manifestation of God—as the reflection of the divine attributes of the First and the Last. The pentagram temple consists of five lines arranged to create six chambers. As such, it symbolizes the sum of Há' and Váv, or 5 and 6. The two signs of Há' and Váv constitute the name *Huva,* which is identical with the first and the last sign—the Temple.

From various early and later writings we can infer close connections between this 11, 111, and 1111. The first number signifies the divine Essence (*Huva* = He) that is reflected in the Temple of Revelation, that is, the Báb. The second is the name of the Báb, 'Alí. The third, as the Báb notes extensively, refers to the expression, *Báb ẓáhir* (The Báb is manifest) because numerically they are identical. The most extensive discussion of the relation and meaning of 1, 11, 111, and 1111 can be found in the Báb's "Tafsír-i-Váv," pp. 249–65. The letter Mím often refers to the station of Muḥammad (the other component of the name of the Báb), and the square ladder could refer to the spiritual ascent to God as well as to the next Revelation. See also al-Búní, *Shamsu'l-Ma'árif,* p. 92.
64 This is extensively explained by the Báb in the Tablet of Nineteen Temples. See the Báb, *Panj Sha'n,* pp. 405–47.

65 The Báb, "Tafsír-i-Váv," Collection, p. 251.
66 For further discussion of "Bahá" as the Most Great Name and its relation to other scriptures see Lambden, "The Word Bahá."
67 Bahá'u'lláh has extensively explained the mystery of reversal of the letter Váv in the Islamic sign of the Most Great Name in relation to the concept of progressive revelation.
68 The Báb, *Risáliy-i-Ithbát-i-Nubuvvat-i-Kháṣṣih.*
69 The Báb, *Qayyúmu'l-Asmá'* (Súrih of *Ḥúríyyih*), INBA 3:53.
70 *Al-Ismayn* (Twin Names) refers to the Báb Himself, Who is both 'Alí and Muḥammad. The Báb, *Tafsír-i-Súriy-i-Kawthar,* INBA 53:181.
71 The Báb, *Tafsír-i-Súriy-i-Kawthar,* INBA 53:179–80.
72 The Báb, *Tafsír-i-Súriy-i-Baqarih* II, INBA 69:381.
73 Qur'án 70:9.
74 Sometimes the triangle is used to refer to the first three, sometimes to the last three; while the square may refer to the first four or the last four stages.
75 The Báb, *Qayyúmu'l-Asmá'* (Súrih of *Tathlíth*), INBA 3:184. The Báb's frequent references to the unity of binary structures within Himself is also a reference to Imám 'Alí's Sermon of the Twin Gulfs. See Lawson, "Coincidentia Oppositorum."
76 The Báb, Kitábu'l-Asmá', chapter on the name of God, *Aknaz* (the Most Hidden Treasure), INBA 29:66.
77 The Báb, "Sharḥ-i-Ḥadíth-i-Abú Lubayd-i-Makhzúmí," Collection, p. 147, also INBA 98:40–41. For further discussion of this tradition see Gulpáygání, *Fará'id,* pp. 31–36.
78 Qtd. in Bahá'u'lláh, *Kitáb-i-Íqán,* p. 254.

4 : THE STRUCTURE OF THE QAYYÚMU'L-ASMÁ'

1 See Lawson's apt use of the term "exploded meaning" or "explosion of meaning" in relation to the commentaries of the Báb, in "Dangers of Reading."
2 The Báb, *Tafsír-i-Súriy-i-Kawthar,* INBA 53:99.
3 The Báb, *Tafsír-i-Súriy-i-Kawthar,* INBA 53:99–100.
4 The Báb, *Tafsír-i-Súriy-i-Kawthar,* INBA 53:121.
5 Qur'án 103.
6 For further discussion of the Commentary on Súrih of the Afternoon, see Lawson, "Dangers of Reading."
7 The Báb, *Tafsír-i-Súriy-i-Va'l-'Aṣr,* INBA 14:121, 165.
8 The Báb, *Tafsír-i-Súriy-i-Va'l-'Aṣr,* INBA 14:126.
9 For example, see the Báb, *Tafsír-i-Súriy-i-Va'l-'Aṣr,* INBA 14:166; *Ṣaḥífiy-i-'Adlíyyih,* pp. 20–33; *Tafsír-i-Bismilláh,* INBA 64:76; *Tafsír-i-Súriy-i-Tawḥíd,* INBA 14:212–13; *Tafsír-i-Ḥadíth-i-Man 'Arafa Nafsah faqad 'Arafa Rabba,* INBA 14:480; *Tafsír-i-Sirr-i-Há',* INBA 86:152–53, 153–54.
10 The Báb, "Tafsír-i-Du'á'-i-Ṣabáḥ," Collection, p. 30.

11 See, Lawson, "Interpretation as Revelation," p. 233; Mohammadhosseini, *Haḍrat-i-Báb*, p. 733; MacEoin, *Sources*, p. 47.
12 The Báb, *Tafsír-i-Súriy-i-Baqarih* I, INBA 69:341. I thank Parviz Moini for bringing this point to my attention.
13 The Báb, *Tafsír-i-Súriy-i-Baqarih* I, INBA 69:156–159. Italics added.
14 Qur'án 2:35.
15 The Báb, *Tafsír-i-Súriy-i-Baqarih* I, INBA 69:263–65.
16 Qur'án 2:40.
17 The Báb, *Tafsír-i-Súriy-i-Baqarih* I, INBA 69:277.
18 Qur'án 2:49.
19 Yazíd was the second Caliph of the Umayyad Dynasty.
20 The Báb, *Tafsír-i-Súriy-i-Baqarih* I, INBA 69:286.
21 Qur'án 2:60.
22 The Báb, *Tafsír-i-Súriy-i-Baqarih* I, INBA 69:296.
23 Qur'án 2:143.
24 The Báb, *Tafsír-i-Súriy-i-Baqarih* II, INBA 69:390.
25 See, for example, Lawson, "Interpretation as Revelation."
26 MacEoin, *Sources*, p. 55. 'Abdu'l-Bahá's reference is in *Traveler's Narrative*, p. 2.
27 MacEoin, *Sources*, p. 46.
28 The Báb, *Ṣaḥífiy-i-'Adlíyyih*, p. 3.
29 The Báb, *Selections*, p. 119 (*Dalá'il-i-Sab'ih*, p. 29).
30 MacEoin, *From Shaykhism to Babism*, pp. 157–58. MacEoin's argument is supported by Lawson in his "Interpretation as Revelation," pp. 232–53.
31 The Báb, qtd. in Mázandarání, *Ẓuhúru'l-Ḥaqq* 3:285, also in INBA 91:174. Mullá Ḥusayn identified this tablet as one written in Bú<u>sh</u>ihr and addressed to Mírzá Ibráhím-i-<u>Sh</u>írází. Another identification is made by Afnán on the basis of the letters of the Báb in the possession of the Afnán family. Thus he identifies the letter as addressed to the uncle of the Báb, Siyyid 'Alí, and written in Muscat. See Abu'l-Qásim Afnán, *'Ahd-i-A'lá*, pp. 439–40.
32 Qur'án 2:185.
33 The Báb, *Qayyúmu'l-Asmá'* (Súrih of *Kitáb*), INBA 3:74–76.
34 Fayḍ-i-Ká<u>sh</u>ání, *Navádiru'l-A<u>kh</u>bár*, p. 258.
35 The Báb, Majmú'iy-i-Á<u>th</u>ár 4:108.
36 See, for example, 'Arab-Bá<u>gh</u>í, *Tuḥfatu'l-Mahdíyyah*.
37 For details of this trial and decree, see Momen, "Trial of Mullá 'Alí Basṭámí."
38 In a provisional translation of a chapter of the Qayyúmu'l-Asmá', Momen has used the same fact to argue that all the text of the Qayyúmu'l-Asmá' could not have been revealed in forty consecutive days. He notes that both the clerical decree against the text and the early refutation written by Karím <u>Kh</u>án-i-Kirmání quote only up to chapter 65, but he concludes that, therefore, on the departure of Basṭámí and the other Letters of the Living, only half of the book had been revealed (Momen, "The Súrat al-Dhikr"). How-

ever, this argument can only show that the copies taken by the Letters may have been incomplete copies, but it does not prove that the full text was not yet revealed. We already saw that the Báb complains that for ten months the Qayyúmu'l-Asmá' has been among the people and yet not a single correct copy has been *completed*. Thus we should expect that the earliest copies taken by the Letters might well have been incomplete.

39 The Báb, *Tafsír-i-Súriy-i-Baqarih* II, INBA 69:382–83.

40 Related to this issue, MacEoin writes: "In the Persian Bayán, the Bab indicates that he is to be buried 'in one of the twin shrines,' which . . . may be a reference to Mecca and Medina" (*Rituals*, p. 24). However, here (Persian Bayán 9:1) the Báb is not speaking of His own burial. He is speaking of His son Aḥmad, who died in infancy: the remains of the one who is "taken" (i.e., derived, created) from the Point. This fact is stated more explicitly in another part of the Persian Bayán (5:1). Clearly the two shrines are the two sacred places in Shiraz, the birthplace of the Báb and His House; the sacred remains of the Báb's son are to be taken to one of these shrines. The Báb explains the reason for this: so that people on their pilgrimage will remember that the Báb was a human being Who was born and was followed by His son; thus the Bábís will not forget His servitude to God. Curiously, in just the paragraph before the one quoted, MacEoin correctly states that the Báb has affirmed that all former shrines are rendered null in His Dispensation, yet MacEoin then goes on to interpret the twin shrines as Mecca and Medina. MacEoin's translation mistake is not new; Nicolas made the same mistake earlier.

41 The Báb, *Qayyúmu'l-Asmá'* (Súrih of *Huva*), INBA 3:83.

42 The Báb, *Qayyúmu'l-Asmá'* (Súrih of *Dhikr*), INBA 3:223.

43 Qur'án 2:255, 3:2.

44 The Báb, qtd. in Mázandarání, *Ẓuhúru'l-Ḥaqq* 3:223–24. Many thanks to Dr. Muhammad Afnan for informing me of the identity of the recipient of this historic tablet. The tablet as it is quoted in Mázandarání's book is incomplete. The full text can be found in *Khoosh-i-Há'i az Kharman-i-Adab va Honar* 6, pp. 10–14. However, in both these copies instead of "And He prefaced each súrih with two of the verses of the Qur'án," it has: "And He prefaced each súrih with one of the verses of the Qur'án." This latter rendering does not fit the point that is discussed by the Báb. In addition, the form of the sentence does not fit such a reading. In at least two other copies the text refers to two verses and not one verse, and the sentence then makes perfect sense. One of them can be found in INBA 58:177, while the other is in Majmú'iy-i-Áthár 10:73.

45 The Báb, Khuṭbiy-i-Dhikríyyih, qtd. in Mázandarání, *Ẓuhúru'l-Ḥaqq* 3:290.

46 The Báb, *Tafsír-i-Bismilláh*, INBA 64:38.

47 See, for example, the Báb, Persian Bayán 3:16.

48 The Báb, *Qayyúmu'l-Asmá'* (Súrih of *Varaqa*), INBA 3:153–54.

49 The Báb, *Qayyúmu'l-Asmá'* (Súrih of *Dhikr*), INBA 3:223–24.

50 The Báb, *Tafsír-i-Ḥadíth-i-Ḥaqíqat,* INBA 53:33.
51 The Báb, qtd. in Mázandarání, *Ẓuhúru'l-Ḥaqq* 3:223–24.
52 The Báb, *Tafsír-i-Bismilláh,* INBA 64:34–35.
53 The Báb, *Tafsír-i-Bismilláh,* INBA 64:35.
54 The Báb, *Tafsír-i-Bismilláh,* INBA 64:37–38.
55 The Báb, *Tafsír-i-Bismilláh,* INBA 64:45.
56 The Báb, *Tafsír-i-Bismilláh,* INBA 64:48.
57 The Báb, *Qayyúmu'l-Asmá'* (Súrih of *Akbar*), INBA 3:114.
58 The Báb, *Qayyúmu'l-Asmá'* (Súrih of *Ṭayr*), INBA 3:174.
59 See, for example, the Báb, *Tafsír-i-Súrih-i-Kawthar,* INBA 53:179; Persian Bayán 8:5.
60 The Báb, *Selections,* p. 54 (*Qayyúmu'l-Asmá'* [Súrih of *Ḥúríyyih*], INBA 3:52).

5 : THE QAYYÚMU'L-ASMÁ' AS INTERPRETATION

1 Browne, "Some Remarks on the Bábí Texts," p. 261.
2 Qur'án 3:45.
3 The Báb, *Qayyúmu'l-Asmá'* (Súrih of *Khalíl*), INBA 3:150.
4 The Báb, *Qayyúmu'l-Asmá'* (Súrih of *Ḥayy*), INBA 3:58–59.
5 The Báb, *Qayyúmu'l-Asmá'* (Súrih of *Naṣr*), INBA 3:60.
6 The Báb, *Selections,* pp. 41–42 (Qayyúmu'l-Asmá' [Súrih of *Mulk*], INBA 3:3–4).
7 The Báb, *Qayyúmu'l-Asmá'* (Súrih of *Mulk*), INBA 3:3.
8 Amanat renders this title as the "Súrih of al-Malik" (the King). In Arabic, *malik* and *mulk* are spelled the same. Amanat, *Resurrection and Renewal,* p. 203.
9 The Báb, *Qayyúmu'l-Asmá'* (Súrih of *Mulk*), INBA 3:3.
10 Qur'án 42:51 and 43:3.
11 The Báb, *Qayyúmu'l-Asmá'* (Súrih of *Raḥmah*), INBA 3:126.
12 See, for example, Browne, "Some Remarks," p. 261, and MacEoin, *Sources,* pp. 56–57.
13 The Báb, *Qayyúmu'l-Asmá'* (Súrih of *Yúsuf*), INBA 3:10.
14 Shoghi Effendi, *God Passes By,* p. 23.
15 The Báb, *Qayyúmu'l-Asmá'* (Súrih of *Yúsuf*), INBA 3:10–11.
16 The Báb, *Qayyúmu'l-Asmá'* (Súrih of *Yúsuf*), INBA 3:10.
17 The Báb, qtd. in Mázandarání, *Ẓuhúru'l-Ḥaqq* 3:223–24
18 The Báb, *Qayyúmu'l-Asmá'* (Súrih of *Ṣiráṭ*), INBA 3:31.
19 The Báb, *Qayyúmu'l-Asmá'* (Súrih of *'Arsh*), INBA 3:27.
20 The Báb, *Qayyúmu'l-Asmá'* (Súrih of *Núr*), INBA 3:33–34.
21 The Báb, *Qayyúmu'l-Asmá'* (Súrih of *Má'*), INBA 3:38.
22 The Báb, *Qayyúmu'l-Asmá'* (Súrih of *A'ẓam*), INBA 3:166.
23 The Báb, *Qayyúmu'l-Asmá'* (Súrih of *Dhikr*), INBA 3:120.
24 The Báb, *Qayyúmu'l-Asmá'* (Súrih of *Ḥill*), INBA 3:44.

25 Qur'án 34:17.
26 The Báb, *Qayyúmu'l-Asmá'* (Súrih of *Sábiqín*), INBA 3:229.
27 The Báb, *Qayyúmu'l-Asmá'* (Súrih of *Qarábah*), INBA 3:49.
28 The Báb, *Qayyúmu'l-Asmá'* (Súrih of *Qarábah*), INBA 3:49–50. Part of this passage is in *Selections*, pp. 52–53.
29 The Báb, *Qayyúmu'l-Asmá'* (Súrih of *Ḥúríyyih*), INBA 3:52–53. Part of this passage is in *Selections*, p. 54.
30 See also Mehri Afnan, "Maqám-i-Zan."
31 Qur'án 12:28.
32 This is a reference to Qur'án 17:40 and 53:27.
33 The Báb, *Qayyúmu'l-Asmá'* (Súrih of *Ḥúríyyih*), INBA 3:54.
34 The Báb, *Qayyúmu'l-Asmá'* (Súrih of *Ḥayy*), INBA 3:59.
35 The Báb, *Qayyúmu'l-Asmá'* (Súrih of *Ḥujjah*), INBA 3:90.
36 The Báb, *Qayyúmu'l-Asmá'* (Súrih of *Af'idah*), INBA 3:118.
37 The Báb, *Qayyúmu'l-Asmá'* (Súrih of *Raḥmah*), INBA 3:127.
38 The Báb, *Qayyúmu'l-Asmá'* (Súrih of *Qalam*), INBA 3:145.
39 The Báb, *Qayyúmu'l-Asmá'* (Súrih of *Jihád*), INBA 3:202; (Súrih of *Mujallal*), INBA 3:187.
40 The Báb, *Qayyúmu'l-Asmá'* (Súrih of *Mujallal*), INBA 3:186–87.
41 The Báb, *Qayyúmu'l-Asmá'* (Súrih of *Mujallal*), INBA 3:188.
42 The Báb, *Qayyúmu'l-Asmá'* (Súrih of *Sábiqín*), INBA 3:229.
43 The Báb, *Qayyúmu'l-Asmá'* (Súrih of *Dhikr*), INBA 3:223–24.

6 : THE SANCTUARY OF THE HEART AND THE PATH TO TRUTH

1 The Báb, Persian Bayán 1:1.
2 The Báb, *Tafsír-i-Ḥadíth-i-Ḥaqíqat,* INBA 53:32–34.
3 The Báb, *Tafsír-i-Ḥadíth-i-Ḥaqíqat,* INBA 53:32–33.
4 The Báb, *Tafsír-i-Ḥadíth-i-Ḥaqíqat,* INBA 53:33.
5 The Báb, *Tafsír-i-Ḥadíth-i-Ḥaqíqat,* INBA 53:32.
6 The Báb, *Tafsír-i-Ḥadíth-i-Ḥaqíqat,* INBA 53:33.
7 The Báb, *Tafsír-i-Ḥadíth-i-Ḥaqíqat,* INBA 53:34. Part of the passage is quoted in Bahá'u'lláh, *Kitáb-i-Íqán,* p. 102.
8 The Báb, *Tafsír-i-Ḥadíth-i-Ḥaqíqat,* INBA 53:34.
9 The Báb, *Dalá'il-i-Sab'ih,* pp. 58–59.
10 The Báb, *Panj Sha'n,* p. 11.
11 The Báb, *Panj Sha'n,* p. 12.
12 Qur'án 24:34.
13 The Báb, *Panj Sha'n,* p. 295.
14 The Báb, *Dalá'il-i-Sab'ih,* pp. 58–59. The same point is frequently discussed in other works of the Báb. See, for example, the Báb, *Panj Sha'n,* pp. 294–97, 321; and *Kitábu'l-Asmá',* INBA 29:28.
15 The Báb, INBA 98:175.

16 The Báb, Kitábu'l-Asmá' 4:7 (Princeton copy, pp. 163–64).

17 In a tablet addressed to Yaḥyá Azal, the Báb emphasizes the fact that the Báb is the Morn of Eternity and that all believers without exception are merely mirrors who have no light of their own. He writes: "Today, from the inception of the Revelation of the Bayán until the advent of Him Whom God shall make manifest, all attainment of exaltation by anyone is a token reflection of the exalted station of the Point of Unity and the Dayspring of the Morn of Eternity. How beloved it hath been, and continueth to be, before God that in each Revelation pure mirrors will reflect the Tree of Truth. But the mirrors are not illumined by themselves, independent of the Primal Will, for had they been radiant by themselves, they would have been speaking before the Day of Revelation. . . . All the mirrors abide by His bidding, return unto Him, utter His glory, and seek shelter beneath His shadow" (*Panj Sha'n*, pp. 135).

18 Kant, *Critique of Pure Reason.*

19 Kant, *Critique of Pure Reason*, pp. 287–483.

20 The Báb, *Panj Sha'n*, pp. 388–90.

21 The Báb, *Panj Sha'n*, p. 389.

22 The Báb, *Panj Sha'n*, p. 391.

23 The Báb, *Panj Sha'n*, pp. 391–92.

24 The Báb, *Tablet to Mírzá Ḥasan*, INBA 53:199.

25 The Báb, *Tablet to Mírzá Sa'íd*, INBA 14:439.

26 Qur'án 39:30.

27 The Báb, *Panj Sha'n*, p. 393.

28 Bahá'u'lláh, *Seven Valleys and Four Valleys*, pp. 18–21.

29 'Abdu'l-Bahá, *Makátíb* 2:2–55. See also Momen, "'Abdu'l-Bahá's Commentary."

30 Keven Brown, "'Abdu'l-Bahá's Response."

31 'Abdu'l-Bahá, *Makátíb* 2:40–42.

32 Cf. Moojan Momen's discussion, in "Relativism," of 'Abdu'l-Bahá's tablet, which focuses on the two opposing positions analyzed by 'Abdu'l-Bahá but does not discuss the third position, which is a resolution and synthesis of the two.

33 'Abdu'l-Bahá, *Makátíb* 2:42–43.

34 See Kant, *Critique of Pure Reason, Critique of Practical Reason*, and *Critique of Judgment.*

7 : THE PRIMAL WILL AS THE UNITY OF SUBJECT AND OBJECT

1 The Báb, Persian Bayán 4:1.

2 The Báb, Persian Bayán 2:8.

3 The Báb, *Panj Sha'n*, pp. 99–104.

4 Bahá'u'lláh, *Tablet to Jamál-i-Burújirdí*, INBA 35:39.

5 The Báb, Persian Bayán 7:19.
6 The Báb, *Panj Sha'n*, pp. 40–41.
7 The Báb, Persian Bayán 2:14.
8 Mázandarání, *Ẓuhúru'l-Ḥaqq* 3:121.
9 The Báb, *Qayyúmu'l-Asmá'* (Súrih of *Kitáb*), INBA 3:77.
10 Weber, *Protestant Ethic*. "Asceticism" in Weber's specific sense, as used here, does not mean practices of deprivation and self-denial.
11 The Báb, *Tafsír-i-Súriy-i-Kawthar*, INBA 53:189.
12 See, for example, Ghazzálí, *Incoherence of the Philosophers*.
13 See, for example, Morewedge, "Logic of Emanationism."
14 See Ghazzálí, *Incoherence of the Philosophers*.
15 See, for example, Fárábí, *On the Perfect State*.
16 The Báb, *Tablet to Mírzá Sa'íd*, INBA 14:434–35, 437.
17 The Báb, *Panj Sha'n*, pp. 388–89.
18 The Báb, *Ṣaḥífiy-i-'Adlíyyih*, p. 16.
19 The Báb, *Tafsír-i-Súriy-i-Tawḥíd*, INBA 14:218.
20 The idea of the True Indivisible Being, which in Islamic philosophy is attributed to Aristotle, is present in Plotinus' *Enneads* 5.2.1. The idea that the objects of knowledge are present in the divine knowledge, as an argument for the thesis of the unity of existence, can be found throughout Ibn 'Arabí's work, *The Bezels of Wisdom;* Fayḍ-i-Káshání's *Kalimát-i-Maknúnih* also contains explicit affirmations of this point. Shaykh Aḥmad has written extensive criticism of both works. For further discussion on this topic, see Izutsu, *Sufism and Taoism;* Ra'fati, " Ideas of Ibn 'Arabí"; and Keven Brown, "'Abdu'l-Bahá's Response."
21 Aḥsá'í, *Javámi'u'l-Kalim* 2:166–74.
22 The Báb, Persian Bayán 3:12. 'Abdu'l-Bahá has referred to this discussion in a tablet dealing with the same issue (*Makátíb* 1:276). The translation can be found in "'Abdu'l-Bahá's Tablet."
23 The Báb, *Tafsír-i-Ḥadíth-i-Ḥaqíqat*, INBA 53:32.
24 For information relating to Mírzá Sa'íd, see Mohammadhosseini, *Haḍrat-i-Báb*, pp. 816–17.
25 See also Ra'fati, "Ráhnamá'í baráy-i-Muṭáli'iy-i-Basiṭu'l-Ḥaqíqah."
26 The Báb, *Tablet to Mírzá Sa'íd*, INBA 14:429–30.
27 The Báb, *Tablet to Mírzá Sa'íd*, INBA 14:430.
28 The Báb, *Tablet to Mírzá Sa'íd*, INBA 14:432–35.
29 The Báb, Persian Bayán 3:13.
30 The Báb, *Ṣaḥífiy-i-'Adlíyyih*, p. 17. Provisional translation provided by the Research Department of the Universal House of Justice.
31 See Fárábí, *On the Perfect State;* Morewedge, "Logic of Emanationism."
32 The Báb, *Tablet to Mírzá Sa'íd*, INBA 14:436–39.
33 The Báb, Persian Bayán 1:1.

34 The Báb, Persian Bayán 1:1.

35 For example, in his translation of this part of the Persian Bayán ("It is for the Will, and through the manifestation of His own Self, that God hath created, out of His Self, eighteen souls, ere the creation of all things,") MacEoin has replaced the word "eighteen" with "seventeen." Although he does not give any reason for this alteration, it is reasonably clear that he has assumed that "eighteen" was a typographical error and thus he has tried to translate the text according to his assumption of what it must be. However, all the original and authentic versions of the Persian Bayán consistently give "eighteen"—not "seventeen." It would seem that the term "first believer," which is the referent of "Him" in that paragraph, has been assumed to be the first Letter of the Living and thus only seventeen other Letters could be created out of him. See MacEoin, *Persian Bayán.*

36 The Báb, Majmú'iy-i-Á<u>th</u>ár 5:63–64. Mullá Ḥusayn's full name was Muḥammad-Ḥusayn, which consists of eight Arabic letters.

37 The Báb, *Risáliy-i-I<u>th</u>bát-i-Nubuvvat-i-<u>Kh</u>áṣṣih,* INBA 14:382–85.

8 : THE STAGES OF DIVINE CREATIVE ACTION

1 See Ra'fati, "Marátib-i-Sab'ih."

2 The Báb, *Tablet to Mírzá Sa'íd,* INBA 14:438.

3 Aḥsá'í, *<u>Sh</u>arḥu'l-Favá'id,* pp. 33–89.

4 The Báb, *Tablet to Mírzá Sa'íd,* INBA 14:426–27.

5 The Báb, *Tafsír-i-Ḥadí<u>th</u>-i-Imám Riḍá',* INBA 14:401.

6 The Bab, *Risálah Fi'l-Ghiná,* in *Safinih-i-'Irfán* Book 1, p. 88.

7 Bahá'u'lláh, *La'áli'l-Ḥikmah* 2:275.

8 The Báb, *Tafsír-i-Súriy-i-Baqarih* I, INBA 69:263–64.

9 The Báb, *Tafsír-i-Bismilláh,* INBA 64:36.

10 See, for example, the Báb, *Tafsír-i-Súriy-i-Va'l-'Aṣr,* INBA 14:105–6, and *Tablet to Mírzá Sa'íd,* INBA 14:437–38.

11 The Báb, *Risálah fi'n-Naḥv,* INBA 67:124.

12 The Báb, Collection, pp. 72–73.

13 The Báb, Majmú'iy-i-Á<u>th</u>ár 10:185–92. In this work the Báb chooses to use the significant verb *vahaba* (*vhb*, bestowed) to demonstrate this spiritual grammar.

14 See Momen, *Introduction to Shi'i Islam.*

15 The Báb, *Ṣaḥífiy-i-'Adlíyyih,* pp. 16–17.

16 Aḥsá'í, *Rasá'ilu'l-Ḥikmah,* pp. 56, 151.

17 Bahá'u'lláh in the Tablet of Wisdom defines the essence of nature as the Will (*Tablets of Bahá'u'lláh,* p. 142).

18 Saiedi, *Logos and Civilization,* pp. 59–61.

19 The Báb, Persian Bayán 4:3.

20 The Báb, Persian Bayán 4:3.

21 The Báb, Persian Bayán 4:3.
22 The Báb, "Fi's-Sulúk II," Collection, p. 457.
23 The Báb, Persian Bayán 4:3.
24 See, for example, The Báb, *Tafsír-i-Súriy-i-Va'l-'Aṣr,* INBA 14:182; *Tafsír-i-Bismilláh,* INBA 14:98.
25 See, for example, Ibn al-'Arabí, *Bezels of Wisdom,* pp. 163–71.
26 For an introduction to this subject, see Rahman, *Islam,* pp. 85–99.
27 See, for example, Aḥsá'í, *Rasá'ilu'l-Ḥikmah,* pp. 187–92. I have discussed aspects of the thesis of the unity of existence and the problem of Destiny in *Logos and Civilization,* pp. 69–78, 84–88.
28 The Báb, *Tafsír-i-Sirr-i-Há',* INBA 86:115.
29 The Báb, *Tafsír-i-Há',* INBA 86:115.
30 The Báb, *Tafsír-i-Há',* INBA 86:116.
31 The Báb, *Tafsír-i-Há',* INBA 86:116–17.
32 The Báb, *Tafsír-i-Ḥadíth-i-'Allamaní Akhí Rasúlu'lláh,* INBA 14:422.
33 'Abdu'l-Bahá, *Makátíb* 2:161.
34 The Báb, *Tafsír-i-Bismilláh,* INBA 14:74.
35 Note that Bahá'u'lláh's Four Valleys also end with the heart. As He explains, the station of the heart is the station of the mystery of Destiny. He states that the people who have reached the summit of the heart become the pure mirrors of the divine attributes (*Seven Valleys and Four Valleys,* p. 61).

9 : THE EPISTLE OF JUSTICE AND THE ROOT PRINCIPLES OF RELIGION

1 The Báb, *Ṣaḥífiy-i-'Adlíyyih,* p. 34. For more information on the Interpretation of the Letter Há', see Mohammadhosseini, *Haḍrat-i-Báb,* pp. 774–81.
2 The Báb's reference to the time of sorrow and isolation is not only a reference to His house arrest in Shiraz, but also to His stage of self-decreed withdrawal.
3 In the printed edition of the Epistle of Justice: Root Principles, there is a mistake in regard to this statement. Instead of *mustanír gashtih* (shone forth) is printed *mustatir gashtih* (is hidden). But *mustatir gashtih* does not make sense here. Several other copies use the correct wording.
4 The Báb, *Ṣaḥífiy-i-'Adlíyyih,* pp. 3–4.
5 In His later writings, the Bab uses the five stages of the Tradition of Truth to refer to the first five years of His mission. But in this earlier text, He uses the same Tradition to discuss the revelation of His Persian writings, which begins not in 1260 but in 1262. Here the first statement, "Pierce the veils of glory," signifies the inception of the year 1262.
6 The Báb, *Ṣaḥífiy-i-'Adlíyyih,* p. 31.
7 Qur'án 14:24.
8 The Báb, *Ṣaḥífiy-i-'Adlíyyih,* p. 38.
9 The Báb, *Tafsír-i-Há',* INBA 14:279–80.

10 The Báb, *Sharḥ-i-Du'á'-i-Ghaybat,* INBA 60:103–4.
11 See, for example, Aḥsá'í, *Sharḥu'z-Zíyárat* 1:80–81.
12 The Báb, *Ṣaḥífiy-i-'Adlíyyih,* p. 34.
13 The Báb, *Ṣaḥífiy-i-'Adlíyyih,* p. 5.
14 The Báb, *Ṣaḥífiy-i-'Adlíyyih,* pp. 5–7.
15 The Báb, *Ṣaḥífiy-i-'Adlíyyih,* p. 7.
16 The Báb, *Ṣaḥífiy-i-'Adlíyyih,* pp. 7–9.
17 The Báb, *Ṣaḥífiy-i-'Adlíyyih,* pp. 9–12.
18 The Báb, *Ṣaḥífiy-i-'Adlíyyih,* p. 14.
19 The Báb, *Ṣaḥífiy-i-'Adlíyyih,* p. 15. Authorized translation provided by the Research Department of the Universal House of Justice.
20 The Báb, *Ṣaḥífiy-i-'Adlíyyih,* p. 15.
21 The Báb, *Ṣaḥífiy-i-'Adlíyyih,* p. 18.
22 The Báb, *Ṣaḥífiy-i-'Adlíyyih,* p. 17.
23 The Báb, *Ṣaḥífiy-i-'Adlíyyih,* p. 21.
24 The Báb, *Ṣaḥífiy-i-'Adlíyyih,* pp. 18–19.
25 See, for example, Aḥsá'í, *Sharḥu'z-Zíyárat* 1:21–22. See also Bahá'u'lláh, *Epistle,* p. 113.
26 Therefore both MacEoin's and Amanat's presentations of these stages are inaccurate. See MacEoin, *Sources,* p. 69, n. 104; and Amanat, *Resurrection and Renewal,* p. 189.
27 Bahá'u'lláh, qtd. in *Epistle,* p. 113.
28 The Báb, *Ṣaḥífiy-i-'Adlíyyih,* pp. 23–26.
29 The Báb, *Ṣaḥífiy-i-'Adlíyyih,* p. 23.
30 The Báb, *Ṣaḥífiy-i-'Adlíyyih,* p. 35.
31 The Báb, *Ṣaḥífiy-i-'Adlíyyih,* p. 35.
32 The Báb, *Sharḥ-i-Du'á'-i-Ghaybat,* INBA 60:108.
33 The Báb, *Ṣaḥífiy-i-'Adlíyyih,* pp. 32, 38.

10 : RESURRECTION AND HISTORICAL CONSCIOUSNESS

1 The Báb, Persian Bayán 6:1.
2 The Báb, *Tablet to Mullá Báqir,* in Gulpáygání and Gulpáygání, *Kashfu'l-Ghiṭá',* Appendix, p. 9 (qtd. in Shoghi Effendi, *God Passes By,* p. 30).
3 See Saiedi, *Logos and Civilization,* pp. 126–30.
4 The Báb, Persian Bayán 4:6.
5 The writings of Bahá'u'lláh are also based on such a historicization of these same categories. For example, in the Book of the River, Bahá'u'lláh writes that "in every age and century, as He desireth, the Unique Hidden One and the Eternal Essence manifesteth that true River and real Sea and causeth it to flow, adorning it with a new temple and a new vesture" (qtd. in Saiedi, *Logos and Civilization,* p. 60).
6 The Báb, *Kitábu'l-Asmá',* INBA 29:66.

7 The Báb, *Selections,* p. 117 (*Dalá'il-i-Sab'ih,* p. 65).
8 The Báb, *Selections,* p. 125 (*Dalá'il-i-Sab'ih,* pp. 1–2).
9 The Báb, *Selections,* p. 126 (*Dalá'il-i-Sab'ih,* pp. 2–3).
10 The Báb, *Panj Sha'n,* pp. 23–24.
11 See Hegel, *Lectures.*
12 The Báb, *Tafsír-i-Ḥadíth-i-'Allamaní Akhí Rasúlu'lláh,* INBA 14:419–23.
13 The Báb, "Fi's-Sulúk II," Collection, p. 454.
14 The Báb, *Tablet to Mullá Báqir,* in Gulpáygání and Gulpáygání, *Kashfu'l-Ghiṭá',* Appendix, p. 3.
15 The Báb, *Selections,* pp. 77–78 (Persian Bayán 7:19).
16 See, for example, the Báb, *Tafsír-i-Há',* INBA 86:118–19.
17 The Báb, *Ad'íyi-i-Haftigí,* INBA 58:79–80.
18 Qur'án 42:11.
19 The Báb, *Tafsír-i-Ḥadíth-i-Ḥaqíqat,* INBA 53:33.
20 The Báb, *Tafsír-i-Súriy-i-Baqarih* I, INBA 69:205.
21 The Báb, *Ṣaḥífiy-i-'Adlíyyih,* p. 18.
22 See Feuerbach, *Essence of Christianity.*
23 See, for example, Lewis, *The Assassins.*
24 The Báb, *Selections,* pp. 106–7 (Persian Bayán 2:7).
25 Gen. 1:26–28.
26 The Báb, Persian Bayán 4:11.
27 The Báb, *Selections,* p. 89 (Persian Bayán 5:4).
28 The Báb, *Selections,* pp. 107–8 (Persian Bayán 2:7).
29 The Báb, *Qayyúmu'l-Asmá'* (Súrih of *Mulk*), INBA 3:4.

11 : HISTORY AND THE PERSPECTIVE OF UNITY

1 Nabíl-i-A'ẓam, *Dawn-Breakers,* p. 31.
2 MacEoin, *Sources,* p. 88.
3 The Báb, Persian Bayán 3:16.
4 See the Báb, *Khuṭbiy-i-Jiddah,* INBA 91:69–72; Mázandaráni, *Ẓuhúru'l-Ḥaqq* 3:289; and MacEoin, *Sources,* p. 52.
5 The Báb, Persian Bayán 8:12. I would like to thank Parviz Moini for sharing this perceptive idea with me.
6 The Báb, Arabic Bayán 9:10.
7 Qur'án 55:2–4.
8 On the concept of the "Perfect Human Being," see Saiedi, *Logos and Civilization.*
9 The Báb, Persian Bayán 3:17.
10 The Báb mentions that His book can be called either *Bayán* (Exposition) or *Bayyán* (One who exposes). See Kitábu'l-Asmá' (Princeton copy), chapter on the name of God, *al-Abyan.*
11 The Báb, Persian Bayán 3:17.

12 The Báb, Persian Bayán 1:1.
13 The Báb, Persian Bayán 1:1.
14 In the Persian Bayán we see the same point reaffirmed in new ways; see, for example, 3:12.
15 The Báb, *Selections,* p. 126 (*Dalá'il-i-Sab'ih,* pp. 2–3).
16 The Báb, Persian Bayán 1:2.
17 The Báb, Persian Bayán 1:2. This complex passage has been mistranslated by Amanat, who has thought that "hidden names" refers to the fourteen souls, whereas it refers to the four Gates. As the Báb has explained in various writings, the Most Great Name of God is represented by the fourth name which is a well-guarded and hidden name. That name refers to the station of the four Gates. The fourteen sacred souls represent the three names of God that have been manifest (see Amanat, *Resurrection and Renewal,* p. 191).
18 The Báb, Persian Bayán 1:1.
19 The Báb, Persian Bayán 1:15.
20 The Báb, Persian Bayán 1:2.
21 The Báb, *Qayyúmu'l-Asmá'* (Súrih of *Yúsuf*), INBA 3:10–11.
22 Shaykh Aḥmad-i-Aḥsá'í frequently discussed this question. His work, "Infallibility and Return," is an extensive discussion of the topic. See Aḥsá'í, "Al-'Iṣmah va'r-Raj'ah," in *Javámi'u'l-Kalim,* pp. 14–111.
23 The Báb, Persian Bayán 7:3.
24 The Báb, Persian Bayán 5:18.
25 The Báb, Persian Bayán 2:19.
26 The Báb, *Selections,* p. 87 (Persian Bayán 6:16).
27 The Báb, Persian Bayán 3:3.
28 The Báb, Persian Bayán 6:13.
29 The Báb, Persian Bayán 3:13.
30 The Báb, Persian Bayán 8:1.
31 The Báb, *Selections,* p. 105 (Persian Bayán 4:12).
32 The Báb, Persian Bayán 4:16.

12 : COMMUNITY AND THE PRIMAL UNITY

1 The Báb, Persian Bayán 1:1.
2 The Báb, Persian Bayán 1:1.
3 The Báb, Arabic Bayán, unity 1.
4 The Báb, Persian Bayán 1:1.
5 The Báb, Persian Bayán 2:6.
6 The Báb, Arabic Bayán, unity 1.
7 The Báb, Persian Bayán 4:18.
8 Saiedi, *Logos and Civilization,* pp. 123, 127–30, 198. Amanat identifies these "eight unities" (8 x 19 = 152) as the numerical value of the word *Quddús,* but

the value of *Quddús* is 170. Amanat, *Resurrection and Renewal,* p. 244 and n. 232.

9 The Báb, Persian Bayán 8:3.
10 The Báb, *Selections,* p. 84 (Persian Bayán 6:15).
11 The Báb, *Selections,* pp. 80–81 (Persian Bayán 8:19).
12 The Báb, Persian Bayán 2:2.
13 The Báb, *Kitábu'l-Asmá',* INBA 29:103
14 The Báb, *Tablet to Mullá Báqir,* in Gulpáygání and Gulpáygání, *Kashfu'l-Ghiṭá',* p. 6. Part of the passage is quoted in Bahá'u'lláh, *Epistle,* p. 153.
15 The Báb, Persian Bayán 2:1.
16 The Báb, Persian Bayán 2:1.
17 The Báb, *Panj Sha'n,* p. 390.
18 The Báb, *Panj Sha'n,* p. 391.
19 This tradition is frequently mentioned in the writings of Shaykh Aḥmad. See, for example, his interpretation of the *Bismilláh* in *Rasá'ilu'l-Ḥikmah,* p. 137.
20 Qtd. in Aḥsá'í, *Rasá'ilu'l-Ḥikmah,* p. 135.
21 The Báb, Persian Bayán 3:8.
22 The Báb, Persian Bayán 5:1.
23 The Báb, Persian Bayán 8:8.
24 The Báb, *Qayyúmu'l-Asmá'* (Súrih of *Yúsuf*), INBA 3:10–11.
25 The Báb, Persian Bayán 1:2.
26 The Báb, *Tafsír-i-Súriy-i-Va'l-'Aṣr,* INBA 14:172–73, *Risáliy-i-Ithbát-i-Nubuvvat-i-Kháṣṣih,* INBA 14:387–92.
27 Qur'án 10:10.
28 Qur'án 20:130.
29 Qur'án 47:15.
30 Qur'án 47:15.
31 The Báb, "Tafsír-i-Kullu'ṭ-Ṭa'ám," Collection, pp. 229–30.
32 The Báb, Persian Bayán 4:8.
33 The Báb, Persian Bayán 8:5.

13 : ETHICS AND LAWS IN THE BAYÁN

1 See Abu'l-Qásim Afnán, *'Ahd-i-A'lá,* pp. 99–100; Mohammadhosseini, *Haḍrat-i-Báb,* p. 765; and MacEoin, *Sources,* p. 62.
2 In this sense, the beginning passage of Bahá'u'lláh's Kitáb-i-Aqdas, which speaks of the inseparable twin duties of recognition of the Manifestation and observing His ordinances, is the essence of the Bayán's approach to the issue.
3 The Báb, *Fí's-Sulúk I,* INBA 67:145–48. For further discussion of this tablet, see Lawson, "The Báb's Epistle."
4 Abú Ṭálibi'l-Ḥusaynáví was the brother of Siyyid Javád-i-Karbilá'í.

5 The Báb, "Fi's-Sulúk II," Collection, pp. 454–55.
6 The Báb, "Fi's-Sulúk II," Collection, p. 456.
7 See, for example, Mill, *Utilitarianism.*
8 Kant, Immanuel, *Critique of Practical Reason* pp. 30–52, 114–37.
9 A good critique of the Kantian theory of love in the context of his ethics can be found in Schopenhauer, *Basis of Morality.*
10 The Báb, "Fi's-Sulúk II," Collection, pp. 456–57.
11 The Báb, "Fi's-Sulúk II," Collection, p. 457.
12 The Báb, "Fi's-Sulúk II," Collection, p. 457.
13 The Báb, "Fi's-Sulúk II," Collection, p. 458.
14 The Báb, "Fi's-Sulúk II," Collection, p. 458.
15 The Báb, "Fi's-Sulúk II," Collection, p. 458.
16 Reference is to Qur'án 17:23.
17 The Báb, "Fi's-Sulúk II," Collection, p. 459.
18 The Báb, "Fi's-Sulúk II," Collection, p. 459.
19 The Báb, "Fi's-Sulúk II," Collection, p. 459.
20 The Báb, "Fi's-Sulúk II," Collection, p. 463.
21 The Báb, "Fi's-Sulúk II," Collection, pp. 463–64.
22 The Báb, "Fi's-Sulúk II," Collection, p. 466.
23 The Báb, Persian Bayán 4:16.
24 The Báb, Persian Bayán 3:12.
25 In the Four Valleys, Bahá'u'lláh mentions three of these stages—soul, intellect, and heart. Bahá'u'lláh omits the category of essential body and creates a new category, love, which mediates between intellect and heart. Thus while both intellect and soul are imprisoned within the realm of oppositions, the category of love transcends such otherness. But in the relation of love there still remains a trace of otherness, which is in turn transcended in the category of heart (*Seven Valleys and Four Valleys,* pp. 54–57).
26 The Báb, Persian Bayán 7:2.
27 The Báb, Persian Bayán 5:19.
28 The Báb, Persian Bayán 2:16.
29 The Báb, Persian Bayán 7:2.
30 Bahá'u'lláh, Kitáb-i-Aqdas, par. 1.
31 The Báb, Persian Bayán 7:2.
32 The Báb, Persian Bayán 6:7.
33 The Báb, Persian Bayán 9:4.
34 The Báb, *Selections,* pp. 88 (Persian Bayán 5:4).
35 The Báb, Persian Bayán 4:11.
36 The Báb, Persian Bayán 9:10.
37 The Báb, Arabic Bayán 9:11.
38 The Báb, Persian Bayán 6:2.
39 The Báb, *Kitábu'l-Asmá',* INBA 29:621–25.

40 The Báb, *Kitábu'l-Asmá',* INBA 29:626.
41 The Báb, Persian Bayán 6:3.
42 The Báb, Persian Bayán 3:17.
43 This same principle is reaffirmed in Bahá'u'lláh's Kitáb-i-Aqdas. See Saiedi, *Logos and Civilization,* pp. 253, 279–80, 284–86.
44 The Báb, Persian Bayán 5:14.
45 The Báb, *Kitábu'l-Asmá',* INBA 29:626.
46 The Báb, *Kitábu'l-Asmá',* INBA 29:630.
47 The Báb, Persian Bayán 4:16.
48 The Báb, Persian Bayán 6:19.
49 The Báb, Persian Bayán 6:19.
50 The Báb, *Kitábu'l-Asmá',* INBA 29:152.
51 The Báb, Persian Bayán 7:18.
52 The Báb, Persian Bayán 9:4.
53 The Báb, *Kitábu'l-Asmá',* INBA 29:85–92.
54 The Báb, *Kitábu'l-Asmá',* INBA 29:423–24.
55 The Báb, Persian Bayán 4:16.
56 The Báb, Persian Bayán 6:3.
57 The Báb, Persian Bayán 7:6.
58 The Báb, Persian Bayán 6:11.
59 The Báb, Persian Bayán 6:16.
60 The Báb, *Kitábu'l-Asmá',* INBA 29:426.
61 The Báb, Persian Bayán 8:11.
62 The Báb, Persian Bayán 5:3.
63 The Báb, Persian Bayán 5:3.
64 The Báb, Persian Bayán 5:3.
65 The Báb, Persian Bayán 8:18.
66 The Báb, Persian Bayán 8:6.
67 The Bahá'í symbol of the Greatest Name includes two of these temples, which refer to the Báb and Bahá'u'lláh.
68 The Báb, Persian Bayán 5:10.
69 The Báb, *Tafsír-i-Súriy-i-Ḥamd,* INBA 14:32–37. For a translation of some of these parts of the tablet, see MacEoin, *Rituals,* Appendix 3, pp. 101–4.
70 The Báb, Persian Bayán 5:10.
71 The Báb, Persian Bayán 7:2.
72 The Báb, Persian Bayán 8:18.
73 The Báb, Arabic Bayán 8:7.
74 The Báb, Persian Bayán 7:19.
75 MacEoin has misconstrued this law through mistakes in translation. He writes: "In the *Chahár Sha'n,* the believer is instructed to stand each month facing the moon and to recite the following verse: 'The glory . . . ' It is preferable to recite this verse 142 times (to the number of the name *al-Qá'im*)"

(*Rituals*, p. 13). However, what he translates as "It is preferable to recite this verse 142 times (to the number of the name *al-Qá'im*)," is something else, entirely unrelated to the previous statement about facing the moon and reciting a verse. The mistranslated part is actually the beginning of a new paragraph in which the Báb begins to address a different question. After finishing the discussion of facing the moon and reciting a verse, the Báb writes: "Now, regarding the person thou hast mentioned, whose name is equal to the name of the beloved Qá'im: Say! Protect it thou before thyself. . . ." (*Kitábu'l-Asmá'*, INBA 29:508).

76 See Saiedi, *Logos and Civilization*, pp. 271–74.
77 The Báb, Persian Bayán 5:4.
78 The Báb, Persian Bayán 5:9.
79 The Báb, Persian Bayán 5:9.
80 Bahá'u'lláh, *Seven Valleys and Four Valleys*, pp. 42–43.
81 The Báb, Persian Bayán 5:4.
82 MacEoin, *Sources*, p. 92.
83 The Báb, *Kitábu'l-Asmá'*, INBA 29:383–86.

14 : THE LAW OF THE SWORD AND THE TWIN REVELATIONS

1 Shoghi Effendi, *God Passes By*, p. 25. This interpretation of the writings of the Báb is the subject of numerous Bahá'í works. Three major examples are Bahá'u'lláh's Kitáb-i-Badí', 'Abdu'l-Bahá's *Traveler's Narrative*, and Shoghi Effendi's *God Passes By*.
2 The Báb, Arabic Bayán 6:15.
3 Bahá'u'lláh, *Kitáb-i-Badí'*, pp. 114–15.
4 This statement of the Báb is read in two ways. In one, it is read without attention to the previous two statements in which the Báb orders Azal to obey Him Whom God shall make manifest without question. In this reading, the Báb's statement is translated as saying: "Should God make manifest glory [that is, exaltation, victory] in thy time, then manifest the eight paths with His permission." The second reading, which corresponds to the earliest reading of the tablet by a defender of Azal (namely, the author of *Nuqṭatu'l-Káf*), takes the statement as the continuation of the reference to God's making manifest Him Whom God shall make manifest and thus the statement is rendered as: "Should God make [him] manifest, out of his glory, then manifest the eight paths with his permission." However, even the first reading is indirectly affirming the same point that is made in the second. According to the Báb, the realization of glory and the exaltation of the Bábí Faith is an event which happens through or after the advent of Him Whom God shall make manifest. Logically, the fact that, on one hand, the Bab categorically says in the Bayán that between His own martyrdom and the advent of the Promised One there will be no more binding writings, and, on the

other hand, in this tablet the Báb apparently allows Azal to manifest the rest of the Arabic Bayán, can only make sense if it is understood that such a completion of the Arabic Bayán could only take place after the revelation of the Promised One and through His inspiration and permission.

5 The Báb, *Kitábu'l-Asmá'*, INBA 29: 273–74.

6 Káshání, *Nuqṭatu'l-Káf,* p. 244. It should be noted, however, that various internal textual evidence leaves no doubt that the author of the text is not Ḥájí Mírzá Jání Káshání.

7 The Báb, Persian Bayán 3:16.

8 The Báb, *Panj Sha'n,* pp. 255–56.

9 The Báb, *Panj Sha'n,* p. 280.

10 Bahá'u'lláh, *La'áli'l-Ḥikmah* 2:23. I would like to thank Khazeh Fananapazir who noted this point in one of his Internet postings.

11 The Báb, *Panj Sha'n,* p. 279.

12 The Báb, *Panj Sha'n,* p. 6.

13 For a detailed discussion of this issue, see Muhammad Afnan, "Ayyám-i-Buṭún."

14 Káshání, *Nuqṭatu'l-Káf,* pp. 260, 252, 255.

15 Káshání, *Nuqṭatu'l-Káf,* pp. 207–8.

16 Káshání, *Nuqṭatu'l-Káf,* p. 209.

17 For a discussion of the Báb's statement addressed to Yaḥyá, see Ishráq Khávarí, *Raḥíq-i-Makhtúm* 2:187; Muhammad Afnan, "Ayyám-i-Buṭún," p. 36; and Saiedi, *Logos and Civilization,* pp. 191–97.

18 It is noteworthy that the authors of *Hasht Bihisht* name six of the claimants as merely examples of those who have claimed to be Him whom God shall make manifest and then say that "it reached a stage where whoever would wake up in the morning would clothe himself with such claim . . . thus in all directions diverse lords and various gods appeared." In other sections, they name additional claimants. See Kirmání and Rúḥí, *Hasht Bihisht,* pp. 302–3, 319–20.

19 Bahá'u'lláh, *Kitáb-i-Badí',* pp. 102–4, and *Áthár-i-Qalam-i-A'lá* 2:34.

20 *Tashdíd* is the diacritic for a long consonant.

2 The Báb, *Tablet to Mullá Báqir,* in Gulpáygání and Gulpáygání, *Kashfu'l-Ghiṭá',* Appendix, p. 9.

22 MacEoin, "Hierarchy, Authority, and Eschatology," pp. 134–35.

23 Qtd. in Gulpáygání and Gulpáygání, *Kashfu'l-Ghiṭá',* p. 309. For more detailed discussion of this issue see Bahá'u'lláh, *Kitáb-i-Badí',* pp. 114–15.

24 The Báb, *Lawḥ-i-Haykalu'd-Dín* 6:15.

25 The Báb, Arabic Bayán 6:15.

26 The Báb, Persian Bayán 6:15.

27 The Báb, Persian Bayán 3:7.

28 See, for example, MacEoin, "Hierarchy, Authority, and Eschatology," p. 105, and *Sources,* p. 120.

29 Zunúzí, "Su'ál va Javáb," in Mázandarání, *Ẓuhúru'l-Ḥaqq* 3:33.
30 The Báb, "Tafsír-i-Váv," Collection, p. 251.
31 The Báb, Persian Bayán 6:3.
32 The tablet is also part of the book Panj Sha'n. However, earlier writings of the Báb, including His works written in Mákú, also refer to the tablet.
33 The Báb, Tablet to Aḥmad-i-Azghandí, Collection, p. 204.
34 Afnan and Hatcher, "Western Islamic Scholarship."
35 Zabihi-Moghaddam, "Babi-State Conflict" and *Váqi'iy-i-Qal'iy-i-Shaykh Ṭabarsí.*
36 Qur'án 9:29.
37 MacEoin, "Babi Concept of Holy War," p. 109.
38 The Báb, Persian Bayán 6:1.
39 The Báb, *Selections,* p. 119 (*Dalá'il-i-Sab'ih,* p. 29).
40 MacEoin, "Babi Concept of Holy War," pp. 106–7.
41 The Báb, *Dalá'il-i-Sab'ih,* pp. 51–52.
42 MacEoin, "Babi Concept of Holy War," p. 109.
43 Zabihi-Moghaddam, "Babi-State Conflict."
44 MacEoin, "Babi Concept of Holy War," p. 108.
45 MacEoin, "Babi Concept of Holy War," p. 109.
46 The Báb, Persian Bayán 8:15.
47 Bahá'u'lláh, Kitáb-i-Aqdas, par. 139–40.
48 The Báb, Persian Bayán 7:19, and Arabic Bayán 8:7.
49 The Báb, Persian Bayán 5:5.
50 The Báb, Persian Bayán 4:5.
51 MacEoin, "Babi Concept of Holy War," p. 108.
52 The Báb, Persian Bayán 4:5.
53 The Báb, *Selections,* p. 77 (Persian Bayán 2:16).
54 The Báb, *Panj Sha'n,* p. 437.
55 The Báb, Arabic Bayán 11:5.
56 Muhammad Afnan, "Dar báriy-i-Aḥkám-i-Bayán," p. 43.
57 Bahá'u'lláh, in Mázandarání, *Asráru'l-Áthár* 4:22. See also Saiedi, *Logos and Civilization,* pp. 242–57, 304–10.
58 The Báb, *Selections,* pp. 101–2 (Persian Bayán 3:13).
59 The Báb, Persian Bayán 6:8.
60 The Báb, Persian Bayán 6:8.
61 The Báb, Tablet to Aḥmad-i-Azghandí, Collection, p. 191. This tablet discusses a number of issues including the various Qur'ánic signs of the Day of Resurrection.
62 The Báb, *Tablet to Mullá Báqir,* in Gulpáygání and Gulpáygání, *Kashfu'l-Ghiṭá',* Appendix, pp. 1–2.
63 The Báb, *Tablet to Mullá Báqir,* in Gulpáygání and Gulpáygání, *Kashfu'l-Ghiṭá',* Appendix, p. 3.

64 The Báb, *Tablet to Mullá Báqir,* in Gulpáygání and Gulpáygání, *Kashfu'l-Ghiṭá',* Appendix, pp. 3–5. Part of this passage is quoted in Shoghi Effendi, *God Passes By,* p. 30, and Bahá'u'lláh, *Epistle,* p. 141.

65 The Báb, *Tablet to Mullá Báqir,* in Gulpáygání and Gulpáygání, *Kashfu'l-Ghiṭá',* Appendix, p. 6. Part of this passage is quoted in Bahá'u'lláh, *Epistle,* p. 153.

66 The Báb, *Tablet to Mullá Báqir,* in Gulpáygání and Gulpáygání, *Kashfu'l-Ghiṭá',* Appendix, p. 7.

67 The Báb, *Tablet to Mullá Báqir,* in Gulpáygání and Gulpáygání, *Kashfu'l-Ghiṭá',* Appendix, p. 7.

68 The Báb, *Tablet to Mullá Báqir,* in Gulpáygání and Gulpáygání, *Kashfu'l-Ghiṭá',* Appendix, pp. 7–8 (qtd. in Shoghi Effendi, *World Order,* p. 101).

69 The Báb, *Tablet to Mullá Báqir,* in Gulpáygání and Gulpáygání, *Kashfu'l-Ghiṭá',* Appendix, p. 8 (qtd. in Bahá'u'lláh, *Epistle,* p. 155).

70 The Báb, *Tablet to Mullá Báqir,* in Gulpáygání and Gulpáygání, *Kashfu'l-Ghiṭá',* Appendix, p. 9.

71 The Báb, *Tablet to Mullá Báqir,* in Gulpáygání and Gulpáygání, *Kashfu'l-Ghiṭá',* Appendix, p. 9 (qtd. in Shoghi Effendi, *God Passes By,* p. 30).

REFERENCES

Works by the Báb

Ad'íyi-i-Haftigí (Weekly Prayers). Iran National Bahá'í Archives 58:72–95.

Bayán-i-Fársí (Persian Bayán). N.p., n.d.

Al-Bayánu'l-'Arabí (Arabic Bayán). N.p., n.d.

Collection of the Writings of the Báb. Manuscript copy dated 27 Muḥarram 1331.

Dalá'il-i-Sab'ih (The Seven Proofs). N.p., n.d.

Fi's-Sulúk I (On the Virtuous Journey I). Iran National Bahá'í Archives 67:145–48.

"Fi's-Sulúk II" (On the Virtuous Journey II). Collection, 452–66.

Khuṭbiy-i-Jiddah (Sermon of Jiddah). Iran National Bahá'í Archives 91:60–73.

Kitábu'l-Asmá' (Book of Divine Names). Iran National Bahá'í Archives, vol. 29.

Kitábu'l-Asmá' (Book of Divine Names). Manuscript. Princeton University Archives. Islamic Manuscripts, Third Series, vol. 30.

Kitábu'l-Fihrist (Indexical Tablet). Manuscript.

Kitábu'r-Rúḥ (Book of the Spirit). Manuscript.

Kitáb-i-Panj Sha'n (Book of the Five Modes of Revelation). N.p., n.d.

Lawḥ-i-Haykalu'd-Dín (Tablet of the Temple of the Faith). N.p., n.d.

Majmú'iy-i-Áthár-i-Ḥaḍrat-i-A'lá. 10 vols. Manuscript.

Qayyúmu'l-Asmá'. Iran National Bahá'í Archives. Vol. 3.

Risálah fi'l-Ghiná (Treatise on Singing). In *Safiniy-i-'Irfan* Book 1. Darmstadt: Asr-i-Jadíd, 1998. 85–95.

Risálah fi'n-Naḥv (Treatise on Grammar). Iran National Bahá'í Archives 67:121–25.

Risáliy-i-Ithbát-i-Nubuvvat-i-Kháṣṣih (Epistle on the Proofs of the Prophethood of Muḥammad). Iran National Bahá'í Archives 14:321–92.

Ṣaḥífiy-i-A'mál-i-Sanih (Epistle on the Devotional Deeds of the Year). Manuscript.

Ṣaḥífiy-i-Bayna'l-Ḥaramayn (Epistle Revealed between the Twin Shrines). Manuscript.

Ṣaḥífiy-i-Furú'-i-'Adlíyyih (Epistle of Justice: Branches). Manuscript.

Ṣaḥífiy-i-Makhzúnih (Hidden Treasured Epistle). Manuscript.

Ṣaḥífiy-i-Raḍavíyyih (Epistle of Riḍá'). Manuscript.

Ṣaḥífiy-i-'Adlíyyih (Epistle of Justice: Root Principles). N.p., n.d.

Selections from the Writings of the Báb. Trans. H. Taherzadeh et al. Comp. Research Dept. of the Universal House of Justice. Haifa: Bahá'í World Centre, 1976.

Sharḥ-i-Asmá'u'lláh (Tablet on the Names of God). Iran National Bahá'í Archives 98:11–20.

Sharḥ-i-Du'á'-i-Ghaybat (Commentary on the Occultation Prayer). Iran National Bahá'í Archives 60:57–54.

"Sharḥ-i-Ḥadíth-i-Abú Lubayd-i-Makhzúmí" (Interpretation of the Tradition of Abú Lubayd-i-Makhzúmí). Collection, 139–57.

Sharḥ-i-'Ilmi'l-Ḥurúf (Tablet on the Science of Letters). Iran National Bahá'í Archives 67:203–4.

Tablet to Aḥmad-i-Azghandí. Collection, 176–211.

Tablet to Mírzá Ḥasan-i-Vaqáyi'-Negár. Iran National Bahá'í Archives 53:193–99.

Tablet to Mírzá Sa'íd. Iran National Bahá'í Archives 14:426–40.

Tablet to Mullá Aḥmad. Collection, 547–76.

Tafsír-i-Áyiy-i-Núr I (Commentary on the Verse of Light I). Iran National Bahá'í Archives 14:495–98.

"Tafsír-i-Áyiy-i-Núr II" (Commentary on the Verse of Light II). Collection, 10–26.

Tafsír-i-Bismilláh (Commentary on *Bismilláh*). Iran National Bahá'í Archives 64:33–34; 60:1–56.

"Tafsír-i-Du'á'-i-Ṣabáḥ" (Commentary on the Morning Prayer). Collection, 26–39.

Tafsír-i-Há' (Commentary on the Letter Há'). Iran National Bahá'í Archives 53:81–125.

Tafsír-i-Ḥadíth-i-'Allamaní Akhí Rasúlu'lláh 'Ilma má Kán va 'Allamtuhu 'Ilma má Yakún (Interpretation of the Tradition attributed to 'Alí, "My Brother, the Apostle of God, taught me the knowledge of that which hath been, and I taught Him the knowledge of that which will be"). Iran National Bahá'í Archives 14:418–25.

Tafsír-i-Ḥadíth-i-Ḥaqíqat (Commentary on the Tradition of Truth). Iran National Bahá'í Archives 53:32–34.

Tafsír-i-Ḥadíth-i-Imám Riḍá' (Commentary on the Tradition of Imám Riḍá'). Iran National Bahá'í Archives 14:400–402.

Tafsír-i-Ḥadíth-i-Man ʿArafa Nafsah faqad ʿArafa Rabbah (Commentary on the Tradition "He Hath Known God Who Hath Known Himself"). Iran National Bahá'í Archives 14:474–82.

"Tafsír-i-Kullu'ṭ-Ṭaʿám" (Commentary on All Food). Collection, 211–33.

Tafsír-i-Sirr-i-Há' (Commentary on the Mystery of Há'). Iran National Bahá'í Archives 86:154–92.

Tafsír-i-Súriy-i-Baqarih I (Commentary on the Súrih of the Cow I). Iran National Bahá'í Archives (INBA): 69:156–377.

Tafsír-i-Súriy-i-Baqarih II (Commentary on the Súrih of the Cow II). Iran National Bahá'í Archives 69:377–410.

Tafsír-i-Súriy-i-Ḥamd (Commentary on the Súrih of Praise). Iran National Bahá'í Archives 14:32–37.

Tafsír-i-Súriy-i-Kawthar (Commentary on the Súrih of Abundance). Iran National Bahá'í Archives 53:91–193.

Tafsír-i-Súriy-i-Tawḥíd (Commentary on the Súrih of Unity). Iran National Bahá'í Archives 14:209–21.

Tafsír-i-Súriy-i-Va'l-ʿAṣr (Commentary on the Súrih of the Afternoon). Iran National Bahá'í Archives 14:105–208.

Tafsír-i-Súriy-i-Yúsif (Commentary on the Súrih of Joseph). See *Qayyúmu'l-Asmá'*.

"Tafsír-i-Váv" (Interpretation of the Letter Váv). Collection, 249–65.

General References

ʿAbdu'l-Bahá. "ʿAbdu'l-Bahá's Tablet on the Unity of Existence." *Journal of Bahá'í Studies* 11.3/4 (2001): 25–29.

———. *Makátíb*. 2 vols. Cairo: Kurdistánu'l-ʿIlmíyyah, 1910–1912.

———. *A Traveler's Narrative Written to Illustrate the Episode of the Báb*. Trans. Edward G. Browne. Wilmette, IL: Bahá'í Publishing Trust, 1980.

Afnan, Abu'l-Qasim. *ʿAhd-i-Aʿlá: Zindigáníy-i-Haḍrat-i-Báb*. Oxford: OneWorld, 2000.

Afnan, Mehri. "Maqám-i-Zan dar Áthár-i-Haḍrat-i-Nuqṭiy-i-Awlá va Mashá-hír-i-Zanán dar ʿAhd-i-Aʿlá." *Khushiha'i az Kharmani Adab va Honar* 6. Darmstadt: Society for Persian Letters and Arts, 1995. 207–26.

———. "Naẓarí bar Mundaraját-i-Risáliy-i-Dalá'il-i-Sabʿih." *Safiniy-i-ʿIrfán* Book 2. Darmstadt: Asr-i-Jadíd, 1999.

Afnan, Muhammad. "Dar báriy-i-Aḥkám-i-Bayán va Khitábát bih Ahl-i-Bayán dar Kitáb-i-Musṭatáb-i-Aqdas." *Safiniy-i-ʿIrfán* Book 1. Darmstadt: Asr-i-Jadíd, 1998. 39–52.

———. "Kushishí dar Muridí Shinásá'íy-i-Áthár-i-Haḍrat-i-Nuqṭiy-i-Awlá."

Khushiha'i az Kharmani Adab va Honar 6. Darmstadt: Society for Persian Letters and Arts, 1995. 39–46.

Afnan, Muhammad. "Sha'n-i-Tafsír dar Á<u>th</u>ár-i-Hadrat-i-Nuqṭiy-i-Awlá." *Khushiha'i az Kharmani Adab va Honar* 6. Darmstadt: Society for Persian Letters and Arts, 1995. 94–120.

Afnan, Muhammad, and William S. Hatcher. "Western Islamic Scholarship and Bahá'í Origins." *Religion* 14 (1985): 29–51.

Aḥsá'í, <u>Sh</u>ay<u>kh</u> Aḥmad. "Al-'Iṣmah va'r-Raj'ah." *Javámi'u'l-Kalim*. N.p., n.d. 14–111.

———. *Rasá'ilu'l-Ḥikmah*. Beirut: Dáru'l-'Álamíyyah, 1993.

———. *<u>Sh</u>arḥu'l-Favá'id*. N.p., n.d.

———. *<u>Sh</u>arḥu'z-Zíyárati'l-Jámi'ati'l-Kabírah*. 3 vols. Kirmán: Sa'ádat, A.H. 1397.

Amanat, Abbas. *Resurrection and Renewal: The Making of the Babi Movement in Iran, 1844–1850*. Ithaca: Cornell University Press, 1989.

Amini, Tooraj. "Majlis-i-Munáẓiriy-i-Báb bá 'Ulamáy-i-Tabríz." Unpublished paper.

'Arab-Bá<u>gh</u>í, Ḥusayn. *Tuḥfatu'l-Mahdíyyah fí Aḥváli'l-Ḥujjah*. Urmíyih: Ḥaqírí.

Arjomand, Said A. *The Shadow of God and the Hidden Imam: Religion, Political Order, and Societal Change in Shi'ite Iran from the Beginning to 1890*. Publications of the Center for Middle Eastern Studies 17. Chicago: University of Chicago Press, 1984.

Azal, Yaḥyá. *Al-Mustay<u>gh</u>iẓ*. N.p., n.d.

———. *Mutammim-i-Bayán*. N.p., n.d.

Bahá'u'lláh. *Á<u>th</u>ár-i-Qalam-i-A'lá*. Bombay: Náṣirí, A.H. 1314. Vol. 2.

———. *Epistle to the Son of the Wolf*. Trans. Shoghi Effendi. Wilmette, IL: Bahá'í Publishing Trust, 1962.

———. *Gleanings from the Writings of Bahá'u'lláh*. Trans. Shoghi Effendi. Rev. ed. Wilmette, IL: Bahá'í Publishing Trust, 1952.

———. *The Kitáb-i-Aqdas: The Most Holy Book*. Haifa: Bahá'í World Centre, 1992.

———. *Kitáb-i-Badí'*. Prague: Zero Palm Press, 148 B.E. (1992).

———. *The Kitáb-i-Íqán: The Book of Certitude*. Trans. Shoghi Effendi. Wilmette, IL: Bahá'í Publishing Trust, 1950.

———. *La'áli'l-Ḥikmah*. Brasil: Editora Bahá'í, 1990. Vol. 2.

———. *Majmú'iy-i-Alváḥ-i-Mubárakiy-i-Ḥaḍrat-i-Bahá'u'lláh*. Ed. Muḥyi'd-Dín Ṣabrí. Wilmette, IL: Bahá'í Publishing Trust, 1978.

———. *The Seven Valleys and the Four Valleys*. Trans. Marzieh Gail and Ali Kuli Khan. Wilmette, IL: Bahá'í Publishing Trust, 1991.

Bahá'u'lláh. *Tablet to Jamál-i-Burújirdi*. Iran National Baha'i Archives 35:39–41.
———. *Tablets of Bahá'u'lláh Revealed after the Kitáb-i-Aqdas*. Comp. Research Dept. of the Universal House of Justice. Trans. H. Taherzadeh et al. 2nd ed. Wilmette, IL: Bahá'í Publishing Trust, 1988.
Balyuzi, H. M. *The Báb*. Oxford: George Ronald, 1973.
Behmardi, Vahid. "Muqaddami'í dar báriy-i-Sabk va Síáq-i-Á͟thár-i-Mubár-akiy-i-Ḥaḍrat-i-Rabb-i-A'lá bar Asás-i-Ṭabaqih bandí." *Khushiha'i az Kharmani Adab va Honar* 6. Darmstadt: Society for Persian Letters and Arts, 1995. 47–67.
———. "Ṣaḥífiy-i-Bayna'l-Ḥaramayn." *Safiniy-i-'Irfan* Book 1. Darmstadt: Asr-i-Jadíd, 1998. 18–38.
Brown, Jacob Vahid. "Textual Resurrection: Book, Imam, and Cosmos in the Qur'án Commentaries of the Báb." *Lights of 'Irfán: Papers Presented at the 'Irfán Colloquia and Seminars*, vol. 5. Wilmette, IL:'Irfán Colloquia, 2004. 41–58.
Brown, Keven. "'Abdu'l-Bahá's Response to the Doctrine of the Unity of Existence." *Journal of Bahá'í Studies* 11: 3/4 (2001): 1–24.
Browne, Edward Granville. "The Babis of Persia." *Journal of the Royal Asiatic Society*, 1889. Reprinted in *Selections from the Writings of E. G. Browne on the Bábí and Bahá'í Religions*. Ed. Moojan Momen. Oxford: George Ronald, 1987.
———. Introduction to *A Traveller's Narrative Written to Illustrate the Episode of the Báb*. Cambridge, 1891. Reprint. Amsterdam: Philo Press, 1975.
———. "Some Remarks on the Bábí Texts Edited by Baron Victor Rosen in Vols. 1 and 6 of the Collections Scientifiques de l' Institut des Langues Orientales de Saint Petersbourg." *Journal of the Royal Asiatic Society* 24 (1892): 261.
———. *The Tarikh-i-Jadid or New History of Mirza 'Ali Muhammad the Báb*. Cambridge: Cambridge University Press, 1893.
al-Búní, Aḥmad ibn. *S͟hamsu'l-Ma'árif va Laṭá'ifu'l-'Avárif*. N.p., n.d.
Coleridge, Samuel T. "Aids to Reflection." *The Collected Works of Samuel Taylor Coleridge*. Ed. John Beer. 16 vols. Princeton: Princeton University Press, 1969–2002. Vol. 9.
Comte, Auguste. *The Positive Philosophy*. London: George Bell and Sons, 1896.
Dabashi, Hamid. *Authority in Islam: From the Rise of Muhammad to the Establishment of the Umayyads*. New Brunswick, NJ: Transaction Publishers, 1989.
Durkheim, Emile. *The Elementary Forms of the Religious Life*. New York: Free Press, 1955.

Edgerton, Robert B. *Sick Societies: Challenging the Myth of Primitive Harmony*. New York: Free Press, 1992.

Fáḍil-i-Mázandarání, Mírzá Asadu'lláh. *Asráru'l- Á<u>th</u>ár*. 5 vols. Tehran: Mu'assisiy-i-Millíy-i-Maṭbú'át-i-Amrí, 124–29 B.E. (1968–73).

———. *Kitáb-i-Ẓuhúru'l-Ḥaqq*. Tehran: [Ázúrdigán]: n.d.

Fárábí, Abú Nasr. *Al-Farabi on the Perfect State*. Oxford: Clarendon, 1985.

Fayḍ-i-Ká<u>sh</u>ání, Mullá Muḥammad Muḥsin. *Kalimát-i-Maknúnih*. Tehran: Faráhání, n.d.

———. *Navádiru'l-A<u>kh</u>bár fí ma yata'llaqu bi Uṣúli'd-Dín*. Tehran: Mu'assisiy-i-Muṭáli'át va Taḥqíqát-i-Farhangí, A.H. 1370.

Fayḍí, Muḥammad 'Alí. *Ḥaḍrat-i-Nuqṭiy-i-Awlá*. Hofheim: Bahá'í Verlag, 1994.

Feuerbach, Ludwig. *The Essence of Christianity*. New York: Harper, 1957.

Freud, Sigmund. *The Future of an Illusion*. New York: Liveright, 1949.

Gadamer, Hans-Georg. *Truth and Method*. New York: Seabury Press, 1975.

Ghazzálí, A. Ḥámid Muḥammad. *The Incoherence of the Philosophers/Taháfut al-falásifah: A Parallel English-Arabic Text*. Trans. Michael E. Marmura. Provo, UT: Brigham Young University Press, 1997.

Gulpáyigání, Mírzá Abu'l-Faḍl. *Fará'id*. Cairo, 1898.

Gulpáygání, Mírzá Abu'l-Faḍl, and Mírzá Mihdí Gulpáygání. *Ka<u>sh</u>fu'l-<u>Gh</u>iṭá' 'an Ḥíyali'l-A'dá'*. N.p., n.d.

Hegel, Georg W. F. *Lectures on the Philosophy of Religion*. 3 vols. Berkeley: University of California Press, 1984–85.

Heller, Wendy M. "The Religious Foundations of Civil Society." Parts 1, 2. *Journal of Bahá'í Studies* 10.1/2, 10.3/4 (2000): 27–70; 25–56.

Ibn al-'Arabí. *The Bezels of Wisdom*. Trans. R. W. J. Austin. New York: Paulist Press, 1980.

I<u>sh</u>ráq <u>Kh</u>ávarí, 'Abdu'l-Ḥamíd. *Má'idiy-i-Ásmání*. 9 vols. Tehran: Mu'assisiy-i-Millíy-i-Maṭbú'át-i-Amrí, 128–29 B.E. (1972–74). Vol. 2.

———. *Muḥáḍirát*. 2 vols. Hofheim: Bahá'í Verlag, 1987. Vol. 2.

———. *Raḥíq-i-Ma<u>kh</u>túm*. 2 vols. Tehran: Mu'assisiy-i-Millíy-i-Maṭbú'át-i-Amrí, 128–29 B.E. (1965). Vol. 2.

Izutsu, Toshihiko. *Sufism and Taoism: A Comparative Study of Key Philosophical Concepts*. Berkeley: University of California Press, 1983.

Jung, Carl. *Aion: Researches into the Phenomenology of the Self*. Trans. R. F. C. Hull. 2nd ed. Bollingen Series 20. Princeton: Princeton University Press, 1959.

———. *Psychology and Alchemy*. Trans. R. F. C. Hull. Princeton: Princeton University Press, 1968.

Kant, Immanuel. *Critique of Judgment*. Indianapolis: Hackett, 1987.

Kant, Immanuel. *Critique of Practical Reason*. Indianapolis: Bobbs-Merrill, 1956.

———. *Critique of Pure Reason*. Trans. Norman Kemp Smith. New York: St Martins Press, 1965.

Káshání, Ḥájí Mírzá Jání. *Nuqṭatu'l-Káf*. Leiden: Brill, 1910.

Kirmání, Ḥáj Karím Khán. *Izháqu'l-Báṭil*. Kirmán: Sa'ádat, A.H. 1371 (1973).

Kirmání, Mírzá Áqá Khán, and Shaykh Aḥmad Rúḥí. *Hasht Bihisht*. N.p., n.d.

Kuhn, Thomas S. *The Structure of Scientific Revolutions*. Chicago: University of Chicago Press, 1970.

Lawson, B. Todd. "The Báb's Epistle on the Spiritual Journey towards God." *Lights of 'Irfán: Papers Presented at the 'Irfán Colloquia and Seminars*, vol. 3. Wilmette, IL: 'Irfán Colloquia, 2002. 49–57.

———. "Coincidentia Oppositorum in the Qayyum al-Asma: The Terms 'Point' (nuqta), 'Pole' (qutb), 'Center' (markaz), and the Khutbat al-Tatanjiya" <http://www2.h-net.msu.edu/~bahai/bhpapers/vol5/tatanj/tatanj.htm>.

———. "The Dangers of Reading: Inlibration, Communion, and Transference in the Qur'án Commentary of the Báb." *Scripture and Revelation: Papers presented at the First Irfan Colloquium, Newcastle-upon Tyne, England, December 1993, and the Second Irfan Colloquium, Wilmette, USA, March 1994*. Ed. Moojan Momen. Bahá'í Studies Series, vol. 3. Oxford: George Ronald, 1997. 171–255.

———. "Interpretation as Revelation: The Qur'án Commentary of Sayyid 'Alí Muhammad Shírází, the Báb (1819–1850)." *Approaches to the History of the Interpretation of the Qur'án*. Ed. Andrew Rippin. Oxford: Clarendon, 1988. 223–53.

———. "The Term 'Remembrance' (dhikr) and 'Gate' (báb) in the Báb's Commentary on the Sura of Joseph." *Studies in Honor of the Late Hasan M. Balyuzi*. Ed. Moojan Momen. Studies in the Bábí and Bahá'í Religions, vol. 5. Los Angeles: Kalimát Press, 1988. 1–64.

Lambden, Stephen. "The Sinaic Mysteries: Notes on Moses/Sinai Motifs in Bábí and Bahá'í Scripture." *Studies in Honor of the Late Hasan M. Balyuzi*. Ed. Moojan Momen. Studies in the Bábí and Bahá'í Religions, vol. 5. Los Angeles: Kalimát Press, 1988. 65–183.

———. "The Word *Bahá*: Quintessence of the Greatest Name of God." *Journal of Bahá'í Studies* 8.2 (1997–1998): 13–45.

Lewis, Bernard. *The Assassins: A Radical Sect in Islam*. New York: Basic Books, 1968.

MacEoin, Denis M. "The Babi Concept of Holy War." *Religion* 12 (1982): 93–129.

MacEoin, Denis. "Early Shaykhí Reactions to the Báb and His Claims." *Studies in Bábí and Bahá'í History,* vol. 1. Ed. Moojan Momen. Los Angeles: Kalimát Press, 1982. 1–47.

———. "From Shaykhism to Babism: A Study in Charismatic Renewal in Shí'í Islam." PhD diss. University of Cambridge, 1979.

———. "Hierarchy, Authority, and Eschatology in Early Bábí Thought." *In Iran.* Ed. Peter Smith. Studies in Bábí and Bahá'í History, vol. 3. Los Angeles: Kalimát Press, 1986.

———. *The Persian Bayán, Sayyid 'Ali Muhammad Shirazi, the Bab: Ongoing Translation.* <http://bahai-library.org/provisionals/Bayán.html#exordium>.

———. *Rituals in Babism and Baha'ism.* Pembroke Persian Papers, vol. 2. London: British Academic Press, 1994.

———. *The Sources for Early Bábí Doctrine and History: A Survey.* Leiden: E. J. Brill, 1992.

———. "The Trial of the Bab: Shi'ite Orthodoxy Confronts Its Mirror Image." <http://bahai-library.com/unpubl.articles/bab.article.html>.

Majlisí, Mullá Muḥammad Báqir. *Biḥáru'l-Anvár.* Trans. 'Alí Daváni. Tehran: Dáru'l-Kutubu'l-Islámíyyah, A.H. 1363. Vol. 13.

Martin, Douglas. "The Mission of the Báb: Retrospective 1844–1944." *The Bahá'í World 1994–95.* Haifa: Bahá'í World Centre, 1996.

Mill, John Stuart. *Utilitarianism.* Indianapolis: Bobbs-Merrill, 1979.

Mohammadhosseini, Nosratollah. *Haḍrat-i-Báb.* Dundas, ON: Institute for Bahá'í Studies in Persian, 1995.

———. *Ḥaḍrat-i-Ṭáhirih.* Quebec: Association for Bahá'í Studies in Persian, 2000.

Momen, Moojan. "'Abdu'l-Bahá's Commentary on the Islamic Tradition: 'I Was a Hidden Treasure . . .'" *Bahá'í Studies Bulletin* 3.4 (1985): 4–37.

———. *An Introduction to Shi'i Islam: The History and Doctrine of Twelver Shí'ism.* Oxford: George Ronald, 1985.

———. "Relativism: A Basis for Bahá'í Metaphysics." *Studies in Honor of Hasan M. Balyuzi.* Ed. Moojan Momen. Studies in the Bábí and Bahá'í Religions, vol. 5. Los Angeles: Kalimát Press, 1988. 185–217.

———. "The Súrat al-Dhikr of the Qayyúm al-Asmá' (Chapter 108): A Provisional Translation and Commentary." Forthcoming.

———. "The Trial of Mullá 'Alí Basṭámí: A Combined Sunní-Shí'í Fatwá against the Báb." *Iran* 20 (1982): 113–43.

Morewedge, Parviz. "The Logic of Emanationism and Sufism in the Philosophy of Ibn Sina (Avicenna), part 2." *Journal of the American Oriental Society* 92.1 (1972): 1–18.

Nabíl-i-Aʻẓam (Muḥammad-i-Zarandí). *The Dawn-Breakers: Nabíl's Narrative of the Early Days of the Bahá'í Revelation*. Trans. Shoghi Effendi. Wilmette, IL: Bahá'í Publishing Trust, 1932.

Nicolas, A. L. M. *Le Béyan Persan*. 4 vols. Paris: Librairie Paul Geuthner, 1911–14.

Plotinus. *Enneads*. Cambridge: Harvard University Press, 1966.

Ra'fati, Vahid. "The Ideas of Ibn 'Arabí in the Bahá'í Writings." In *Maḥbúb-i-'Alam*. N.p.: Andalíb, n.d. 139–57.

———. "Marátib-i-Sabʻih va Ḥadi<u>th</u>-i-Ma<u>sh</u>íyyat." *Safiniy-i-'Irfán* Book 1. Darmstadt: Asr-i-Jadíd, 1998. 53–98.

———. "Ráhnamá'í baráy-i-Muṭáliʻiy-i-Basíṭu'l-Ḥaqíqah." *Safiniy-i-'Irfan* Book 2. Darmstadt: Asr-i-Jadíd, 1999. 20–37.

Rahman, Fazlur. *Islam*. Chicago: University of Chicago Press, 1966.

Ra<u>sh</u>tí, Siyyid Káẓim. *Risálat as-Sulúk Fíl-<u>Ak</u>hláq wa-l-Aʻmál*. Ed. Vahid Behmardi. Wurzburg: Ergon Verlag, 2004.

Rawls, John. *A Theory of Justice*. Cambridge: Harvard University Press, 1971.

Saiedi, Nader. *Logos and Civilization: Spirit, History, and Order in the Writings of Bahá'u'lláh*. Bethesda: University Press of Maryland, 2000.

Sawyer, John F. A. *Sacred Languages and Sacred Texts*. New York: Rutledge, 1999.

Schopenhauer, Arthur. *On the Basis of Morality*. Providence, RI: Berghahn Books, 1995.

Shoghi Effendi. *God Passes By*. Wilmette, IL: Bahá'í Publishing Trust, 1944.

———. *The World Order of Bahá'u'lláh: Selected Letters*. Rev. ed. Wilmette, IL: Bahá'í Publishing Trust, 1991.

Weber, Max. *Economy and Society: An Outline of Interpretive Sociology*. New York: Bedminster Press, 1968. Vol. 1.

———. *The Protestant Ethic and the Spirit of Capitalism*. London: Unwin, 1984.

Zabihi-Moghaddam, Siyamak. "The Babi-State Conflict at Shaykh Tabarsi." *Iranian Studies* 35.1–3 (2002): 87–112.

———. "Pírámún-i-Kitáb-i-Ḥaḍrat-i-Báb." *Pazhuheshnameh* 4 (1998): 130–59.

———. *Váqiʻiy-i-Qalʻiy-i-<u>Sh</u>ay<u>kh</u> Ṭabarsí*. Darmstadt: Asr-i-Jadíd, 2002.

Zeller, Eduard. *A History of Greek Philosophy from the Earliest Period to the Time of Socrates*. 2 vols. London, 1881.

INDEX

CPSIA information can be obtained
at www.ICGtesting.com
Printed in the USA
BVHW040532060821
613736BV00011B/917

9 781554 580569